EPISTEMOLOGY AND METHOD IN LAW

This book seeks to question the widely held assumption in Europe that to have knowledge of law is simply to have knowledge of rules. There is a knowledge dimension beyond the symbolic which reaches right into the way facts are perceived, constructed and deconstructed. In support of this thesis the book examines, generally, the question of what it is to have knowledge of law; and this examination embraces not just the conceptual foundations, methods, taxonomy and theories used by jurists. It also examines the epistemological schemes used by social scientists in general in order to show that such schemes are closely related to the schemes of intelligibility used by lawyers and judges.

Contents: The scope of legal epistemology; *Scientia iuris*; Methodologies in law; Institutions and concepts; Facts and law; Taxonomy in law; Theories of liability; Schemes of intelligibility in social science.

Author: Geoffrey Samuel is a Professor of Law at the Kent Law School and a visiting professor at the Sorbonne. He specialises in the law of obligations, comparative law, legal epistemology and legal theory. His other publications include *The Foundations of Legal Reasoning* (Maklu, 1994) and the *Law of Obligations and Legal Remedies* (Cavendish, 2nd edn, 2001).

This book is dedicated to Bernard Rudden,
Emeritus Professor of Comparative Law, University of Oxford,
to whom I owe so much.

Epistemology and Method in Law

GEOFFREY SAMUEL
Kent Law School, UK

Routledge
Taylor & Francis Group
LONDON AND NEW YORK

First published 2003 by Ashgate Publishing

2 Park Square, Milton Park, Abingdon, Oxon OX14 4RN
711 Third Avenue, New York, NY 10017, USA

Routledge is an imprint of the Taylor & Francis Group, an informa business

First issued in paperback 2016

Britih Library Cataloguing in Publication Data
Samuel, Geoffrey, 1947–
Epistemology and method in law. – (Applied legal philosophy)
1. Law – Methodology 2. Knowledge, Theory of
I. Title
340.1'1

Library of Congress Cataloging-in-Publication Data
Samuel, G. H.
Epistemology and method in law / Geoffrey Samuel.
p. cm. -- (Applied legal philosophy)
Includes bibliographical references and index.
ISBN 978-1-85521-599-3
1. Semantics (Law) 2. Law--Methodology. 3. Knowledge, Theory of. I. Title. II. Series.

K213 .S259 2002
340'.14--dc21

2001048705

Transfered to Digital Pinting in 2010

ISBN 978-1-85521-599-3 (hbk)
ISBN 978-1-138-26741-1 (pbk)

Contents

Series Preface

The objective of the Applied Legal Philosophy series is to publish work which adopts a theoretical approach to the study of particular areas or aspects of law or deals with general theories of law in a way which focuses on issues of practical moral and political concern in specific legal contexts.

In recent years there has been an encouraging tendency for legal philosophers to utilize detailed knowledge of the substance and practicalities of law and a noteworthy development in the theoretical sophistication of much legal research. The series seeks to encourage these trends and to make available studies in law which are both genuinely philosophical in approach and at the same time based on appropriate legal knowledge and directed towards issues in the criticism and reform of actual laws and legal systems.

The series will include studies of all the main areas of law, presented in a manner which relates to the concerns of specialist legal academics and practitioners. Each book makes an original contribution to an area of legal study while being comprehensible to those engaged in a wide variety of disciplines. Their legal content is principally Anglo-American, but a wide-ranging comparative approach is encouraged and authors are drawn from a variety of jurisdictions.

Tom D. Campbell
Series Editor
Centre for Applied Philosophy and Public Ethics
Charles Sturt University, Canberra

Preface

This book has been long in gestation and perhaps even longer in writing. But it has not been easy to try to produce a work for readers who may have knowledge neither of the continental (civil) law tradition nor of the main schools of Western legal theory, yet would like to go beyond the standard introductory works to legal method. In going beyond the standard works, the general question that this book seeks to answer is this: what does thinking like a lawyer actually involve? The focus is mainly on English cases and so the book is aimed at those primarily interested in the methods of common lawyers. Yet its ambitions are wider: it is also designed as a contribution to comparative law inasmuch as it is concerned with the 'law' question. For if one does not know what it is to have knowledge of law, then it becomes difficult to know what one should be comparing. Most important, however, it is propounding a thesis that knowledge of law is more than just knowledge of rules. If there is one issue that underpins the search for knowledge beyond the rules, it is the awareness that to date no one has been able to model the legal mind for artificial intelligence purposes. This work is a direct response to that failure, although I am fully aware that there is nothing in this book that will be of direct benefit to AI.

The book has benefited immensely from both public and private criticism of my earlier work. I should therefore like to take this opportunity to thank those colleagues who have written reviews and provided commentary. Many weaknesses have been addressed and, if not always fully and successfully strengthened, they will I hope be treated as part of a continuing dialogue. Needless to say, then, that the book does contain a few sections that have, to a greater or lesser extent, seen the light of day elsewhere. The influence of many will be found in the pages that follow. Where that influence is conscious, I have attributed ideas as fully as I can. Nevertheless, there will be many omissions. To go some way in combating this weakness, the bibliography ranges wider than the actual note references and thus inclusion in the list is a recognition of influence and absorption. Even so, this bibliography probably does not fully represent all those who have contributed to my thinking.

My family have patiently suffered late-night absences and disappearances to French faculties and to them I offer my warmest thanks. Many thanks also to all those colleagues here and abroad, often named by me elsewhere, for their help and support. John Bell and Pierre Legrand do, however, deserve special mention here. Finally, I would like to acknowledge the superb editing carried out by the publishers. They not only improved the style of my English, but on occasions corrected my French. A special thanks to real professionals.

Geoffrey Samuel
Kent Law School

List of Cases

Common Law Cases

Continental Law Cases

List of Roman Law References

Gai institutionum

Institutiones (Institutes of Justinian)

List of Statutes

English Statutes

English Statutory Instruments

European Statutes

List of Abbreviations

AC	Appeal Cases (Third Series)
AJCL	American Journal of Comparative Law
All ER	All England Law Reports (Butterworths & Co)
APD	*Archives de philosophie du droit*
App Cas	Appeal Cases (Second Series)
BGB	*Bürgerliches Gesetzbuch*
BW	*Burgerlijk Wetboek* (Netherlands Civil Code)
C	Code of Justinian
CA	Court of Appeal
CC	*Code civil* (France)
CE	*Conseil d'État*
Ch	Chancery Division (Third Series)
Ch D	Chancery Division (Second Series)
CJQ	Civil Justice Quarterly
CLJ	Cambridge Law Journal
CLP	Current Legal Problems
CLR	Commonwealth Law Reports
D	Digest of Justinian; and also Dalloz
DS	Dalloz-Sirey
EC	European Community
EG	Estates Gazette
EGLR	Estates Gazette Law Reports
EHRR	European Human Rights Reports
ER	English Reports
EU	European Union
FLR	Family Law Reports
G	*Institutes* of Gaius
HL	House of Lords
ICLQ	International and Comparative Law Quarterly
IECL	International Encyclopedia of Comparative Law
IJSL	International Journal for the Semiotics of Law
J	*Institutes* of Justinian
JCP	*Jurisclasseur périodique*
JLH	Journal of Legal History
KB	King's Bench (Third Series)

LC	Lord Chancellor
LGR	Knight's Local Government Reports
LJCP	Law Journal Common Pleas
LJ Ex	Law Journal Exchequer
LJQB	Law Journal Queen's Bench
Ll Rep	Lloyd's List Law Reports
LQR	Law Quarterly Review
LR...CP	Common Pleas Cases (First Series)
LR...Eq	Equity Cases (First Series)
LR...Ex	Exchequer Cases (First Series)
LR...HL	English and Irish Appeals (First Series)
LR...QB	Queen's Bench Cases (First Series)
LS	Legal Studies
LT	Law Times Reports
MJ	Maastricht Journal of European and Comparative Law
MLJ	Malayan Law Journal
MLR	Modern Law Review
NBW	*Nieuw Burgerlijk Wetboek* (Netherlands Civil Code)
NCPC	*Nouveau code de procédure civile* (French)
NILQ	Northern Ireland Legal Quarterly
NJW	*Neue Juristische Wochenschrift* (Germany)
OJLS	Oxford Journal of Legal Studies
P	Probate Division (Third Series)
PC	Privy Council
PECL	Principles of European Contract Law
PL	Public Law
QB	Queen's Bench (Third Series)
QBD	Queen's Bench (Second Series)
RIDC	*Revue internationale de droit comparé*
RLR	Restitution Law Review
RSC	Rules of Supreme Court
SLR	Statute Law Review
Swiss CO	Swiss Code of Obligations
UWAL Rev	University of Western Australia Law Review
WLR	Weekly Law Reports
ZEuP	*Zeitschrift für Europäisches Privatrecht*

Introductory Remarks

The thesis that will be advanced in this book, in summary, is this. It will be argued that the assumption that knowledge of law consists of knowledge of rules – that is to say, normative propositions capable of being expressed in symbolic language (natural and mathematical language) – is inadequate. Such a rule-model epistemological thesis fails, it will be argued, to take account of fact construction in legal thought. In pursuing this thesis, however, the book will embrace wider issues than fact construction: it will look at legal reasoning and legal method more generally.

The idea that facts are part of legal knowledge is not, of course, an idea that will cause surprise to most lawyers.[1] What might be more controversial is the idea that the way facts are constructed internally, leading to the way that they are thus viewed, is capable of creating a normative dimension quite separate from any normative aspect attaching to a legal rule. Sometimes this fact construction can be seen as a kind of precategorisation: that is to say, it is a preliminary categorisation before the facts are formally assigned to an established legal category. It is a matter of how facts are viewed, of how particular aspects are emphasised; thus it may be a matter of emphasising a whole as opposed to its parts, or vice versa. It will be argued that this 'non-symbolic' knowledge might well be more dynamic than it at first sight appears.[2] How facts are actually constructed at this precategorisation stage might well be an active step in the process of reaching a solution in a case and thus the construction – and reconstruction – of facts is as important as any search for, or an application of, a rule.

Given this idea of construction and reconstruction, the facts of a case are not, then, 'real' facts. They are not real-life (for want of a better term) situations, but are, to use a term fashioned by the philosopher of science Giles-Gaston Granger, 'virtual facts'.[3] The notion of virtual facts has been developed by Granger to explain the role of fact in the laboratory experimentation; such facts, for example, are those that underpin the 'law' that objects of different weight fall at the same speed. These facts are 'ideal' inasmuch as they are 'true' only in laboratory conditions. In the actual real world objects may not fall at the same speed, owing to a range of factors such as wind that are not present in the laboratory. Granger goes further than this: he makes the point that science is not an activity that takes natural phenomena for 'real' fact. Or, put another way, the object of science is not the phenomena of the real world; the object consists of the schematic construction or abstract model of this real world and science itself is the exploitation of such models to explain and predict the phenomenon modelled.[4] This epistemological thesis is equally – or perhaps one should say analogously – applicable to law since this is a discourse or 'science' (*intellectus*) which does not operate directly on the facts (*res*). What lawyers do is to construct a model of the social world and it is, arguably, this model which acts as the bridge between the social and legal worlds. The model is both the *res* (object of knowledge) and the *intellectus* (knowing subject).

This model allows one to appreciate that the object (*res*) of the *intellectus* is not the factual situation itself. The direct object of legal analysis is not a car crash involving this and that particular type of vehicle; nor is it the actual transaction involving a delivery of a cargo of rotten oranges. Nor, again, is it the particular type of spikes built, or holes dug, on a specific individual's land so as to interrupt a neighbour's ballooning activities or his water supply. Facts are abstracted versions of these events in which a car is interchangeable with a van and oranges with bananas, just as spikes can be replaced by holes. Legal factual situations are constructed out of legal institutions which are capable of being amenable to legal rules. These legal institutions are those concepts – in particular *res* (thing) and *persona* (person) – which have the ability of functioning at one and the same time in the 'real' and the legal worlds. These institutions are in turn supported by a range of other, seemingly descriptive, concepts such as fault, damage and interest, which again function at one and the same time in the real and the legal spheres. It is the central thesis of this present work, as we have already suggested, that the construction itself may determine the rules to be applied. The object of legal science is, in other words, the constructed legal model of facts. It is a world of persons, things, interests, fault, expectations, damage, causation and the like.

This is not to deny that law can be seen in terms of texts, that is to say normative propositions stated in natural language. In fact the very existence of statutory texts and law reports setting out applicable rules indicates that it would be idle to deny the existence of linguistic propositions. The point to be made, however, is that there is more to legal knowledge than just rules, in the same way that there is more to the natural and social sciences than just 'laws'. For example, research in the field of artificial intelligence (AI) is beginning to indicate that perception may well itself be founded not just on symbolic, or propositional, knowledge but equally on non-propositional knowledge.[5] Knowledge may be determined by the way one 'sees' an object and such an object can often be seen in different ways by different people.[6] Thus an ambiguous representation like the Necker cube, a 'three-dimensional' pictorial representation actually drawn two-dimensionally on paper, can be perceived in two different ways. It can be seen with a front face at the lower left or with a top surface at the upper right.[7] Similarly, institutional representations of legal facts can be 'seen' in different ways. A case involving the accidental destruction by fire of a building can be perceived as a problem involving two individuals (owner of building and contractor working on the building who actually causes the fire) or simply as a matter of risk between two insurance companies.[8] The purpose, therefore, of this enquiry is to justify and to develop in more depth the ideas outlined in this introductory essay.

However, this present enquiry will range far wider than this central thesis. Time will be spent analysing the idea of a legal epistemology and its relationship with other areas of legal philosophy and legal theory. Such an analysis will in turn involve an examination of the history of legal ideas and the development of different kinds of methods. Indeed, epistemology goes much further than this. The various schemes, systems, concepts and categories used by lawyers are central areas of investigation, as are the range of reasoning methods employed by those involved in solving legal problems. The relationship between law and fact, as we have mentioned, will of course be central; but this will involve the examination of cases and judgments and so this present work will be an enquiry into legal method. Yet is there such a notion as *legal* method? Or is the methodology one that can be related to reasoning and argumentation techniques used in general? And, even if there is a legal method, does the methodology vary between different classes of jurists? Do judges reason in the same way as law professors or legislators? This takes one into the area of professional viewpoints, another important aspect of epistemology. What kinds of knowledge models do the various sub-groups within law employ when they go about their legal business? Does the law professor need a quite different model than the practitioner working within the busy law centre?

This enquiry will, of course, be a work of theory and methodology, but arguably not of philosophy. The aim is not to provide any kind of moral underpinning of law even although a moral framework certainly could be said to have epistemological implications. Indeed, an investigation into the 'ontological' (what exists) basis of law – the constructed legal world – may well in its turn betray certain moral implications. Yet the purpose of this present enquiry is to try to provide an account of legal knowledge. The chapters that follow will try to construct a model which will explain the *intellectus et res* of legal discourse. In addition to this theoretical dimension, this enquiry will also attempt to provide a methodological account of law and legal reasoning, particularly from the position of non-symbolic or non-propositional knowledge. Accordingly, in the later chapters, there will be an emphasis on decided cases. Such an emphasis will, it must be said, focus on cases taken from English law because this is a system that, more than any other (save perhaps Roman law and the *mos Italicus*), seems to have the most 'direct' relationship with facts. The common law thus presents the greatest challenge to anyone claiming that legal systems function in relation to 'virtual' facts.

This emphasis on cases from the common will not, it is hoped, prevent this work from being viewed, equally, as a contribution to comparative law. Now 'comparative law' as a discipline implies, evidently, that one has an epistemological foundation for both 'comparison' and 'law'. Yet much of the literature on comparative law seems unaware of the importance of this epistemological dimension.[9] What this present enquiry will attempt to do, therefore, is to show how the construction and reconstruction of models of 'institutional' facts have a vital role to play in comparative legal studies. Comparative law is not just about the comparison of legal texts and normative propositions; it is also about the way, say, a Roman, a French and an English lawyer structure factual situations. A bottle of orange juice explodes in a supermarket just as the customer is handing it to the person at the check-out point. Is this a problem involving the legal relationship between the supermarket owner and the customer covered in orange juice? Or is it a problem of damage done by a thing (orange juice) under the control of another? What if someone then slips on the orange: is this still a problem of damage done by a bottle of orange juice or is it now a matter of dangerous premises? These different 'images' could give rise to quite different legal situations each capable of being compared one with another. In one sense, of course, this may be a matter of comparing textual rules; and so article 1384 of the *Code civil* can be compared with the Occupiers' Liability Act 1957. But the ability to construct and reconstruct the facts so as to emphasise the *personae* (owner and customer) on the one hand or the *res* (bottle or premises) on the other ought to indicate that comparative law is equally capable of being a matter of comparing factual models.[10]

One primary aim is, then, to look beyond the rules of law. Rules, for this exercise, are the propositions to be found in statutes, the principles to be found in legal maxims or induced out of decided cases, and the descriptive statements of what the law is, or said to be, in textbooks and manuals. To go beyond these rules is neither to deny their existence – indeed, quite the opposite – nor to downgrade their importance as a means of access to legal knowledge and the solving of legal problems. It is simply to add a further dimension to the study of law, a dimension that is often left out of introductory and general textbooks on law because the rules themselves have come to represent for positive law subjects the sum total of the knowledge required.[11] Books on contract, for example, or works in which contract law forms a part, are almost entirely devoted to setting out descriptively the rules on contract formation, vitiating factors, discharge and so on. Between the propositions cases will of course be described and analysed, but often with the aim either of illustrating a previously described rule or of inducing a principle. And while an increasing number of textbooks do devote space to theory and aims, these are more or less ancillary to the chapters setting out the actual rules, principles and cases.

There are of course exceptions to the descriptive textbook. The Law in Context collection[12] represents a major attempt to provide an alternative approach to the traditional textbook; and comparative works such as those to be found in the *International Encyclopedia of Comparative Law* analyse by definition a range of alternative models of private law. Books on jurisprudence exclusively concentrate on the theoretical worlds beyond positive law. Equally, many edited works and collections of essays are designed to reach those parts into which the standard manuals do not have the will or mandate to enter. Moreover, at one time, courses on Roman law were intended to provide an introduction to institutional and conceptual thinking while at the same time initiating law students into legal rules, maxims and case law examples. Nevertheless, comparative law and jurisprudence are rarely encountered in the early years of legal study; and Roman law has slipped out of most of the law schools in the United Kingdom and on the continent (with some exceptions). An introduction to legal knowledge is, therefore, likely to take the form of an introduction to legal propositions, that is to say legal rules.[13] Of course many law schools take students beyond the rules inasmuch as law is placed in its social, political and (or) economic context. In this sense, then, to go beyond the rules is by no means revolutionary. However, these contextual approaches, while undoubtedly looking well beyond the rules, rarely ever question the rule thesis itself as a form of legal knowledge. In other words the representation of legal knowledge in the form of language propositions is rarely challenged. What this present work aims to do is to challenge the rule model itself as the sole means of access to the solving of case law problems. While doing this, however, it aims to inform upon the history of legal method and legal ideas and upon the conceptual and classification schemes employed by lawyers within the European tradition.

The general question, then, that this book will attempt to investigate is this: what is it to have knowledge of law? This is not the first book to seek an answer, since a pioneering work in 1985 by Professor Christian Atias set out to investigate this very question.[14] However, the question has not, arguably, been properly investigated by a common lawyer and so there is room for a reflection on what it is to have legal knowledge by a jurist from 'the other' tradition. Moreover, it is increasingly being recognised by some comparative lawyers that the foundation of their enterprise is essentially epistemological.[15] To be able to compare law one must know what it is that one is comparing. What is meant by the term 'law' in comparative law? Legal epistemology is the starting point for comparatists for a commitment to theory.[16]

Of course one might respond to this comparative law question by reminding the comparatist that there is much literature by legal theorists and legal philosophers on the concept and nature of law. In addition, given that methodology forms an important practical aspect of scientific knowledge, one might equally add that there is no dearth of books on legal method. Within both the common law and civil law worlds there are many works covering the whole field of methodology, from introductory texts to sophisticated monographs on the theoretical dimensions of legal reasoning and argumentation. However, these works are not strictly epistemological investigations. They do not set out to investigate legal knowledge 'across an analysis of cognitive structures acting as the basis for a legal tradition'.[17] They are not works studying 'knowledge on knowledge, its nature, its methods, its value, its conceptualisations'.[18]

The question of what it is to have legal knowledge does, then, overlap with legal theory and legal philosophy. One should not be surprised therefore that the three areas – epistemology, theory and philosophy – have been brought together under the single Anglo-American heading of 'jurisprudence'.[19] Or, put another way, jurisprudence could be said to be concerned, *inter alia*, with legal epistemology.[20] However, epistemology needs to be differentiated from, if not jurisprudence itself, then from legal theory and legal philosophy. Jurisprudence is too broad a category since the philosophy of law covers the nature of law and legal values.[21] And while, in one sense, legal epistemology will need to concern itself with definitions of law and with the value system which law displays or reflects, in another sense epistemology is more focused. It seeks to understand the nature of the cognitive relationship between knowing subject (*intellectus*) and object of knowledge (*res*).[22] Epistemology seeks to establish a theory, or at least a model, which will explain the *res* (law) in relation to the *intellectus* (mind) and the *intellectus* in relation to the *res*.

In doing this, legal epistemology will draw its inspiration from the natural sciences to the extent that these sciences are continually preoccupied with knowledge models and with the validity of these models. Science seeks to understand the world by constructing abstract 'structures' which both (seemingly) describe and predict the physical world. These structures have their own formal qualities which, while mirroring the physical phenomena, are nevertheless abstracted from them. Of course, law is not a natural phenomenon. It is, at best, a social science and this implies that it is subject to all the epistemological difficulties which attach to social science. Legal epistemology will therefore have to confront these more general difficulties. With respect to this wider epistemological issue, a contribution by a French social science theorist is particularly noteworthy, all the more so since it has attracted the attention of a leading philosopher of science.[23] Jean-Michel Berthelot claims to have isolated a definitive number of schemes of intelligibility which, he estimates, lie at the heart of differences of approach, of method and (or) of theory as between different social scientists.[24] His identification and isolation of these fundamental starting points for analysis could well represent something of a breakthrough in social science epistemology. Now, whether or not these schemes will ultimately prove to be definitive and comprehensive is a matter of debate.[25] What is of importance is that these schemes have a particular relevance for law, since Berthelot's schemes might well provide a definitive synchronic model or models of legal knowledge.

However, the synchronic model is only one approach to epistemology. Another, equally important, approach is the diachronic. This approach looks at knowledge as an historical phenomenon and, once again, French epistemology has made a major contribution in a model proposed by Robert Blanché. He has suggested that all the natural sciences pass through a series of stages to end up at an axiomatic stage.[26] This scheme, it will be suggested, is also of relevance to law. Yet where law may be different is in respect of the definitive nature of the four-stage process set out by Blanché; for it will be argued that the idea of an axiomatic stage is itself an historical phenomenon. It could be that there is now a fifth, post-axiomatic stage which represents the current state of legal science.[27] This fifth stage, assuming its existence, could act as the context for the epistemological thesis that will be advanced in this present work. That is to say, the post-axiomatic stage is one where law is no longer viewed as a two-dimensional set of linguistic propositions. It is a stage representing complexity and epistemological constructivism. This work is thus offering a 'post-axiomatic' thesis of legal knowledge.

Notes

1 See, for example, Ivainer (1988).

2 The term 'non-symbolic' knowledge is used here in the sense described by Delacour (1995). Symbolic knowledge is knowledge that can be reduced to symbols which are representations of the knowledge simplified so as to facilitate communication, conservation and treatment by, for example, digital machines (pp. 33–4). Natural language and mathematical figures and symbols are the main forms of this kind of knowledge. Non-symbolic knowledge, in contrast, is a matter of 'images, of emotional states, of conceptual structures, of prototype models often untranslatable by a linguistic expression' (p. 35).

3 Granger (1995, p. 49).

4 Ibid., p. 70.

5 See Delacour (1995). The idea of non-propositional knowledge, which is similar to Delacour's idea of non-symbolic knowledge, comes from Bechtel and Abrahamsen (1991, pp. 147–75).

6 Bechtel and Abrahamsen (1991, pp. 160–61).

7 Ibid., p. 160.

8 Cf. *Photo Production Ltd* v. *Securicor* [1980] AC 827.

9 Cf. Legrand (1995a).

10 See also Samuel (1998b).

11 Susskind (1987, pp. 149–55).

12 Now published by Butterworths & Co.

13 Twining and Miers (1999).

14 Atias (1985). See also Atias (1994).

15 See in particular Legrand (1999b, p. 32).

16 Legrand (1995a).

17 Ibid.

18 Busino (1998, p. 4).

19 Jolowicz (1963, pp. 1–11).

20 Lloyd and Freeman (1994, p. 6).

21 Bergel (1999, no. 4).

22 The use of Latin terms might appear at first sight somewhat unnecessary. However, not only was Latin the language of knowledge until after the Enlightenment, but a whole range of Latin expressions themselves have acted as the object of knowledge, particularly in the history of legal ideas. *Intellectus* is a term that expresses perception, understanding and intellect, while *res* means a 'thing' both in a tangible and an intangible sense.

Res, as will be seen, was a term of the utmost importance in Roman law, but, equally, it had its own epistemological dimension as well; it was a remarkably general term which could encompass a physical object, such as a cabbage, or something far more amorphous such as 'affair'.

23 Granger (1995, pp. 90–92).

24 Berthelot (1990, pp. 43–85; 1996, pp. 78–82); Berthelot (2001a, 2001b).

25 Cf. Berthelot (1996, p. 81).

26 Blanché (1983, p. 65).

27 See also Samuel (1998a).

1 The Scope of Legal Epistemology

The word 'epistemology' is derived from the Greek words *épistémè* and *logos*, the first meaning science and the second signifying a theoretical and critical study of something.[1] Thus, linguistically, legal epistemology means the theoretical study of legal science. In the English language, and in English philosophy, the word 'epistemology' is used to mean a theory of knowledge. However, in some continental languages 'epistemology' has a narrower meaning inasmuch as it is restricted to the critical study of the natural sciences. In France, for example, *épistémologie* has gradually become separated from philosophy and from the general theory of knowledge. It has come to mean a reflection on science in the same way as aesthetics has become a reflection on art and moral philosophy a reflection on ethics.[2] Accordingly, in continental thought, epistemology is closely associated with the theory and philosophy of the sciences.[3]

However, as Robert Blanché observed, the reflection is not necessarily philosophic: 'it does not necessarily get one to abandon the scientific demands'; it allows itself, instead, 'to be integrated into the domain of science'.[4] All the same, what is important is that this integration does not result in a confusion between epistemology, science and the object of science. Epistemology must study the principles, the hypotheses and the results of the various sciences with the purpose of determining their value as a scheme of knowledge discourse.[5] This means that it should in theory leave out of the account everything that science takes as its object. Thus an epistemological study of meteorology, under pain of confusing two levels of language, ought strictly to look only at the discourse (the science) and methods of meteorologists and not at the atmosphere, climates and weather (the object of the science). Epistemology, then, concerns itself with scientific discourse 'treated as a system of signs combining between themselves according to certain rules independent of what they can evoke'.[6] This separation is, however, by no means clear-cut and, as we shall see, particularly problematic when it comes to legal science.

The Domain of Epistemology

Legal epistemology will thus involve a reflection on the activity of legal science or, if the notion of a legal science is unacceptable, on what it is to have knowledge of law. An important question, however, is whether an epistemological investigation of law is valuable or even possible. Can one really compare a subject like law with the hard sciences? Certainly, one can reflect upon the nature of legal knowledge, but Richard Susskind claims that legal epistemology 'falls firmly within the bounds of jurisprudence'.[7] Consequently, one might ask how a work on legal epistemology will differ from work already done under the heading of jurisprudence. Christian Atias has responded to these reservations by arguing that, if one takes a narrow view of epistemology and restricts it simply to the study of the natural sciences, then it is to be doubted if a true epistemological reflection is possible. Yet, if one envisages epistemology as an investigation of knowledge in a more general sense, it becomes possible to study 'the modalities according to which legal assertions are grounded and made'.[8] One can take legal knowledge as an object of study and one can study 'the modalities according to which assertions *concerning* (*portant sur*) the law are grounded and produced' (emphasis in original).

Epistemology and Jurisprudence

Accordingly, an epistemological investigation of law will differ from traditional introductory textbooks to jurisprudence in several ways. First, an epistemological approach to law will reflect, if only very briefly, upon the whole phenomenon of legal knowledge and legal science from its inception to the present. In science itself the progress of each science is accomplished by inventions, discoveries and revolutions, yet always on the basis of previously accumulated knowledge. And this is 'why the study of the history of science is an absolute requirement for anyone who wants to understand and interpret the sense and scope of existing discoveries'.[9] Of course, it may be that law is very different from natural science and that it is not a discipline that has suffered from crises and revolutions.[10] Yet there have certainly been internal developments within legal thought as any history of, say, contract will show.[11] Now even in science it is said that the 'successive developments of basic concepts is not in essence dependent upon circumstances extrinsic to science itself'; instead, the actual linking together of discoveries 'is dependent in the final analysis on an *internal movement* of concepts' (emphasis in original).[12] And if this is true it does provide a link between the history of science and the history of law. Both might be said to be the histories of discourse schemes which, while clearly reacting to circumstances extrinsic to the schemes, nevertheless have consistent histories of their own internal developments. Consequently, an epistemological approach to law will, almost by necessity, be in part a work of historical jurisprudence. The modern – and 'post-modern' – cannot, in other words, be explained without reference to the whole of the past.

Secondly, there have been few if any theories of law that have attempted to capture the whole phenomenon of law. That is to say, there are few books on jurisprudence that deal at one and the same time with the history, methods, institutions, concepts, habits of thought, internal structures (and so on) of law. Until recently, this did not matter in a direct practical sense. However, with the advent of artificial intelligence (AI), the question of what it is to have knowledge of law has become important inasmuch as the existing theories of legal knowledge have proved inadequate. AI researchers using existing jurisprudential theories have completely failed to produce any AI programme that mirrors the legal intelligence of a human jurist. The problem is that research into AI and law has been dominated by the theoretical assumption that legal knowledge is propositional; that is to say that it consists of knowing rules and principles and that legal reasoning involves the application of these propositions to factual situations.[13] This is the approach that is now in crisis,[14] since one cannot talk about artificial legal intelligence if there is confusion about what it is to have legal intelligence.[15] More generally, however, it might be argued that the time is right for a reconsideration of legal reasoning and methodology within the whole cultural tradition of Western law.[16] Is there something culturally and (or) scientifically specific about Western legal knowledge? At any rate, what is needed, according to some writers, is theories aimed at revealing the deep structures of a knowledge discourse.

Yet the malaise goes much further than the AI community. There is a general disillusionment with what has been called the 'modernist' view of law.[17] Current Anglo-American jurisprudence has failed in its task of providing an adequate answer to the question of what it is to have legal knowledge,[18] and thus what is needed is a new body of work which will, amongst other things, examine the foundations of legal reasoning.[19] This examination should propose a conceptual structure that might act as the basis for the formulation of a theoretical model of legal reasoning that will stand as an alternative to those that have been proposed to date. What is needed is a new approach that will fill or, more modestly, try to go some way in filling, the gap that has been revealed as a result of research into artificial intelligence and law.

Indeed, this gap was specifically identified by Richard Susskind in his own research on expert systems and law and it has also been noticed by others. We actually know rather little 'about the philosophical, theoretical and methodological ideas and principles adopted by the Roman lawyers'.[20] And, given that when it comes to the development of the main trends of Western legal theory 'so many roads in law lead us back to Rome by way of the Commentators',[21] this is a serious gap. Susskind makes a similar point, even although he is viewing the situation from the position of an expert systems analyst keen to exploit modern jurisprudential theory. He observes that, 'while current legal theory, being carried out within a rule-based paradigm ... offers guidance for rule-based modelling, it has little to say directly about conceptual modelling'.[22] There is, therefore, 'unequivocal help available neither from legal theory nor from the primary or secondary sources of law' when it comes to the task of developing a conceptual model of legal knowledge that could be of value.

A third way an epistemological work will differ, then, from traditional works on jurisprudence is that it will concern itself with reasoning and method in the context of a legal science itself conceived within a specific history of legal thought. It will look at the tools used by lawyers and, if only briefly, the way these tools have been developed. It will look, in an introductory way, at how Roman law has acted as a fundamental source book (*Corpus Iuris Civilis*) of legal knowledge in Western Europe and how this source book, when subjected over the centuries of its second life to differing intellectual methods, has revealed a wealth of vital information about what it is to have legal knowledge. Admittedly, any emphasis on Roman law creates difficulty when it comes to an understanding of Western legal science. On the one hand, as Walter Ullmann has pointed out, it would be no exaggeration to think of the *Corpus* of Roman law as being, until quite recently, the sum total of juristic wisdom.[23] Yet, on the other hand, there is the difficulty of the relationship between English law and Roman law. At one level, the relationship is a distant one; the history of English law is traditionally seen as being a history quite independent of the *Corpus Iuris*.[24] At another level, however, the relationship is more complex. At the level of a history of legal ideas – that is to say at the level of the *Corpus Iuris* as a science (a discourse) rather than an object of science (a set of rules or whatever) – it becomes possible to make connections because this type of history is very different from a history of chronological events. The development of ideas can, according to Robert Blanché, only be grasped from within.[25] And once one looks at the inner relationships between Roman, English and, say, French law the picture that emerges is one that may owe as much to a difference between the teaching and practice of law, or to *a priori* and experimental knowledge, as to differences in time and space.

Epistemology and Comparative Law

Legal knowledge thus requires comparison between different legal systems. Accordingly, another way a work on legal epistemology will differ from traditional works on jurisprudence is in the way it will concern itself with some theoretical problems of comparative law. This present enquiry does not have as its objective the formulation of a theory of comparative law, but in its concern for the development of reasoning models it will go some way in fulfilling Rudolfo Sacco's goal of legal comparison as a science. According to Sacco, the goal of legal comparison is the revealing of differing models and legal knowledge is, in turn, derived from the details of this difference.[26] In looking, then, at the differences and the similarities between the reasoning and methodological models of, say, common law and French law, one is not just engaging in an exercise of comparative law. One is also moving towards the production of a theoretical model.

In the context of the EU, such a theoretical model is of importance. For, whatever the future holds in political terms,[27] it is unlikely that the momentum towards increasing harmonisation of laws will cease completely and thus the pressure for a new 'common law' (*ius commune*) of Europe will continue.[28] Any model of legal reasoning proposed in this present work, if drawn from both the English (Common Law) and the Continental (Civil Law) traditions, and whatever its strengths and weaknesses, will at least have a relevance in respect of the theoretical foundation of any new *ius commune*. This is not actually to say that Europe is on the brink of a new *ius commune*. The *mentalité* of the continental lawyer, as Pierre Legrand elegantly emphasises, might well be different from that of the English lawyer.[29] Yet this difference should not be allowed to hide the fact that law, or Western law at any rate, is about relations between people and between people and things, and it is in this notion of *relation* that a common structural basis can be found to underlie legal method.[30] One is not talking here of empirical relations between people and property. One is talking of structural relations between legal institutions, and it is in the system of these structural relations that the categories, concepts and notions used by lawyers gain their meaning.

Epistemology and comparative law can thus combine to take one beyond the rule model. One important aim of legal epistemology is to re-emphasise[31] the possibility of an alternative jurisprudential model that might challenge, or at least act as an alternative to, the rule theory of legal knowledge. Such a model will stop well short of claiming to provide a *philosophy* of law. What it aims to do is to provide an *epistemological* model which will be of relevance both to 'black-letter' (comparative) lawyers interested in problem solving[32] and to jurisprudence researchers interested in linking legal theory to positive law and to comparative law. Now whether any alternative model will prove useful, in a *ius commune* sense, to, say, AI or to the EU is a difficult and ambitious matter. However, one thing is certain, given the crisis facing AI. The idea that 'all that was required to produce a legal expert system was to take a group of lawyers off for a weekend to "get the rules from them"' is finished.[33] What is needed now is a model of legal intelligence that transcends legal rules: for legal theorists seem to have forgotten that lawyers have always been able to cope with rule change without major reprogramming. Discovering how they are able to do this will be the challenge facing any work on legal epistemology.

Epistemology and Viewpoints

Lawyers, of course, are not the only group necessarily to have knowledge of law. One of the valuable contributions of the American Realist movement of the prewar years is that the perception of law changes according to the person, or class of persons, perceiving.[34] As Oliver Wendall Holmes put it, 'if we take the view of our friend the bad man we shall find that he does not care two straws for the axioms or deductions [from principles or ethics], but that he does want to know what the Massachusetts or English courts are likely to do in fact'.[35] Holmes's point is simple but important. The German-educated legal scientist will probably view law as a scientific system of principles and axioms from which legal solutions can be drawn using deductive logic.[36] Legal knowledge for such a jurist is, then, a matter of concise propositions systematically arranged in an abstract world of concepts. The burglar, in contrast, is unlikely to carry such a knowledge structure in his or her head; to him or her, law is a matter of policemen, courts and court officials, prison officers and the like. Equally, the knowledge structure of the policemen and the prison officials will probably be different from that of the judge. The policemen may see law in terms of good and bad behavioural acts, whereas the judge in a criminal court will think in terms of procedures, instructions to juries and rules of criminal law.

The point to be stressed here is that there is no single idea of what it is to have legal knowledge. Much will depend upon what Twining has called the 'standpoint' or 'point of view in an observational sense'.[37] This point of view might depend upon one's role *vis-à-vis* law or it might involve the adopting of 'some principle or ideology or intellectual system, as when someone approaches a subject from the standpoint of a utilitarian or a Marxist'.[38] Twining was talking here in the context of a general theory of law, but his observations are particularly relevant for epistemology. For the forms and modes (*modalités*) through, and on, which the assertions about law are made and grounded are likely to be very different depending upon the standpoint of the person making the assertion. Furthermore, these standpoints will probably vary, not just with one's role or ideology, but equally with one's position in the professional sphere of law. For although it may seem, from the point of view of the bad man, that the judge, the practitioner, the legislator and even the law professor will share a similar view of legal knowledge (for example, they might all view law in terms of rules to be applied), on closer investigation it will soon become evident that the different categories of jurist do not use exactly the same knowledge.[39] Indeed, the difference between the teaching and the practice of a science is well known to philosophers of science, and such differences can be traced to differing epistemological structures.[40]

The problem, of course, is where an epistemological reflection on law ought to start. There is no reason in principle why one should not begin with the bad man, since the one person likely to have contact with law in its widest form – the police, officials, lawyers, courts, prisons and the like – is the person who has passed through the penal system. However, if one makes an analogy with medicine, such an approach would be similar to attempting to gain knowledge of medical science through the forms and modes of thought of a patient. And the difficulty with this standpoint is that it would conceal as much as it would reveal about what it is to have knowledge of medical science. Certainly, one could gain certain insights into medicine as a social system in the factual (empirical) sense; that is to say, one would gain insights into doctors, hospitals, aftercare provisions and so on taken as a social whole. But would such a standpoint give one an insight into diagnosis, viruses, bacteria, drugs and their causal effects? If epistemology is to be a reflection on science, it would need to reflect upon medical science as an object of knowledge in itself. The behaviour of doctors, nurses, surgeons and other officials, as experienced by a patient, as valuable as this might be for medical science, or at least aspects of it, is not medical science as an object in itself. For, as Granger put it, 'scientific knowledge of the kind concerned with experience of the real world always consists of constructing abstract schemes or models of this experience, so as to allow one to exploit, by means of logic and mathematics, the relations between the abstract elements of these models, so as to infer in the end properties corresponding with sufficient precision to the empirical properties directly available'.[41]

Epistemology and Science

Doctors, surgeons and nurses can all to a greater or lesser extent be described as adhering to medical science. But can the same be said of the range of professionals involved with law? Is there such a thing as legal science? And, if so, does such a science transcend national systems or is it an ideology attached to particular national and (or) cultural systems? Much of course will depend upon what one means by science in this context.[42] Jurists have certainly constructed conceptual schemes and models from which they try to exploit the relations between the abstract elements so as to infer solutions to problems. And they have even tried to use mathematical logic in their quest for objective certainty within the legal system. But, as Bergel points out, this kind of method has proved a myth when it comes to law.[43] Mathematical logic implies a particular kind of methodology involving a deductive approach founded upon axioms themselves expressed in highly precise symbols which are entirely different from reasoning ideas such as *bona fides* and 'duty of care' upon which much legal reasoning is based. In addition, there is the problem of legal and scientific truths. A court of law, as an English judge once pointed out, is not an institution engaged in 'establishing an absolute scientific truth'. It 'is engaged in determining what is the proper result to be arrived at, having regard to the evidence before it'. And this involves 'a course of reasoning which could never establish a positive truth of science'.[44]

These observations do not, it has to be said, undermine the notion of a legal science as a scheme of thought, or discourse, that employs weaker abstract concepts than the mathematical sciences. However, the epistemologist must be aware of the dangers that lie in wait for those keen to make use of such a science. The problem with law as a science is that it is a social rather than a natural science and the difference between the two is one of object. The natural sciences may not take natural phenomena as their direct object; yet such natural phenomena act as an independent means of verification of scientific models. The social sciences, in contrast, take humans as their phenomenon to be modelled and this means that the social scientist is always modelling a phenomenon that includes his own behaviour. Moreover, the phenomenon itself cannot be verified in the same way since the behaviour of humans is much more chaotic and complex than the behaviour of, say, comets. Theories about behaviour can easily become theories influencing behaviour, with the result that they become ideologies. Epistemology thus loses its claim to knowledge. As Granger has warned, 'the formation of the concepts in the system constituting the theory comes up against the temptation of reproducing pure and simply those naive and immediate notions upon which we fasten in the actual practice of life'. For, 'a theory dealing with human facts is constantly menaced, if one is not careful, with becoming an ideology, substituting myths for concepts and prescriptions for descriptions'.[45]

Weak social science concepts can, nevertheless, still be useful for analysing social facts and for acting as elements in a model that has its own internal coherence.[46] Take, for example, the thesis advanced by Franz Pringsheim that between Roman and English law there exists what he called an 'inner relationship'.[47] This inner relationship was according to Pringsheim, a 'natural relationship' arising from a similarity of 'spirit' between the Romans and English and it could not be fully explained by rational considerations. Today, for the epistemologist, notions such as 'spirit' are far too weak to be useful as knowledge concepts; they rely too much on what Granger might call 'recourse to images, subjective impressions or universalising myths'.[48] Yet Pringsheim's article remains valuable. Not only does it remind the modern jurist that in terms of methodology there does seem to be a close similarity between the methods of the classical Roman jurists and those of the modern common lawyers.[49] But it raises the possibility that perhaps all legal systems pass through stages of development which manifest themselves in terms of 'spirit'. Now 'spirit' may well be most suspect. However, epistemologists have noticed that the natural sciences do seem to go through stages of development and that is why one is able to speak of a distinction between deductive and inductive science. 'Deduction and induction mark two stages in the development of science,' said Robert Blanché, 'the stages themselves being framed within an initial stage and a final stage'. In fact all the sciences seem to 'follow, in distinguishing themselves only by their degree of advancement, a similar course, passing or being called to pass, successively through the descriptive, inductive, deductive and axiomatic stages'.[50] Might it not be said that Pringsheim was, if only crudely, anticipating this epistemological observation?

Whatever the answer, it would seem that, if one is going to talk in terms of a legal science, one has to envisage it via a constructive form. That is to say, it has to be envisaged through a 'structure' which mediates between fact and science (law), allowing the legal scientist both to make legal sense of the facts and to discover solutions from transformations within the structure. Such a structure is what one calls a 'model'.[51] What, then, is the basis for such a legal model? This, of course, is the fundamental question that should motivate and direct any work on legal epistemology. However, before one can begin to think in terms of developing knowledge models, the discipline of law itself needs to be re-examined since this discipline acts as the reason for posing, in the first place, the knowledge question. Yet what is the basis of legal knowledge? Is it a matter of method and only of method, or is it a matter of something more substantive? And, method or substance, is this knowledge something that can be gleaned only from the history of legal thought or is it a discourse, like mathematics or a foreign language, that can be absorbed, seemingly, by the mind quite independently of history? These are questions that will have to be explored, at least in outline, before anything of substance can be said about legal knowledge.[52] Moreover, given the theoretical nature of the question, the existing theoretical map of law, equally, will need to be studied in outline.[53] The existing diachronic and the synchronic aspects of legal knowledge are, in other words, the starting point for any epistemological investigation of law.

Approaches to Epistemology

One of the jobs of jurisprudence is to fashion an epistemology of law.[54] Yet care must be taken here and not just because in the Anglo-American world the word 'epistemology' has a wider meaning than it does in some of the other European languages. The term 'jurisprudence', in its precise English meaning, is unknown in some civil law countries of continental Europe. (The French term *jurisprudence* means, of course, case law.) In fact, instead of thinking in terms of a very general category, civil lawyers tend to think via a number of separate subjects: general theory of law, philosophy of law, legal epistemology, legal science, sociology of law and so on. Some of these topics interrelate and overlap; but in France there is a sharp difference between general theory and philosophy of law, since the concerns of the two areas are perceived as being very different. Philosophy is seen as being a matter of metaphysics and values, that is to say of the non-technical elements of law, and its starting point is from a metajuridical standpoint; it aims to understand law within a total vision of the world.[55] General theory, in contrast, is concerned with law as a technical discipline; it deals with the normative structure of law in terms of its aims and functions and with the structure, methods and procedures of legal thought.[56] Legal epistemology is more difficult to detach from both general theory and philosophy of law, since the two are intimate parts of legal knowledge itself. Yet as far as strict epistemology is concerned a thinker such as Kant is a philosopher rather than an epistemologist, since his central concerns are with metaphysics rather than the fundamental notions of science.[57]

The Philosophical Approach

Nevertheless, the first approach to legal knowledge is via what might be termed a philosophical viewpoint, using philosophy in its more precise sense of a concern with metaphysics. There are two ways of envisaging this philosophical approach. First, one can view philosophy from the position of science; the question here is whether science is simply part of philosophy or whether it is a body of knowledge detached from philosophy. Is the scientist pursuing scientific research involved in a philosophical pursuit? Secondly, one can abandon any notion of science and see law simply as part of philosophy. From this position law is an art rather than a science.

This debate first surfaces in Roman law inasmuch as the Roman jurists saw themselves as 'real' rather than 'sham' philosophers.[58] They pursued justice (*justitia*) and law itself was envisaged within, and drawing part of its authority from, a total vision of the world which itself was governed by 'natural law' (*ius naturale*).[59] The civil law (*ius civile*) of the Roman state was part of a total knowledge system founded in the *ius gentium* (law of peoples) and *ius naturale*.[60] Law was an art (*ars*), the art of what is good and fair,[61] and this art was in turn founded, via the *ius gentium*, on natural reason (*ratio naturalis*).[62] Later civil lawyers and philosophers developed (or some would say distorted) this idea of a *ius naturale* into a grand universal system of general legal axioms based upon the natural law precept of human reason.[63] Modern versions of this approach are rooted in ideas such as universal values, goods and (or) rights and it is these values, goods or rights which ultimately give law its authority.[64] *Lex injustia non est lex* is a theme that continually underpins such a philosophical approach, although the more sophisticated natural lawyers are often cautious here; the notion of universal human rights is seen as a more effective way of expressing the limits of governmental power.

The Synchronic Approach

To become a lawyer, then, one does not need to take a course in legal history. That is evident from empirical observation inasmuch as legal history is neither a core subject nor a compulsory element in most universities in the Anglo-American world, if not in Europe as a whole.[65] Legal philosophy is able to provide reasoning schemes, capable of rising above their historical origins, within which one can seemingly understand law as a discourse (*ratio naturalis* abstracted from history). Indeed, legal theorists are prepared to reject the historical dimension as a fundamental element of actual legal practice. From an internal point of view, lawyers 'want theories not about how history and economics have shaped their consciousness but about the place of these disciplines in argument about what the law requires them to do or have'.[66] For theories 'that ignore the structure of legal argument for supposedly larger questions of history and society are ... perverse', as they 'ignore questions about the internal character of legal argument, so their explanations are impoverished and defective, like innumerate histories of mathematics'.[67]

In the natural sciences, this direct approach which neglects the temporal dimension in favour of treating a knowledge scheme as it is offered in all its *actualité* is said to be the approach subscribed to by the majority of scientists.[68] Certainly, most legal practitioners would probably regard law as a static or synchronic knowledge structure and this outlook is reinforced by two interrelating and highly successful epistemological assumptions. The first is that legal knowledge consists of legal rules; the second is that these legal rules are identifiable in terms of their particular sources and independent of all other social norms arising from other, non-legal sources. Both of these epistemological assumptions are to be found in what became known as the theory of positivism.

The natural law paradigm was dominant until the end of the 18th century, when it was replaced by a new paradigm, that of positivism. Law was no longer envisaged in terms of a total world system, but as a set of rules 'posited' (*ius positivum*) by a ruler (emperor, king, Parliament and so on). From a historical position, the roots of positivism can be traced back to several ideas already evident in the later Roman sources. These ideas are, first, what pleases the prince has force of law,[69] second, that legislation is a command[70] founded upon sovereignty (*imperium*),[71] and third that all law flows from the emperor (*omnia principis esse intelligantur*).[72] In the later civil law these ideas were developed in conjunction with the higher philosophical value of natural reason, with the result that the 'fundamental assumption on which the idea of a law of Nature rested was that there was a dualism in the realm of law'.[73] With codification this view was undermined; it was not nature that was the source of the codes but the will of the legislator. In other words the command theory of legislation had the effect of undermining the very project upon which codification had been based and what 'was originally projected as a stable statement of natural law ended in natural law's eclipse'.[74] In this new philosophy there was simply no room for ideals, 'except to the extent that they received concrete embodiment in rules actually in force and were consistent with the notion of law as a system with a changing content'.[75]

Broadly speaking, there were two main forms of positivism. In 19th-century England John Austin, building upon the work of

Jeremy Bentham and Thomas Hobbes, developed what might be called empirical positivism: law was no more nor less than the commands of a sovereign, backed by sanctions.[76] Herbert Hart, criticising Austin, fashioned a more sophisticated form of empirical positivism in his 1961 book, *The Concept of Law* (Hart, in the Preface, described his book as an essay in descriptive sociology). Law was a system of two interrelating types of social rules, the union of primary (obligation imposing) and secondary (facultative) rules. These legal rules are endowed with their legality as a result of being ultimately traceable to a rule of recognition which, in turn, is empirically discoverable by the behaviour of top officials (judges, civil servants, legislators and so on) who act 'as if' there is a rule of recognition. Hart accepts, it must be said, that the rule thesis of law is not unproblematic.[77] But, according to Hart, a legal system is a system that *uses* rules 'as standards for the appraisal of ... behaviour' and thus the definition of law is to be found through reference to this functional element.[78]

On the continent positivism took a metaphysical (Kantian) form whose most perfect expression is to be found in the work of Hans Kelsen. This theorist was keen to fashion a science of law purified of all extraneous material, and for him the object of his science was the norm.[79] Law was a logical pyramid of 'oughts' (norms), each norm being grounded in a higher norm, with the whole edifice resting upon the *Grundnorm*. This *Grundnorm* is an entirely rational and *a priori* supposition. When compared with Hart's positivism, Kelsen's structure might look similar to Hart's hierarchy, in that both are ultimately grounded in a fundamental 'ought' (*Grundnorm* and rule of recognition). But there are fundamental differences: norms are not empirical, whereas rules are, and thus German theorists make an important distinction between norms and rules.[80] Nevertheless, the overriding feature of positivism is that legal knowledge consists of normative propositions (empirical or rational) whose validity is in no way dependent upon the moral or social content of these propositions. To have knowledge of law is simply, then, to have knowledge of these rules or norms, irrespective of their content. Scientific positivism of the Kelsenian kind goes, epistemologically speaking, further: the positivist hierarchy is itself a science in that it is an independent rationalisation which has norms as its object. Kelsen has, in other words, gone far in providing one kind of epistemology of law.

Both the philosophical and the scientific (positivist) approach to law are metaphysical to the extent that both are 'idealised' conceptions of 'law'.[81] But the 20th century, building on ideas of the German Historical School (itself using ideas and notions having roots in the Roman sources), was to see a remarkable change of viewpoint. Law came to be seen as a social practice. The immediate roots of sociological jurisprudence are to be found, perhaps ironically, in a school noted for its conceptualism rather than for its contribution to sociology. Yet the German Historical School, for all its abstract and conceptual scientific jurisprudence, grounded these structures, not in some universal theory of natural law, but in the *Volksgeist* of each nation.[82] Law was an emanation of the spirit of the people. In fact disillusionment with conceptualism led Rudolf von Jhering to develop a jurisprudence of interests;[83] and this was taken up by the American jurist Roscoe Pound, who saw law and legal rights as a matter of protected social interests.[84] According to this approach, knowledge of law is not so much about 'rights' but about the interests and social data that these rights reflect.[85] The Marxists went much further and developed a political and social critique founded upon class interests. Legal knowledge, according to some Marxists, was simply a superstructure built upon this economically determined class basis. Some Marxists, however, were more sophisticated in their analysis of the relations between legal institutions (property, contract) and economy. According to Karl Renner's vision, law is more than a mere superstructure inasmuch as its institutions – *persona* and *dominium* – are the means by which the right of the capitalist becomes a form of *imperium* (public power). Ownership takes over the function of regulating power and employment and thus acts as the means of private domination, the power of the capitalist class over the labour class.[86]

Sociological jurisprudence did not stop with economic and social interests. The American Realist movement rejected the notion of law as some idealised model of rules, norms, concepts or whatever.[87] Law was about the behaviour of officials and what courts actually do.[88] Thus, according to this theory, knowledge of law is not about deduction from abstract rules; it is about judicial behaviour in all its aspects – from the construction of facts to the social and political values of the judges and other officials.[89] Critical legal theory has pushed the Marxist and Realist theses to their logical conclusion: there is no such thing as a specifically legal knowledge.[90] This may seem an extreme conclusion, yet it cannot be dismissed by the epistemologist; for, as we shall see, it is by no means certain that, from the position of schemes of intelligibility, law is so easily distinguishable from the other social sciences.

The Diachronic Approach

We have already mentioned that, with regard to the sciences, the question of approaches to epistemology is far from uncontroversial. Jurisprudence soon reveals that similar controversies are to be found with respect to law. These controversies may not be formulated within the framework of a conscious epistemological investigation, for we have seen that jurisprudence is more concerned with the broad question of the nature of law rather than with the narrower issue of legal knowledge. But the philosophical debates are of direct relevance since they often reveal, even if under a slightly different form, old problems which have tormented the knowledge debate. Epistemology cannot escape either from philosophy or, perhaps, from history. Accordingly, an alternative approach to the synchronic is the diachronic: that is to say, an historical and evolutionary approach to the structure of legal knowledge. However, before any epistemological assessment can effectively be attempted, something must be said about the broad development of legal science in Europe.

Legal Epistemology and Legal History

Just where an historical account of legal thought should start is itself a controversial question. From a professional, and historical, point of view probably the only feasible starting point is Roman law as it was rediscovered at the end of the Dark Ages. For, as we have briefly seen, it was the Romans who developed a system of legal reasoning based upon a set of categories, institutions and relationships through which one could comprehend social reality. Law for the Romans became a kind of 'reality imposed upon social reality putting it into order, and ending up by becoming more "true" than the facts'.[91] Indeed, as Watson has argued,[92] to have knowledge of a legal system is not a matter of just knowing rules, but of knowing how the system is structured. And it is in this respect that Roman learning is fundamental, since Roman law not only proved adaptable to a range of completely different economic systems – slavery, feudalism and capitalism – but operated successfully in states of a variety of political or religious persuasions. This 'transplantability' is due in part to the fact that Roman law as it appears in the sources, and thanks to the teaching manuals, 'divides naturally into self-contained and self-referential blocks' and it is these blocks that have proved so adaptable.[93] These blocks also enabled (Roman) law to be considered as forms of knowledge existing in their own right with their own logic (using the term in a loose sense) and independent of the facts of society. Roman law, in other words, is a self-contained form of knowledge.

Roman Sources

Now this is not to ignore the historical fact that customary systems, including the English common law, developed independently of Roman learning. But, today, not only is it accepted that common law thinking has been influenced by Roman law over the centuries, but abstract conceptions such as legal theory and legal science are conceptions that transcend national systems. At this higher level, as has already been observed, 'so many roads in law lead us back to Rome by way of the commentators on Roman law'.[94] More recently, Berman has argued that to have knowledge of the Western legal tradition one must study the legal thought of the medieval Papal Revolution, since it was the medieval papacy that developed the governmental institutions and bureaucratic apparatus needed to make the system work. And this apparatus included a professional judiciary trained in the medieval canon and Roman law. Thus, for Berman, all Western legal systems, including the common law, 'have common historical roots from which they derive not only a common terminology and common techniques but also common concepts, common principles, and common values'.[95] Moreover, it is often only possible to understand the distinctive qualities of the common law and other 'customary' systems by reference to the continental civil law tradition based on Roman law. To have knowledge of the separateness of English and American law, one must have knowledge of Roman learning.

Roman law itself is not, however, adequate as a mass of source material to understand the development of a Western legal science, for over the centuries professional jurists have brought to bear on the texts, and on the commentary that these texts produced, quite different methods. In classical Roman law (27BC–250AD approximately) the method was rooted in concrete problems and cases; the Romans were practical lawyers concerned only with actual situations and they proceeded from hypothetical facts to hypothetical facts. The *Digest* (a collection of juristic case law) is, accordingly, full of cases of actual situations and in giving advice on these cases 'the jurists hypothetically varied the actual facts of the situations presented to them, and considered what the legal effect of such hypothetical variations would be'.[96] It is only in the textbooks written for students, the Institutes (*institutiones*), that one finds law as a set of written propositions systematically arranged and simplified for clarity and ease of assimilation. *Scientia iuris* (a term to be found in the Roman sources) was assimilated knowledge to be distinguished from the *ars* (art) of deciding cases and knowing what is good and fair (*ars boni et aequi*).

Glossators and Post-glossators

The medieval jurists who took up again, and developed, the Roman law in the first European law faculties seemingly continued the Roman methodology.[97] The first group of jurists, academics working mainly in the law faculties of Northern Italy in the 11th and 12th centuries, attracted the name 'Glossators' because they annotated (glossed) the newly discovered Roman law texts with interpretative comments explaining difficult terms and notions and cross-referencing one text with another. As Professor Carbasse explains, the 'method of the Glossators was identical to that of the grammarians: textual explanation'.[98] The methodology was particularly precise. Working on the rediscovered Roman law materials, the master would read the texts stopping 'at each important or difficult word to offer an explanation of it: a *gloss* (from a Greek word meaning both "language" and "word")'. In addition the Glossators began to collect together scattered texts on the same subject and thus they also laid the foundations for what today we would call the textbook tradition.[99] In the 13th century, a second school of medieval jurists set about adapting Roman law to the social and political circumstances of their time. The Post-glossators, while still remaining close to the actual Roman texts, broke away from the structure and paragraphs of the *Digest* and *Code* by producing commentaries and opinions which were to transcend as well as influence the multitude of local and customary laws throughout Europe.[100] Although the Roman sources remained the starting point and fundamental authority for these opinions and commentaries, the great jurists of the period such as Bartolus went far in laying the foundation for modern Western legal theory and legal reasoning. Their work was to form a 'common law' (*ius commune*) of Europe.

However, the scholastic methodology that they used was more self-conscious in form than had been the Roman method which no doubt inspired it. And, more importantly from a scientific point of view, the object of study was not so much factual situations as the cases to be found in the Roman texts. The object of legal science thus became, at least for the Glossators, not the factual situations thrown up by society but the texts of Roman law.[101] Legal knowledge was a closed body of knowledge and all that one needed to know about law was to be found in the *Corpus Iuris Civilis* (the source book of Roman law). Nevertheless, the medieval jurists continued the tradition of starting out from particular factual situations in order to work towards solutions arising out of those facts (*ex facto ius oritur*: law arises out of fact, as one medieval jurist put it). The method was dialectical (*dialectica*) in that arguments for (*pro*) and against (*contra*) were part of the process by which irrelevant and unreasonable possibilities were excluded; and this dialectical method involved in turn the use of classification (*divisio*), distinction (*distinctio*) and debate (*disputatio*). This methodology proved particularly fruitful in conjunction with the 'new logic' (*logica nova*) that was being disseminated throughout Europe with the rediscovery of Aristotle's works on the syllogism. Knowledge was a matter of categorisation, interpretation and analysis.

Humanists

At the end of the Middle Ages this casuistic approach was to give way to one which emphasised (Roman) law as a rational science (*scientia iuris*) rather than an art (*ars boni et aequi*). Law was a product of the mind. This process had started with the later medieval jurists whose work was progressing beyond the interpretative glosses (*glosae*) attaching to each section and paragraph of the *Corpus Iuris Civilis*; but the revolution came with a movement known as Humanism. The Humanist jurists brought to the Roman legal sources new methods which took interpretation beyond the texts themselves and into the wider world of the humanities – into the historical, philosophical and linguistic circumstances surrounding the Roman material. What did the words mean and what was the rationality behind them? Was there not a basic simplicity behind the Roman texts which had been obscured, not just by the mass of medieval glosses, but by the corrupt additions and alterations of the late Roman lawyers who had compiled the *Digest*?

The programme of the Humanist jurists was to search for the purity of reason in Roman law, a purity which they believed had been obscured by the 'acquisitive pettifogging' and repellent 'jargon which passed among the lawyers for Latin' of the medieval scholastics.[102] In fact the new approach was more a reaction to the cumbersome procedures of the casuistic methods which even Justinian had recognised were unsuitable for legal education.[103] Now of course the results of such cumbersome methodology had been, and remained, ideal for practitioners, in that they provided a rich source of material for dealing with the diverse and detailed problems of everyday legal life. A legal science obsessed with factual problems is a science fashioned for practitioners. But in the university lecture hall it was possible for a teacher to take the whole academic year to comment on just several passages of Roman law.[104] What the New Learning offered was, seemingly, a much more efficient way of learning law. And the Roman work that best understood and represented this efficiency was the *Institutiones*, the elementary textbooks, which stressed system over detail. As the Humanist Duarenus (1509–59) warned, even a library full of commentaries cannot answer every case which might arise in practice. What is needed is a system capable of formulating general principles which, once established, can be used to cope with each individual concrete case (*in universalibus methodus, in singularibus exercitatio*).[105] With the Humanists, legal science, in the modern sense of the term 'science', had been born.

Natural Lawyers and the Codes

During the 17th and 18th centuries the German professors, often trained in mathematics as well as law, continued the work of the Humanists and reconstructed the Roman law into global and autonomous systems from which legal solutions could be extracted using increasingly rigorous deductive methods. Law was no longer to be induced out of the concrete facts of cases, but facts were to be subsumed under the rationalised system of intellectual discipline of law (*ex iure factum oritur*: fact is deduced from law). This transposition into the legal domain of a mode of reasoning which was essentially mathematical in its approach had, evidently, important consequences for legal method.[106] It oriented legal science towards a conceptual hardening whereby deduction became explicable only because of the existence of 'structures' from which necessary consequences could be discovered. These structures were finally given concrete expression in the great European codes and the effect of these codes was to force practitioner, judge and professor all to see legal knowledge as a model of interrelated and systematised rules and principles. In turn the model of rules was founded upon the will of the legislator which, in its turn, represented the will (*volonté*) or spirit (*Volksgeist*) of the people.

The effect of the codes was to erase Roman law as a formal source of knowledge. From the moment of their arrival, the object of legal science was only the codes, together with other legislative rules, that is to say the positive law emanating from the centralised legislature.[107] And closely associated with this scientific assumption was the deductive method. In order to find solutions in particular cases one only had to apply the model of rules to the facts in question; the rule constituted the major premise, the established facts as perceived by the rule the minor premise and the court decision the solution.[108] Of course, there would be difficult cases where the rule would need interpretation. However, the methodology here was also straightforward. The role of the court was to discover the intention of the legislator either through its *volonté* as expressed for example in *les travaux préparatoires* (French model) or through an elaborate structure of scientific concepts. This latter model consisted of an abstract model of norms through which both court and legislator functioned and which gained its constitutional legitimacy from a fundamental norm (*Grundnorm*) (German model).[109] In short, the mission of the judge was to submit himself only to the written text of legislative law (*lex, la loi*). Where the law was clear, deduction and not interpretation was the method (*de claris non fit interpretatio*); where the text was less clear, one searched only within the written language of *la loi*.[110]

Positivists

The legal theory which developed out of this scientific view of law attracted, as we have seen, the label 'positivism', from the medieval Latin term *ius positivum,* itself a development of the classical term *ius positum*. Law was a set of rules posited by the constitutionally valid ruler. This view of law became all-consuming in that both theory and practice (method) were swallowed up by a science which saw as its object only the written manifestation of the will of the legislator.[111] Knowledge of law thus became knowledge of the 'sources of law'. One must not, of course, underestimate the practical importance of such a thesis, since one fundamental issue that jurists will always have to face is the distinction between legal and non-legal rules, a question which seemingly always leads back to the source of the rule. Moreover, it has to be stressed that such a scientifically oriented view of law does not of itself imply that the foundation of law is grounded in, and only in, the will of the ruler. One can still distinguish, as the Romans did, between *ius civile* (positive law) and *ius naturale*. However, 'when interest in the philosophy of law was revived towards the end of the nineteenth century, the only hope of advance seemed to lie in putting the investigation upon a purely positive basis by clearing the ground of the fictions and assumptions which, under the name of natural law, were blamed for having made philosophy suspect in the minds of lawyers'.[112] Natural law was an ideal and not a positive system. Or, to put it another way, a rule is either a legal rule or it is not.

Retreat from Positivism

Leaving aside the debate about natural law as opposed to positive law – a debate that never actually died[113] – the most effective retreat from positivism and the *mos geometricus* resulted from the one great epistemological weakness of positivism as a theory about the nature of law. Positivism could never adequately explain the reasoning processes of the judge other than in terms of the syllogism and (or) of interpretational discretion. Where the law was clear, the syllogism (seemingly) applied; where it was unclear, the judges interpreted the language of the legal text to be applied so as to create a further premise to add to the logic of the application process. As Hart put it, the discretion left to the judge by the language of the rule may be very wide; 'so that if he applies the rule, the conclusion, even though it may not be arbitrary or irrational, is in effect a choice'.[114] Positivism stops at the discretion of the judge. This is a serious gap, since one cannot have a science without a method,[115] and if the method is suspect it would seem to follow that so is the science. Can one really have knowledge of law simply in having a knowledge of the sources and the positive rules flowing from these sources?

The theorists who attempted to look beyond the positive rules were the American Realists.[116] American Realism came in a variety of different forms, but its main point of focus was the court process and in this respect the school offers a radical departure from the traditional positivism which emphasised knowledge of law as knowledge of formal rules. The centre of the legal world is not, according to the Realists, the mass of rules: it is to be found, instead, 'in specific court decisions (i.e. judgments, orders, and decrees) in specific lawsuits'.[117] Law is what officials do about disputes.[118] This reorientation of the object of legal knowledge had profound implications not just for the value of rules themselves – the legal concepts as described by legal rules were seen as transcendental nonsense[119] – but also for facts. The way in which judge and (or) jury interpret fact is as much a matter of prejudice and uncertainty as is the interpretation of vague paper rules, for humans are fallible and so witnesses are not reliable and jurors and judges are unconsciously prejudiced.[120] The key to legal knowledge is, then, the behaviour of deciding cases and it is thus decisions which form the object of legal knowledge. Or, put another way, there 'is no science of law apart from the science of legal decision, and no law but case law'.[121]

As a philosophical or an epistemological thesis, American Realism is not without its problems.[122] Nevertheless, it will always remain central to legal epistemology inasmuch as it puts the emphasis on the reasoning processes of those who have to interpret and apply the law. It opens up, in other words, the law to psychological, sociological and ideological theories in such a way as to marginalise the rule thesis. Law is a cognitive process that might pretend to be founded upon propositional knowledge (rules) applied objectively to factual situations via the logic of the syllogism, but in truth it is a decision-making process that is rooted in the values and beliefs of those who make the decisions. And these values and beliefs are, in turn, determined by a whole range of social, political and psychological factors. Values and ideology can, then, make just as much a claim to be the object of a legal science as any set of codified or uncodified rules and this means that the social upbringing and educational developments of judges can justifiably claim to be part of legal knowledge.[123]

Epistemological Weakness of Realism

Now, the idea of legal values as an object of knowledge does not create any inherent difficulty at one level, since such values can be more or less identified and described.[124] Indeed, such values can be translated into a plausible theory of judicial decision making founded upon the politics and ideology of judges.[125] However, just as positivism excludes from the picture the cognitive and intellectual aspects of the reasoner, so Realism eclipses any kind of knowledge system outside of the application and decision-making process. Ideologically, this is dangerous, in that it is a fundamental aspect of traditional Western legal thought – particularly with respect to criminal law – that law as an objective system of knowledge be knowable in advance of any court proceedings. And this ideology is part of legal knowledge itself in that it is expressed as a fundamental maxim: *nulla crimen sine lege* (no crime without posited rule).[126]

An epistemological thesis that says that law as a system of objective knowledge is unknowable will, then, always be a contradiction – and not just in terms of legal education (since students in Western law schools do not spend all their time looking at the cognitive aspects of legal officials), but in terms of analytical tools that can, if only imperfectly, be objectively described. It is actually possible to have knowledge of article 1384 (or whatever) of the French Civil Code and to apply it to facts. Of course, this is not to say that article 1384 is a normative piece of propositional knowledge. It might, for instance, be a structural relationship between person and thing that inserts itself, or is 'discovered', in particular factual situations. Nor is it to say that it is applied via the syllogism; it might be applied because of a value judgment or some other psychological reason. But the code or other set of rules remains a discourse capable of acting as an objective discourse (*res*) to which the mind (*intellectus*) can respond. Even if the concepts and language are transcendental nonsense and (or) are incapable of acting as a means to truths (except in a relative sense), it is possible to have knowledge of the French Civil Code. Equally, it is possible to say that most French lawyers have knowledge of it as well. A realist or decisionist theory will go far in explaining the cases involving the application of the code, but such theories simply do not explain the discourse as it is passed from one generation to another. It is similar to an epistemology of science that explains science only in terms of what scientists do in laboratories. Scientific epistemology must also explain what goes on in the lecture hall and how such information taught is used in relation to the objects of scientific discourse and issues such as truth and falsity.

New Hermeneutics

However, the re-emphasis of the role of the judge provided the opportunity to question, not only what judges actually did when they reasoned, but also what they ought to do. With regard to the reasoning process itself, positivism and legal science had resulted in an emphasis on abstract formalisation. It was a question of analytical reasoning whereby the reasoner started out from axiomatic – that is to say, necessary and incontestably true premises – to arrive at equally necessary conclusions. As Bergel points out, the syllogism became the general support for the application process; yet 'mathematical logic involves an axiomatic stage in the presentation which requires an explicit and rigorous definition of all the notions and propositions utilised for the proofs'.[127] Can law be so divorced from social reality? Does a judge really reason on the basis of a model so abstracted from everyday social life?

These questions led some jurists to look at alternative forms of reasoning and, in particular, to focus on the logic of argumentation.[128] Instead of deduction, which emphasised form over content, was not law a matter of induction and dialectical reasoning – that is to say, a matter of persuasion and conviction with regard to the substance of the matter in issue? In emphasising legal reasoning as argumentation writers such as Perelman[129] and Bergel[130] do not claim that the syllogism has no role. It remains 'the general support of reasoning, but the choice of premises presupposes each time a debate'. That is to say, no 'premise can be admitted without admitting at the same time the opposite premise, so that no conclusion can be retained without having envisaged the opposite conclusion and without having operated a choice between two possible conclusions'.[131] Certainly, the identification of legal reasoning with axiomatic logic would give it the certainty and rigour that argumentation and dialectical reasoning lacks. But 'the reduction of law to equations is a myth', since it implies that the language of law is symbolisation and calculus when in truth it consists of terms like 'public policy' and 'good faith'.[132] Moreover, the reduction of law to formal logic would be contrary to its essential purpose. The function of law is to regulate social life and thus legal reasoning cannot divorce itself from the values attached to the conclusions reached by the reasoners.[133]

This New Rhetorician's thesis does not, however, deny the notion of discretion and choice on the part of the judge and to this extent his new rhetoric approach to legal reasoning is perfectly reconcilable with Hart's positivism. Hart and the New Rhetoricians might be said to be describing different aspects of the same system. However, some other legal philosophers have, in contrast, advanced the thesis that judges do not have discretion when they reason. Ronald Dworkin argues, for example, that ideally a judge 'must construct a scheme of abstract and concrete principles that provide a coherent justification for all common law precedents and, so far as these are to be justified on principle, constitutional and statutory provisions as well'.[134] Having constructed such a scheme out of what has gone before, the judge must interpret this scheme in order to arrive at a solution; he is not entitled to 'strike out in some new direction of his own'.[135] Moreover, in constructing what has gone before, he cannot invent a better history than the one that exists in the legal sources, since his duty is to interpret legal history as he finds it.[136] The implication flowing from this thesis is that there are right and wrong answers in legal reasoning; and even if this uniquely right answer thesis, in practice, looks far too idealistic, Sartorius makes the observation that it is a question of viewpoint. In any particular case a judge is simply not entitled to act as if there is no uniquely correct answer.[137] Now, the epistemologist might well question this thesis on the basis that judges simply do not reason in this way, but that would be to confuse philosophy with epistemology. Writers like Dworkin are not claiming that all judges actually reason in the way he alleges; indeed, Dworkin specifically talks in terms of the superhuman judge (Hercules). Such philosophers are claiming that this is how the ideal judge ought to reason.

In terms of a retreat from positivism and legal science, the right answer thesis suggests, if not a model of axioms, at least a structure capable of acting as an interpretative (hermeneutical) model from which the correct solution in any case can be found. Is this, then, not a return to structural models of rules rather than a theory actually founded on adjudication? Two points must be made in response to this apparent contradiction. First, whether or not writers such as Dworkin are actually offering a genuine epistemological thesis (as opposed to a philosophical one), the fact remains that it is impossible to escape from reasoning models when dealing with epistemological issues. Scientific thought and reasoning are all about the construction of models from which the scientist can make deductions, calculations, developments and the like. As Granger asserts, to 'understand means, in this respect, to fit a fact or a law into a system of concepts where they appear as coming from this system; more generally, it means inserting a theory into a larger ("more comprehensive") theory within which it then becomes a particular case'.[138] Following this view, it can be said that Dworkin not only talks in terms of a series of concepts (rights, principles and rules) but, as we shall see, also tries to situate his thesis within a more general theory of interpretation. Secondly, the thesis or model proposed by writers like Dworkin is much more open-ended than the axiomatic constructions of the German-influenced legal scientists; judges are bound to take account of both rules and principles. These latter propositions may well be situated as much in moral and political ideals as in positive legal models and thus, to this extent, these adjudication-theory writers might be said to situate themselves within the *ius naturale* tradition, rather than in strict positivism. What Dworkin does share with the positivists is the view that knowledge of law is knowledge of propositions (rules and principles). The difference, then, between the natural law tradition and the positivists becomes one of defining what propositions count as 'legal' propositions and what propositions do not.

History, Theory and Comparative Law

A historical approach to epistemology needs to take account not just of legal theory but also the contextual background in which such theories have been fashioned. One major distinction, accordingly, between Hans Kelsen and Ronald Dworkin is that the former was trained within the German model whereas the latter is the product of the common law. The historical developments in both traditions are, as is common knowledge, very different. The common law lacked both a Roman law and a university tradition, with the result that it is a creation of practice; the role of the professors, and of a legal science, has been marginal.[139] It would seem evident, given the dichotomy between the teaching and practice of a science, that the epistemological models might well be different. Yet legal philosophy is largely indifferent to legal traditions to the extent that it is a subject that seeks to rise above both history and tradition in order to fashion theories about the nature of 'law'.

When one turns to comparative law, on the other hand, one finds a subject that is, or should be, sensitive to difference. Comparing civil law and common law, Pierre Legrand has emphasised the particular importance of *difference* in questions of legal epistemology; such questions 'do not simply raise issues of abstract reasoning' since one must also consider 'matters of social order'. If one were to assume a common European code on some given area of law, says Legrand, the 'common lawyer will never approach the reading, interpretation, and the application of the code in the same way as her Italian counterpart'. Equally, 'the common lawyer will never be able truly to understand how the Italian lawyer approaches and appreciates the code'. For the '*summa differentia* will, simply, never give way: epistemological congruence is a chimera'.[140]

The Legrand thesis is, it has to be said, controversial and not without serious problems,[141] yet it is also a valuable thesis in two particular ways. First, it helps remind the epistemologist that legal knowledge within the EU might not be uniform and that, when viewed from the position of a *scientia iuris,* there may well be different stages or levels of 'development'. Such difference of stages could be a key to the formulation of a comprehensive model of knowledge. Secondly, Legrand's thesis sharply and usefully distinguishes the work of comparatists from the preoccupations of legal theorists. Theory has had the effect of masking, to some extent, the historical and cultural differences between legal systems and this has had both beneficial and detrimental effects on the epistemological investigation of law. It is beneficial in that theory has facilitated the flow of ideas between the various systems and traditions; thus the Pandectist construction of a *scientia iuris* acted as the basis for English legal theory (jurisprudence) at the end of the 19th century.[142] Anglo-American theorists, for their part, are now having their influence on continental thinking.[143] It is detrimental, in that the imposition of one set of ideas, formulated within a particular cultural tradition, on a system of legal thinking conceived within a different cultural tradition can be distorting.

For example, Van Caenegem makes the point that, when one thinks of a divergence between common law and the civil law, the tendency is to see the former as diverging from the latter. The common law is the odd one out amongst an EU dominated by codified systems. Yet these codifications are the result of a legal science based upon a 'holy book', namely the *Corpus Iuris Civilis*. 'It is amazing and probably unique,' observes Van Caenegem, 'that the medieval world suddenly accepted the great law book of a society that had been gone for centuries as its ultimate authority, and entirely reshaped its own law through scholastic glosses, disputations and commentaries on this venerable relic of a defunct world.' And, of course, he is able to conclude that, seen in this light, 'the English way of developing existing rules, modernising the courts and their procedures and gradually building up new case law or occasionally appealing to the lawgiver, but for the rest letting the professionals get on with their daily task of pleading and adjudicating, appears much more normal'.[144] Codification, and the hermeneutical tradition that both preceded it and attached to it, is not necessarily synonymous with legal knowledge. It may be one form of legal knowledge, but it is by no means unique.

Roman Law and Common Law

There is, however, an irony to the divergent traditions of which Van Caenegem himself is only too aware. He makes the point that the Romans knew nothing about codes and developed their law in a piecemeal fashion. 'The idea,' he says, 'that the law was contained or even half hidden in some old book and had to be ascertained by the exegetical method was quite alien to the Roman world.'[145] The irony is that it is possible to conclude that the original Roman law mind had more in common with the English law mentality than with the modern civilian mind. Indeed, one Romanist has, as we have seen, talked of an 'inner relationship' between English and Roman law.[146] However, care must be taken here since there are both similarities and differences. The development of the two systems through a law of actions undoubtedly 'led legal practitioners in Rome and England to think not so much in terms of rights as in terms of types of action, and to interest themselves more in the concrete *facts* which fell within the various actions or writs rather than in elaborating the substantive law into a *system* based on some rational method'.[147] But, as we shall see, the Roman jurists did produce an institutional system for students within which this 'procedural thinking' was encapsulated. And this system, which was arguably the means by which Roman law was transplanted into modern Europe,[148] was based upon a symmetry that had much less meaning in the common law.

In fact, the English forms of action were in many ways very different from Roman law actions and gave rise to a different taxonomical structure. Debt, trespass, nuisance, trover, account and the like would have been unfamiliar structures to a mind that rigidly distinguished between actions *in rem* and *in personam*.[149] More interesting, in some ways, is the later history of the common law. For, with the abolition of the forms of action in the middle of the 19th century, English law found itself without any internal structure. Consequently, 'substantial categories had to be adopted in order to give the law some appearance of system, and those categories, so far as the common law of obligations and moveable property were concerned, were contract and tort'.[150] Given that this 'Romanisation' is a continuing process – unjust enrichment as a category separate from contract and tort has only quite recently been recognised[151] and the fashioning of a *ius publicum* category is still going on, if problematic – the epistemologist has to be wary when it comes to constructing the objects of knowledge. 'Contracts' clearly have to be understood not just in the context of Roman thinking but also across English forms of action. What is thus constructed may, then, have to be appreciated within a more complex model than the 'contract' envisaged in the *Code civil*, which does not carry the baggage of trespass, debt and other remedies – remedies that often had an *in rem* flavour alongside the *in personam* relationship.[152] In short, the whole 'inner relationship' thesis is in need of some sophisticated concepts if it is to move from being a mere creative metaphor to an epistemological focal point. That said, both Roman and common lawyers have much to contribute to a better and more precise understanding of methodology, if only because they represent stages where it may just be possible to escape the all-pervading modernist idea that the object of legal science is the legal proposition. Roman law and common law offer an alternative to the *ars hermeneutica*.

Internal versus External Approaches to Epistemology

Natural law theory, positivism and sociological jurisprudence each have their own separate epistemological implications. Yet what they share is a synchronic discourse that is not as such dependent upon time and place. This may seem a curious statement with regard to sociological jurisprudence,[153] but what is meant is that a sociological approach to law represents a scheme of knowledge dependent, not on construction, but upon viewpoint. As Cotterrell explains:

> The numerous approaches to legal analysis which can be categorised as sociological in the broadest sense are unified only by their deliberate self-distancing from the professional viewpoint of the lawyer. It is implicit in the aim of empirical legal theory that law is always viewed 'from the outside', from the perspective of an observer of legal institutions, doctrine and behaviour, rather than that of a participant, although participants' perceptions may be taken into account as data for the observer ... Behind such an objective usually stands the motive of adopting an epistemological standpoint from which a radical critique of and challenging to lawyers' professional conceptions of law becomes possible.[154]

Natural law and positivism are, by contrast, internal perspectives. They approach legal rules in terms of their formal sources as defined by criteria internal to legal knowledge itself. Thus even if legal rules are said to be based upon sources external to law – for example morality as a source of law – one can still talk of an internal perspective inasmuch as it is law itself defining the criterion of morality as source. Now, one can evidently talk about internal and external epistemologies, yet the problem with both the philosophical and the empirical (sociological, economics and so on) viewpoints is that they are extremely limited in their epistemological functions. Positivism, for all its scientific rigour, could account for case law decisions in only two ways: either rules were applied to facts via the syllogism or they functioned, particularly in hard cases, through judicial discretion. Where a rule was ambiguous there was scope for interpretation and this left the door open to a Realist approach which, although able to explain interpretation through, say, political values,[155] could not easily theorise *legal* knowledge.[156] The end result was to deny the existence of legal knowledge. Yet this denial seems to be contradicted both by history (the history of legal thought) and by social institutions (law courts, law faculties and so on). The challenge, then, for the epistemologist is to rethink the possibility of legal knowledge.

Epistemology and Adjudication

When one examines jurisprudence as a subject it is, of course, not short of theories about law. Yet one problem with many textbooks on jurisprudence is that they contain relatively little actual law in the traditional meaning of the term. There are few statutes, cases or law review articles devoted to contractual mistake, criminal procedure and so on. Now one response to this lack of 'law' is to say that jurisprudence is a subject beyond the 'black-letter', or doctrinal, legal texts; jurisprudence functions on a meta-rule level. The danger here for the epistemologist is that the practitioner gets left out of the knowledge model. A comprehensive theory of legal knowledge, if it is to be genuinely comprehensive, needs to be more integrated with the 'science' (practice) of law. As Blanché has expressed it:

> Epistemology is, in relation to science, a secondary process, bearing upon a primary activity. It is a reflection on science in the same way that aesthetics has essentially become a reflection on art and moral philosophy a reflection on ethics ... The reflection on science is not ... necessarily philosophic, it does not necessarily get one to abandon the scientific demands, it allows itself to be integrated into the domain of science. On one condition however: that it makes sure that it leaves out of account those things that the science takes for itself as its object ... Under pain of confusion between the levels of the language, it must, then, consider only the scientific *discourse*, treated as a system of signs combining between themselves according to certain rules independent of what they can evoke ... But the separation between the science itself and its object is never as clear-cut as theory requires ...[157]

An epistemological theory of law thus needs to go much further than merely speculating about the sources and nature of legal rules. It has to incorporate a theory of adjudication since, at the very least, the application of rules to factual situations involves the categorisation of these situations to make them amenable to the law. Before one can apply the legal rules one must categorise the facts, but before one can categorise the facts one must apply the legal rules. This objective no doubt appears ambitious and perhaps a little daunting. The point that needs to be emphasised, however, is that the objective of an epistemological model is simply the articulation of the requirements which will endow the competent jurist with his or her skills. This is relevant to the comparatist, as Louise Rayar, an accomplished legal translator, has asserted:

> Without comparing legal systems, we would have no idea of the conceptual differences between systems and could not assess the usefulness of foreign terms as translations. The possible existence of a common ground (a 'common sense') between the source language term and legal terms available in the target language needs to be established. I think of it as applied comparative law. It should be conducted at a systematic and conceptual level, as well as at the word level. Systematic comparison involves the structure and organization of a particular legal area. At the conceptual level, the difference in legal concepts, institutions and solutions is studied. It is not sufficient to study a system merely at the level of its terminology. Kisch has said it much more elegantly in French: '*La connaissance des termes, ou plutôt de leurs définitions, vous laisse dans l'ignorance par rapport au système, à la structure, à l'économie de la science*', adding: '*le droit étranger ne s'apprend pas par l'étude d'un vocabulaire juridique.*' Or: one does not learn about foreign law by studying its legal vocabulary.[158]

Rayar is making the important point, from the view of a comparative lawyer, that legal rules (propositional knowledge) are not enough. One needs to get at the structures underpinning systems of legal thought.

Interpretation and Fact

One might note, in particular, Rayar's emphasis on the structure and organisation of a legal area. Such structures are not simply a matter of organising the law under different headings and into different categories; they are also fundamental to the understanding of facts. As a French professor has pointed out, 'the jurist can hardly study the facts without seeing them through a pre-categorisation' and 'the function of the categorisation is not to describe reality, but to subject it to the most appropriate legal regime'.[159] Or, as the scientist would put it, 'facts are never evident' since they 'have sense only in relation to a system of thought, through a pre-existing theory'.[160]

What the epistemologist must appreciate, however, is, as Amselek has noted, that the organisation of facts is not the same as the interpretation of legal texts:

> To categorise objects, facts, acts and situations is to subsume them under concepts (in particular specifically legal concepts). It is to give them a conceptual clothing fabricated out of our spirit: between raw fact – data immediately perceived – and categorised fact, there is this intermediate clothing which is not purely neutral and transparent but which has on the contrary a certain 'vision of the world', as the modern philological and neo-humboldtian theories put it. But all intermediation operated by the mental processes does not necessarily amount to interpretation. No doubt before categorising facts with regard to concepts used in legal regulation, the written text which acts as the vehicle for this regulation must be interpreted … but after the categorisation itself, the actual labelling of facts is no longer interpretation.[161]

This epistemological thesis stands in stark contrast to the one advocated by Ronald Dworkin. This legal philosopher, whose great merit is that he has shifted the emphasis of legal philosophy off positivism and onto adjudication, holds the view that law itself is interpretation. To support this view, Dworkin has had recourse to the analogy of the chain novelist. 'We can find an even more fruitful comparison between literature and law,' he says, 'by constructing an artificial genre of literature that we might call the chain novel.' And he explains:

> In this enterprise a group of novelists writes a novel *seriatim*; each novelist in the chain interprets the chapters he has been given in order to write a new chapter, which is then added to what the next novelist receives, and so on. Each has the job of writing his chapter so as to make the novel being constructed the best it can be, and the complexity of this task models the complexity of deciding a hard case under law ...[162]

This is a striking analogy and one that legal epistemology cannot afford to ignore. But it cannot easily be reconciled with Amselek's assertion that fact categorisation is not a matter of interpretation. As both Atias and Amselek indicate, a simple distinction between fact and law no longer suffices to explain the process by which law is applied to a factual situation. Categorisation of fact is clearly central, but a 'vision of the world' or 'pre-categorisation' model seemingly assumes a vital function. Just what acts as the foundation for this vision or model is something that should be central to the epistemologist, and the starting point is legal classification itself. Here, then, is the project of legal epistemology. It is as much about the facts as about the law in a textual sense, since to know law is to know how to handle and view facts in a particular way. Yet the project has been to a large extent obscured by legal philosophy which, by emphasising the rule model, has equally emphasised a particular scheme of intelligibility. Legal philosophy has become identified with hermeneutics.

Thus the problem with the Dworkin thesis, for the epistemologist at any rate, is that it locates legal knowledge in the interpretation of normative propositions (that is to say rules and principles). There seems little room for facts as such. Now Amselek does not appear to be denying the importance of the text (normative proposition) or its interpretation; but what he seems to be saying is that there is an aspect to legal knowledge – an intermediate stage – that lies between the facts and the text. This intermediate stage can be seen as one of legal 'construction' of the factual situation so as to bring it into contact with the interpreted text. This 'construction' stage is not itself a matter of interpretation. This view is not, it must be said, shared by all French jurists. Ivainer seemingly agrees with Atias and Amselek that there is a pre-categorisation stage whereby facts are brought into contact with the normative system of rules,[163] but he regards this as a hermeneutical exercise and he openly talks of the interpretation of facts.[164] What the epistemologist needs to do is to try to separate the exercise of interpretation, which always is in danger of becoming nothing more than an ideology,[165] from schemes or abstract models of the facts. These schemes or models may be social constructions and thus no less influenced by ideology. But, if they can be isolated in a 'scientific' manner from the interpretation of rules and principles, there is at least the possibility of being able to determine in a more precise way how these facts are constructed in terms of their own elements and relationships. Are facts capable of being the object of an epistemological model independent of any particular set of normative propositions?

Science and Object of Science

One problem facing those wishing to equate law with the sciences, or even to free facts from the interpretation process, is that law is the object of its own science. As Atias has observed:

> The positive sciences have owed their success to the systematic research into the relations between phenomena, the laws of nature. Now the law itself contains such laws. This is not the science of law, it is the law which determines the consequences attached to the non-performance of a contract or to such and such wrong. In consequence, the law is its own science ... The great merit – rarely recognised – of Hans Kelsen is to have emphasised both the common tendency to confuse law and science of law and the necessity for their distinction ... He thus emphasised one of the reasons which have hindered the development of legal epistemology, that is the difficulty of distinguishing the science of law – exclusive object of this epistemology – from other neighbouring activities.[166]

The problem is exacerbated, as we shall see later in this work, by the historical basis of both law and legal science being founded in the same book, the *Corpus Iuris Civilis* of Roman law. The law itself, or what is traditionally seen as the law (that is to say, rules, statutes and case law examples), and the scientific rationalisation of this knowledge (*scientia iuris*) were one and the same as far as the medieval universities were concerned. In other words there was, and remains, a confusion between language (law) and meta-language (legal science). The system of signs becomes confused with the object that these signs are attempting to rationalise. Indeed, they can become one and the same discourse.

Facts thus become part of positive law. They become part of the normative rule. A jurist looking at the tort (delict) of negligence in, for example, Roman and English law finds that a term such as 'foreseeability' (*providere*) is merged within particular factual situations. The result is that the factual situation itself cannot easily be understood outside of this notion of foreseeability while, in turn, the notion itself conjures up particular factual situations. Take the following examples. A farmer sets fire to his field to burn off the stubble and the fire spreads, because of the wind, to neighbouring land and destroys the neighbour's vineyard.[167] A ship accidentally releases crude oil into a harbour and the oil spreads to a nearby wharf, where it catches fire, owing to welding operations, and the wharf is destroyed.[168] In both of these situations the opinion of jurist or judge, as recorded in texts, is that the person who occasions the spread of fire or oil will be liable if they lacked skill when furnishing the opportunity for damage.[169] Ought they to have foreseen that the act or omission which was to occasion the harm might cause harm to a neighbour? It is of course possible to formulate an abstract normative proposition which gives expression to these cases,[170] but the proposition is of itself empty and it is the examples that give it content. The examples thus become part of the normative proposition to be 'interpreted' either through analogy (is the dropping of branches by a pruner onto a passer-by analogous to the spreading of fire or oil?) or through the induction of a normative principle. One might note how, in the law of the United Kingdom, the restating of the tort of negligence in terms of a general proposition was in the end achieved only by incorporating directly into the proposition, as a metaphor, the notion of a 'neighbour'.[171]

The point to be made about this merging of normative proposition with fact description is that it endows facts with a normative propensity and rules with a descriptive dimension. This confuses even more the distinction between science and object of science, since what appears to be the 'object', facts, becomes part of the 'science', that is to say the rules. This has an impact in turn on other legal propositions. For example, the doctrine of precedent, if conceived as a normative proposition, dictates that like cases should be decided alike. Yet, the moment that facts are merged with a normative proposition, the proposition itself becomes hopelessly ambiguous, since no two sets of facts are ever the same. Distinction always becomes a possibility, however striking the analogy. A spreading fire is not the same as spreading oil or falling branches. This may not matter in the everyday practice of decision making, where the doctrine of precedent seemingly functions in a 'commonsense' fashion.[172] But the result is a paradox: precedent works as a practical method, but not as a coherent epistemological theory. The epistemologist cannot therefore be satisfied with a general account of legal method via a standard textbook on legal precedent. Such works are undermined, epistemologically speaking, by the failure properly to distinguish science and object of science.

Teaching and Practice of Law

Another, although associated, epistemological distinction of importance in science is between the teaching and practice of science. 'The teacher has to master the contents of what is to be taught' and this involves 'a more general vision of the discipline to be taught, in terms of the organising principles, the areas of thought, the conceptual threads'. It 'is a question of seeing the discipline not as a patchwork without unity, each element corresponding to a concept, but as an expressive mosaic made up of concepts each relating one to another'.[173] Now, the great advantage of working with a system of precedents where rules are facts and facts are rules is that the method has a certain fact-matching simplicity. A problem about damage caused by spreading fire can be researched via the keyword 'fire' and all of the retrieved fact situations about fire can be matched to the problem in hand. Law becomes classed according to the alphabet: and what is more logical than the alphabetical system used in dictionaries?[174] The problem, of course, is that law becomes irreducible. A dictionary has nothing to say over and above the definition of each individual word, in that the juxtaposition of each word is of no significance.[175] A dictionary, in other words, never becomes more than the sum of its parts.

As far as the practitioner is concerned, this lack of classification *ratio* may not matter. Indeed, patchwork structure and the lack of unity may have no impact whatsoever, provided that the retrieval system is adequate. The practitioner faced with a problem of damage caused by spreading fire needs a concept that corresponds with fire and not much more in order to get started. This is not to say, of course, that such a practitioner will not have to go beyond fire; but any progression will probably be made step-by-step via concepts operating within the fire precedents themselves. Even notions such as foreseeability will probably be tied to specific factual elements such as wind or tide and thus the reasoning model itself will remain within the factual boundaries of the fire precedents.

The teacher could, equally, teach law through an alphabetic listing of factual situations. Indeed, law teaching in the early law faculties of Europe was, to some extent, along these lines, since the *Digest* of Roman law did not conform to any recognisable conceptual structure. The practical problem with this approach is that it was extremely time-consuming and with the end of the medieval age the new methods introduced by the Humanists could cover 'twenty times as much ground'.[176] The epistemological point here is the reduction of knowledge to more simplified symbolic forms of representation which will facilitate communication and allow the knowledge to be more easily absorbed by the mind.[177] The key to this was the development of more abstract concepts which could at one and the same time be expressed in language, be manipulated with ease and be capable of storing a large amount of 'factual' information. Accordingly, it is not surprising that the role of the academic changed from commenting in ever more detail on particular texts in the Roman sources to searching within these texts for key concepts capable of being abstracted out of their factual contexts. As we shall see later in Chapter 4, the Romans themselves had gone far in undertaking this exercise with their works specifically written for students; the *Institutes* were textbooks which stood in contrast to the practitioner works.

Recurring Problems

How might one summarise all of these problems of epistemology? There are, as this chapter has attempted to show, problems surrounding the domain, approaches, viewpoints, schematic methods and so on. One particular area of contention is the history of legal science (assuming for the moment that law is a science). Can one have knowledge of law which is not dependent upon history? The history of the sciences in general is revealing inasmuch as it indicates that there are a number of recurring problems with this kind of question.[178] How do conceptions and theories of law develop? Is it a matter of internal development governed by some kind of inner logic or are such developments dependent upon historical contexts? The problem here is not just between an 'internal' and 'external' account of a knowledge discourse; it is also a matter of historical paradox. The paradox became evident in the sciences with the anti-historical character of Descartes's scientific (analytical) method. Descartes provided the basis both for rising above history and for establishing a starting point from which a history of science became possible.[179] Theories must become *passées* in order that a history of such theories can exist in the sense that one can be conscious of movement.[180] Positivism and the rule model is a knowledge structure that indeed allows jurists seemingly to escape from the historical baggage that attaches to law. This is why positivism, unlike natural law, appears much less historical in the way that it is presented in the jurisprudence textbooks. Yet positivism provides the very starting point for seeing natural law theory as *passée*. In fact, of course, positivism has a history which parallels that of natural law and which can equally be traced back to Roman law. Dworkin's own anti-historical thesis has the effect of, or at least would like to have the effect of, consigning positivism to history. The history of legal science is a history of theorists attempting to provide anti-historical theories.

What the history of science shows, then, is that the subject itself – that is to say the history of science – is characterised by problems and paradoxes that cannot be resolved. Indeed it is these recurring difficulties that give the subject its *raison d'être*. Legal epistemology is therefore a vehicle for grasping these problems with the objective, not of resolving them, but of appreciating how they inform and underpin methodology and law as a 'science'. Of course, whether law is actually a science is one of these very problems. And the search for a response to this question will simply reveal other problems and paradoxes.

Notes

1 Virieux-Reymond (1972, pp. 7–8).
2 Blanché (1983, p. 119).
3 Atias (1994, p. 3).
4 Blanché (1983, p. 120).
5 Atias (1994, p. 3).
6 Blanché (1983, p. 120).
7 Susskind (1987, p. 46).
8 Atias (1994, p. 4).
9 Granger (1995, p. 114).
10 Atias (1985, pp. 199–202).
11 See, for example, Gordley (1991).
12 Granger (1995, p. 115).
13 Note on this point Thiry's comment about the weakness of modern philosophy when it comes to epistemology: Thiry (1996, p. 153).
14 See, generally, Dreyfus (1992).
15 See, generally, the papers in Thomasset and Bourcier (1996).

16 Particularly as there may even be a direct link between Roman law and the Western scientific tradition: Acot (1999, pp. 55–6).
17 'When one talks of the "modern" epoch it is to designate the period which extends from the end of the Middle Ages until the French Revolution. Historians talk next of the "contemporary period"; but legal and political philosophers and theorists have now started to talk confidently of *post-modernism* to describe the time we are now entering, which suggests that, with regard to intellectual thought at least, they think we are not yet fully out of the influence of modernist times' (Arnaud, 1991, p. 102).
18 On this issue, the present work owes a great debt to Atias (1985).
19 For example, with regard to analogy: Araj (1996).
20 Strömholm (1985, pp. 46, 67).
21 Jones (1940, p. vii).
22 Susskind (1987, p. 154).
23 Ullmann (1975a, pp. 46–7).
24 Van Caenegem (1971, paras 20ff).
25 Blanché (1983, p. 38).
26 Sacco (1991a, pp. 8, 10).
27 Cf. Millon-Delsol (1993, pp. 120–24).
28 See, for example, Van Hoecker and Ost (2000).
29 Legrand (1997a, 1998, 1999b).
30 Izorche (2001, p. 91).
31 See Samuel (1994).
32 Cf. Markesinis (1990).
33 Leith (1993).
34 On the American Realist movement in general, see Duxbury (1997).
35 Holmes (1897), extracted in Lloyd and Freeman (1994, p. 670).
36 On German legal thinking, see Wieacker (1995).
37 Twining (1973), extracted in Lloyd and Freeman (1994, p. 672).
38 Ibid.
39 See Atias (1994, pp. 21–8).
40 See, generally, Astolfi and Develay (1996).
41 Granger (1995, p. 70).
42 Which is much more ambiguous than it might at first seem: Berthelot (2001a, p. 249).
43 Bergel (1999, p. 273).
44 Viscount Simon LC in *Hickman* v. *Peacey* [1945] AC 304, 318.
45 Granger (1995, p. 99).
46 See, generally, Berthelot (2001a).
47 Pringsheim (1935, pp. 347ff).
48 Granger (1995, p. 111).
49 Zweigert and Kötz (1998, pp. 186–7).
50 Blanché (1983, p. 65).
51 Piaget (1988, p. 103).
52 Knowledge of the historical outline of the civilian tradition, if not the common law tradition, is not assumed. For an excellent introduction to the history of legal thought, see Jones (1940); this monograph remains an astonishingly sophisticated and elegant work still ahead of its time. Indeed, Jones is still the only work in English that might be considered a work on

legal epistemology; it has been, needless to say, an important influence on this present enquiry. See also Wieacker (1995).

53 Equally, an outline knowledge of legal philosophy and legal theory is not assumed. Jones (1940), once again, provides a good background, although it evidently does not deal with the present-day theorists. Lloyd and Freeman (1994) provide an excellent selection of extracts from the modern Anglo-American writers.

54 Lloyd and Freeman (1994, p. 6).

55 Bergel (1999, no. 4).

56 Ibid., p. 4.

57 Blanché (1983, p. 29).

58 D.1.1.1.1.

59 This notion of 'natural law' has, however, been seen as a possible starting point for the modern scientific mind: Acot (1999, p. 55).

60 D.1.1.1.2.

61 D.1.1.1pr.

62 D.1.1.9.

63 See, generally, Wieacker (1995, pp. 199–256).

64 See, for example, Finnis (1980).

65 But cf., for example, Carbasse (1998), Rouland (1998).

66 Dworkin (1986, p. 13).

67 Ibid., p. 14.

68 Blanché (1983, p. 34).

69 D.1.4.1.

70 D.1.3.7.

71 D.2.1.3.

72 C.7.37.3.

73 Jones (1940, p. 205).

74 Kelly (1992, p. 313).

75 Jones (1940, p. 206).

76 See Jolowicz (1963, pp. 15–27, 101–18).

77 Hart (1961, pp. 10–13).

78 Ibid., p. 96.

79 See now Kelsen (1997).

80 Stamatis (1995, p. 276).

81 Jones (1940, pp. 203–34).

82 Jolowicz (1963, p. 127).

83 Fassò (1976, pp. 149–54).

84 Jolowicz (1963, pp. 175–9).

85 For an overview of Pound's journey from Savigny to social interests, see Pound (1923).

86 Renner (1949, pp. 117–18).

87 Lloyd and Freeman (1994, pp. 655–729) and references therein.

88 See, for example, Cohen (1935).

89 Frank (1949, p. 46).

90 Lloyd and Freeman (1994, p. 936).

91 Ellul (1982a, p. 27).

92 Watson (1981, pp. 14–22).

93 Ibid., p. 15.

94 Jones (1940, p. vii).
95 Berman (1983, p. 539).
96 Weir (1992b, p. 1617).
97 Wieacker (1995, p. 45).
98 Carbasse (1998, p. 142).
99 Jones (1940, p. 14).
100 Ibid., pp. 144–5.
101 Van Caenegem (1987, p. 124).
102 Jones (1940, p. 29).
103 Justinian, *Constitutio Deo Auctore*, 11.
104 Jones (1940, p. 32).
105 Quoted in Jones (1940, p. 34 n. 2).
106 Pédamon (1985, pp. 15–16).
107 Stamatis (1995, p. 20).
108 Timsit (1986, pp. 106–7).
109 Stamatis (1995, pp. 24–7).
110 Ibid., p. 21.
111 Atias (1985, pp. 30–36).
112 Jones (1940, p. 205).
113 See, for example, Finnis (1980).
114 Hart (1961, p. 124).
115 Barreau (1998, p. 51).
116 See, generally, Lloyd and Freeman (1994, pp. 655–729).
117 Frank (1932, p. 578).
118 Llewellyn (1951, p. 12).
119 Cohen (1935).
120 See, generally, Frank (1949, pp. ix–xi).
121 Jones (1940, p. 195).
122 For some very general criticisms, see Jolowicz (1963, pp. 134–40).
123 Jones (1940, p. 196).
124 See Stein and Shand (1974).
125 See, for example, Griffith (1997).
126 The ideological aspect of this maxim is, however, evident in its history: it goes back only to the 19th century and grew out of the idea that basic rights could be stated as declarations in constitutional form: Carbasse (1990, p. 319).
127 Bergel (1999, no. 249).
128 See, generally, Manuel Calvo García (1994, pp. 167–246).
129 See, generally, Perelman (1979).
130 Bergel (1999, nos 257–8).
131 Ibid., no. 253.
132 Ibid., no. 252.
133 Perelman (1979, p. 8); Bergel (1999, no. 252).
134 Dworkin (1977, pp. 116–17).
135 Dworkin (1985), extracted in Lloyd and Freeman (1994, p. 1322).
136 Ibid., p. 1323.
137 Sartorius (1971), extracted in Lloyd and Freeman (1994, pp. 1365–7).
138 Granger (1995), p. 111).
139 Van Caenegem (1987, p. 53).

140 Legrand (1995c, p. 83).
141 One particular problem is the regressive nature of the theory. If a common lawyer can never think like an Italian lawyer and vice versa, it would seem to be arguable that a lawyer from Welsh-speaking North Wales could not think like an English lawyer born and bred in London. Yet if England is to be equated with North Wales, does it not follow that parts of Belgium can be equated with France, and so on? These kinds of question do not undermine the thesis, but they do seriously weaken it as an epistemological model. Culture is too weak a concept to act as an epistemological model in itself. The other problem with the thesis is that it cannot be falsified by external phenomena and thus some would say that it is not a scientific theory as such. It is, in other words, in danger of being seen as an ideology. In fact the epistemological position is more complex: see Berthelot (2001a).
142 See, for example, Holland (1924).
143 See, for example, Manuel Calvo García (1994, ch. VIII).
144 Van Caenegem (1987, p. 126).
145 Ibid., p. 125.
146 Pringsheim (1935).
147 Zweigert and Kötz (1998, p. 186).
148 Watson (1994).
149 D.44.7.3pr.
150 Weir (1972, no. 67).
151 *Kleinwort Benson Ltd* v. *Glasgow CC* [1999] 1 AC 153.
152 Milsom (1981, p. 263); Ibbetson (1999, p. 18).
153 Cf. Pound (1923).
154 Cotterrell (1983, pp. 242, 243).
155 See, for example, Griffith (1997).
156 This allows Hart to marginalise the rule-sceptic: Hart (1961, p. 150).
157 Blanché (1983, pp. 119, 120, 122).
158 Rayar (1993, p. 5).
159 Atias (1985, p. 129).
160 Astolfi and Develay (1996, p. 25).
161 Amselek (1995a, p. 24).
162 Dworkin (1986, p. 229).
163 Ivainer (1988, pp. 157–61).
164 Ibid., pp. 22–3, 84–6.
165 Granger (1995, p. 99).
166 Atias (1985, pp. 33, 40).
167 D.9.2.30.3.
168 *The Wagon Mound (No 1)* [1961] AC 388.
169 This foreseeability point is made clear in Roman law by the following text: D.9.2.31.
170 See, for example, CC art. 1382.
171 *Donoghue* v. *Stevenson* [1932] AC 562.
172 Cf. *R* v. *Bow Road Justices, Ex p Adedigba* [1968] 2 QB 572.
173 Astolfi and Develay (1996, p. 114).
174 Bonardel (1996, p. 3).
175 Ibid., p. 5.

176 Jones (1940, p. 32).
177 Delacour (1995, pp. 29–34).
178 Acot (1999, p. 30).
179 On Descartes, see Pheby (1988, pp. 14–16).
180 Ibid., pp. 17–18.

2 *Scientia Iuris*

The brief survey of the history of legal 'science', undertaken in the last chapter, is evidently useful to the extent that it traces how the modern discourse of law has been developed over the centuries. One can follow the progress from a vision of law based on the *ius naturale* to a conception of law as nothing more than a *ius positum*. Equally, one can chart the evolution (or revolutions?) in legal methods from the dialectical and inductive approaches of the medieval jurists to the deductive logic of the *mos geometricus*. These historical progressions remain of importance to the extent that they inform the modern philosophical debates about the nature and definition of law. Thus natural law theory tends to be presented as a historical phenomenon inasmuch as its roots are in the writings of Roman and medieval jurists and philosophers. Positivism, in contrast, is seen as 'modern' inasmuch as it is associated with thinkers reacting against the older conceptions. But this is really a philosophical rather than a historical debate and thus history itself is contributing to the epistemological model only in an indirect way. History allows one to see, paradoxically, that positivism is as much a historical phenomenon as natural law. Yet, when one turns to epistemology in the natural sciences, history does have its own distinct contribution to make to modern scientific knowledge. Accordingly, in addition to the synchronic approach to epistemology, one must examine in more depth the diachronic.

Nevertheless, the relationship between 'legal science' and science itself – that is to say science in the natural sciences sense – is an ambiguous one. Much depends upon exactly what is meant by 'legal science'. When understood in terms of a history of codification in Europe, there is no escaping some relationship. The institutional system, as we shall see later, in Chapter 4, acted as the structural foundation for all the codes. However, *scientia iuris* can also be understood as a notion quite independent of the Roman classification scheme. Instead of deriving its force from what might be called the internal (Roman) law point of view, legal science can take the natural sciences as its starting point. Accordingly, just as legal philosophy looks to the tradition of philosophy, so legal science can look to zoology, physics and mathematics for its central paradigms.

Science

Over and above the problem of actually defining *scientia iuris*, when one asks what is meant by the term 'science' one comes up against, once again, ambiguity. The Latin word *scientia* did not have the same meaning as the modern term 'science'. It meant knowledge, and *scientia iuris* meant knowledge of law sufficient to permit a jurist to arrive at the right decision.[1] But such knowledge did go beyond a mere catalogue of precedents and legislative commands. The term *scientia* contained within it the idea of a certain rationality allowing relevant knowledge to be easily absorbed by the mind. Science was to be contrasted with chaos.[2] No doubt this idea of making rational sense out of chaos continues to have a relevance with regard to the modern understanding of the word 'science', but equally the modern word has rather a different connotation. As a result of its association with an ever-increasing material understanding of the world, together with technological and medical developments and discoveries, science has become an abstract, if not rather mystical, term for a material activity practised by scientists. The activity can be summed up as industrial and technological and the 'men-in-white-coats' form the popular image of the scientists who stand behind such objects. At an everyday level, science has become associated with technical objects and these objects, impregnated with scientific thinking, have become images for a material rationality.[3]

Science and Technology

It is, however, important to distinguish science from technology. One might inform the other, but technology is rooted as much in technique as in any systematic and rational study of the natural world and beyond. Thus technology has been described as being half-way between technique and science.[4] Technique itself cannot be subordinated to science because 'the first aeroplanes flew before aerodynamics existed and the first plastic materials owed nothing to the theories of chemical synthesis'.[5] Technique, therefore, would appear to be rooted in the concrete world of activity; it is a matter of practice. Science, on the other hand, cannot be defined either as intellectual technique – which is a matter of methodological practice[6] – or as technology, which 'is a special kind of technique (scientific technique)'.[7] As a matter of actual practice, science is about the formulation of 'universal and necessary relations between phenomena, that is to say laws'.[8] This is quite different from technique or technology, in that science is about, not concrete things, but 'reasoned abstractions'.[9]

When looked at from the position of science, rather than from that of technique and technology, this notion of 'reasoned abstraction' is both attractive and problematic. It is problematic inasmuch as the visible face of science has been one of practical discoveries and applications that have had an impact upon societies in a whole number of material ways. And viewed from this position, science begins to lend itself to the kind of definition that one might associate with technology, if not technique. Or, put another way, science can be seen as being associated with a body of researchers who indulge not just in an intellectual activity but also in practical and concrete acts. Yet, as Granger has observed, aqueducts, roads, ships and the like were not seen as 'science symbols' in the ancient world.[10] It was at the end of the 17th century that science became entangled with technique, and modern technical prowess reflects advances in scientific knowledge.[11] Thus the technological and technique face of science is a relatively recent development.

Where the 'reasoned abstraction' proves attractive is in respect of the intellectual foundation of science. One of the fundamental characteristics of the modern idea of science is its complete detachment from concrete reality. Such reality may appear to be the object of science; but science is an abstract scheme completely detached from the world of concrete objects and phenomena. It is only a *representation* of this reality.[12] Science has as its aim the description and explanation of the object that its scheme represents. Its objective is to use this description and explanation to predict and it is in this ability to predict that science has what might be called its dynamic role. Yet this requirement of prediction is also a fundamental control device inasmuch as it acts as a means of verification. If a scientific scheme proves unable to predict accurately, the scheme itself will come into question. Yet, as Granger warns, this requirement of prediction must never be taken too literally simply because science is not concerned with reality itself. Science deals with 'virtual reality', with 'virtual facts'. Accordingly, prediction has to be understood in terms of *virtual* and not *actual* facts.[13] 'The predictive power of a theory is then a true criterion of validity,' concludes Granger, 'but only in the limits that the partially indeterminate character of the virtual fact assigns to this prediction.'[14]

Science and its Object

Professor Granger's definition of science indicates that the old idea of a dichotomy between science and its object is no longer so clear-cut. Science goes far in constructing its own object, that is to say its own version of reality. But the object of a science cannot be so easily dismissed, since it is seemingly difficult to escape from reality's influence on science. Indeed, the whole question of the relationship between science and reality is still a matter of debate. Of course it would be idle to think that this debate can be resolved. Nevertheless, what one can do is to identify two types of object. There are objects of science which are capable of relating to a material or concrete thing which seemingly exists in reality. Equally, there are objects which are only conceptual and thus do not move, explode or metabolise. Mathematical structures, for example, do not get hungry and they do not fly.[15] Thus one can assert that, while a science like mathematics creates its own objects, the natural sciences 'describe, explain and predict the conduct of their objects, but they do not create them'.[16] The result has been expressed by Mario Bunge in the following way:

> If a mathematician postulates the existence of a new conceptual object and does it without falling into contradiction, nobody will be able to refute it, even if his postulate ends up being ignored or considered wanting in interest. In contrast, if a physicist, a biologist or an historian postulates the existence of a concrete object which has not yet been discovered, they are thus acting in the hope of its discovery.[17]

Granger might reply of course that the objects of the empirical sciences are more complex. As he asserts:

> Scientific knowledge arising out of experience always consists of *constructing abstract schemes or models of this experience*, and of exploiting, by means of logic and mathematics, the relations between the abstract elements of these models, so as to deduce from them properties corresponding with sufficient precision to the empirical properties directly observable.[18]

The objects of science are not, then, the actual objects themselves. The objects are contained in the models which are constructed to represent them. This point must be stressed because it indicates how important it is to be aware of the nature of the gap between empirical objects attracting the attention of science and the actual abstractions of science. Bachelard, for example, has claimed that some sciences in the past have encountered epistemological obstacles by being too close to the facts.[19] Other sciences might suffer from not being close enough. What must be appreciated is that the scientific object cannot conserve the same richness as the actual physical object upon which it is based.[20] The question, therefore, is how much of this richness is to be maintained in the abstract model and how much is to be lost. And it is with respect to this question that the scientific scheme or theory itself becomes important. The more abstract the scheme, the less rich the objects. How much of this richness can a scientific theory or model afford to lose before it loses the facility to describe, explain and predict?

Science and Textbooks

This question of the relationship between a scientific theory or scheme and the concrete objects that it is attempting to model is relevant, not just to the practice of science, but also to the communication of scientific knowledge. The function of the teaching of science is to provide students with the means to allow them both to respond to scientific and technical questions in their everyday life and to develop the attitudes and methods of thought employed by scientists in the laboratory.[21] It would seem evident, therefore, that the models used by the practitioners of science should be the same as the ones that inform the teacher. However, things are not quite so simple. The development and perfection of scientific theories are often presented through the results of actual experiments carried out by many individuals over the centuries. This approach gives the impression of a gradual construction of a scientific scheme of thought through the accumulation of personal contributions.[22] The history of science, in other words, is about the gradual building up of a sophisticated methodology allowing humans access to an increasing knowledge of the world around them. Yet some philosophers of science have suggested that this view is largely false. Gaston Bachelard and, later, Thomas Kuhn argued that the history of science is anything but continuous; it is, instead, a history of discontinuity marked by epistemological obstacles (Bachelard) and revolutions (Kuhn).[23]

This historical debate is important in that it calls into question the epistemological validity of the means by which scientific knowledge is transmitted. In particular, it puts under the spotlight textbooks that present science in terms of abstract models of reality, since these models, as we have seen, do not correspond to reality. They correspond only to a certain abstract conception of reality and thus they both explain and do not explain.[24] Once these models are reduced to teaching manuals they assume an authority which goes beyond their original function. Their content becomes, so to speak, 'set in stone'. The result is that the model and its concepts assume a 'depersonalised' and 'de-historicised' status, becoming objects not of explanation and prediction but of teaching. Such a transformation has the effect, according to Jean-Pierre Astolfi and Michel Develay, of turning the model and its concepts into 'truths of nature'.[25] Knowledge is transformed through a process of 'dogmatisation'.[26] Science is no longer a matter of possibility through experimentation, but 'ready-made knowledge' presented as a propositional finality in itself.[27] Thus, far from being facilitative, textbooks on science are always in danger of being obstacles to knowledge.

Textbooks are in danger of being obstacles because they are capable of misstating the nature of scientific knowledge and of eclipsing the transient and relative aspects of its models and theories. Furthermore, it has to be remembered that textbooks have their own particular function, which is to teach rather than to aid the practice of science. The practitioner of science has need of models that continually reflect the fact that scientific knowledge is a matter of 'coming and going between concrete situations and a body of symbolic knowledge'.[28] Now, such models may be local and complex. That is to say, they might well be of a kind that operate at a relatively low level of abstraction where local and concrete objects correspond to their own localised concepts. Such a practitioner model has been described by Astolfi and Develay as a 'patchwork without unity'.[29] The teacher of science, in contrast, has need 'of a more general vision of the discipline to be taught, in terms of organising principles, notional fields and conceptual threads'. He or she needs a universal view of his or her science where every concept can be seen 'in liaison one with another'.[30] The teacher must, in addition, communicate with students and this means that the model by which knowledge is transmitted should be of a kind capable of communication as much as exploration.

History of Science

The history of science has, accordingly, an important status in epistemology since it allows the epistemologist to avoid rather than to perpetuate myths about the internal development of the disciplines. As Blanché has said:

> History offers a good means of analysis in separating, by the date and by the circumstances of their appearance, the various elements which have contributed to form little by little the notions and principles of ... science ... In this way, epistemology is distinguished from the history of science in that this history, for epistemology, is a means and not an end. Supported by history, its research is essentially critical: its goal is to detect, thanks to the lessons that the study of the past brings to bear,

> the elements which have contributed to the formation of the science and scientific ideal itself ... Now such a history, being a history of ideas, cannot be written in the same style as a history of events, for the links are not of the same nature in the two cases ... Whether it is a question of scientific, moral, aesthetic etc., ideas, their history cannot be written, only grasped, so to speak, from the inside ... This is why all history of the sciences other than the purely narrative is already, to some degree, philosophic.[31]

In particular, two philosophers of science, Gaston Bachelard and Thomas Kuhn, have, as we have seen, shown the importance of history in understanding modern science. According to Bachelard, the history of science is not to be understood as an unfolding process of developing knowledge and understanding of the world; rather it is a matter of overcoming obstacles. The history of science is really a question of ruptures rather than continuity. 'The historian of the sciences must take ideas as facts,' writes Bachelard. But 'epistemology must take facts as ideas in inserting them into a system of thought'. Now, a 'fact badly interpreted in an epoch remains a fact for the historian' which becomes 'in the hands of an epistemologist an *obstacle*, a regressive idea'.[32] Scientific knowledge accordingly needs to overcome these obstacles before it can evolve in any progressive way. For example, it was for centuries thought that women were in every way physically inferior to men, and this acted as an obstacle to the understanding, say, of the heart or kidney in human bodies because it was assumed that a woman's organs must be categorically different from those of men. Another example is the striking effect of explosions. This became an obstacle to the understanding of chemical reactions in general, since the striking effect led to explosions being put into a different category than other, more mundane, chemical reactions.

Kuhn views the history of science in a not dissimilar way. According to him, scientific inquiry is predicated on the assumption that the scientific community at any one time knows what the world is like; scientific practice is thus conducted within models which have sprung out of particular scientific world-views which in their time were regarded as the 'normal science'.[33] Kuhn assigned to these models, when viewed historically, the term 'paradigm' and thus the history of science is a history of dominant paradigms.[34] Each paradigm survives as long as it fulfils professional expectations. However, history shows that anomalies occur not only which cannot be explained by the paradigm but which ultimately force a major shift in professional outlook; this shift leads to a new set of professional commitments and a new basis for the practice of science. These 'extraordinary episodes in which that shift of professional commitments occurs,' says Kuhn, 'are the ones known ... as scientific revolutions'.[35] The history of science for Kuhn, then, is a history of revolutions.

Taken together, these two epistemologists suggest that the history of science is one of discontinuity. It is a history of conflicts and not a history of the harmonious discovery of new facts. Nevertheless, these revolutions are not born out of a void and thus they must be understood in terms of the paradigms and obstacles that preceded them. It is in respect of this understanding that the epistemologist is led to reflect upon the issue of continuity and discontinuity. New theories often explain previous doctrines and to this extent the history of science can be seen, equally, as the 'envelopment' of old ideas by the new.[36] Perhaps it is more a question of levels of abstraction; scientific thought moves from one level of rationality to another and, in doing so, produces new categories and concepts.[37] Accordingly, the history of science, 'far from being a chronology of landmark discoveries of facts, or even of a list of inventions of things, is above all a *genealogy* of "categories" which have successively made up the objects of a science'.[38] To paraphrase Granger, this successive development of basic concepts is not in essence dependent upon circumstances extrinsic to science itself. And this is true even if the date and the conditions of their coming to light result to a large extent from the economic, political and ideological circumstances of the society where they are to be found, together with the history and personal psychology of the original scientists. The point to be stressed is that the 'linking together itself of their discoveries is dependent in the final analysis on an *internal movement* of concepts'.[39]

Legal Science

The question for the jurist is, of course, the extent to which the history of the sciences is of any relevance to an understanding of law as a body of knowledge. In particular, to what extent is a historical approach valid in terms of the production of an epistemological model of law? Certainly, the history of law is unlike the natural sciences, in that law is not a discourse which has as its supposed object the facts of the world; it is entirely a history of a 'genealogy of categories' whose function has been to provide a normative system of social regulation. One legal epistemologist has described legal science as being characterised, from a methodological point of view, as having 'atypical objects': that is to say, legal norms or prescriptive propositions which escape the criterion of observability, a criterion which is typical of all empirical phenomena. The legal norm 'is not in fact something of which one can have an *immediate and direct perception* ... without the aid of concepts and theoretical categories'.[40] The history of legal knowledge seems less amenable, then, to an ontological (what exists) basis in some 'objective' world of fact.

However, philosophers of science, as we have seen, no longer conceive the world in terms of objective facts acting as the object of a science which reveals their hidden truths. Facts are scientifically constructed by the model of science itself and it is the history of science that has revealed these differing models.[41] Each science, to the extent that it progresses, tends to modify its own object in order to adapt it to the scientific model in issue.[42] In other words, science and the object of science are by no means so clear-cut as one might have thought. This does not of itself make the history of science relevant to legal knowledge, but it certainly breaks down a number of misconceptions with regard to apparent distinctions between scientific and legal discourse.

Historical Jurisprudence

The history of law has not been ignored by jurisprudence. Indeed, there is a specific school of Historical Jurisprudence associated primarily with the German jurist Savigny, and this school acted as one of the foundations for modern sociological jurisprudence.[43] In developing a thesis that law emerged out of the spirit of the people (*Volksgeist*), Savigny created a 'revolution in legal thinking' by insisting that law is the product of a people and its history.[44] He laid the foundations, in other words, for a cultural approach to law, an approach that is now central to comparative law theory.[45] More directly, however, the Historical School saw law itself as a historical phenomenon.[46] In England, writers such as Sir Henry Maine used legal history to make some important general observations about law,[47] and, while some of these might now be regarded as 'rather wild and largely discredited',[48] it would be a mistake to say that Maine and the viewpoint from which he was writing did not make important contributions to jurisprudence.[49]

Nevertheless, there are two problems associated with historical jurisprudence. First, it is logically impossible to derive from (historical) fact an 'ought' and thus history cannot, in the end, provide much of a philosophical basis to jurisprudence. All it can provide is an explanation of the building blocks of legal thought. This, of course, does not undermine its epistemological value, but it does help explain why historical jurisprudence itself is not alive and well in common law faculties.[50] Secondly, the Historical School itself was motivated primarily by the idea of progress and evolution in law. Historical jurisprudence was a group of theories claiming 'to explain legal change not merely in historical terms but as proceeding according to certain determinate stages, or in a certain pre-determined manner'. And in 'their fully developed form, such theories were essentially a nineteenth century phenomenon and did not long survive the end of the century'.[51] In addition, the belief in science, which motivated the legal evolutionists, is not what it was: the 'distrust of the methods of traditional science has been accompanied by a rejection of general schemes designed to provide explanations of institutional change on a universal basis'.[52]

Scientific Revolutions in Law

However, as Stein points out, 'there can be historical jurisprudence which is independent of social and economic data, and which concentrates on more strictly legal phenomena'.[53] Accordingly, a second relevant question concerns scientific revolutions in the history of legal discourse. Is the history of legal science one of developing continuity or one of obstacles, ruptures and revolutions? This question has received specific consideration from a French jurist. According to Christian Atias, there have been theoretical innovations in law which have overturned legal thinking to such an extent that 'nothing was the same as before'. The appearance and success of concepts such as the legal right, the legal subject, the state and even the consumer 'have had repercussions on many rules, solutions and legal notions'.[54] Equally, the birth of a secular natural law, rational and voluntarist, has been felt in many areas of the law. And, in a similar fashion, the transformation of contract from an empirically based economic operation to an agreement based on the meeting of two abstract wills has modified the fundamental equilibrium of the regime in terms of both formation and execution of this act.[55] However, whether these can actually be seen as revolutions in the Kuhn sense is, according to Atias, questionable. Atias makes the point that there have always been critics of these fundamental legal notions and thus it becomes difficult to talk of 'normal science'; more interesting is the question why some criticisms succeed while others have little effect. At all events, the term 'paradigm' is unsuitable in this context. Instead, it is better to talk of 'anchor points' which are so central to legal knowledge that jurists cannot contemplate the possibility of abandoning them.[56]

Atias does not end the argument with this observation. 'If there is an example of a revolution in legal knowledge,' he writes, 'it ought to be located in the years 1870–1900.'[57] During this period a number of jurists in France inaugurated a new era with the definite tone of a rupture. The immediate cause of this revolution was the German Civil Code which, with its new vision, was calling both the *Code civil* and the 'school of exegesis' (positivistic) interpretative methods which had been applied to it into question. Henceforth the systematisation of legal knowledge along the lines of the German Pandectists and the BGB (German Civil Code) would, according to Atias, revolutionise legal thinking in France to such an extent that one can talk of a 'Copernican revolution'.[58] New methods, new doctrines and new disciplines were to accompany the new century, with the result that the 'way was opened for a positive social science definitively liberated from the experience of jurists and their knowledge'. This was the era of science which was to reduce human nature to nothing more than an object of the 'science of law', a science deprived of its traditional values.[59] 'Legal reality is not what is,' observes Atias, 'but what is scientifically knowable.'[60] François Gény and Hans Kelsen may have had different projects, but between them they produced a rupture in legal thinking inasmuch as, outside the hard sciences, there was little by way of epistemological salvation.[61]

Yet even this revolution is, according to Atias, ambiguous when viewed from Kuhn's theory. The symptoms of crisis are, for sure, to be found in the history of legal knowledge and, once the crisis has passed, the new 'paradigm' seems to produce the results predicted. Positivism and the changed conception of the legal subject might thus be viewed as a scientific revolution.[62] Yet the science of law is of a different nature than the natural sciences, particularly in its susceptibility to ideological influences. It is impossible to make the distinction between periods of normal science and periods of paradigm change, since legal science is permanently open to outside influences. In addition, no legal theory is ever sufficiently and satisfactorily protected against anomalies. Thus the 'science of law must remain open and fragile; it cannot abandon itself to the auto-satisfaction of normal science'.[63] Moreover, it is extremely difficult to show that the everyday reasoning of lawyers has been affected by changes in theory and so it might be better to talk of a permanent revolution in law, at least at the level of theory, which has little in common with Kuhn's thesis.[64]

Stages of Scientific Development

If the history of legal thought seems less amenable to an analysis in terms of internal discontinuity – that is to say, in terms of ruptures and distinct revolutions – it does not follow that the history of the sciences remains irrelevant to legal epistemology. One epistemologist has talked of a history of *mentalités* in Europe.[65] Rather than revolutions, it might be better to see the history of legal knowledge as one of changing mentalities themselves determined by the economic, social and political contexts of the periods in question.

A mentality is a state of mind, a way of seeing the world;[66] and this state of mind is what changes through a process metaphorically described as *unfreezing* and *freezing*.[67] The history of legal thought might, then, be seen as a history of different ways of seeing. For example, the difference between Newton's and Einstein's conception of time is not just a matter of differing theories of the universe; time is envisaged in quite a different way and through differing dimensional structures.[68] It is a matter of the one-dimensional being replaced by a more complex dimensional model.

The idea of dimension and ways of seeing offers another compromise. Piaget has suggested that knowledge is a matter of a continuous and mediating structural development resulting from an interplay between a developing *intellectus et res*. Knowledge is the interrelationship of a subject with an object through a mediating structure.[69] Thus 'knowledge cannot be conceived as predetermined, neither in the internal structures of the subject since they are the result of a real and continuous construction, nor in the pre-existing characteristics of the object since they are known only thanks to the required mediation of these structures and that these enrich and encapsulate them (if only in putting them in the realm of the possible)'.[70] The function of 'genetic epistemology is thus to try to disengage the roots of the various varieties of knowledge right from their most elementary form and following their development to higher levels up to and including scientific thought'.[71] This thesis is not without its critics.[72] However, for the legal epistemologist the idea of knowledge being a matter of evolving structural models is useful in explaining the transformation (revolution?) from the empirical, that is to say a law growing out of fact, to the rational, whereby fact is rejected from legal science. This is what Villey called the rationalisation and systematisation of law.[73] It was a matter of moving from one kind of model rooted seemingly in objects (*res*) to another located purely in the mind (*intellectus*).

Piaget's approach is, then, more subtle than a mere division of scientific stages into the concrete and the abstract. To quote Blanché again:

> Rather than a binary division [between concrete and abstract science] it is necessary to deal here with a continuous development. One should speak more of the distinction between deductive science and inductive science. Mathematics started out by being inductive, and the sciences said to be inductive often take, and always aspire to take, the deductive form. Deduction and induction mark two stages in the development of science, the stages themselves being framed within an initial stage and a final stage. In fact it appears that all the sciences follow, in distinguishing themselves only by their degree of

> advancement, a similar course, passing or being called to pass, successively through the descriptive, inductive, deductive and axiomatic stages.[74]

This analysis of the history of sciences into four stages is particularly useful when one turns to the history of legal science, since it is possible that the history of legal thought can be analysed in terms of Blanché's categories. Accordingly, rather than talk in terms of scientific revolutions, the legal epistemologist might start by examining whether there has been in law a movement towards axiomatisation.

Descriptive and Inductive Stages

Admittedly little epistemological analysis has been undertaken of the methods of the Roman jurists, but the early codes such as the Twelve Tables can be described as 'descriptive' inasmuch as there is little systematic order or abstraction.[75] As to the methods of the classical jurists, these have been characterised in a number of ways – case-oriented, casuistic, dialectical, rhetorical – but the point to be noted is that it was during this period that legal science moved from the descriptive to the 'inductive'. Solutions were discussed and arrived at on the basis of factual examples; but out of these concrete cases the jurists were able to disengage some common denominators. The notion of *culpa* (fault) and foreseeability with regard to wrongful damage is one obvious example,[76] and *conventio* (agreement) in respect of contracts is almost a perfect illustration of induction.[77] Nevertheless, the Romans did not advance beyond the inductive stage, for their distrust of rules as the basis of legal knowledge is evident from a famous observation to be found in the *Digest*: *non ex regula ius sumatur, sed ex iure quod est regula fiat* (the law is not taken from a rule, but a rule is made by the law).[78] The case law itself is often concerned with quasi-normative concepts such as blame, cause and risk (*in causa ius esse positum*, the law is posited in the cause)[79] and this prompted a medieval commentator to observe that 'law arises out of fact' (*ex facto ius oritur*).[80]

The epistemologist might observe that the move from the 'descriptive' to the 'inductive' stage was a key development in that it was providing a conceptual basis upon which one could move to a higher level of rationalisation. Thus one should 'not emphasise too much the separation between the concrete intuition and the abstract conception' since the concrete 'is the abstract rendered familiar through usage'.[81] Interpretation of texts was certainly of importance and often a starting point for the consideration of concrete problems;[82] equally, the Romans were keen to reduce legal knowledge to general propositions for teaching purposes. The *Institutes* are thus works that come close to stating law in terms of rules and principles and this is true also of the final title of the *Digest*, 'rules of law' (*regulae iuris*).[83] Legislation was clearly another area of law that expressed itself in terms of propositions.[84] Yet it would be wrong to locate Roman methodology in the *ars hermeneutica*. The approach was, as we shall see subsequently, in Chapter 4, beyond the descriptive since they had reached a stage of analysing facts via schematic structures which were not only self-referencing and relatively mobile in the way they could escape from the particularities of social fact,[85] but capable of being used as a means of 'constructing' and 'explaining' factual situations.[86] Legal development, as we shall see, was a matter of pushing outwards from the facts.[87] Nevertheless, the failure of the Roman jurists 'to articulate the assumptions and deeper reasons on which the analogies were founded – indeed, their failure even to define the most important legal terms – led to a narrowness, or woodenness, in case analysis'.[88] From the practitioner's viewpoint, Roman law was 'not presented as an intellectual system but rather as an elaborate mosaic of practical solutions to specific legal questions'.[89] Nevertheless, the Roman lawyers, in their desire to simplify for educational reasons,[90] did provide the foundation for what was to become a deductive system based no longer on facts, but on 'rights'.[91]

As for 'the methods of reasoning adopted by the Glossators, it would seem to be clear that 12th and 13th century lawyers did not establish, and did not attempt to establish, complete "systems"'; the 'glossators represent an intermediary stage between the scientific – "geometric" or "axiomatic" – methodology of later legal reasoning, and the older tradition based on the ancient art of rhetoric'.[92] The methodology of the medieval scholars is often referred to as scholasticism, but this hides a developing set of techniques that start out from *glosae*, pass through *expositio per modum quaestionis*, *disputatio* and *dialectica*, to arrive at the *logica nova*.[93] Much of the work of the medieval doctors was built upon Greek and Roman sources and methods, yet what gave scholasticism its particular characteristics is that it 'presupposes the absolute authority of certain books ... , but paradoxically, it also presupposes that there may be both gaps and contradictions within the text; and it sets as its main task the summation of the text, the closing of gaps within it, and the resolution of contradictions'.[94] The most striking feature of scholasticism was the use of the dialectical method which, according to Berman and Wieacker, was the foundation of the modern scientific method.[95]

It is tempting to think that the medieval jurists were taking up where the classical Roman jurists left off, and in one sense this is true. Villey thus talks of the Glossators having respect for the texts and conserving the method of the Roman jurists.[96] However, the medieval jurists were faced with an epistemological problem that was rather different from the one facing the Roman jurists. The medieval lawyers 'took it for granted that the different texts could be reconciled, for they accepted without question Justinian's assurance that the Digest contained no contradictions which could not be resolved *subtili animo* (*Const. Tanta,* 15)'.[97] And so the object of their science was no longer social facts as such but legal texts. They were not analysing the world; they were interpreting the writings of others with the result that there was a subtle shift from an exercise in rationalising the chaos of fact[98] to one that involved the analysis of words and concepts. Their technique, although similar to some of those to be found in the *Digest* (for example the use of genus and species), was, as a result, more developed in a formal sense. For scholasticism placed much greater emphasis on the techniques of categorisation and Aristotelian logic; it was much richer and more complex than anything the Romans had produced.[99] More importantly, however, it shifted the emphasis off the facts as the basis of legal knowledge towards the idea that law was a matter of rules (*regulae*). A *regula,* as Peter Stein has shown, was seen by the Glossators as a means of transmission of legal knowledge and of extending its scope where the same *ratio* was to be found (*ubi eadem ratio, ibi et eadem iura*).[100] In addition, this emphasis on the interpretation of texts gave rise to a much greater definition of notions used by the Romans such as *interesse*.[101] These moved from being tools of social description to notions that were more normative, in that they became part of the textual knowledge. They became 'scientific' and thus more assertive in an 'ought' sense.

It was the Post-glossators who shifted some of the attention back onto social facts. Not that Bartolus and Baldus denied the power of rules, but they 'recognised that a study of the last titles of the Digest and Sext was no substitute for the detailed analysis of the titles dealing with particular topics'.[102] They therefore set about analysing the actual social and political problems of their day, using Roman law and the scholastic methodology which had become associated with the way one thought about law (not just Roman law but also the *ius speciale*). It was the Post-glossators who transformed the feudal property ideas of northern France, based essentially on seisin (possession), into the Roman conception of absolute titles founded on *dominium*.[103] This kind of exercise is of particular relevance to the epistemologist, in that it shows how the Post-glossators were moving away from 'mere interpretation' towards the development of structural models in the sense that Piaget describes the development of the scientific mind. These structures were not, as such, deductive, in that they were founded on propositions divorced from the empirical. They functioned within the facts in order to take them to a stage where they began to function creatively in a slightly more rarefied manner than the level at which the Romans had operated, thus endowing these facts with a more defined and structured institutional flavour. In Roman law, for example, the notion of *persona* did not as such have a clear institutional role in any definitional sense. What endowed towns with 'legal personality' was the law of actions rather than the law of persons.[104] In the hands of the Post-glossators, the group who could act within the institutional plan had become the *persona ficta*,[105] and the *utilitas publica* had 'gained a new lease of life' as the public interest.[106] *Persona* and *utilitas* were coming together in a structural sense, not just as focal points for rules, but as a means of actually constructing social fact.

Deductive Stage

The end of the medieval world is, for legal thinking, marked by two 'revolutions'. First was the nominalist revolution associated with William of Ockham,[107] whereby all universal terms (men, forests and the like) were merely names and had no real (ontological) existence; only individual humans and individual trees existed.[108] This nominalism had profound effects upon thinking at all levels. In the natural (and later the social) sciences it laid the foundations for the increasing exclusion of metaphysics from analytical thinking and this was to give rise to a methodology which can be described as analytical reductionism.[109] Things were to be reduced to their individual parts. One might note that this kind of problem was not unknown to the Roman jurists and thus the germ of the nominalist debate could be said to be in the Roman legal sources.[110] But, according to Villey, Ockham and the other nominalist thinkers changed radically the conception of law. After Ockham, only individuals exist, and nothing but individuals, and thus law was not something that attached to society – *ubi societas ibi ius* – but to individuals.[111] It is the individual and not society that is the source of law, and society, according to the later modernist thinkers such as Hobbes,[112] was simply the result of a contract freely made by individuals.[113] This 'nominalist education ... has the consequence of restricting our catalogue of values only to those values of interest to individuals – or to groups fictionally conceived as individuals'.[114]

The second revolution was the arrival of Humanism, which had the effect of giving rise to a new kind of legal science. The emphasis on the individual went hand-in-hand with an emphasis on human reason (*ratio*). Not that the Post-glossators were against reason as such; but the medieval world primarily thought in terms of authority (*nemo jurista nisi Bartolista*) and what mattered was the authority of the glosses and commentaries.[115] And these glosses and commentaries were for the main part attached to the passages in the Roman texts. 'As commentary was piled upon commentary,' writes Walter Jones, 'all pretence of interpreting the texts was thrown aside.'[116] What was needed was a new methodology to clear the ground, so to speak.[117] One way to cut through the accretions was to appeal to the original (Roman) texts themselves on the basis of *ratio iuris*; accordingly, it was with the Humanists of the 16th century that an interest in law as *regulae iuris* revived.[118] The textual emphasis shifted from the *Digest* to the *Institutes* of Justinian and the methodological concerns moved from dialectics to law as an art (*ius civile in artem redigere*).[119] The Humanists wanted to transform the law – 'to wrench it away from the law faculty pedants, the Bartolist technicians, the specialist lawyers'[120] – so as to make it accessible to ordinary citizens. The new learning which developed law into an *ars* was no longer one of piecemeal interpretation and commentary on isolated texts nor the analysis of individual cases with their single points of law; it was a matter of building a logical structure of rules.[121] As Jones comments:

> The need for a more intelligible statement of the principles of the law, and the growing dissatisfaction with the arrangement or lack of arrangement found in the Digest, resulted in the publication of one work after another professing to supply the true *ars juris* which all were seeking. No law book was complete which did not bear the word *methodus* or *methodice* on its title-page.[122]

The epistemological importance of this new method was striking but simple. It took law from the inductive to the deductive stage of legal science. In terms of cognitive structures, deduction 'becomes explicable only at the moment when it takes a constructive form, that is to say when it tends to set up a "structure" whose transformations would accordingly allow the rediscovery of general laws as much as particular ones, but by virtue of *necessary* consequences of the structure and no longer by virtue of the generality of diverse but only enclosed propositions'.[123] The direct foundations for this structure were, as Villey observed, laid by the school of jurists who heralded the end of the medieval world. Legal science had become a science located in the mind (*ratio*) and no longer a matter of induction from social reality and from nature. It could now be systematised. Indeed, 'it could even take the form (as Grotius at least tended towards) of an axiomatised system, deduced from principles of reason'.[124] Henceforth the law resided in rules and in the systematised doctrinal works.

Axiomatic Stage

In Germany this rationalism was taken to an even higher degree of formal systematisation:

> The science of the expository approach [*l'exégèse*] and of the commentary on the texts which had dominated up to [the Enlightenment] gave way to doctrinal syntheses aiming to regulate and to reconstruct the legal order into a global and autonomous system. The works of Christian Wolff and his pupil Daniel Nettelbladt merit particular mention in this respect. Starting from superior principles founded on reason and human nature, these two authors constructed with wholly mathematical logic a body of rules even more exact, interrelated one to another, and forming a pyramidal whole as coherent as rational. This transposition, in the legal domain, to a mode of reasoning which was essentially deductive, applied in a rigorous manner and independently of all consideration drawn from experience or from social life could be labelled *mos geometricus*; it had important consequences for legal method. It orientated German legal science towards a kind of 'conceptual hardening' (Holleaux) which foreshadowed the work of the Pandectic school and which still characterises today, at least in some respects, the German legal spirit.[125]

In terms of epistemology there had been a shift from consensus amongst the doctors to coherence at the level of the legal model. What mattered was the rigour of the intellectual structure and thus *scientia iuris* (in the civil law) was a matter no longer of *ars judicandi* but of inference. Solutions were to be deduced from hardened and systematised models given their ultimate expression in legislative codes:

> The courts are entrusted with the duty of establishing the facts from which flow the legal consequences to apply having regard to the legal system in force. Once the facts are established, a legal syllogism is enough, whereby the rule of law constitutes the major premise, the established facts as envisaged by the conditions of the rule the minor premise and the court decision the conclusion ... This implies that for each situation submitted to the judge there would be a legal rule applicable, that there would be only one and that this rule would be devoid of any ambiguity ... The legal system is, at the end of the day, assimilated to a deductive system constructed on the model of axiomatic systems existing in geometry or arithmetic.[126]

And if axiomatisation 'is the perfection of deductive theory',[127] then it is possible to see that what the Humanists started the German professors finished. The German Civil Code (BGB) has been described as a 'legal calculating machine par excellence'.[128] This axiomatisation of law, as we saw in the last chapter, proved to be a myth, in that law cannot be reduced to mathematical logic because of the open-ended nature of many of its concepts. There are too many gaps in the intellectual system, with the result that the coherence can never be rigorous enough to allow solutions to be deduced from the model without the intervention of human interpretation. Conceptual coherence gives way to hermeneutics. However, given the retreat from positivism and the renaissance of dialectics and argumentation theories, the question for the epistemologist is this: what, if anything, comes after Blanché's final, axiomatic stage: a new, fifth stage, or a retreat into some previous stage?

The Retreat from Science

The historical survey of legal method and reasoning, in focusing largely on the civil law tradition, has of course left open the question of methodology in the common law. Furthermore, in adopting what could be seen as a 'progressive' epistemological framework (descriptive, inductive, deductive, axiomatic), the suggestion is that the history of legal method is, from the position of a scientific ideal, a matter of increasing rationalisation, comprehension and precision. Yet the inference (coherence) thesis is more complicated, inasmuch as it is part of an ideology about the political role of the judges. Is not their job only to apply rather than to make the law? Does not judicial discretion undermine the certainty, if not the rule, of law? The interpretation thesis of legal method helps overcome these questions in effecting a compromise between rules and their application. The role of the judge is not to make law but to interpret it. And while the positivists are prepared to accept that the ambiguity of language leaves a margin of discretion, the new hermeneutical theorists take a more severe view.[129] The concept of an axiomatic legal science might be on the wane, but only to the extent that it is being replaced by an art of interpretation founded, it would seem, upon an 'axiomatic' structure of rights and duties.

Dialectics and the Common Law

The thesis that legal solutions can be deduced entirely from codes of axiomatic propositions is no longer a dominant one in civilian legal thought. As Bergel has wirtten, 'the reduction of law to equations is a myth', since it 'comes up against insurmountable difficulties of method and against the objectives of every legal system'. The idea that law can be expressed in terms of the symbols of calculus 'is irreconcilable with legal method' because the 'law is full of departures from logical solutions deduced from an axiom' and these 'exceptions result from other preoccupations, other principles and other axioms of which the sheer number, the complication and the differing intensity make impossible an expression of positive law in mathematical form'.[130] Moreover, the 'reduction of law to a formal logic would ... be contrary to the essential purpose of any legal system' which is 'to regulate social life' and the 'dynamic force of facts is out of sequence with the rhythm and direction of deductions from formal logic'.[131] One is, it would seem, forced back into history inasmuch as it 'has been shown that the ancient jurists and those of the Middle Ages – from the Talmudists to the Greeks and Romans then the Italian Glossators – proceeded not by rigid deduction from pre-established rules, but by debate leading, thanks to rhetoric and dialectical argument in the Aristotelian sense, to conclusions that were only probable ones founded upon argumentation'.[132] Scholasticism rather than axiomatics lies at the heart of legal reasoning,[133] and such methodology 'explains just as much the legal processes in the "common law" as in the Romano-Germanic legal systems'.[134]

Perelman, Bergel and others seem to be suggesting that it is the common law, rather than the *mos geometricus*, which holds the epistemological key to methodology. Villey makes a similar point in saying that the common law was spared the Humanist revolution, which he saw as the intellectual event which led to the *mos geometricus* and the codes; as a result, the common lawyers preserved the (inductive?) methods of the Roman and medieval jurists.[135] However, while there may be something of an 'inner relationship' between Roman and English methods, the rationality of the later civil lawyers has not been without influence. The idea that legal method is grounded in the rule model is, it seems, the starting point for the English judiciary, although pragmatism and experience, rather than logic, is said, as we shall see, to be the main guide. Accordingly, the expectation of some academic commentators is that the English judiciary should be conducting the search for principle not with less, but with greater, vigour. According to Professor Birks:

> The realists and post-realists have done a good job of debunking legal science. In the United States where Jerome Frank and his intellectual successors did their most serious damage, it has never recovered and now lets in floods of law and economics in the hope of filling the broken vessel.[136]

And he is of the following view:

> A sound taxonomy, together with a keen sense of its importance, constant suspicion of its possible inaccuracy and vigorous debate on its improvement, is an essential precondition of rationality. All these

> are wanting in the common law systems. Until that is put right, the realists and the fundamentalists of the school of critical legal studies will continue to play from a winning hand.[137]

The influence of deductive, if not axiomatic, thinking is, therefore, not necessarily either a thing of the past or a unique characteristic of civilian legal science, since there is, as we have just seen, pressure from some quarters for English law to become more 'rational' and 'logical'. Yet the difficulty with this view of legal technique is that it is making a fundamental assumption about the nature of legal knowledge as a discourse that is at one and the same time isolated from and yet interpretative of facts.

Axiomatics and the Common Law

Professor Birks provides an example. He criticises the House of Lords decision in *Spring* v. *Guardian Assurance*,[138] where an employer was held liable for economic loss caused to a former employee by an inaccurate reference, on the basis that the liability was framed in negligence rather than defamation. Professor Birks makes the point that the effect of the decision is to change the law of defamation by reducing the behavioural requirement of the defendant from malice to carelessness. 'This is a conundrum of disorderly categories,' he claims, since the two categories of negligence and defamation intersect; defamation is based on the invasion of the interest to reputation while negligence is founded upon behaviour. 'The law,' he says, 'cannot tolerate, or should not be able to tolerate, torts named so as to intersect.'[139] Now this may seem logical enough at one level. The difficulty, however, is that it assumes that the facts are neutral, in that they will simply display particular kinds of 'interest' and 'behaviour'. What a post-axiomatic epistemologist might say is that this is far too simplistic. For a start, 'interest' itself is being constructed by Birks in a particular way; it is being used in relation to reputation, whereas it could equally be applied to the actual damage suffered by the plaintiff, namely the economic loss caused through a failure to secure a job.[140] In other words, *Spring* v. *Guardian Assurance* is not a case about the reputation interest at all. There is no reason why the tort of negligence for misstatement cannot be extended to cover the loss of an expectation (the failure to secure a job). And such an extension is no more illogical *vis-à-vis* the tort of defamation than the attaching of liability to any other 'thing' that does damage.

Furthermore, the idea that invasion of a protected interest on the one hand and the display of fault on the other should constitute two independent 'wrongs' is to create a system that is bound to intersect.

Each time a legal liability is explained entirely on the basis of the invasion of an interest, a normative structure is implicitly being established which would inevitably cause its own logical contradictions when compared with liabilities founded on fault. Why should it be harder for the plaintiff in a personal injury claim to obtain damages than a plaintiff in a defamation action? Is reputation a more valuable interest than a limb? Why should the expectation interest in respect of securing employment be less well protected than an interest in reputation?

Easy and Hard Cases

Rather than plead for the return to an axiomatic science of law free from apparent internal contradictions, it might be more in keeping with modern ideas about scientific thought to be as flexible with regard to the facts as with regard to the law. One way Anglo-American lawyers have handled this difference between logic and practicality is, since the Realists, to approach legal reasoning in terms of easy and hard cases, a distinction seemingly ignored in France, if not in civilian legal science in general.[141] Nevertheless, the difference has been well explained by a civilian, Joxerramon Bengoetxea, in his work on legal reasoning in the European Court of Justice (ECJ). According to him, the 'term "clear case" refers to a situation of isomorphy in which the applicability of a legal rule or a set of legal rules to certain facts is clear and unproblematic'.[142] And in 'these cases of isomorphy, where the facts of the case clearly fit into the operative facts of the legal rule, which attaches a legal consequence to those facts, judicial action can be accounted for by pointing to the fact that a rule is being almost unreflectively applied'.[143] The hard case, according to this rule model thesis, gives rise to a different epistemological process:

> But problems arise when hard cases have to be decided and those decisions justified. What if no valid norm seems to govern the case? Which norm has to be chosen? What if a norm which tendentially governs the case leads to undesirable consequences? How must a norm be interpreted in order to obtain the best possible result? It is clear that all these questions take us to the domain of axiology, morality, or politics and yet legal justification is not expected to question the very system of law nor the ideology of adjudication embodied therein, i.e. the postulate that legal decisions have to be grounded on legally relevant sources, a postulate that embodies the rule of law ideal.[144]

An analogous approach has been to distinguish between formal and substantive reasoning. Professors Atiyah and Summers argue that judges use these two types of reasoning and they offer the following definitions. A 'substantive reason is a moral, economic, political, institutional, or other social consideration', whereas a 'formal reason is a different kind of reason'. A formal reason 'is a legally authoritative reason on which judges and others are empowered or required to base a decision or action, and such a reason usually excludes from consideration, overrides, or at least diminishes the weight of, any countervailing substantive reason arising at the point of decision or action'.[145] This is not exactly a mirror image at the level of reasoning of the distinction between the hard and easy case, but it does emphasise in terms of method two kinds of technique. The formal reason is more likely to be framed as a matter of inference inasmuch as a solution is being deduced from the existence of a normative proposition that is in complete isomorphic conformity with the facts as constituted by the court. The result is inferred from the rule thus blocking off an 'interpretative' analysis. Where there is no such isomorphic rule pattern to govern the facts then the judges will adopt the Perelman approach of legal argumentation.

Argumentation

Such arguments can themselves be analysed in terms of form and substance. At the level of form, one can class arguments into different kinds such as the argument *a fortiori, a minor, a pari, a contrario* and so on.[146] Equally, they can be approached in terms of skill and substance. The basic skills aspect to legal argumentation is not to be underestimated. Propositions of law can be absorbed by the mind usually without too much difficulty, but the application of such propositions is an entirely different matter and the convincing of a third party adds an even further dimension. Argumentation, which is in form fundamental to Western legal thinking under the principle of contradiction,[147] thus entails that law has a dynamic aspect. It involves a rational process of social influencing.[148]

Argumentation entails a number of quite complex skills.[149] From a strategic point of view, a knowledge of the diverse types of argument is vital to the preparation and orientation of a case.[150] Arguments based upon precedent (time) are different from those founded upon social justice (norm), just as arguments founded on analogy and metaphor (image) are not the same as those using deductive methods (logical inference). Equally, arguments based upon the status of a witness (authority) are to be distinguished from those founded upon the hidden implications of words or facts (interpretation). Interpretation, in turn, must be distinguished from justification. On an even more general level, arguments focusing on ends (teleological) are to be contrasted with those going to the means (logical). At this general level one can also talk of arguments based on an appeal to facts – for example, an appeal to statistics to support a claim – or upon presuppositions. An example of the latter is when one appeals to implicit moral or social values. The debate surrounding capital punishment can rely on one or other of these approaches. A politician may support the death penalty on the basis that (say) 80 per cent of the electorate is in favour, or that statistics prove that it is a deterrent. Alternatively, the politician may seek support for capital punishment in the supposed principle of morality that the taking of one life deserves the taking of another. Opponents of capital punishment will, equally, challenge the appeal to facts with either an argument disputing the facts (for example, that it is not a deterrent) or an appeal to moral value. Particularly important for the jurist, when it comes to argumentation strategy, is the selection, isolation and categorisation of facts.[151] The debate surrounding abortion, for example, depends largely upon whether a foetus is classified as a 'person'; equally, the extension of the tort of negligence into the area of consumer law depended in part on whether or not a pair of underpants was to be classified as a 'product'.[152] Syllogistic logic weaves in and out of these forms of arguments. For example, if it is accepted that the will of the majority is always to be followed, then the argument in favour of capital punishment appears settled the moment one establishes as fact the majority in favour (if p, then y). Similarly, the moment it is accepted that the foetus is a person, the harder it becomes to resist the inference that termination of pregnancy amounts to the killing of a human.

There is also a tactical skill in argumentation.[153] The purpose of an argument is to transfer a conviction to another with the object, in law at any rate, of securing a particular result. The transfer will no doubt base itself largely on the quality of the justification(s) used to support the argument. Nevertheless, the way an argument is formally constructed and, if there is more than one, the order in which they are presented, may well have a bearing on their force. The use of language (rhetoric) may have a relevant role in this respect (*bene dicendi scientia*). Furthermore, given that argumentation is about convincing another party, the tactician will no doubt wish to try to use to his or her advantage any prejudices or predispositions that this other party may have. Tactical skills often blend into those used at the strategic level; one might, for example, make a strategic decision to concentrate more on the dismantling of an opponent's argument than upon the positive aspects of one's own case. Yet such an approach might rely on the tactical undermining of an argument by an opportunist riposte that may have no logical connection with the actual argument being undermined.[154] The association of a local authority's behaviour, in asserting what it believed was its right of ownership in excluding a local rugby club which had undertaken a tour of apartheid South Africa, with the Nazi regime might serve as an example.[155] It was an argument by association which had only the barest connection with the legal question at issue and, indeed, could equally have been applied to the behaviour of the other party in the case. This approach to argument has a particular relevance in a legal system which favours orality and the jury, since cross-examination presents the opportunity to create vivid impressions. And, if the case is before a jury, these impressions may be more effective when aimed at the minds of those for whom argumentation and reasoning may not be a professional skill.

The creation of impressions is not, however, something which should be dismissed in any investigation of argumentation skills: for such images are in themselves a form of communication and they raise the question of a distinction between symbolic and non-symbolic knowledge. That is to say, the distinction between mental representations as linguistic propositions (symbolic) and mental representations as images and intellectual structures incapable of being translated into linguistic expressions (non-symbolic).[156] The association of a local authority's use of power with the use of power by the Nazi government no doubt raises all sorts of problems when viewed as a rational argument. It also directs attention to the nature and acceptability of legal arguments. But its force as an image cannot be denied.[157] Moreover, whether or not flawed in the particular circumstances of the actual case, it would be wrong to dismiss this form of argumentation as having no basis in logical reasoning. It is an example of reasoning by analogy inasmuch as the abuse of *imperium* for political repression is being transposed to the assertion of *dominium* for (what was perceived as) vindictive repression. That said, the argument is of a type that directs attention onto the kind of analogies that are permitted and onto those that would have no relevance.[158] Would such an argument have been acceptable in, say, a contract case? Could, for example, a lawyer seriously argue that the oppressive vindication of a contractual right is analogous to political repression, and thus should be subject to judicial intervention? Or what about criminal law? Could a prosecuting lawyer argue that the court should punish the defendant for 'behaving like a Nazi'? If not, what limits the use of analogies? If, alternatively, argumentation can function relatively independently from the area of substantive law in issue, does this mean that legal argumentation is a form of legal knowledge in itself? These questions can lead the epistemologist in a number of distinct directions.

Argumentation and Reasoning

The first direction is argumentation based on inference. Legal argumentation is often identified with legal reasoning and to an extent the identification of the two in the realm of law is of itself a revealing phenomenon. However, they must also be differentiated. The word 'reasoning' suggests a sophisticated activity where solutions are *inferred* from intellectual discourse systems whose paradigm example is mathematics and its deductive logic. Here the methodology is more one of *demonstration* rather than argumentation; it is a question of *modus ponens* where a conclusion follows necessarily from a premise. 'If *p*, then *q*; it is *p*, thus it must be *q*.' Argumentation, on the other hand, is an everyday activity where one person hopes to convince another of the superiority of some plan, policy and so on. Reasoning may form part of argumentation inasmuch as inference is a form of argument; argumentation may form part of reasoning inasmuch as it is an intellectual activity based upon justifications. Argumentation may well use inference, but the latter is not a reliable guide to the ultimate solution arrived at by a court, since a court can always refuse to accept the premise upon which the inference is founded.

This distinction between reasoning (inference) and argumentation is well brought out in a relatively recent case. In *Harbour Assurance Ltd* v. *Kansa General International Insurance Co Ltd*,[159] one party to a contract brought an action for a declaration that an arbitration clause contained in the insurance contract was void for illegality since the contract itself was void. The court of appeal refused to accept the argument – or more accurately the conclusion based on inference – that if the contract was void then each clause must be void. Hoffmann LJ's response to the inference claim was to undermine the model itself:

> Mr. Longmore's argument is extremely simple. He says that the question raised on the pleadings is whether the retrocession agreement was void ab initio. The arbitration clause formed part of the retrocession agreement. Therefore the issue must involve the validity of the arbitration clause itself.[160]

And he continued:

> Mr. Longmore calls this logic. I call it over-simplification. The flaw in the logic, as it seems to me, lies in the ambiguity of the proposition that the arbitration clause 'formed part' of the retrocession agreement. In one sense of course it did. It was clause 12 of a longer document which also dealt with the substantive rights and duties of the parties. But parties can include more than one agreement in a single document.

> They may say in express words that two separate agreements are intended. Or the question of whether the document amounts to one agreement or two may have to be answered by reference to the kind of provisions it contains ... There is no single concept of 'forming part' which will provide the answer in every case.[161]

Another important difference is that argumentation, unlike reasoning, implicitly implies an activity involving more than a single person; it is a social activity.[162] However, because its base is wider than a rigorous model from which necessary solutions are inferred, argumentation was, from the time of Descartes, increasingly excluded from science since science could never be content with opinions which were only probable.[163] Uncertainty in an intellectual system was a sign of scientific weakness of the system itself. This downgrading of argumentation, the effects of which can still be felt inasmuch as rhetoric (formerly an honourable part of argumentation) remains a pejorative term, was to have a major impact, as we have seen, on the movement towards an axiomatic stage of legal science. However, with the retreat from positivism and from the *mos geometricus*, argumentation has been forced in other directions.

Policy

One of these other directions is to abandon traditional legal concepts and to appeal to 'policy'. Thus in one case Lord Denning asserted:

> In previous times, when faced with a new problem, the judges have not openly asked themselves the question: what is the best policy for the law to adopt? But the question has always been there in the background. It has been concealed behind such questions as: Was the defendant under a duty to the plaintiff? Was the relationship between them sufficiently proximate? Was the injury direct or indirect? Was it foreseeable, or not? Was it too remote? And so forth.[164]

A policy argument has been defined as a substantive justification 'to which judges appeal when the standards and rules of the legal system do not provide a clear resolution of a dispute'.[165] It differs from what might be called normal legal authority reasons in that 'the appeal is to the values which could justify a rule, or an interpretation of it, and the argument centres on the balancing of conflicting values'.[166] Policy arguments have been described by one leading United Kingdom judge as belonging to 'a less formalistic age' where more than one 'solution is logically defensible', and where 'good sense, fairness and respect for the reasonable expectations of contracting parties suggests that the best solution' is one which 'at least has the merit of promoting more sensible results than any other solution'.[167] Not surprisingly, such an approach can lead to conflicts of views and such a conflict was quite recently in evidence when two judges offered rather different policy values. In the court of appeal, Scott LJ declared that the 'authorities seem to me to leave the developing law, if not at the crossroads, at least at the junction of two diverging roads'.[168] And this encouraged him to state:

> The choice between the two roads cannot, in my opinion, be made simply by reference to binding authority. Binding authority can be found to justify either. The choice should, I think, be a matter of policy. Ought the law to treat married women who provide security for their husband's debts, and others in an analogous position, as requiring special protection? The position of married women today, both generally and vis-à-vis their husbands, is very different from what it was ... But ... in the culturally and ethnically mixed community in which we live, the degree of emancipation of women is uneven.[169]

However, in the House of Lords, Lord Browne-Wilkinson countered with the following observation:

> On the other hand, it is important to keep a sense of balance in approaching these cases. It is easy to allow sympathy for the wife who is threatened with the loss of her home at the suit of a rich bank to obscure an important public interest viz., the need to ensure that the wealth currently tied up in the matrimonial home does not become economically sterile. If the rights secured to wives by the law renders vulnerable loans granted on the security of matrimonial homes, institutions will be unwilling to accept such security, thereby reducing the flow of loan capital to business enterprises. It is therefore essential that a law designed to protect the vulnerable does not render the matrimonial home unacceptable as security to financial institutions.[170]

Policy arguments are, as Bell indicates, normally to be found in the 'hard case' and for the positivist their existence would indicate ambiguity in the rule. In such situations of ambiguity judges support their discretionary judgment with arguments of policy which may be based on social, political, economic values or some values outside of the rule system. Sometimes such arguments can be fairly 'simplistic' as was the case in Lord Denning's judgment in *Spartan Steel & Alloys* v. *Martin & Co*. In this case, which involved economic loss caused by the negligent interference with the electricity supply by a contractor working in the street, Lord Denning offered as a justification for refusing compensation for such loss the following policy argument:

> The second consideration is the nature of the hazard, namely, the cutting of the supply of electricity. This is a hazard which we all run. It may be due to a short circuit, to a flash of lightning, to a tree falling on

> the wires, to an accidental cutting of the cable, or even to the negligence of someone or other. And when it does happen, it affects a multitude of persons; not as a rule by way of physical damage to them or their property, but by putting them to inconvenience, and sometimes to economic loss. The supply is usually restored in a few hours, so the economic loss is not very large. Such a hazard is regarded by most people as a thing they must put up with – without seeking compensation from anyone. Some there are who install a stand-by system. Others seek refuge by taking out an insurance policy against breakdown in the supply. But most people are content to take the risk on themselves. When the supply is cut off, they do not go running round to their solicitor. They do not try to find out whether it was anyone's fault. They just put up with it. They try to make up the economic loss by doing more work next day. This is a healthy attitude which the law should encourage.[171]

Now to claim that this reasoning is 'simplistic' is not to claim that it is either wrong or out of touch with the values of society. The point is that it is really rather far removed from legal entitlement and the reasoning would be difficult to justify in terms of legal logic. To deny someone a claim simply to deter them from running around to their solicitor is to risk putting the law of remedies entirely upon the foundation of what the judges consider to be reasonable claims. In short, policy becomes a means not of structuring argumentation but of reducing it to a 'commonsense' discretion. Accordingly another direction in which one can restrict argumentation is to reject policy completely as a valid form of legal argument.

The Rights Thesis

Ronald Dworkin is one such writer specifically to reject policy as a means of arriving at a legal decision. In comparing policy with principle, Dworkin states that policy arguments justify a decision by showing that the decision advances or protects some collective goal of society as a whole; arguments of principle, in contrast, justify a decision by showing that it respects or secures some right.[172] Now, with respect to the *Spartan Steel* case, Dworkin offers an alternative approach to arriving at the decision: 'suppose ... that a judge successfully justifies a decision in a hard case, like *Spartan Steel*, on grounds not of policy but of principle'; in other words, 'that he is able to show that the plaintiff has a *right* to recover ... damages'.[173] This rights thesis, according to Dworkin, 'provides a more satisfactory explanation of how judges use precedent in hard cases than the explanation provided by any theory that gives a more prominent place to policy',[174] since it 'provides that judges decide hard cases by confirming or denying concrete rights'.[175] In order to demonstrate this thesis, Dworkin invents a judge of superhuman skill. This judge, he says, 'must construct a scheme of abstract and concrete principles that provides a coherent justification for all common law precedents and, so far as these are to be justified on principle, constitutional and statutory provisions as well'.[176]

It would be tempting to claim that all that Dworkin is doing is setting up another 'axiomatic' model from which the right answer is to be inferred. The logic model gives way to the hermeneutic structure. In truth, Dworkin is not doing quite this. His starting point is not the abstract model as such but the actual practice of adjudication; he sees the role of the judge as being involved in an interpretative exercise similar to the author of a chapter in a chain novel (discussed in Chapter 1). The right answer is not inferred from the model of abstract and concrete principles. Interpretation, says Dworkin, is not like physics since it is not based on a model that represents something 'out there'.[177] It is based on an internal constraint that weighs upon all legal reasoners that subscribe to his integrity model of law. Such subscribers are analogous to the writers taking part in the chain novel exercise; they are subscribing to the integrity model because they all wish to produce a single novel which is as coherent and as perfect as possible. Dworkin's reasoning model is phenomenological in that it represents the internal viewpoint of the interpreter.[178]

Accordingly, Dworkin does not claim that this interpretative model represents legal knowledge. It is not as such an epistemological structure. Rather, it is the actual act of interpretation which represents legal knowledge and thus law itself is an 'interpretive concept'.[179] Judges, therefore, decide what the law is not by reference to an object detached from the judiciary, but 'by interpreting the practice of other judges deciding what the law is'; and so general 'theories of law ... are general interpretations of ... judicial practice'.[180] Dworkin has, then, 'not devised an algorithm for the courtroom' nor has he produced an epistemological foundation for an artificial intelligence programme. 'No electronic magician', he specifically asserts, 'could design from my arguments a computer program that would supply a verdict everyone would accept once the facts of the case and the text of all past statutes and judicial decisions were put at the computer's disposal.'[181] Equally, knowledge of law is 'not exhausted by any catalogue of rules and principles, each with its own dominion over some discrete theatre of behaviour'.[182] It is a question of attitude.

This thesis has two general merits for legal epistemology. First, it has the merit of suggesting that law is more than simply a matter of legal propositions and this is something in itself valuable. Secondly, however, it indicates the limits of the hermeneutical approach to legal knowledge. The world beyond the rules and principles can be grasped only by a concept – attitude – and this is a concept that is fundamentally weak in an epistemological sense (although not necessarily in the philosophical sense). It cannot act as a model for legal reasoning since, as Dworkin himself asserts, it cannot act as the basis for an AI programme. And it cannot act as an AI programme because, arguably, it has nothing to say about facts.

Legal Science and Codification

Law as interpretation – the hermeneutical scheme (cf. Chapter 8) – would certainly appear to have destroyed the Enlightenment idea of *scientia iuris*. Yet can the codes be dismissed so easily? When one turns from the natural and mathematical sciences to the discipline of law, or more precisely when one turns from scientific models to the codes, one finds that the codes have seemingly been designed for several functions. They are abstract models for the solving of concrete problems; they are directives to the citizens at large; and they are the means by which legal knowledge is transmitted from one generation to another. In short, they are designed as unique 'scientific' models for use in the law office, in the living room and in the lecture theatre. They are eclectic models that bridge the gap between the teaching and practice of law. This has prompted the observation that the distinction between law and the science of law disappears once one has reached the stage of codification, since the purpose of a code is to reduce law to an inference model.[183] Put another way, legal science, *jurisprudentia rationalis*, seemingly obliterates all epistemological distinctions between legal practice, legal theory and legal teaching.

Epistemology and Social Science

Yet are the codes genuine scientific models? Whatever one's view of the relationship between the natural sciences and the human sciences, this question is by no means a simple one. Certainly, one can dismiss the social sciences as 'pseudo-science', or even as an abuse of language, on the basis that they have no solid conceptual foundation. The social sciences, it could be said, consist of a multitude of schemes of intelligibility (cf. Chapter 8), all of which are characterised by a rather weak power of validation.[184] It is often impossible to separate such schemes from ideological and philosophical interpretation, with the result that conceptual structures soon give way to myth and prescription.[185] Equally, however, it can be argued that the codes are really rather different structures from the schemes of intelligibility that are used by the social sciences in general. The codes are constructions that are not designed to describe, explain and predict a social phenomenon as empirical object. They are models developed to create an artificial social 'reality' that exists independently from the social phenomenon that is of interest to, say, the sociologist. In other words, when lawyers and sociologists each construct their own models of social reality they are not involved in the same exercise. Lawyers use a code, consciously or unconsciously, as an object in itself; the code is an alternative 'reality' consisting of normative relationships. Sociologists, in contrast, might end up, like natural scientists, in producing an abstract model of society, but the model is not designed to be an alternative society as such. It is an attempt to elicit information about the society itself.

What is true of the code is also true of the *Institutes* of Gaius. This work, which will be considered in more depth later, in Chapter 4, represented a 'great leap forward in the systematic presentation of private law'.[186] This Roman jurist published a student textbook whose scheme of arrangement was to become the foundation for the modern civil codes. Now, Gaius may have thought that he was producing a descriptive scheme of Roman society,[187] but the success of his scheme of arrangement is due mainly to the fact that it was a self-referencing model that created its own elements and relationships which were normative in effect. When describing, say, the contract of sale, it is easy to think that Gaius was simply describing a commercial aspect of Roman society. Yet what he was doing was recreating a world of *personae* and *res* and establishing between these mediating elements normative abstract relationships such as contract. Today the normative element is inherent in the relationship itself; contract creates 'rights' and 'duties' between the parties. In Gaius, the normative aspect is more indirect; it is provided by the third mediating element of the *actio* which has the effect of turning a seemingly descriptive bond (*iuris vinculum* according to Justinian) into a normative relationship. Civil codes are, then, more developed, in the axiomatic sense, versions of Gaius. They are more like mathematical models except that the elements and relationships are very different. In the place of symbols which have no direct connection with the real world, there are mediating elements (institutions) which relate to the social world as non-symbolic mental states. Mental states are not, according to Jean Delacour, limited to arbitrary symbolic representations constrained only by their own syntax; there are also 'images' and abstract 'schemes' which are non-symbolic.[188]

Symbolic and Non-symbolic Models

The codes are abstract schemes of institutional elements and normative relationships which appear, then, to function like mathematical models but which actually operate rather differently. Where a legal code differs from a mathematical model is in the way the conceptual elements and the relationships between them can only operate through the intervention of a human 'interpreter'. The idea of interpretation must be used carefully here because it is not just a question of interpreting the language of the code provisions. It is also a matter of 'interpreting', in effect constructing, 'facts'. The point to be made is that the code, being a non-symbolic model, is incapable of inferring predictions and solutions simply as a result of any internal syntax inherent in the model itself. There must always be human intervention, save perhaps where the code provision is essentially mathematical in its construction.

Take, for example, the following provision to be found in article 1134 of the *Code civil*: 'Contracts must be performed in good faith.' Can this provision be used to infer a solution to the situation to be found in a well-known English case? The facts of the case were stated by Dillon LJ:

> The plaintiffs run a library of photographic transparencies. The defendants are engaged in advertising. On 5 March 1984 Mr Beeching, a director of the defendants, wanting photographs for a presentation for a client, telephoned the plaintiffs, whom the defendants had never dealt with before. He spoke to a Miss Fraser of the plaintiffs and asked her whether the plaintiffs had any photographs of the 1950s which might be suitable for the defendants' presentation. Miss Fraser said that she would research his request, and a little later on the same day she sent round by hand to the defendants 47 transparencies packed in a jiffy bag. Also packed in the bag, among the transparencies, was a delivery note which she had typed out ...[189]

Dillon LJ explained that, having received the photographs the defendants put them to one side where they were temporarily forgotten. The result of this oversight was that the photographs were not returned to the plaintiffs until 2 April. Dillon LJ continued:

> The plaintiffs thereupon sent an invoice to the defendants for £3,783.50 as a holding charge for the transparencies. The invoice was rejected by the defendants, and accordingly in May 1984 the plaintiffs started this action claiming £3,783.50, the amount of the invoice. That is the sum for which the judge awarded the plaintiffs judgment by his order now under appeal.[190]

The appeal judge then explained as follows:

> The sum of £3,783.50 is calculated by the plaintiffs in strict accordance with condition 2 as the fee for the retention of 47 transparencies from 19 March to 2 April 1984. It is of course important to the plaintiffs to get their transparencies back reasonably quickly, if they are not wanted, since if a transparency is out with one customer it cannot be offered to another customer, should occasion arise. It has to be said, however, that the holding fee charged by the plaintiffs by condition 2 is extremely high, and in my view exorbitant. The [trial] judge held that on a quantum meruit a reasonable charge would have been £3.50 per transparency per week, and not £5 per day ...[191]

Now, the first point that needs to be made is that there is nothing in the facts themselves that dictates that a solution to the problem is to be determined by reference to a provision about good faith (even assuming that article 1134 represented English law). Nevertheless, one of the appeal judges thought that the provision was relevant:

> In many civil law systems, and perhaps in most legal systems outside the common law world, the law of obligations recognises and enforces an overriding principle that in making and carrying out contracts parties should act in good faith. This does not simply mean that they should not deceive each other, a principle which any legal system must recognise; its effect is perhaps most aptly conveyed by such metaphorical colloquialisms as 'playing fair', 'coming clean' or 'putting one's cards face upwards on the table'. It is in essence a principle of fair and open dealing. In such a forum it might, I think, be held on the facts of this case that the plaintiffs were under a duty in all fairness to draw the defendants' attention specifically to the high price payable if the transparencies were not returned in time and, when the 14 days had expired, to point out to the defendants the high cost of continued failure to return them.[192]

What the appeal judge was doing here was to construct a model of facts so as to produce an image – a pattern – that conformed in structure to the kind of pattern contained in article 1134. The pattern of this article did not force itself onto the facts. The judges could have easily inferred that the behaviour of the defendants was such that they had only themselves to blame. This was a commercial relationship and so, if the defendants failed both to read the small print of the contract and to return the photographs, it was no business of the courts to intervene. As article 1134 also states: 'Agreements legally made take the place of legislation for those who make them.' Indeed, as an earlier English appeal judge observed: 'If there is one thing more than another which public policy requires, it is that men of full age and competent understanding shall have the utmost liberty of contracting and that their contracts, when entered into freely and voluntarily, shall be held sacred and shall be enforced by courts of justice.'[193] The trial judge in the photographs case did not, then, make the wrong inference. He simply applied a different image.

A second point that emerges out of this photographs case is that other quite different, solutions were possible. The court could simply conclude that the onerous term was not incorporated into the contract. Thus Dillon LJ was of the view that the 'question is therefore whether condition 2 was sufficiently brought to the defendants' attention to make it a term of the contract which was only concluded after the defendants had received, and must have known that they had received the transparencies and the delivery note'. And he concluded:

> At the time of the ticket cases in the last century it was notorious that people hardly ever troubled to read printed conditions on a ticket or delivery note or similar document. That remains the case now. In the intervening years the printed conditions have tended to become more and more complicated and more and more one-sided in favour of the party who is imposing them, but the other parties, if they notice that there are printed conditions at all, generally still tend to assume that such conditions are only concerned with ancillary matters of form and are not of importance. In the ticket cases the courts held that the common law required that reasonable steps be taken to draw the other parties' attention to the printed conditions or they would not be part of the contract. It is, in my judgment, a logical development of the common law into modern conditions that it should be held, as it was in *Thornton* v. *Shoe Lane Parking Ltd* [1971] 2 QB 163, that, if one condition in a set of printed conditions is particularly onerous or unusual, the party seeking to enforce it must show that that particular condition was fairly brought to the attention of the other party.[194]

Another possibility is mentioned by Bingham LJ:

> In reaching the conclusion I have expressed I would not wish to be taken as deciding that condition 2 was not challengeable as a disguised penalty clause. This point was not argued before the judge nor raised in the notice of appeal. It was accordingly not argued before us. I have accordingly felt bound to assume, somewhat reluctantly, that condition 2 would be enforceable if fully and fairly brought to the defendants' attention.[195]

These possibilities can of course be seen as species of the generic term 'good faith'. That indeed is the reason why Bingham LJ refers to the codified systems. Equally, however, they can be seen as solutions flowing from different institutional patterns. Thus, for example, the inclusion of a term within a contractual relationship is one that is largely determined by the form of the contractual document and (or) the time that the term is brought to the other party's attention. This is a much more formal pattern than simply saying the plaintiff was lacking in good faith. The penalty clause point can equally be viewed as having its basis in a different pattern. For example, it could be viewed as the attempt by one party to use contract as a means of punishment or as a method of securing an unjustified enrichment. Assuming for the moment that all these different ways of analysing the case could be reduced to a code,[196] it is evident that there is nothing in the code itself that determines which actual provision is to be used to settle the case. Is it to be a matter of good faith (article 1134) or a question of a penalty (article 1152)? The human 'interpreter' must make the choice. And this choice is not just a choice between two or more articles in a code. The way the facts are 'constructed' is equally important, since these facts must produce an image which matches the images to be found in the code.

The Scientific Inadequacy of the Codes

The codes, therefore, are scientific models only in a rather limited way. They are schemes of thought riddled with 'imperfections' and 'impressions', and this renders them uncertain as intelligent systems. Or, put another way, codes as intelligent systems do not contain enough information for them to be able to arrive at unquestionably correct conclusions.[197] Such uncertainty probably renders them incapable of being seen as scientific models in any hard sense of the term 'science'. What codes do have, however, is a legal science dimension inasmuch as they can, seemingly, describe, explain and, to a certain extent, predict. Of course this description, explanation and prediction is effective only within the artificial boundaries of legal knowledge. And such legal knowledge is constructed out of the very institutions that act as the pillars of the code. Yet there is a scientific aspect to such epistemological constructions and this is what makes the notion of codification so ambiguous. What the codes offer, then, is a synchronic model of legal knowledge that, although not fully reliable in any logical sense, at least attempts to coalesce legal history, legal practice and legal education. What it cannot do is to include within itself its own case law. And it cannot do this because the construction of normative patterns within facts arguably involves a cognitive and epistemological process that is not a matter of syllogistic logic. In other words, the codes fail as scientific models in the full sense because they fail at the level of methodology. The cognitive and epistemological assumptions upon which they were originally based were incorrect.

Notes

1 Zenati (1991, p. 95).
2 D.22.6.2.
3 Granger (1995, pp. 14–17).
4 Goffi (1988, p. 26).
5 Ibid.
6 Ibid., p. 23.
7 Ibid., p. 25.
8 Ibid., pp. 26–7.
9 Ibid., p. 27.
10 Granger (1995, p. 14).
11 Ibid., p. 15.
12 Ibid., p. 46.
13 Ibid., p. 49.
14 Ibid.
15 Bunge (1983, p. 58).
16 Ibid., p. 59.
17 Ibid., p. 60.
18 Granger (1995, p. 70), emphasis in original.
19 Bachelard (1938, p. 44).
20 Granger (1995, p. 72).
21 Astolfi and Develay (1996, p. 23).
22 Ibid., p. 24.
23 See Bachelard (1938) and Kuhn (1970).
24 Astolfi and Develay (1996, pp. 29–30).
25 Ibid., p. 44.
26 Ibid., p. 46.
27 Ibid., p. 55.
28 Ibid., p. 106.
29 Ibid., p. 114.
30 Ibid.
31 Blanché (1983, pp. 36–8).
32 Bachelard (1938, p. 17).
33 Kuhn (1970, pp. 1–9).
34 Ibid., pp. 10–11.
35 Ibid., p. 6.
36 Bachelard (1934, p. 62).
37 Blanché (1975, p. 152).
38 Granger (1995, p. 114).
39 Ibid., p. 115, emphasis in original.
40 Villa (1990, p. 84), emphasis in original.
41 Granger (1995, pp. 70–75).
42 Blanché (1983, p. 121).
43 Jones (1940, p. 55); Jolowicz (1963, pp. 123–9). And see, generally, Stein (1986).
44 Jolowicz (1963, p. 127).
45 See Legrand (1999a).
46 Wieacker (1995, p. 330).

47 See, generally, Cocks (1988).
48 Twining (1974, pp. 149, 160).
49 Samuel (1991).
50 Stein (1986, p. 293).
51 Stein (1980, p. 122).
52 Ibid., p. 124.
53 Stein (1986, p. 304).
54 Atias (1994, p. 95).
55 Ibid.
56 Ibid., pp. 95–6.
57 Ibid., p. 96.
58 Ibid., p. 98.
59 Ibid., p. 101.
60 Ibid., p. 102.
61 Ibid., p. 103.
62 Atias (1985, pp. 199–201).
63 Ibid., p. 201.
64 Atias (1994, p. 103).
65 Barreau (1998, pp. 21–8).
66 Mucchielli (1985, p. 16).
67 Ibid., pp. 73–4.
68 Piettre (1994, pp. 66–75).
69 Besnier (1996, p. 25).
70 Piaget (1988, p. 5).
71 Ibid., p. 6.
72 See, for example, Barreau (1995, pp. 12–14).
73 Villey (1975, pp. 513–40).
74 Blanché (1983, p. 65).
75 Strömholm (1985, pp. 46, 54).
76 D.9.2.31.
77 D.2.14.1.3.
78 D.50.17.1.
79 D.9.2.52.2.
80 Stein and Shand (1974, p. 104).
81 Blanché (1973b, p. 54).
82 See, generally, D.50.16.
83 See, generally, Stein (1966, pp. 74–89).
84 D.1.3.7.
85 Watson (1981, pp. 14–22).
86 Samuel (1994, pp. 35–7).
87 Ibid., pp. 193–6.
88 Berman (1983, p. 139).
89 Ibid., p. 150.
90 Watson (1994).
91 Villey (1975, pp. 400–540); Samuel (1994, pp. 171–80).
92 Strömholm (1985, pp. 122, 123).
93 See Samuel (1994, pp. 43–6).
94 Berman (1983, p. 131).
95 Ibid., pp. 151–64; Wieacker (1995, p. 45).

96 Villey (1975, pp. 523–4).
97 Stein (1966, pp. 131–2).
98 See D.22.6.2.
99 Wieacker (1995, pp. 36–7).
100 Stein (1966, pp. 141–2).
101 Wieacker (1995, p. 37, n. 40).
102 Stein (1966, p. 154).
103 See, for example, Zenati and Revet (1997, pp. 133–48).
104 Cf. D.50.16.16.
105 Canning (1987, p. 189; and p. 265 for original Latin).
106 Ullmann (1975b, p. 110).
107 1290–1349. But note that this association has recently been seriously challenged: Tierney (1997).
108 See also Samuel (1994, pp. 54–5).
109 Laurent (1994, pp. 25–33).
110 See D.41.3.30.
111 Villey (1975, pp. 203–10); but cf. Tierney (1997), pp. 13–42.
112 1588–1679.
113 Villey (1975, pp. 649–61).
114 Ibid., p. 400.
115 Jones (1940, p. 17).
116 Ibid., p. 22.
117 Ibid., p. 32.
118 See, generally, Kelley (1970).
119 Stein (1988, p. 75).
120 Villey (1975, p. 516).
121 Strömholm (1985, p. 161).
122 Jones (1940, p. 39).
123 Piaget (1988, p. 103).
124 Villey (1975, p. 538).
125 Pédamon (1985, pp. 15–16). See in particular Wieacker (1995, pp. 243–56).
126 Timsit (1986, pp. 106–7).
127 Blanché (1980, p. 85).
128 A.B. Schwarz quoted in Zweigert and Kötz (1998, p. 145).
129 On the new hermeneutical theorists, see Manuel Calvo García (1994, pp. 167–246).
130 Bergel (1999, p. 273).
131 Ibid., p. 274.
132 Ibid., p. 275.
133 Perelman (1979, pp. 6–8).
134 Bergel (1999, p. 275).
135 Villey (1975, p. 700).
136 Birks (1996b, p. 4).
137 Ibid.
138 [1995] 2 AC 296.
139 Birks (1996b, p. 6).
140 The damage suffered by Mr Spring was serious: *The Guardian*, Jobs & Money section, 4 March 2000, p. 33.

141 Atias (1994, p. 83).
142 Bengoetxea (1993, p. 184).
143 Ibid., p. 186.
144 Ibid., p. 146.
145 Atiyah and Summers (1987, pp. 1–2).
146 See, for example, Robaye (1991, pp. 97–131).
147 See, for example, *Nouveau code de procédure civile*, art. 16.
148 Oléron (1996, pp. 4–5).
149 Ibid., pp. 64–124.
150 For a general discussion of legal argumentation, see MacCormick (1978).
151 See, generally, Izorche (2001).
152 *Grant* v. *Australian Knitting Mills Ltd* [1936] AC 85 (PC).
153 Oléron (1996, pp. 111–24).
154 Ibid., pp. 190–91.
155 *Wheeler* v. *Leicester CC* [1985] AC 1054, 1080.
156 Delacour (1995, pp. 34–42).
157 For some further examples from English cases, see Samuel (2000a, pp. 190–91, 192).
158 Atias (1994, p. 80).
159 [1993] QB 701.
160 Ibid., p. 722.
161 Ibid., p. 722.
162 Oléron (1996, pp. 4–5).
163 Perelman and Olbrechts-Tyteca (1988, p. 2).
164 *Dutton* v. *Bognor Regis UDC* [1972] 1 QB 373, 397.
165 Bell (1983, pp. 22–3).
166 Ibid., p. 23.
167 Steyn LJ in *Watts* v. *Aldington* (1993) *The Times* 16 December, quoted by Auld LJ in *Jameson* v. *CEGB* [1998] QB 323, 336.
168 *Barclays Bank plc* v. *O'Brien* [1993] QB 109, 137.
169 At p. 139.
170 *Barclays Bank plc* v. *O'Brien* [1994] 1 AC 180, 188.
171 [1973] 1 QB 27, 38.
172 Dworkin (1977, p. 82).
173 Ibid., p. 85.
174 Ibid., p. 87.
175 Ibid., p. 101.
176 Ibid., pp. 116–17.
177 Dworkin (1985, p. 83).
178 Ibid., p. 235.
179 Ibid., pp. 87, 410.
180 Ibid., p. 410.
181 Ibid., p. 412.
182 Ibid., p. 413.
183 Dubouchet (1990, p. 62).
184 Granger (1995, p. 98).
185 Ibid., p. 99.
186 Stein (1984, p. 127).

187 Ibid.
188 Delacour (1995, p. 65).
189 *Interfoto Picture Library Ltd* v. *Stiletto Visual Programmes Ltd* [1989] QB 433, 434–5.
190 At p. 435.
191 At p. 436.
192 Bingham LJ, at p. 439.
193 Sir George Jessel, in *Printing and Numerical Registering Co* v. *Sampson* (1875) LR 19 Eq 462, 465.
194 *Interfoto*, at pp. 438–9.
195 At pp. 445–6.
196 See, for example, CC, art. 1152.
197 Bouchon-Meunier and Nguyen (1996, p. 9).

3 Methodologies in Law

Legal science implies a legal method, in that there can be no science without method.[1] The problem, however, is not just to relate method to science as a state of mind, but to identify and to isolate the various methods and techniques and to relate them to objects which form the object of science. If science is a constructed representation of reality, how do the methods and procedures of science relate, if at all, to reality? How are they more 'real' as a means of 'knowing' reality than the methods and procedures associated with myths, religions and other ideologies?[2] How is science 'better' in its methods, techniques and procedures from other discourses and theories? More particularly, if law is a science, why are the procedures it adopts with respect to deciding cases superior to, say, trial by ordeal or trial by combat? Should a jury who decide the guilt of a defendant through recourse to a ouija board be condemned for using the wrong methods?[3] The scientist might reply that scientific methods have as their object a rigorous representation of the real and that the methods themselves are about the 'interrogation' of nature in order to render the scientific investigator its master.[4] The representation and the methods are themselves continually to be tested against the criteria of validity. 'A piece of knowledge concerning an experiment is scientific,' says Granger, 'only if it matches the particular conditions by which it has been obtained, sufficient for it to be reproduced by the same conditions.'[5]

Inductive Reasoning in Roman Law

It has already been suggested in the previous chapter that, if scientific method is a process of development from the descriptive and inductive to the deductive and axiomatic, then the methods of the Roman jurists can be classed in the former. Roman jurists took legal science into the inductive stage. That they never really went beyond this stage is evident from a number of texts, the chief amongst them being the observation that rules were not the source of law. They were only brief summaries of what the law is.[6] What actually formed the source of law in the knowledge sense is more difficult to determine, in that the Romans were not interested in formulating definitions and theories. Indeed, they were of the view that all definitions were dangerous.[7] However, what seems clear is that the search for solutions to particular litigation problems was to be found within the circumstances of each case; *in causa ius esse positum*, observed one jurist before analysing the facts of a relatively complex accident case.[8] The law (*ius*) is to be found in the causal aspects of facts.

Inductive Methodology

The movement from the descriptive to the inductive may seem a modest development in the overall scheme of things. Yet, while the BGB and the work of the Pandectists reveals a level of juristic intellectual achievement rarely matched in rigour and logical consistency, it would be an error to think that the inductive stage of legal science was, and remains, somehow lacking in sophistication. As Blanché has asserted, an 'axiomatic stage remains rather hollow if it is not built upon a pre-existing deductive theory, which itself has scientific value only if it organises a vast mass of laws inductively acquired after a long exploration of phenomena'.[9] Indeed, it may well be that it is the inductive stage of science that is the most sophisticated in terms of intellectual development, for it is within this stage that one passes from the particular to the universal and this passage itself is based on degrees of rationality. One passes from one degree of inductive rationality to another, each degree producing new categories and new principles.[10] The inductive stage is anything but static. It is continually 'reorganising itself in taking into account new departures from foundations gradually expanding as rational structures more and more complex are established'.[11]

A good example of this inductive movement is provided by the law of contracts. Roman law did not develop a general theory of contract; it thought in terms of specific contracts based on particular transactions such as sale, hire, pledge and stipulation.[12] Each specific contract had its own legal action and it was the empirical nature of the transaction – the sale, hire, deposit and so on – which acted as the *causa* of the contract.[13] However, the classical jurist Ulpian writes that there can be no contract without there being within the facts 'agreement' (*conventio*).[14] Agreement, therefore, takes the structure of contract to a new degree of inductive rationality. Contract does not arise from agreement; that idea took flight, as one might expect, only during the deductive stage of legal science. It is the nature of the transaction as much as the agreement which gives rise to the legal obligation.[15] But it does allow the Roman jurists to group contracts together under a general heading of *obligationes ex contractu*.[16] This category can then in turn be used to give a degree of internal coherence to a range of transactions which in themselves always remain empirically independent.[17] Bare agreements never gave rise to legal actions in Roman law, since they lacked a factual cause.[18] Yet there is no doubt that they set in train an inductive movement which was capable of being developed into a rational scheme of contract.[19] The internal force required to propel scientific thought into a deductive stage gathers its force within the inductive period.

Given this richness of the inductive stage, it is surprising, perhaps, that there is little by way of systematic study into the methods and thought processes of the Roman jurists.[20] There are hints of the movement between degrees of inductive rationality. Thus one comparatist and legal historian, Stig Strömholm, writes:

> It has been put forward that the 'style of reasoning' of the Roman lawyers in the long period of development accessible to modern scholarship underwent different stages characterised, in particular, by different degrees of freedom in relation to the strict wording of statutory texts. From an archaic period of strict adherence to the letter of the law, particularly in the then wide field of sacral law, the lawyers, it is said, developed in the sense of greater freedom; towards the end of Antiquity, in the bureaucratic atmosphere characteristic of the centralized and theocratic late Empire, lawyers would have reverted to a narrow formalisation. Further, it is claimed that different attitudes were adopted with regard to different sources of law. The greatest freedom reigned in the field of customary law and in those areas where legal solutions were essentially founded on the writings of private jurists, whereas the interpretation of formal enactments was more cautious.[21]

Strömholm, on the whole, puts an emphasis on *interpretatio*. This is clearly important. Indeed, we have already seen the importance of hermeneutics as a philosophical method. Moreover, Strömholm's discussion of the Greek influence is also very relevant since the Roman jurists themselves, particularly Gaius, stress the structure of law in terms of genus and species.[22] However, systematisation in Roman law went some way beyond the arrangement of material in teaching manuals. In addition to the genus and species hierarchy of categories so characteristic of the *institutiones*, systematic thinking can be found to be functioning, admittedly more obscurely, within the facts themselves. This more concrete form of systems thinking consisted of building within the facts structural models that acted as the basis for both reasoning and problem solving.

Roman Case Law

The practical examples bequeathed to the modern world via the *Digest* of Justinian[23] are not, as such, actual case law decisions. They are academic discussions of practical examples by jurists and their relative brevity limits, perhaps, the amount of insight that can be gained into Roman legal reasoning.[24] Nevertheless, the Roman jurists were both teachers and practitioners and the structure of the 'case law' discussion is such as to allow considerable insight into the way they reasoned from within the facts.

A man sold some oxen on the basis that the buyer could try them out; one of the oxen gored a slave of the buyer and the jurist was asked who should be liable for this damage. The jurist replied that the seller would not be liable if the buyer had actually bought the oxen or if the slave had suffered the goring through his own fault. But if the buyer had not yet bought the animals and the goring was due to some vice in the ox, then the seller would be liable.[25] Two loaded wagons were being dragged up Capitol Hill by mules and the first cart tipped up; the drivers tried to hold the wagon to make it easier for the mules but it began to roll back towards the second cart. The drivers, fearing for their own safety, jumped out of the way, and the wagon rolled back, striking the second cart which in turn rolled back and crushed a slave boy. The owner of the slave asked the jurist against whom he might have an action for damages based on *culpa* (blameworthiness) and the jurist replied, by way of introduction, that it depended on the actual circumstances of the case in question (*in causa ius esse positum*).[26] If the first wagon hit the second because the drivers had let it go when they need not have done so and the mules were physically not strong enough to hold it, then an action would not lie against the owner of the mules. It would lie against the drivers. The letting go of the wagon was, said the jurist, equivalent to a driver failing to control an ass or to a person throwing or discharging something which caused damage. On the other hand, if the drivers had had to jump out of the way for their own safety, and the mules had backed away because they had been frightened by something, then the owner of the mules, and not the drivers, would be the one against whom an action would lie. Again, if neither the mules nor the men were the cause of the accident (*in causa essent*) because the mules could not hold the weight, or had slipped, and the men were not strong enough to support the weight, then no action would lie. Moreover, no action could be brought against the owner of the mules of the second wagon since they did not go back on their own accord but because they were hit.

These examples could be multiplied endlessly. However, they illustrate the tone of Roman legal reasoning. In order to determine liability one searched within the circumstances of the case in order to discover whether or not a remedy (*actio*) would be available and against whom. Now it is evident that one major determinant of liability is the existence of fault together with cause and so one can reasonably assert that the facts are being analysed by the jurist in order to discover if there is blameworthiness on the part of any individual. It is therefore possible to say that one is simply analysing the facts in order to apply a rule about the slightest negligence giving rise to liability for wrongful damage caused.[27] The jurist is searching, in other words, to discover if a minor premise (fact) exists which, when put alongside the major premise (rule of negligence),[28] will logically produce the solution. Legal reasoning is, it could be argued, syllogistic.

However, great care should be taken before arriving at this conclusion. Certainly, the Roman jurists were perfectly capable of thinking in terms of rules and propositional statements. Indeed, not only is there a specific title in the *Digest* devoted to rules of law (*regulae iuris*),[29] but there is in addition one dealing with the actual interpretation of words.[30] Moreover, there are plenty of examples in the *Digest* of a jurist starting out from a statutory rule – from a major explicit premise – and working towards particular fact situations.[31] Yet the jurists in these examples use the facts in such a way as to create new legal situations. Take, for example, the Roman rule about noxal liability. If a slave kills with the knowledge (*scientia*) of his owner, the owner will be liable, but if he did not have knowledge he will be liable only up to the value of the slave.[32] The jurists, understandably, needed to interpret the word 'knowledge' and they state that this means any situation where the owner could have prevented the act of the slave.[33] Yet it soon becomes evident that this proposition is fairly meaningless in itself. It is simply a short summary of the situation. Accordingly, the *Digest* goes on to look at a number of factual situations. What if (*quid si*) the slave did not obey the owner? Or what if he is over the other side of a river when the owner sees him commit the killing? It is evident from the sheer emphasis on these kinds of examples in the *Digest* that, for the Roman jurists, it is in such factual situations that the fine distinctions about knowledge reside. It is by posing these factual examples that the jurists arrive at the conclusion that it is 'more appropriate to say' that 'knowledge' should mean that a person was unable to prevent the act.[34]

In the examples to be found in the *Digest*, 'fault', 'damage' 'knowledge' and the like are descriptive terms and it is the factual situation itself which gives rise to the 'right (*ratio*) answer' in respect of the availability of a remedy. Moreover, such words are not the only focal points for factual analysis, as the examples themselves indicate. The mere fact of being an owner of a slave or a mule is another determinant of who might be liable in an action for damages. What if a prospective owner saw the killing by the slave before he actually became owner of the slave? In this situation the owner cannot be personally liable, since he was not the owner at the time of the act.[35] With respect to damage caused by animals, the noxal liability of the owner had its origin in an old rule which emphasised the damage (*pauperies*) rather than any wrong.[36] But by classical times it was ownership and damage that had become the key.[37] The mere causing of damage by an animal was likely to give rise to a legal remedy provided the victim was not himself at fault.[38] What if a borrower of property sees this property damaged as a result of an act of an animal? The borrower would have an action against the owner of the animal provided he had sufficient interest in the claim, that is to say if he might be facing an action brought against him by the lender.[39]

What emerges from these concrete examples is not so much a set of rules as a set of focal points operating within the facts themselves. Damage, cause, ownership, interest and fault are what might be called quasi-normative concepts inasmuch as they fulfil a double function: they are descriptive on the one hand, but obligation-creating on the other. The descriptive aspect evidently arises out of the facts themselves. The normative dimension, however, results not just from the moral flavour attaching to fault and knowledge, but also from the fact that ownership and interest relate to other aspects of the law. Ownership brings into play the law of property and interest relates to the law of actions. The normative dimension thus arises partly from a structure of legal connections (*iura*) functioning at the heart of the facts themselves.

Constructing the Facts

This last point can be illustrated by reference to several other examples. The first concerns a will wrongfully obliterated by the deliberate (or possibly negligent) act of some person.[40] The jurist Ulpian first of all invites one to consider whether a legal action will lie and he follows this question by noting that, according to another jurist whom he quotes, the action will not be available because it is impossible to estimate the damage. Ulpian agrees that, from the testator's position, this opinion is true, but he goes on to point out that from the position of the heir or legatees the situation is different; an action will be available because the will is equivalent to a signed document acknowledging a debt. Like the examples quoted earlier, this problem and its analysis appears to be functioning at the factual level. Certainly, the method does not start out from a major premise, nor does it talk of ascertaining the relevant rule or principle as the means to obtaining a solution. All the same, the analysis does not rest at the level of wills and damage. What is being constructed by Ulpian is a model of relations between abstracted legal subjects (*quis*, heir, legatee), an abstracted legal institution (the *actio*), an abstracted notion of a legal object (thus a will becomes interchangeable with an IOU) and an abstracted notion of damage (which exists only by virtue of an economic rationality conceptualised into law via the notion of an *interest*). The methodology may look as though it is dealing only with the hard facts of social reality, but in truth Ulpian is manipulating elements and relations that exist in their own rationalised world. He is dealing in abstractions which have been rendered familiar only by constant use.

In addition, the method employed is one of argumentation rather than inference from a single rule. Ulpian is not saying that the jurist he quotes is wrong. He is simply saying that, if one considers the problem from a different angle, it is possible to arrive at a different conclusion. In fact, this is quite a common technique of the Roman jurists and is the reason why it is possible to claim that their methods owed more to rhetoric than to logic.[41] Jurists used each other's opinions as vehicles for discussing particular factual problems. The later jurist would extend legal knowledge, so to speak, either by expanding, or at least altering to some extent, the factual situation posed by the earlier jurist[42] or by proposing an alternative solution to the one advanced by the earlier jurist.[43] Now the technical point at issue here is that decisions depended upon the facts of a case only in the sense that the facts responded to a series of relationships between people, things and legal remedies (*actiones*). And so, in order to determine if a person had an *actio*, the point of the discussion would be to see where, in the case of a compensation claim for example, responsibility could be located. In turn, as we have seen with the wagon case, this would be dependent upon how particular individuals had behaved in relation either to other people directly or to particular things which had the potential of causing damage or injury. Indeed, if one returns to the wagon problem, these structural relationships between things allow one to raise questions not seemingly dealt with by the jurist. For example, what if the wagon had rolled backwards because the owner of the stones, or the owner of the wagon, had overloaded the vehicle? Or what if the slave boy had been killed by badly packed stones falling off the wagon? There is no doubt that the person at fault in overloading, or badly packing, the wagon could be sued in an action for wrongful damage.[44]

Ownership of property also gave people the right to bring actions if their property got damaged. But what if the owner had pledged the property to a creditor? In this situation the owner would have an action as a result of his legal connection with the thing damaged, while the creditor might have an action on the basis of his factual interest in the thing remaining undamaged.[45] Equally, the owner of a valuable cup would have an *actio* against an engraver if the latter caused the breakage through want of skill.[46] However, if the owner of the cup had agreed with the engraver to take the risk of damage, the owner would not have the action. These relationships between people, things and actions seemed empirical enough and often they involved commonsense notions such as cause and blame (*culpa*). Yet one must not be misled by the facts-of-the-case approach. Behind all of the different factual situations there were a limited number of reference points which would be used both to 'construct' the facts and to determine the question of liability. Accordingly, throughout all of the discussions one finds notions such as damage, blame, risk, agreement, ownership, possession (and the like) being used as a means not only of solving problems but of describing them. The technique was not a matter of a major and a minor premise constructed independently of the facts. It was a matter of building a set of formal reasoning relationships within the facts themselves.

One final example illustrates this technique. Ulpian asks who will have the action for theft if a letter he sends to another is intercepted before it arrives.[47] The first thing one needs to know, according to the jurist, is to whom did the letter belong: was it the sender or the addressee? If the sender had given it to the slave of the addressee, then the latter would be the owner because he would acquire it through the slave. The same would be true if the letter was given to the addressee's agent, especially if the addressee had an interest (*interfuit*) in becoming the owner. However, if the sender had sent the letter on the understanding that it would be returned to him, then he would retain ownership. These seemingly concrete situations having been raised, Ulpian returns to the question of who had the action and states that it is the person who had an interest in the letter not being stolen, that is to say the person who benefited from its contents. This leads to another question. Can the messenger bring the action? Ulpian replies that he might well have an action in that, if he were responsible for carrying it safely, he would have a personal interest in the letter being delivered. For example, if the messenger had expressly undertaken to look after the letter, or if he was to be paid for delivering it, he would be strictly responsible for the letter in the same way as an innkeeper or shipmaster. And as they had the action for theft, so should the messenger.

Law as a Conceptual Scheme

This example illustrates very clearly how the law of delict (tort) is dependent upon other areas of the law such as the law of property and the law of contract. Indeed, if one turns to the section in the *Digest* dealing with the law of property, one will actually find two things. One will discover, first of all, a rule dealing with the very problem of ownership and the sending of letters followed, immediately afterwards, by a factual problem indicating that the rule is too brief to be of much value.[48] When the letter has been stolen, the question of the person who will have the action for theft, a question for the law of obligations, is dependent upon the law of property. Ownership might, in its turn, be dependent, *inter alia*, on the law of persons (status). If the messenger is a slave, the addressee will automatically acquire ownership; if he is not a slave, possession might be acquired by the addressee, since one can acquire possession through another person (*persona libera*). However, it transpires that it is not ownership as such which is the key; it is the person who has the *interest*. Here one is moving from the law of property to the law of actions where, on the whole, only persons with an interest are entitled to bring a legal claim.[49] Having used, then, the law of property as a means by which one can determine the interest, this notion of an interest can be used in turn as a means of bringing into play the law of contract (paid messenger) and the law of quasi-delict (strict liability of innkeeper and shipmaster). Liability under one obligation (contract, quasi-delict) becomes, via the notion of an interest, the reason for claiming under another (theft).

The example of the stolen letter is, therefore, revealing in the way it shows how reasoning, even when operating within the facts themselves, makes use of concepts such as property (ownership, possession) and interest. In turn these concepts, while remaining within the facts, also transcend the problem in hand to reappear in other areas of the law. *Dominium* (ownership) is indeed *furtum* (theft),[50] but the link between the two is much more complex, since facts themselves are complex. Who can bring a claim for damages arising out of the theft depends just as much upon connections between people and actions (interests, damage) and upon connections between people and people (contract). Moreover, obligations themselves interrelate, particularly when the facts disclose more than two legal parties. The question to be answered is whether sender or addressee has the *actio furti*, but the role and status of the messenger soon takes over as an important focal point. Not only might the status or obligation position of the messenger be important in deciding the remedy question as between sender and addressee, but the messenger himself becomes a party who might be entitled to sue. The action is one in delict (tort), yet the law of contract assumes an important role in the analysis of the facts. Did the messenger expressly undertake to keep the letter safe?

How can one characterise this kind of legal reasoning? First, one might note how legal reasoning is a matter, not of applying pre-established legal rules as such, but of pushing outwards from the facts.[51] It is a question of starting with sender and addressee and working from them towards the third party. Of course, in doing this, the jurist was working within a highly structured model of legal relations between people (contract and delict) and between people and things (ownership and possession) and this model could be seen to be one that contained a mass of rules. As we shall see in the next chapter, the Romans actually produced institutional manuals that came close to setting out law as a structured set of propositions. However, it was not rules as such that were employed as the main tools of analysis in the actual 'case law' problems; far more important, in the problem of the stolen letter, was the role of notions such as interest, possession and payment. The Romans, in other words, were the ones who developed the mediating elements between the 'science' (law) and its object (fact). These facts were not, of course, real facts in the sense that law was a science explaining and predicting a phenomenon. The mediating elements were the 'bricks' which actually went far in constructing the facts. And these elements, or 'bricks', as we have insisted, are not really rules. They are focal points through which one moves from the world of fact to the world of law and vice versa.

Deductive Reasoning and the Codes

In moving from Roman law to the codes one is moving, as we have seen, from the inductive to the deductive stages of legal science. Now, the codes, seemingly, contain no information about the methods by which solutions are to be inferred from their provisions. This information is assumed. However, the methodological assumption traditionally to be found in Western legal systems is that of deductivism. Legal rules are universal normative propositions forming abstract problem-solving knowledge; cases are specific factual problems in need of solving according to the abstract knowledge. The syllogism is the traditional methodological means by which a solution to the case is inferred from the abstract knowledge. This logical assumption is of course historically determined in one sense.[52] It stems in particular from the *mos geometricus*. In another sense it could be said to rise above history, in that logic has a knowledge value that is synchronic in its structure; it has a truth value that is independent of time and place. The geometry of the law, in other words, was always inherent in legal knowledge even if, say, the Roman jurists were unaware of it in any mathematical sense.[53]

Deductive Methodology

In truth it is not fully correct to say that the codes are devoid of methodological information. A code represents, or at least was once thought to represent, the abstract legal knowledge as a formal set of axioms, these axioms being structured in such a way as to be, supposedly, fully comprehensive. That is to say, any factual situation which seemingly raises a question of legal rights or interests will fall within the architecture of the code. Accordingly, given that axioms are statements for which no proof is required, a code thus acts (or was once seen to act) as a closed totality from which logical inferences can be made. However, the success of the codes as scientific models clearly depends not just on axiomatisation of legal knowledge but also upon the effectiveness of the syllogism as the foundation of legal method. Now, the effectiveness of formal deductive logic as legal method is to be found in the syllogism's abstract capacity to infer new information from given information. In law this means that the solution to concrete problems can be inferred from, and only from, the given information contained in the code. Method and substance combine to assert that a code, or a set of codes, is a repository for all legal knowledge.

When viewed, in turn, from the position of the syllogism, two basic requirements are necessary in order for formal deductive logic to be a comprehensive and effective method.[54] First, the knowledge discourse must have reached a stage where it is capable of being fashioned into an abstract structure or model. 'Deductivism becomes explicable only at the moment when it takes a constructive form,' wrote Piaget. And he continued: 'that is to say when it tends to set up a "structure" whose transformations would accordingly allow the rediscovery of general laws as much as particular ones, but by virtue of *necessary* consequences of the structure and no longer by way of diverse generalities simply categorised into boxes'.[55] Secondly, the deductive model must be a perfectly constituted list of axioms and theorems capable of subsisting when abstracted from all empirical reality. The system, in other words, must be reducible to a self-referencing structure of symbols. The utilisation of these symbols must, in turn, be a constitutive element of the deductive structure. They must be developed enough to permit the movement from one configuration of symbols to another by virtue of, and only by virtue of, the abstract system itself.[56] In short, the 'structure' has to be coherent enough to allow for solutions to be arrived at without the need to have reference to knowledge models or methods independent of the structure itself.

The most perfect kind of deductive model is, accordingly, one whose symbols are completely and totally divorced from all exterior sources. This is evidently not true of the codes since the symbols they use are those of natural language. Natural language is by its nature very different from mathematical symbols, since language is open-textured. Or, put another way, as an intelligent system it is plagued by elements which are themselves intrinsically imperfect; they cannot be characterised in a precise and sure fashion.[57] In addition, the very complexity of the social world that the deductive system is attempting to model, together with imperfections in the knowledge itself, means that all knowledge models are only approximations.[58] Words such as 'damage', 'fault' and 'good faith' are, as we have seen, vague to say the least, and thus they give rise to uncertainties or gaps in the deductive structure. That said, knowledge itself is often presented under the form of propositions in natural language and can, accordingly, be presented in the form of propositional logic ('if *a*, then *b*') which, in turn, can be translated into a syllogism. For example:

1 Major premise: cotton grows well where it is hot and dry.
2 Minor premise: England is cold and humid.
3 Conclusion: cotton does not grow naturally in England.

The conclusion is 'new' knowledge inasmuch as it can be obtained without recourse to empirical observation.[59] Moreover, the knowledge is reliable because both 'cotton' and 'England' are reasonably precise terms. However, because natural language is a system in itself, there are a number of dangers when it is used to give expression to other knowledge systems. In particular, the words employed must keep their same signification in the major and minor premises. If they do not, then the conclusion will be absurd, as the following example[60] indicates:

1 Major premise: a mouse eats cheese.
2 Minor premise: a mouse is a word of one syllable.
3 Conclusion: words of one syllable eat cheese.

In addition, care must be taken not to confuse genus and species:

1 Major premise: cats eat meat.
2 Minor premise: cats are animals.
3 Conclusion: animals eat meat.

This conclusion might not be quite as absurd as words eating cheese, but it is equally wrong inasmuch as it does not accord with reality. Not all animals eat meat.

The methodological weakness of the codes are then to be found in the use of natural language and in the original assumption that code provisions could be treated as axioms. They are 'axioms' in the sense that the proposition expressed in the code does not have to be proved or justified. But, as Timsit has observed, the syllogistic assumption originally made by the code 'implies that for each situation submitted to the judge there would be a legal rule applicable, that there would be only one and that this rule would be devoid of all ambiguity'.[61] Such an assumption is clearly misconceived. For not only does a single factual situation often give rise to a choice of rules, but fact complexity and linguistic ambiguity is what lies at the heart of the hard case. One could argue, then, that the notion of law as a science died with the failure of deduction as a methodology. Legal method is, instead, a matter of argumentation and such a mental process relates, not so much to any model or scheme in the scientific sense, but to a model in the artistic sense. Legal method is about the art of distinguishing.[62]

Professional Viewpoints

This art of distinguishing is a method to which we shall have to return in later chapters since it forms part of a scheme of analysis that needs detailed examination from a variety of viewpoints. Before looking at these in more detail, however, some general comments must first be made with regard to professional viewpoints. For example, one of the epistemological conclusions flowing from the distinction between the teaching and practice of science is that, although the professor of physics and the laboratory researcher may both be scientists, their epistemological outlook is not the same. The professor needs a global vision of his or her subject, whereas the researcher may be working to a more fragmented and localised structure of knowledge. The same difference is undoubtedly to be found in legal science. Indeed, the range of different categories of knowledge viewpoints may be even wider in law, in that one needs to distinguish not just between professor and practitioner, but between judges, legislators, practitioners and, perhaps, between different kinds of law professors.[63] In addition to these 'internal' viewpoints, there are the knowledge structures associated with those involved with law but whose epistemological visions are 'external' to legal science; for lawyers, of course, are not the only group necessarily to have knowledge of law.

Critical Viewpoints

The internal and external viewpoints can, then, be reflected within the field of professionals working with law. The police and social workers working alongside professional lawyers may well share certain viewpoints, but equally they are likely to view legal knowledge from the outside. The same is true, as we have seen (Chapter 1), with academics. The sociologist will deliberately distance him- or herself from the viewpoint of the professional lawyer. Law from this position will be a 'science' tied to other human activities. There is an obvious truth to this connection just as there is for the physical sciences: it is unlikely that the theory of relativity would have been conceived by a 16th-century magician working in some far-off land.[64] The history of money and accounting, for example, clearly has close connections with the fashioning of the institutional plan by Gaius and its re-adoption by later civilians.[65] The danger is one of slipping from connection to determinism. Are scientific theories determined by factors external to the relevant science? This debate is a central one in comparative law, where Watson argues that the connections between social facts and the success of Roman law in Europe is a tenuous one.[66] How is it, he says, 'that law texts written in a very different place and very different time can be recycled so readily'?[67] This view has not gone unchallenged. But the point to make here is that the external viewpoint can provide only a certain insight into epistemological issues in law. It cannot explain the actual workings of the internal movement within legal knowledge models any more than sociological accounts of the development of motor vehicles can fully explain the workings of the internal combustion engine.

Sometimes, however, such external viewpoints can become 'incorporated' into the professional viewpoint. This can happen in a number of ways. For example social theories can be adopted by legislators and translated into statutes. Alternatively, the external viewpoint can become a legal theory. Thus the law and economics school has tried

> to develop a moral theory that goes beyond classical utilitarianism and holds that the criterion for judging whether acts and institutions are just or good is whether they maximize the wealth of society. This approach allows a reconciliation among utility, liberty, and even equality as competing ethical principles. The approach seems to have played an important role in the growth of the common law, which is not surprising when the limitations of common law as a means of redistributing, as distinct from creating, wealth are taken into account.[68]

Furthermore, incorporation is possible via the reasoning of judges, often through policy arguments. Such an approach, as we have seen, is not above criticism. But recourse to another discipline like economics or political theory can appear attractive, in that it seems to underpin law with an independent rationality. The danger, however, is that one can end up replacing one set of normative propositions with another and legal reasoning can thus slip easily into ideology (that is to say, false or at least biased accounts of social reality). Liberal ideology might find itself being played off against market economics.[69] In terms of knowledge, one moves from law to politics or economics and this has the effect of draining law of its own particular knowledge base. Of course it may be that law and legal argumentation are empty – or relatively empty – forms of knowledge waiting for an input from adjoining social science disciplines. Griffiths accordingly takes the view that judicial decisions cannot be politically neutral because judges are placed in positions where they have to make political choices; they are part of the 'established authority'. And from 'all this flows ... judicial attitudes such as tenderness towards private property and dislike of trade unions, strong adherence to the maintenance of order, distaste for minority opinions, demonstrations and protests, indifference to the promotion of better race relations, support of government secrecy, concern for the preservation of the moral and social behaviour to which it is accustomed, and the rest'.[70] Here the input is unconscious in that the judge is not deliberately making reference to a framework of 'conservative and illiberal' views. Tenderness towards private property or the dislike of demonstrations will normally be justified by reference to some legal device like the tort of trespass or the tort of nuisance. Yet, as we have seen with the policy arguments used by judges, judges may deliberately have recourse to arguments beyond legal rules. They may justify a decision openly and directly on some ground that is rooted in a discipline beyond the strict legal rule of legal notion. The question, of course, is the extent to which such reasoning forms part of legal knowledge.[71]

Historical Viewpoints

Another, equally complex, viewpoint is that of history. History is complex in this respect since history as a knowledge discipline stands both inside and outside law. Or, put another way, the historical viewpoint merits special attention since it can be both internal and external at one and the same time. For example, the history of Roman law can be grasped from within in the sense that its notions, concepts and techniques can be traced from the Roman world to modern times. That is to say, its internal development as a science can be traced in terms of its internal rationality.[72] Yet, in doing this, it is necessary to adopt an external position as well. For, as Tierney states, to 'interpret a whole tradition of thought, a scholar needs to understand sympathetically the various stages of its development "from the inside", as it were, from within the world of a particular time and place; but he also needs to stand outside the tradition, perceiving connections and adaptions over long periods of time that the makers of the tradition themselves could not be aware of'.[73] Thus a 'twelfth-century canonist naturally did not know that some of his ideas constituted an "anticipation" of fifteenth-century conciliar theory'.[74]

In addition, there are the external factors outside the legal tradition, which many regard as forces that create the system of law itself. 'The "rediscovery" of Roman law,' wrote Walter Ullmann, 'concerned not the law, which was being studied in any case, but its underlying ideas'; and without 'the familiarity with Roman law its ideological wealth would not have been grasped'.[75] This idea that 'law is the product of those forces that created the society to which the law is to apply'[76] may seem an evident historical point. Yet, as we have seen, the position is not quite as simple as it might at first appear. Certainly Roman law may well have been grasped for its ideological wealth, but this ideology was in part epistemological as well. It was part and parcel of legal knowledge itself inasmuch as the institutional system was founded upon a model that stressed ownership, obligation and individual responsibility.[77] This knowledge point has been developed to some extent by Alan Watson. He sees teaching manuals as one of the main vehicles for the transmission of legal knowledge and he claims 'that modern legal systems, common law and civil law alike, and their spread over many territories in several continents, are inconceivable without the input of Nutshells [teaching manuals] often written in far off times and in far-away places'.[78]

More provocatively, as has been mentioned, Watson casts doubt on the idea of a close interrelationship between society and its legal system by asking in 'what sense does Gaius' *Institutes* reflect the society of pagan Rome and with some modifications, Christian Byzantium?'[79] There is not 'one scrap of evidence that the *Institutes* [of Justinian] is in any way indicative of the specific religious, political, economic or social conditions of early Byzantium'. If it had been, asserts Watson, 'it would have been influential in the west only with difficulty'.[80] The historical emphasis here is very much on the internal viewpoint. Pierre Legrand, in challenging this thesis, asserts that, just because there is an appearance of adoption or transplantation, it does not follow that what is actually 'transplanted' is the rule from an alien culture. According to

Legrand, 'a crucial element of the ruleness of a rule – its meaning – does not survive the journey from one legal system to another'.[81] The transplant does not actually happen, since the key element of the rule, that is to say its meaning, 'stays behind so that the rule that was "there", in effect, is not itself displaced over "here"'.[82] *Extra culturam nihil datur.*[83]

This debate is by no means sterile for the epistemologist. It goes to the heart of legal knowledge and to the idea that law might be a coherent and independent discipline. If Watson is right, one key to this legal knowledge is to be found in the *Institutes* and in the subsequent teaching manuals usually based upon Gaius' structure (cf. Chapter 4). Of course, one does not have to accept Watson's epistemological view that knowledge of law is knowledge of rules. Legrand makes the point that Watson is talking about rules as bare propositional statements and saying that it is these bare propositional statements that get transplanted across centuries and across frontiers – an epistemological assumption that Legrand finds most impoverished. 'The problem,' says Legrand, 'is that in the way the reasoning promotes a most exacerbated positivism it fails to grasp and express the multi-layered nature of the interaction between the constituents of a social totality.'[84] But the epistemologist must take seriously the *possibility* of a legal knowledge that, like scientific knowledge, transcends particular legal systems. Just what constitutes that knowledge is evidently the central question. But, whatever the answer, the internal historical viewpoint has a contribution to make to this question, even if this contribution is difficult to reconcile with those arising out of the external historical viewpoint.

Comparative Viewpoint

Watson and Legrand are not just offering a historical view. They are also writing from the position of a comparative lawyer from where they claim, or vigorously dispute, that the transplanting of rules from one system to another has been extremely common, fertile and lacking in social difficulty. Whatever the merits of the two viewpoints, the claims are of epistemological importance inasmuch as they indicate that comparative law can offer a critical set of models through which legal knowledge assumptions can be questioned. One might not agree with Watson's views on legal transplants, but he is offering a model of legal knowledge. Now the 'goals of legal comparison as a science' are 'to know the differences existing between legal models, and to contribute to knowledge of these models',[85] but only 'comparison reveals to us certain details of the different models under consideration'.[86] Comparison, it would seem, is not just a viewpoint, but a method and, as epistemologists have continually asserted, there 'is no science without method'.[87]

The question, however, is whether the comparative viewpoint is anything more than a method. Legrand is of the view that it is. He asserts that to 'espouse the view of comparative-analysis-of-law-as-method and take it to its logical conclusion is to deny, in sum, any substantive content to comparative work about law and to ensure that it ultimately loses its status as a discrete, autonomous intellectual domain'.[88] What the comparative viewpoint can offer is a means of highlighting 'the accidental and contingent character of rules, practices and assumptions', which in turn can emancipate 'the student from the idea that these are necessary, just and unchallengeable'.[89] The role of comparative law is thus primarily epistemological. It concerns itself with law as a form of knowledge. The difficulty, however, is that, the moment one is emancipated from the narrow formalist idea of law-as-rules capable of being compared in a neutral way, one is to some extent emancipated from the comparatist viewpoint. The comparatist becomes a social theorist investigating the culture and mentalities of societies and their legal traditions.[90] The internal viewpoint can become eclipsed by the external. This may be no bad thing, of course. Yet, if care is not taken, it can have an impact upon comparative law's epistemological ability to mediate between legal history, legal theory and positive law. In other words, care must be taken, at least by the legal epistemologist, not to emancipate comparative law from all of its epistemological functions, one of which is to investigate the possibility of an 'internal' epistemological model (which may or may not be rule-based).

Indeed, once the epistemological function of comparison is fully appreciated, the idea that one is making comparisons only between different legal systems is exposed as far too simplistic. The Realist observation that definitions of law depend upon a point of view applies equally to an internal view of law, that is to say as between those who work within law as a professional science or discipline. Different categories of jurist use different kinds of legal knowledge.[91] This may be evident with respect to, say, the legal historian *vis-à-vis* the commercialist, but it might equally be true as between judge and legislator or practitioner and professor.[92] Have the epistemological differences been eclipsed by the rule thesis, which has had the effect of imposing a common model of legal knowledge on all those who work within the law? It is in respect of these internal differences that the idea that comparative law is a matter of comparing rules is unhelpful. For if it transpires that the different actors within law do utilise rather different knowledge conceptions, this will serve to illustrate how legal epistemology is more complex than the dominant legal philosophers have suggested. Even if law is language, it is unlikely that the words uttered by legislators, by judges and by academics have the same signification.[93] Comparative law is not, then, just a matter of comparing one set of rules, institutions or concepts in one system with those in another. It is about comparing all aspects of legal knowledge both within and without any single legal system. It is about comparing judge with legislator, professor with practitioner, supreme court with courts of first instance, *persona* with *res*, and so on.

View of the Judiciary

From a comparative law position, it might seem difficult to formulate a common viewpoint for all judges in all legal families, but even as between the civil and the common law judge the differences can appear considerable. Differences with respect to formal sources, to history and to ideology have led to a distinction between *le pouvoir judiciaire* and *l'autorité judiciaire* which in turn relates to the distinction between non-codified and codified systems.[94] Moreover, the historical tradition of the *mos geometricus* gave rise to an ideology whereby the methodological role of the civilian judge was traditionally one of *inference*, with the judge supposedly acting as little more than a machine, whereas that of the common law judge was one of *argumentation* and *interpretation*.[95] The civil codes, in other words, had already judged. Today, however, this dichotomy has much less meaning and many would argue, or imply, that all judges within the Western legal tradition are involved in much the same enterprise.[96] This enterprise is generally seen as one of *ars hermeneutica*, the art of interpretation, although the German view is that argumentation in support of judicial solutions must be supported by objective justification.[97] One cannot talk of a legal science unless it is scientific.

One cannot talk, either, as we will see (Chapter 8), of a single scheme of intelligibility. Alongside the hermeneutical scheme there are others that are equally important. Moreover, one cannot talk of a single corpus of judges. In the civil law system there may be different status categories within the profession and (or) differing specialisations. The investigating magistrate and the *parquets* may well have rather different knowledge foundations than the judge in a first instance court; the *Cour de cassation* judge will quite possibly have a more restricted appreciation of political science than the judges in the administrative courts hierarchy. Judges in the *tribunaux de commerce* have a different background from those in the ordinary courts. They may share much that is common; yet the differences, particularly, for example, between public law and private law judges, may be significant. Even in English law differences can be found between the various divisions of the High Court. Thus a judge in the family division is expected to be familiar with the sociological literature about families and children.[98] Nevertheless, the epistemological questions to be posed of all judges relate to their education, legal formation, practical experience, career structures, sources of relevant knowledge, and relationships with practitioners and advocates.[99] What arguments do they find acceptable and what kinds of legal materials do they find of interest? Do these change over the generations?

In answering these questions the epistemologist cannot simply adopt an internal view of legal knowledge. Judicial values, as Griffith asserts, seemingly influence the outcome of cases.[100] In fact, any epistemological investigation of judicial reasoning models gives rise to a difficult dichotomy. Should the epistemologist be concerned with how judges *ought* to reason or how they *actually* reason? The first will involve theories of legal philosophy, what judges ought to do, whereas the second will not. The second model will be one that reflects what the judges actually do and while this might not be immediately helpful in any normative sense, it could well be valuable in mapping the methods used in arriving at legal solutions. In addition, it may well show how different groups of personnel within law work to different epistemological models.

In looking at judges throughout Europe, it may well be necessary, as we have said, to distinguish between different legal traditions. The common law judge, at one level at least, has been more transparent with respect to the knowledge base to be utilised, mainly no doubt because of the precedent system whereby legal knowledge is contained in the writings of judges. Yet it has been argued that, once one abandons the narrow field of actual judicial decisions, the reasoning processes of French judges might not be so different.[101] Certainly, French jurists themselves have compared unfavourably the style of French judgments with those of the common law tradition;[102] and this is unsurprising since this style is one that is still formalised in terms of a syllogism. But the actual judgment of a French court is only one part of a larger process. If one includes the opinions of the *juge rapporteur* and the advocate general, a much better picture is obtained of the judiciary's own perception of its role.[103] In the common law decisions, the kind of analysis and reasoning to be found in the reports of the French reporting judge and advocate general is included in the judgments themselves. The common law judge is not restricted to expressing his decision and its motivations by set forms of words and so judgments may often be discursive. Nevertheless, differences remain. The English judge has never been regarded as a mere mechanical interpreter of the will of the legislator and thus the style of English judgments has never ideologically needed to be cast in the form of a syllogism.[104] Instead, it reflects the process of argumentation, in that most judgments are constructed to a greater or lesser extent around the arguments advanced by each party's counsel, the judge him- or herself ultimately accepting or rejecting one of them. Of course, judges may often advance beyond this style. They may, for example, give a summary of the law applicable or give a range of hypothetical cases or even attempt to lay down a set of principles. On the whole, however, judgments tend to be restricted to the issues in question and these are set out as a three-way debate involving the barristers and the judge.[105]

The art of the judge in both the civil law and common law traditions can, then, be said to be a matter of searching for the right solution within particular factual situations. This has been described as an art rather than a science. And the judge reaches the height of this art 'from the moment when he will be seen to be employing structural procedures both to construct the factual situation and to choose and devise a normative principle'.[106] The judge is constructing from within. The question, of course, is whether these internal constructions vary, not just in design as between judges from different legal cultures, but equally in the actual elements, or 'bricks' that they use. Does each judge construct his own solution by constructing his own set of facts?

View of the Legislator

One can contrast with the sources of knowledge used by judges the sources used by legislators. Here the range is likely to be much wider: 'all aspects of human nature, of life in society and of the sciences and techniques can be brought into play'.[107] The legislator is more often than not using written legal rules to achieve social, political and (or) economic ends. Laws and regulations dealing with taxation, commercial and labour relations, family law, crime and so on usually result, if not from careful social research (although independent advisory commissions and committees are the source of a 'surprising number' of bills in the United Kingdom), then at least from information and data from outside the scope of traditional legal knowledge itself.[108] Lobby and pressure groups, and the knowledge associated with such institutions, are clearly of importance, as are the educational history, ideological outlooks and professional or other backgrounds of the members of the legislating body and source committees, together with those civil servants and assistants who aid and influence them. More narrowly, most legislators work to a particular model, if not theory, about law itself. And, while this model may be shared by other professionals within law, those who conceive of and draft legislation are likely to be convinced rule theorists, in that written legal propositions are the source medium of most immediate relevance.

Legislators, even as rule theorists, can vary amongst themselves. The elected politician, for example, may well have a different view of how a rule should be drafted than the parliamentary draftsman. Another such variation is between the common law and continental legislator. Comparatists have made much of the different styles of drafting as between the two traditions[109] and this difference of style is more than just a matter of language. The legislator who works at the level of detailed fact – for example in isolating dogs from other domestic animals when it comes to civil liability[110] – is seeing the world in a different way from the legislator who thinks in terms of damage done by things.[111] The attaching of rules to specific objects and specific persons is a different exercise from formulating propositions around the abstract institutions of *persona* and *res* inasmuch as the former has little need of an organising symmetry. One is attempting to control particular descriptive situations rather than to set out a general pattern of liability.[112] Each situation, in other words, travels in a compartment of its own.

View of the Law Professor

It is with respect to this empirical compartmentalisation that the legislator is likely to differ from the law professor. However, in the civil law tradition, the epistemological situation is more complex, in that the influence of the law faculties within the law world has, seemingly, been immense in comparison with the position within the common law. It was the professors, rather than the practitioners, who were the true authors of the great codes of Europe,[113] and it was this *Professorenrecht* which brought law into its deductive and then axiomatic stages. The 'jurist practitioner' was eclipsed by the 'jurist theoretician' and thus technique gave way to science.[114] Today, legal science in the civilian tradition may have moved on from the axiomatic stage to one where interpretation and argumentation have become the dominant methodologies, but the influence of the faculties via doctrine remains a crucial, if unofficial (in the rule-model sense), source of law.

When viewed from the position of legal history, the different viewpoints provide useful insights into legal *mentalités*. As Professor Van Caenegem has noted, 'it is clear that the common law was judge-made, that medieval and modern Roman law ... was professor-made and that an enormous mass of French revolutionary law was legislator-made'.[115] What is particularly interesting about Van Caenegem's lectures on European legal history is that he uses the different professional viewpoints to emphasise different methodological techniques underpinning law. Thus, in comparing Germany with England, Van Caenegem makes the following point:

> The direct and unavoidable consequence of the introduction of the *Corpus Juris* and its medieval accretions – a bulky body of learned books in Latin – was to hand over the law and its study and administration to the only ones who were trained to read, understand and explain Bartolus and Baldus, i.e. the cohort of learned lawyers with university degrees, led by the Professors of Roman law: they henceforth held the key to legal science. It was fatal, for if the law is locked up in sacred books, it is the scholars who can read and understand them who are the masters of the law ...[116]

In terms of technique, the scheme of intelligence that underpinned law was the hermeneutical scheme, that is to say a method that looked beyond the surface of the written text in order to discover deeper and hidden meanings (Chapter 8). Law was about teasing meanings out of the Roman sources and the medieval commentaries that attached to them. The methodology is based upon a pre-existing channel, 'just as in the Freudian interpretation of dreams, the latent content is already there, under the actual dream, in the associations that the dream suggests and in the symbols that it uses'.[117] This hermeneutical tradition is still to be found in the civil law jurisdictions. In France, for example, the academic commentator's main role is to tease out of terse judgments a range of possible meanings. French academics nourish themselves on the study of texts.[118]

In England, on the other hand, the law was not to be found in some 'holy book' and 'hence it did not fall into the hands of a guild of scholarly jurists who had sole access to its bookish sources'.[119] In addition, there was no comprehensive and continuous stream of legislation which might have acted as a means of controlling the output of what had become a very strong set of centralised royal courts. Thus in England 'the law was what the judge said it was, in modern Germany the law was what the professor said it was'.[120] The methodology associated with the judge is, as we have seen, not one that is easily described as hermeneutic, at least in the sense of teasing legal solutions out of texts contained in authoritative books. And even the interpretation of statutes has to be understood within the context of particular factual situations. For 'legislation is given legal effect upon subjects by virtue of judicial decisions, and it is the function of the courts to say what the application of the words used to particular cases or individuals is to be'.[121] Given this emphasis on the judiciary, the academic lawyer has been largely marginalised. Indeed, university law schools, teaching the common law at least, were virtually non-existent until recent times. As Van Caenegem explains, those 'people who wanted to take up a legal career did not go to a university to learn some holy law book by heart and hear from the professors' lips what its exact meaning was; they went ... to live in some Inn of Court and listened to barristers and judges, to learn their law by seeing it in action in the courts'.[122]

Despite this difference of balance between the two professional groups, there remain problems in terms of the relationship between academics and judges not just in England but also in a civil law country such as France. Relations between judges and professors are not as fertile as they might be since the former are too taken with the facts of individual cases while the latter have to construct their more global views of the law on judgments. In France these judgments are too brief[123] and in England too fragmented, if not incoherent.[124] This distinction between the individual case and the rationalisation of the law is particularly important in the common law, since the judges have specifically asserted that it is not the role of the courts to rationalise the law.[125] Such a task is, according to both judges and academics, one for the textbook and article writers.[126] The structure and presentation of positive law is thus an important part of the academic knowledge model and this is one reason why legal dogmatics and legal science are so dominant in continental legal faculties. And even in the common law faculties, the academic writer is said to be pursuing a not dissimilar objective:

> Modern text-books are important ... as guides to the case-law with which they are concerned. But if they are good they are more than mere guides, for they seek not only to arrange the cases systematically but to extract from them the general principles of the law and to show how those principles may be developed. And the same is true, on a smaller scale, of articles in the Law Reviews. Whether acknowledged by the judges or not – and the tendency of judges to acknowledge their indebtedness to legal writers is increasing – opinions stated in text-books and in learned articles are often adopted in the courts and there given the force of law. To deny persuasive authority to text-books today may be to state the formal position in England quite correctly, but it is to conceal the substantial and increasing importance of *la doctrine* in the formation of English law.[127]

However, in addition to the 'black letter' faculty specialists, there are the legal philosophers and legal theorists. And the epistemological models in play here will often be far more extensive than the legal science models employed by the positive law textbook writers. Indeed, 'the jurisprudence teacher is bound to find himself at loggerheads with his colleagues'.[128] The legal historian and the critical lawyer may well, as we have seen, be adopting viewpoints external to law and such external positions may sometimes, perhaps quite often in Anglo-American faculties, be employed by those teaching positive law subjects.[129] Indeed, even academic jurists adopting an internal position (more or less) may still adopt a viewpoint that no judge or legislator would ever take. The problem with the external viewpoint is that it can create difficulties with respect to the relationship between judge and academic. The judge may well find that the kind of objectives being pursued by the professor are of no help in deciding cases,[130] while the academic may discover that his or her freedom is severely restricted by an attitude of servility towards the courts.[131] The epistemologies of the courtroom are not the same as those in the university.[132] It is, of course, easy to believe that the basis of any perceived restricted freedom is the dominance of the judiciary and the legal profession. Yet this might well be misleading. The restrictions arise just as much from the epistemological models constructed by academics themselves inasmuch as the 'process of dogmatisation' can itself become an obstacle to knowledge; or, as one scientific writer has put it, 'the textbooks are the triumph of the anachronism and atrophy of knowledge'.[133]

View of the Practitioner

Practitioners must be distinguished from academics, legislators and judges since they will often be acting to protect a particular interest. No doubt they will share with other 'black-letter' lawyers much substantive and methodological knowledge; yet on one level such knowledge may be much more of a patchwork nature since the questions could well be narrower. Can a remedy be obtained in this factual situation? How should the arguments be presented to achieve this particular end? These questions, it must be said, can be particularly fruitful inasmuch as they can stimulate new and original arguments, remedies, concepts and the like;[134] and so the practitioner may well be analogous to the laboratory researcher. Such 'research' will benefit from ambiguity and gaps in the law and thus, at one level, uncertainty in the systems can be a beneficial part of the practitioner knowledge model. On another level, however, the practitioner may crave legal certainty, since this will aid prediction. In this respect, then, a legal science, in the sense of a scheme of knowledge able to explain and predict, might be a fundamental part of some practitioner knowledge.

Atias has accordingly summed up the knowledge of legal practitioners as being complex. It is composed of legal provisions and regulations and decisions of the courts, together with a 'mass of historical, economic and sociological information which has, or would have, the capacity to influence the legislator or the judge'. In addition, the knowledge will embrace the 'methods and procedures which allow one to take advantage of the different elements thus brought together': for example, 'the methods and procedures which reveal the relevant analogies and far flung comparisons'.[135] It is a model that acts as 'a kind of filter'.[136] Whether this is true of all practitioners is open to question, since the term 'practitioner' covers a multitude of occupations. What is clear is that the knowledge model of a range of practitioners is different from the models to be found in many law faculties in Europe, and this is a point rarely appreciated by legal philosophers. Legal theorists have to date tended to base their theories either on systems of rules (or norms) or upon the activities of judges. A theory fashioned upon the knowledge schemes of practitioners across Europe would doubtless be original.

Concluding Remarks

To talk of legal method, then, is probably misleading. One must think in terms of the plural: methodology in law varies with the status and role of the lawyer, or class of lawyer, in question. This is not to say that there are no shared viewpoints and models. Indeed, one reason why the rule thesis is so successful is that it seemingly acts as a common starting point for all the professionals involved with law. But the model is also misleading in that it masks fundamental differences in epistemological outlook. In the civil law tradition, codification has exacerbated this reductionist tendency, not just in respect of the science itself, but also with regard to methodology. Yet, as Atias suggests, this is as much a matter of jurists choosing to ignore what they know as reacting to the requirements of some scientific criteria.[137] The interest of the client means that practitioners can, and possibly must, live in a world where contradiction is a professional necessity, given the ambiguity in legal texts. The professor, on the other hand, who changes his or her opinion each week about a particular text risks loss of intellectual prestige. Codes do not easily betray these methodological contradictions since they are designed to eclipse the differences of interests in play between the different categories of jurist. Moreover, the rule model deliberately distorts the reality it is seemingly trying to 'model'. Codes speak, for example, of the respect that must be given to contractual agreements simply because the social reality turns out to be rather different.[138] The law constructs its own ideal social reality.

Notes

1 Barreau (1998, p. 51).
2 Granger (1995, p. 42).
3 *R* v. *Young* [1995] QB 324.
4 Barreau (1998, pp. 53–4); Granger (1995, pp. 46–7).
5 Granger (1995, p. 47).
6 D.50.17.1.
7 *Omnis definitio in jure civili perculosa est: parum est enim, ut non subverti posset* (Javolenus, D.50.17.202).
8 D.9.2.52.2.
9 Blanché (1980, p. 84).
10 Blanché (1975, p. 152).
11 Ibid.
12 D.2.14.1.4.
13 D.2.14.7.1.
14 D.2.14.1.3.
15 D.44.7.2.
16 D.44.7.1pr.
17 D.44.7.4.
18 D.2.14.7.5.
19 Zimmermann (1996a, pp. 537–45).
20 Strömholm (1985, p. 67).
21 Ibid., p. 68.
22 Stein (1999, p. 18). And see, for example, G.1.88; G.3.88–9; G.3.183; G.4.1.
23 On which, see Kolbert (1979).
24 J. Bell, book review: (1995a) 15 LS 461, 465.
25 D.9.2.52.3.
26 D.9.2.52.2.
27 D.9.2.44pr.
28 Set out in D.9.2.27.5.
29 D.50.17.
30 D.50.16.
31 See, for example, D.9.2.27.5.
32 D.9.4.2pr.
33 D.9.4.3.
34 D.9.4.4pr
35 D.9.4.4.1.
36 D.9.1.1pr.
37 D.9.1.1.3.
38 D.9.1.2.1.
39 D.9.1.2pr.
40 D.9.2.41pr.
41 Villey (1975, p. 528).
42 See, for example, D.9.2.29.3.
43 See, for example, D.9.2.11pr.
44 D.9.2.27.33.
45 D.9.2.30.1.

46 D.9.2.27.29.
47 D.47.2.14.17.
48 D.41.1.65pr.
49 See, for example, D.45.1.97.1; D.47.23.3.1.
50 'La propriété, c'est le vol' (J.-P. Proudhon, *Qu'est-ce que la propriété?*, 1840).
51 Cf. Samuel (1994, pp. 193–6).
52 Dubouchet (1990, pp. 37–70).
53 Ibid., p. 52.
54 This is not to suggest of course that syllogistic logic and formal deductive logic are synonymous: cf. Susskind (1987, pp. 164–9).
55 Piaget (1988, p. 103), emphasis in original.
56 Oléron (1995, p. 80).
57 Bouchon-Meunier and Nguyen (1996, p. 7).
58 Ibid., pp. 7–8.
59 Cf. Oléron (1995, pp. 52–3).
60 Blanché (1973a, pp. 250–51).
61 Timsit (1986, pp. 106–7).
62 Perelman (1979, p. 9).
63 Atias (1994, pp. 21–8).
64 Acot (1999, p. 42).
65 Degos (1998, p. 29).
66 Watson (1994).
67 Ibid., p. 21.
68 Posner (1983, p. 115).
69 Cf. Lord Hutton in *B (A Minor)* v. *DPP* [2000] 2 WLR 452, 473.
70 Griffith (1997, p. 336).
71 See, generally, Stein and Shand (1974).
72 Granger (1995, p. 115).
73 Tierney (1982, pp. viii–ix).
74 Ibid., p. ix.
75 Ullmann (1962, p. 368).
76 Ibid., p. 367.
77 See, generally, Stein and Shand (1974).
78 Watson (1994, p. 2).
79 Ibid., p. 21.
80 Ibid.
81 Legrand (1997b, p. 117).
82 Ibid., p. 118.
83 Ibid., p. 120.
84 Ibid., p. 122.
85 Sacco (1991a, p. 8).
86 Ibid., p. 10.
87 Barreau (1998, p. 51).
88 Legrand (1995a, p. 264).
89 Ibid., p. 265.
90 See, for example, Bell (1994).
91 Atias (1994, p. 21).
92 Ibid., pp. 21–8.

93 Atias (1985, p. 67).
94 David and Blanc-Jouvan (1994, pp. 20–22).
95 Lobban (1991, pp. 82–98). And see *Copeland* v. *Smith* [2000] 1 WLR 1371, 1376.
96 See, for example, Ivainer (1988); Lasser (1995); Bell (1995).
97 Alexy (1989).
98 *In re L (A Child)* [2001] 2 WLR 339, 375.
99 Atias (1994, p. 23).
100 Griffith (1997).
101 See Lasser (1995).
102 Touffait and Tunc (1974).
103 Lasser (1995, pp. 1355–7).
104 Perrot (2000, pp. 171–2).
105 *Copeland* v. *Smith* [2000] 1 WLR 1371, 1376.
106 Ivainer (1988, p. 320).
107 Atias (1994, p. 23).
108 See, generally, Zander (1999, pp. 1–105).
109 Zweigert and Kötz (1998, pp. 267–8).
110 Animals Act 1971 s. 3.
111 CC, arts 1384–5.
112 Compare, for example, the Contracts (Rights of Third Parties) Act 1999 with the Principles of European Contract Law art. 6:110.
113 Villey (1975, pp. 539–40).
114 Dubouchet (1991, p. 78).
115 Van Caenegem (1987, p. 67).
116 Ibid., p. 85.
117 Berthelot (1990, p. 74).
118 Atias (D.1995.Chron.272) quoted in Legrand (1996a, p. 239, n. 30).
119 Van Caenegem (1987, p. 85).
120 Ibid., p. 86.
121 Lord Wilberforce in *Black-Clawson International Ltd* v. *Papierwerke Waldhof-Aschaffenburg AG* [1975] AC 591, 629.
122 Van Caenegem (1987, p. 60).
123 Tunc (1975, p. 829).
124 See, for example, Birks (1996b).
125 Lord Macmillan in *Read* v. *J Lyons & Co* [1947] AC 156, 175.
126 Wilson (1987, p. 837).
127 Jolowicz (1963, pp. 314–15).
128 Simmonds (1986, p. 1).
129 Samuel and Millns (1998).
130 See, for example, *Hunter* v. *Canary Wharf Ltd* [1997] AC 655, 694.
131 Halpérin (1996, p. 290).
132 See further Wilson (1987, pp. 839–47).
133 Y. Chevallard quoted in Astolfi and Develay (1996, p. 44).
134 Wilson (1987, pp. 835–6); Atias (1994, p. 26).
135 Atias (1994, pp. 26–7).
136 Ibid., p. 27.
137 Atias (1994, pp. 21–2).
138 Ibid., p. 25.

4 Institutions and Concepts

We have already suggested that science is a matter of fitting a fact or a law into a system of *concepts* where the concepts themselves appear to be part of a system that in turn seems to be integrated into the facts.[1] The concept acts as the mediating factor between fact and science. In legal discourse concepts have a similar role. They mediate between the facts of a situation and the rules that are relevant in such a situation. Indeed legal norms – the 'ought' dimension of a rule – are incapable of direct perception, as Villa has noted, 'without the aid of concepts and theoretical categories'.[2] Concepts and categories are thus fundamental aspects of legal knowledge. Their understanding, however, is more complex. Legal concepts can certainly be studied both diachronically and synchronically and it is the purpose of this present chapter to attempt to do just this. Yet, as we have seen with Roman legal reasoning, the way in which legal concepts relate to, and function within, facts is often part and parcel of the construction of those facts themselves. One needs therefore to distinguish between those concepts – 'institutions' that are fundamental to the actual building of the factual situation – and those concepts whose role is to inject into the legal situation a normative dimension. This is the distinction between institutions and concepts. However, it must be borne in mind that in many ways one is making a false distinction, since it could be said that an 'institution' is simply a species of concept.

Legal Institutions

The term 'legal institution' has a variety of meanings. This diversity arises in part from the difficulty of defining the word 'institution' itself; historians, sociologists and lawyers all have rather different conceptions.[3] Even within the discourse of law, the term has a variety of meanings: it is often used, for example, to refer to the empirical manifestations of the law such as the courts, the police, prisons and so on. More narrowly, the term is used to represent the sociolegal concept around which rules are attached.[4] Thus, if one takes a rule such as 'no person shall bring a vehicle into the park', the terms 'person', 'vehicle' and possibly 'park' could be regarded as institutions; they are terms to which rules attach. These sociolegal conceptions can then be expanded to include such notions as the family, the state or even the consumer.[5] In other words, the term 'institution' can represent any person or group that could be said to have 'interests'. Equally, it can apply to 'things' which, although not having their own interests (save perhaps animals), can form the subject matter of an interest inasmuch as a thing is capable of attracting legal relations.[6] If law is to be envisaged in terms of a series of relations flowing between elements – in effect between persons and persons and between persons and things – then the term 'institution' can be applied to the elements of this structure. 'Institution' for the purpose of this enquiry refers to those elements which can exist at one and the same time in the world of social fact and the world of law. Persons and things have a meaning, therefore, both for the sociologist and for the lawyer.

Institutes of Gaius

The term 'institution' has another connotation which at first sight looks rather different from the social focal point for legal rules and relations. The Latin term *institutiones* meant arrangement in an education sense. However, the two meanings are not unconnected. To appreciate the connection one must first recall how the *Digest* of Roman law was a rich source of 'case law' material that bears witness to the vast amount of writing produced by the republican and classical jurists. Parallel to this practical output, however, was another tradition of writing which was to be equally influential on the modern world. The Roman classical jurists produced teaching manuals called 'institutes' (*institutiones*) which were designed to give an overview of the law. These books set out to present the law in the most convenient and economic fashion so that it could be easily assimilated by those who did not have the practical experience of the case law.[7] Classification and arrangement were the techniques adopted to achieve this teaching and transmission aim. The most famous of the *institutiones* was the one written in the second century AD by a relatively unknown jurist of his time, called Gaius.[8] And so successful was his manual that it became the standard work until it was recast into a 'second edition' by the Emperor Justinian in AD 533.[9] It was Justinian's *Institutes* that survived into the modern world, a complete edition of the *Institutes* of Gaius not being discovered until 1816.

There are a number of striking characteristics about the *Institutes* of Gaius that no doubt ensured its success through the centuries.[10] The use of genus and species and of *divisio* developed a methodology in the structuring of knowledge that was to be exploited and consolidated by the medieval jurists and their successors to such an extent that the methodology became in itself a fundamental contribution to legal knowledge.[11] However, it is the institutional structure that is probably the most significant contribution to law.[12] In this exercise, as Peter Stein has observed, Gaius took taxonomy beyond *divisio* to that of *partitio*. That is to say, he took the civil law as a whole and divided it into three component parts.[13] 'All Law,' said Gaius, 'relates either to persons (*personae*), to things (*res*) or to actions (*actiones*)'.[14]

This analysis may seem, at first sight, rather trite. And the way material is actually dealt with in the *Institutes* leaves much to be desired by modern standards. Thus it is by no means clear exactly what Gaius meant by the 'law of persons' (*ius personarum*).[15] Equally, the 'law of things' has been criticised as being at best uneven.[16] Yet it was a scheme of arrangement which not only has left its mark on all the modern codes,[17] but turned out to be something more than a mere scheme of conveniently classifying all the rules of private law under three headings or into three books. There are several reasons for the scheme's success.

First, the actual categories adopted by Gaius proved to be more intellectually fertile than perhaps he himself realised. It may be difficult to gauge from its contents exactly what the Roman jurist meant by the *ius personarum*, yet, as H.F. Jolowicz admits, the category certainly proved suggestive:

> There is the conception that there are some rights which have a person or some facet of personality as their object; there is the allied, but separate, idea that some rights are without patrimonial value; and there is the really different idea that there are various conditions which may be called status, that need description because they influence rights and duties especially by defining capacity and incapacity.[18]

Equally, the *ius rerum* may be uneven, but the idea that there are patrimonial rights which can be contrasted with procedural and personality rights is, again, something that finds expression in modern economic life. Moreover, the inclusion by Gaius of incorporeal things (*res incorporales*) in the law of things went far in laying the foundation for the modern idea of the subjective right.[19] Even the law of actions, which is not to be found in the modern schemes of substantive law,[20] continues to have a relevance inasmuch as the distinction between rights and remedies remains an important dichotomy in Western legal thinking. Indeed, for the common lawyer, the law of actions is still an active category in public and private law.[21]

Secondly, Gaius' scheme was an interrelating system in which each category drew its rational force both from its internal contents and from its systemic relationship with the other categories. Now, admittedly, this aspect of Gaius is not particularly evident in the book itself, since the contents of each category are largely descriptive. That is to say, Gaius simply describes the different kinds of status, things and actions and he makes no attempt to define the various notions. As Stein comments, he 'takes it for granted that they exist as parts of the law, and concentrates on categorising their various forms and on explaining how they occur and how they cease'.[22] However, in categorising legal relations (*iura*) under these headings, he permitted jurists to think beyond the categories themselves towards different kinds of legal situations. Things that were able to be valued in monetary terms could be contrasted with 'things' such as liberty that could not. Substantive 'rights' (*iura*) could be contrasted with remedies (*actiones*).[23]

Thirdly, irrespective of the rational qualities of the categories themselves, the idea of presenting private law as a conceptual whole was in itself a remarkable development. Gaius was, in modern language, a 'Nutshell writer'.[24] The importance of such a development must not be underestimated, since the idea that the whole of the law could be reduced to a relatively short monograph – a 'Nutshell' – has profound implications for knowledge in general. It implies that a complex and disorganised mass of material consisting of legislation, case law, opinion and custom can be contained in a set of propositions. In other words, like legal institutions themselves, the *Institutiones* systematically structured the rules of law and allowed the law to be seen as an organised social phenomenon.[25] The Romans may not have expressed it in this way. The *Institutes* were, for them, textbooks whose primary function was to explain the law in as uncomplicated a way as possible.[26] But the effect of such reductive techniques was clear: the teaching of law could be distinguished from its practice, and legal knowledge could be reduced to linguistic statements. And when this form of knowledge transmission is combined both with the idea of law as a scientific rationality capable of being grasped by the mind[27] and with the technique of induction of abstract rules (*regulae iuris*),[28] a firm foundation for a *scientia iuris* becomes a possibility.

Legal Institutions as Mediating Notions

A fourth reason for the success of Gaius' scheme is to be found in the actual elements of *persona, res* and *actio* that he uses as the foundation of his categories. Each element of the tripartite classification was a mediating notion. That is to say, each element had a meaning at one and the same time in the world of fact and the world of law. And so the sociologist can talk of persons, things and courts as existing in the world of social fact just as the lawyer can speak of legal subjects (*personae*), legal objects (*res*) and legal remedies (*actiones*) as existing in the world of law. The three terms are descriptive as well as conceptual in that they can at one and the same time exist both as elements in a conceptual scheme (law) and as objects (factual realities) of this scheme. As such, 'persons' and 'things' act as bridges between social fact and law. 'Actions' are more ambiguous in this sense since they do not exist in quite the same way as people and things. Nevertheless, it could be said that they have an existence in the physical reality of courts and in the formal procedures of legal processes. This reality also had, for Gaius, a historical dimension, in that the law of actions was a category capable of giving expression to the historical development of Roman law. Furthermore, 'actions' act as a physical manifestation of a dispute between two parties, that is to say between the descriptive and the normative. They act as the empirical expression of the legal relations that bind person to person and person to thing. Or, as Kelley puts it, the notion of an *actio* gives expression to 'the actions and interactions of persons and things, including commerce as well as conflicts over property'.[29]

Indeed, actions were the means of keeping legal 'rights' (*iura*) and legal justice (*suum cuique tribuere*: giving to each what is due)[30] tied to objective social realities. The result was that fundamental legal relations such as ownership (*dominium*) and obligations were never in need of abstract definition in terms of axiomatic propositions. Ownership was largely a matter of whether or not a person was entitled to an *actio in rem*.[31] In other words, although the *Institutes* gave expression to the idea of law as propositions, Roman legal thought had little need of language-defined rules since they had the means of creating *iura* simply through the manipulation of apparent social entities.

Institutional System

Persons, things and actions are 'institutions', then, because they act as social realities around which rules form.[32] Furthermore, as an interrelating body of elements bound together by legal relationships (in particular the relationships of ownership between *persona* and *res* and obligation between person and person) they act as a structure capable of envisaging, at one and the same time, a system of legal and a system of social relations. In fact they go further than this. In addition to acting as elements in a system of legal and social thought, the three institutions are equally capable of forming focal points in political and economic systems. Accordingly, the moment one devises a system of juridical relations between the institutional elements, one is in effect also creating a structure that has some meaning in the worlds of political, social and economic relations. 'This fundamental classification,' writes Kelley, 'entailed not only moral priorities and a means of ordering reality but also a characteristic mode of perceiving, of construing, and potentially of controlling the social field.'[33] Jacques Ellul has put the point differently but no less elegantly. In a perceptive essay on the importance of Roman law, he makes the point that, in addition to bequeathing the notion of the state, the concept of law and the range of judicial techniques, the Romans also provided the modern Western world with a number of legal institutions.[34] These institutions, as others have noticed,[35] are fundamental, not just to legal thought and to legal technique, but also to the relationship between law and social reality. The tripartite institutional plan is the basis for a juristic world quite separate from the world of social reality. 'The law,' says Ellul, 'becomes a kind of reality imposed upon the social situation, putting it into order, and ending up by becoming more "true" than the facts.'[36]

Such an abstraction is of importance to legal knowledge and legal reasoning, in that it immediately suggests that institutions and institutional relations function as systems. Each institution as an element, and each institutional relation as a relation between elements, makes sense within the Gaian scheme only by reference to the other elements and relations. 'Persons' only make sense in relation to 'things' and 'things', particularly intangible things, make sense only in relation to 'actions'. However, the Gaian structure went further than this static model in that the interrelationships between the elements and relations endowed the model with a dynamic aspect. It could, so to speak, alter the very object it was attempting to describe. Legal relations could create institutions as much as institutions could create legal relations. Take for example the notion of *persona*.[37] A legal person represents in the legal scheme a subject able to sue and be sued as an individual entity. Now, if a legal person is an entity capable of bringing or defending a legal *actio* in its own right, then the moment that a person – or more importantly a group of persons (*universitas*) – is granted the procedural power to bring an action in his, her or its own name, this will have the effect of turning that person or group into a legal person.[38] In other words, a legal *persona* can be created indirectly simply through rules attaching to the institution of the *actio*. Admittedly, the texts devoted to legal personality in the Roman sources are fragmented and there is no theory of legal personality as such. Nevertheless, Gaius himself appreciated the effect of endowing towns with the power to bring and defend legal actions, since he observes that towns are treated as private people.[39] Moreover, once towns are regarded as people, it means they must also be capable of having their own patrimony; that is to say, their own fund of tangible and intangible assets and liabilities treated as a single whole.[40]

A similar dynamic characteristic can be found with respect to the legal object, the 'thing' (*res*).[41] The starting point for the institution of a *res* was the piece of tangible property which could be seen and touched (*res corporalis*) and thus represented both a social fact and a legal object. However, as Gaius himself recognised, a *res* was quite capable of being conceived through the obligation relationship between two legal subjects.[42] And so the moment that one person owed to another person a sum of money or some other performance under a contract the debt or performance became a *res* in itself. One person could then lay claim to this *res* as if it was a form of property *owned* by the claimant. Accordingly, a debt was, and remains today, a creature both of the law of obligations and of the law of property. In fact, this duality still causes a certain conceptual confusion since it effectively merges *dominium* with *obligatio*.[43] But some of the conceptual confusion was avoided in Roman law itself through the dichotomy in the law of actions between actions *in rem* and actions *in personam*,[44] which in turn created the fundamental distinction between the law of property and the law of obligations. 'The substance of an obligation,' states the Roman jurist Paul, 'consists not in that it makes some thing or servitude ours, but that it binds another to convey, to do or to perform something.'[45] What needs to be emphasised is that a debt is a form of economic wealth that has been created entirely out of the Gaian system itself. It has no independent existence as a social reality and as a result was an example of a piece of property that was intangible (*res incorporalis*) and existing only because of the existence of the institutional system. As Gaius himself put it: 'Incorporeal things cannot be touched, such as exist only in law, for instance an inheritance, a usufruct, obligations howsoever contracted.'[46]

Legal Theory and the Institutional System

The dynamic possibilities of the institutional system did not, however, stop with the distinction between relations *in rem* and *in personam*. In constructing a system capable of conceiving intangible forms of property (*res incorporales*), Gaius had created a structure in which any kind of asset or interest, including the very notion of a legal relationship itself (*ius*), could be turned into a legal form of property. And once it had become 'property' it could be protected at the level of the law of actions. All legal entitlements were, in other words, forms of property including the entitlements themselves.[47] Now, another way of viewing the law of things is exclusively in relation to the person. The mass of things, intangible and tangible, that each person has can be viewed as a legal entity in itself; such an entity attracted the name 'patrimony' (*patrimonium*).[48] One arrives at a situation where the law of things represents a 'patrimony' that attaches to each person. Accordingly, if one views this situation, not from the law of actions, but from the position of the *persona*, it would appear to follow that all *iura* are things that an individual is entitled to claim as his or her own. The institutional system has created, then, not only new property but its own conceptual framework for viewing all legal claims, from any part of the law, as 'property' claims. At the level of language, *ius* was not just a legal relationship flowing between the elements in Gaius' system: it was a meta-language for the understanding of all law.

This meta-language became more important when the *actio in rem*, the remedy which protected ownership, was extended to include certain rights other than strict ownership. The possibility now existed that certain *iura* could be claimed 'as of right' through the use of the real action. If these *iura* could be claimed 'as of right', why not all *iura*? It has to be said that the Romans never reached this position; the merging of *dominium* and *ius* belongs to the second life of Roman law.[49] But the Gaian system had gone far in laying the foundations for the modern notion of the 'right' by creating a conceptual structure in which certain incorporeal objects could be claimed as if they were physical things. Indeed, one could go further and say that the Gaian system had the potential for conceiving of a 'right' as an institution. Of course, this new 'institution' was no actual institution in the sense that it had an empirical basis in social reality. Rights cannot be compared with persons and things since rights have no physical existence. They are, as we shall see, normative concepts. But the point is that the institutional system had certainly created a notion that could be regarded, if not as an 'institution' in itself, at least as a concept that could replace the institution of the *actio*. Instead of saying 'P has an action', the modern lawyer says, 'P has a right'. The more one treats the relationship between *persona* and *res* as a 'right', the more it seems that the right is a *res* and thus a social reality around which rules collect in an abstract structural sense. Put another way, the *res incorporalis* is always in danger of being mistaken as an institution in its own right.

The dynamic qualities of the Gaian system were thus capable of transforming legal theory. In Gaius' time, although the will of the emperor no doubt had force of law,[50] the *ius privatum*, that is to say Gaius' institutional system, was not seen as dependent upon this will. Private law was part of a structure whose basis was to be found in the *ius naturale, ius gentium* and *ius civile,*[51] and each of these sources was in turn located in the facts of natural and social reality. Thus the *ius naturale* was located in the nature of the world, the *ius gentium* in human reason, and the *ius civile* in custom, praetorian edicts (*ius honorarium*), legal opinion (*responsa prudentium*) and legislation (*lex*).[52] The political input could be found only in the 'institution' of legislation.[53] However, as the classical period gave way to the post-classical and Rome became more and more of a theocracy, the pattern started to change to one of a hierarchy with the emperor at its summit. This was not the result of active rule making as such. It was the result of the logical force of the reasoning model itself. Put another way, the source of law changed. It shifted from being rooted in the natural world and in society to become identified with the emperor who in turn received his power from God.[54]

This shift in the source of law was reflected within the Gaian scheme in a number of ways. First and foremost, the position of the emperor himself was reinforced as a power, not just in terms of Rome, but in the world as a whole (*dominus mundi*).[55] The owner may have been master of his *res*, but the emperor was the master of the *respublica*. More subtly, however, in an institutional model encompassing a law of property which envisaged property relations as consisting of legal (*dominium*) and factual (*possessio*) bonds between people and things, the question is sooner or later going to be posed as to who 'possesses' public property.[56] And, once it is established that the town (*universitas*), the *fiscus* or some other public group could 'possess' public property, or commit delicts,[57] it had to follow from the logical force of the reasoning model that they were legal subjects with the same formal status as human subjects.[58] To use modern legal terms, the state acquired active 'rights' at the institutional level. These rights did not result from a direct intervention through the use of naked political power. Such extreme political interventionism would probably have been fatal to the whole legal system.[59] They were acquired through rational developments within the system itself. However, once these changes of pattern had been effected at the institutional level, they were to have their effects on the concept of law itself. Private law (*ius privatum*) became subjected to a model which saw all law as increasingly defined in relation to the *ius civile* which, in turn, was being increasingly subjected to the *ius publicum*. *Quod principi placuit legis habet vigorem* (what pleases the prince has force of law)[60] became *omnia principis esse intelligantur* (all rights flow from the emperor).[61]

This pattern was to repeat itself in the second life of Roman law. Or, put another way, the Roman pattern with its emperor as theocratic ruler was to prove ideologically useful in consolidating the power of kings in the late Middle Ages.[62] As Brian Tierney has stated:

> Medieval minds were fascinated, captivated by ... the vision of hierarchy. In real life they were ruled by hierarchies of government in church and state. But beyond this they perceived the whole universe as a great hierarchical chain of being. From God authority flowed to an angelical hierarchy in heaven and to an ecclesiastical hierarchy on earth ... Moreover there seemed abundant evidence that the whole of nature was hierarchically ordered ...; among the social insects all the bees of a hive were seen to serve one ruler ... To medieval men, divinely ordained hierarchy seemed, not just an abstract theory, but an observable fact of nature ... It is tempting to dismiss such argumentation as mere gothic fantasy ... But now scientists have again taken to studying the social insects and dominance hierarchies in birds and animals for insights into the natural bases of human behaviour ... The argument from animal hierarchies to human hierarchies may be mere nonsense; probably it is nonsense; but it is not just medieval nonsense. The human mind has never ceased to be fascinated by natural hierarchy; and the point that hierarchical ordering is a near-universal manifestation among human cultures seems self-evident.[63]

Certainly hierarchy appears to have underpinned the later history of Roman law. From the time of the Post-glossators, the law became more and more important as a vehicle for political theory;[64] and such learned law was at the same time used to the advantage of kings to justify and to consolidate their power. Law became dependent upon the king,[65] and knowledge of law became associated with power.[66] This development set the pattern for legal theory: the law evolved into a vehicle for a voluntarist political model where everything flowed from the ruler. In addition, the law was used to class and to categorise.[67] And, when this was put into the context of *societas Christiana*, the ruler, who represented God on Earth, acted as the normative input into the structure. As Ullmann has put it:

> From this supreme being all power was derived and thus order in this world was guaranteed. For order, according to him, consisted of the differences in the grades and ranks of officers, arranged, however, so that each of them stood in direct dependence to his immediate superior officer. The differences in ranks and function and order were expressed by the term hierarchy.[68]

God may now have disappeared, but he was replaced by Hans Kelsen's *Grundnorm*. In other words, the pattern remained the same, with the result that the modern positivist view of law is one whereby all rules are envisaged as conforming to this kind of hierarchical structure. Public law had not just invaded and captured private law.

It had brought every aspect of law – the concept of law, legal science, legal theory, legal epistemology – within its *imperium* and the most compelling evidence of this imperialism is to be found, today, in the effectiveness of Kelsen's epistemology. Kelsen fashioned a pure science of law whereby an 'entire legal system of any country is a mass of linked ought-propositions or norms' in which each 'norm in the system depends for its authority on a superior norm'. And the 'image which results from this account of a legal system … is one of a series of steps which can be ascended or descended'.[69]

Legal Science and the Institutional System

Yet Kelsen's science of law was also destructive of the Roman and medieval idea of law and legal sources since, within this step-like pyramid, all distinctions between different categories of law disappear. The object of legal science is a body of norms. Public and private law, for example, thus disappear and in their place is a pure science of norms. Public law under the guise of *scientia iuris* becomes the means of unifying law and of banishing dualistic categories. For all law comes ultimately from the same source and thus all law is public law. Distinctions between the law of persons and the law of things or between property and obligations are equally rendered irrelevant when it comes to the object of science. This would have been meaningless to the Roman jurists themselves. Yet they provided the elements – *imperium, ius publicum, lex* and the will of the emperor – through which this remodelling could take place. And the model itself was the institutional system whose dynamic interrelationships between persons, things and actions proved, once the power of the state had been incorporated into the law of persons, the structural means for reorganising theory.

It would be tempting, then, to say that the institutional scheme contained the seeds of its own destruction. Yet the model cannot be 'scientifically' dismissed quite so easily, even today: first, because Kelsen's thesis that the object of legal science is a body of norms is not necessarily that helpful when it comes to solving actual legal problems. Legal propositions have to connect with social reality and, as we have seen, they can do this only through institutions. Norms might try to banish categories, but they cannot dispense with persons, things and actions since these are the institutions around which rules (norms) are fixed. In short, a practical legal science – that is to say, a science that can solve actual problems – needs a set of concepts and categories which can relate to facts. One is, effectively, forced back to schemes such as the one to be found in Gaius. Secondly, the institutional model cannot be dismissed for historical reasons. The fact is that the institutional scheme acted as the basic structure for the great codes of Europe and this structure, together with the legal science that attaches to it, cannot be dismantled without dismantling the codes themselves.

Accordingly, the institutional scheme that first found expression in Gaius' introductory textbook to law remains both a model for legal theory and a model for legal science. It represents the link between the analysis of factual situations for the purposes of problem solving and the analysis of law as an abstract system of knowledge. In addition, it holds the key both to the rule model and to the non-rule model, in that the *Institutes* is a work that sees law in terms of propositions fixed around institutions which are forms of knowledge that go beyond rules. Institutions can be rule-described, in that persons, things and actions can all be defined. But their reduction to symbolic knowledge (linguistic definitions) also results in a loss of information, in that institutions belong to, and within, the world of social fact. Not all difficult cases involve the way institutions are imagined, as indeed we have seen from cases already discussed. But many do. And difficult notions such as vicarious liability in the law of obligations or the status of a live musical performance for the purpose of property law are difficult simply because they involve fundamental questions about the nature of a *persona* or a *res*.

Consider, for example, dignity. Is this something that is analogous to a form of property (*res*), that is to say is it a *res* to which the *persona* is entitled? Or is it an integral part of the *persona*? Or, again, is it perhaps an idea that transgresses the categories of positive law to become an essential aspect of the nature of law itself? Law that does not respect the fundamental value of human dignity, it might plausibly be said, is no law at all. Dignity can be treated in any one of these dimensions. Thus in French law it is part of the law of persons and is thus a right of personality,[70] while in English law it is to be found either in the law of tort[71] or in the law of property,[72] and therefore forms part of the law of things. It is more a form of property than personality. Yet if all law, as indeed the Romans insisted,[73] is made for the good of humans, then dignity can be seen as a value underpinning the whole institutional model itself. It becomes a philosophical element within the system and a reason for its existence. Dignity moves from being an element attaching to one or other of the institutions (*persona* or *res*) to become a right in itself. It becomes an element within the whole notion of *ius*. What the idea of dignity illustrates, then, is the central role of the institutional model in law as a knowledge discourse. The model acts as the bridge, not just between the world of social fact and the world of law, but between positive law and legal theory. It is what binds together every aspect of law as a discipline. It is the basis of legal knowledge and that, arguably, is the reason why the system of Gaius has survived into the late 20th century. It is synonymous with law.

Social Science and the Institutional System

During the second life of Roman law, that is to say the period from its rediscovery in the 11th century until the modern codes, the institutional plan was increasingly seen to embody not just the sum total of legal rationality but also a religious and moral dimension. The rational aspect was closely interrelated with the development of systems and classification.[74] This interest in systems did not as such start with the rediscovery of Roman law in the later Middle Ages, although much groundwork was achieved by the medieval doctors of Roman and canon law in synthesising law into a *corpus iuris*.[75] The methods of the scholastics were often focused on detailed distinctions functioning at low levels of abstraction. In other words, they were interested in making distinctions between factual situations and between different kinds of concepts and notions.[76] It was the Humanists, during the 16th century, who shifted attention off the case studies in the *Digest* and onto the general classification scheme of the *Institutiones*, and this inspired later writers to re-order the *Digest* itself.[77] Domat (1625–96) wrote a work entitled *Les lois civiles dans leur ordre naturel* and Pothier (1699–1772) followed a century later with his *Les Pandectes justiniennes dans un nouvel ordre*.

In Germany, as we have seen in Chapters 1 and 2, the influence of the Humanists resulted in a methodological evolution that was to prove a defining aspect of codification itself. University law professors, many of whom had been trained in mathematics and philosophy as well as law, started to reconstruct Roman law into a global and autonomous system. Such a system became detached from the world of social reality to function, like mathematics, in a purified rational domain where solutions could be inferred from such a logical structure in the same manner as solutions could be deduced from mathematical axioms. The institutional system, in other words, was being developed into a deductive mathematical model. This was far from the Roman approach itself. Gaius, as we have seen, had constructed his system around the 'social realities' of people and things and these realities acted as a bridge between the world of fact and the world of law. Even actions were descriptive in that, compared with the modern 'right', they were empirical things in a historical and social sense. All the same, it would be unjust to underestimate the Roman contribution to the systematic nature of the institutional scheme. It has already been demonstrated how *persona, res* and *actiones* were interacting in a creative way so as produce a model that itself could create new elements and relationships.

What the Romans did not attain was a high level of theoretical and conceptual sophistication. That was to be achieved, as has been mentioned, by the later civilians.[78] Equally, the Romans did not invest the institutional scheme with a religious or political dimension. That, again, was the work of the Enlightenment writers. As a French historian has described Domat's *Les lois civiles dans leur ordre naturel*:

> God had established, for the society of men, the natural foundations of order. It was necessary to seek out these foundations and to show how they could be used in a practical way: it was thus in this way that the Christian doctrine of love gave rise to commitments between men. The first species of these commitments arose from the distinctive form of this kind of society, the family ... Other commitments arose from the society established between all persons 'even between the most distant strangers': for example agreement. These basic principles were carefully analysed, and Domat verified their practical application in Roman legislation, which was in his eyes the model of natural law, of immutable justice: thus, via a philosophical journey, Jean Domat arrived at proposing as the ideal law applicable to everyone the Roman legislation of the Code and the Digest.[79]

The *Institutes* of Gaius thus moved from the realm of legal science to that of social science and political and moral philosophy.[80] The tripartite scheme represented the foundation of society as it was to be perceived beyond the legal scheme. The relationships that connected people with things and persons with persons were not simply legal bonds; they were natural connections. They were the bonds that kept society together and thus they provided an empirical object for legal science. *Ubi societas ibi ius*. The point can be expressed another way. Looking at property theory in 19th-century France, Kelley has pointed out that 'if the proprietary theory of human nature – man as *homo economicus* or *acquisitivus* – was a fairly recent discovery of philosophers, it had long been an assumption among civil lawyers'. For it had 'been built into the very structure of law almost from the beginning', that is to say 'at least from the time of Gaius'.[81] Behind the law, there is empirical reality; but behind empirical reality, as perceived by social, moral and economic theory, there is Gaius.

Legal Concepts

Persons, things and actions were fundamental inasmuch as they acted as the starting point for all other legal concepts. Ownership and possession were thus founded in the relationship between *persona* and *res* while *obligatio* was a *vinculum iuris* that bound together two persons. Modern law has moved on inasmuch as it has developed out of this plan not just new notions such as the right, but also the idea that *iura* themselves consist of rules and principles. Yet even these rules and principles (including norms) are not the only focal points of what might be termed normative legal knowledge. Rights and duties, as one has seen in Dworkin's work, have also assumed a central role. Lawyers and legal theorists have, in addition, made use of another concept, that of an interest, sometimes to act as a factual foundation for a right and sometimes as a means for analysing legal claims. Rights, duties and interests have, then, long histories, to a greater or lesser extent going back to Roman law, and thus they warrant specific attention from the epistemologist. They appear to act as the foundation for legal assertions.

Normative and Descriptive Concepts

The policy approach to legal decision making has, as we have seen, come in for specific criticism. Judges should decide hard cases on the basis of rights rather than policy. However, for many legal theorists, rights are simply determined by legal propositions (rules and principles) and thus would appear to have no independent existence. Their normative dimension, in other words, is derived from the rule. Yet to say that a person has a 'right' to something is a statement that is normative in itself; it does not need, as a linguistic proposition, to be justified by reference to any other norm. The same can be said of 'duty'. To assert that D is under a duty to P to do X is a normative statement in itself; yet duty does not appear to have an independent existence as a knowledge element. Like a right, it is derived for many theorists simply from rules and principles. The independent normative flavour to rights and duties can be contrasted with another legal concept, an interest. The notion of an 'interest' seemingly lacks in itself a normative dimension, in that to say that X has an interest to protect does not of itself imply that the interest ought to be protected. Something more needs to be shown. Interest, therefore, can at first sight be termed a descriptive concept. Such a concept seemingly carries no normative implication. Thus to say that it is in the 'commercial interest' of a tobacco company that a reporting restriction order be obtained in respect of legal proceedings concerning the company does not of itself imply that such an order *ought* to be issued; the concept is merely descriptive. And being descriptive such a concept may well have a role and meaning in discourses and disciplines outside of law (for example, in economics and sociology).[82] One might also mention, alongside interests, notions such as 'fault' and 'damage' that are in theory also merely descriptive concepts.

Having said that interest, fault and damage are in theory descriptive, in truth they often play a role that is at once descriptive and normative.[83] For example, to say that D has carelessly caused damage to P is to go far in implying that D ought to compensate P. In other words, the mere juxtaposition of the two descriptive concepts of 'damage' and 'fault' can endow them both with a quasi-normative character.[84] Some systems require a third descriptive concept such as 'interest'[85] or 'proximity'[86] before the required normativity is generated, but the point remains that these descriptive concepts can combine to produce more than the sum of their individual parts. Other useful descriptive concepts are 'legitimate expectation',[87] 'control' (*sous sa garde*)[88] and 'enrichment';[89] and what makes them central to legal analysis is that they function at the level of the facts themselves. They emerge out of the facts to act as bridges between the descriptive (fact) and the normative (law) and thus hold the key to the construction of legal solutions (*ex facto ius oritur*). When combined with the institutions of *persona, res* and *actiones,* which are of course also notions that function at one and the same time at the level of fact and of law, the comparatist can see how legal facts and their solutions are a matter of legal construction (*ex iure factum oritur*).

The notion of an interest (*utilitas, interest*) goes some way, then, in allowing one to say that the roots of legal realism are, ironically, to be found in civilian legal science itself.[90] This realism may not have focused on judges and decision makers as such, but law had its purpose; it was about real persons and real things. Law is about facts and where fact and legal science meet is in the notion of an interest. The role of law is to regulate conflicting interests and a legal claim can thus be seen as, directly or indirectly, a claim to an interest. In fact, Dworkin himself uses the idea of an interest as the empirical basis for his structure of principles. According to him, 'an argument of principle fixes on some interest presented by the proponent of the right it describes, an interest alleged to be of such a character as to make irrelevant the fine discriminations of any argument of policy that might oppose it'.[91]

Rights

Dworkin does not, however, use the notion of a factual interest as the basis of his adjudication thesis. Instead he focuses upon rights. The search for the right answer is the search for the parties' rights amongst the rules and principles that go to make up the reasoning model. In terms of reasoning, the good judge ought not to justify a decision in a case on the grounds of policy. He should do it by confirming or denying concrete rights which themselves result from the judge's interpretation of the scheme of concrete principles that provide a coherent justification for all the legal precedents.[92]

This notion of a legal right is not of course an invention of modern legal theorists.[93] Nevertheless, it has assumed a central role in modern legal thought since it provides a viewpoint for seeing law from the position both of the individual – a central plank of liberal political theory – and of entitlements as 'things' separate from the procedural structure of remedies which enforce them. In the language of the civilian, rights and remedies represent a dichotomy that stretches back to the distinction in the Roman sources between *ius* and *actio*. This separation is important in that one of the objectives of post-Enlightenment legal science was to purge law of its attachment to procedural rules which, although important and deserving of their own codes, were nevertheless no longer to be the formal means of classifying law. The Roman sources themselves, it has to be remembered, had distinguished between ownership (*dominium*) and the remedy (*actio in rem*) for revindicating one's entitlements to a thing (*res*) and Gaius had included obligations (*actiones in personam*) as forms of intangible property (*res incorporales*).[94] To later civilians it seemed obvious that, while law might be closely attached to actions, there was undoubtedly something beyond these remedies that was worthy of classification.[95] Law was made for men, as one text stipulated,[96] and men were bound to each other and to things by legal relationships that were called *iura*.[97]

In fact, although the Romans did not think in terms of rights as a political and epistemological concept as such, the Roman model of law based on *persona, res* and *actio* was individualistic in nature. It was the individual who was the paradigm owner, contractor and actor. This individualistic model was given even greater expression after the so-called 'nominalist revolution' associated with the 14th-century philosopher William of Ockham. Only individual entities actually existed and all group terms (men, forests and the like) were mere names giving expression to abstract ideas that existed uniquely in the mind. From the viewpoint of nominalism, then, society was not a corporate entity (*universitas*) but simply a collection of individuals.[98] Thus for law to have any theoretical basis in social reality it must be attached to, and viewed from, the individual human; only the individual could be the ultimate source of law. It is this nominalist view of law that remains powerful at the theoretical level. Rights theorists such as Dworkin are extremely influential and one reason for the strength of such theories is that the notion of a 'right' acts as a bridge between law and philosophy. Rights can become a vehicle for injecting into, for example, the law of obligations ideas about behaviour and morality. Notions such as promise and fault become the knowledge models through which contractual and extra contractual liability is understood.

Rights, then, have become particularly useful to modern legal thought since they act as the vehicle for bringing together under a single notion all the various entitlements, tangible and intangible, with which a legal system is concerned. An entitlement to one's car (owning) is on the same level as an entitlement to a debt (owing) and both can be placed in a person's patrimony. Indeed, the New Dutch Civil Code has a separate book devoted to all of these economic rights.[99] Yet the term 'right' is, given its association with owning, also valuable for expressing an entitlement free from any social duty or obligation. And so to assert that one has a *right* to one's car is enough to entitle a claim to possession of the car without ever having to show that one *deserves* to be the possessor of such a thing.[100] Right thus carries a connotation of power and it is this aspect of power that has interested legal theorists, since the term can be used as a means of asserting social and political claims.[101] Ronald Dworkin, for example, argues that rights 'are best understood as trumps over some background justification for political decisions that states a goal for the community as a whole'. Accordingly, if 'someone has a right to moral independence, this means that it is for some reason wrong for officials to act in violation of that right, even if they (correctly) believe that the community as a whole would be better off if they did'.[102]

Until recently, with one recent exception,[103] this trump view of a right has not been embraced by actual English judicial reasoning, save in the narrow area of traditional property rights.[104] English judges have preferred to see the independence of the individual in terms of liberty, which, of course, does not have the same power connotation.[105] Indeed, in any legal system where positivist legal theory decrees that the legislator is the supreme source of law, rights can have little place. Nevertheless, the incorporation of the European Convention for the Protection of Human Rights and Fundamental Freedoms ought in theory to revolutionise the English attitude.[106] And it has to be said that the incorporation is certainly having an impact. However, it would be optimistic to say that the English judges are modifying their approach in the direction of the Dworkin thesis. Press freedom, for example, continues to be a matter of balance rather than trumps and newspapers are still being ordered to disclose their sources.[107] Moreover, with respect to statute, 'the law which the court must enforce is the law as it is, even if incompatible with the Convention'.[108] In fact, if rights are to have any real meaning, they will require their own philosophical and epistemological thesis to underpin them. Now, rights need such a theoretical underpinning mainly because they are metaphysical creations. They are the creations of the rational mind and, although the existence or non-existence of rights can be confirmed or denied as social facts (how government officials treat individuals), they cannot be verified in themselves except in relation to law.

Duty

The American theorist Hohfeld saw the term 'duty' as a jural correlative of the term 'right'.[109] If P had a 'right' against D that D should stay off P's land, then D is under a 'duty' to stay off the land.[110] Where there is a right there is a duty. In the world of norms there is logic to this structure, which is why Hohfeld's analysis has retained its rightful place in legal theory. However, when viewed from a diachronic perspective, the interrelating of rights with duties presents a problem in that the two terms result from different structures. The term 'right' is devolved from the Latin word *ius*, which gradually assumed its power (*potestas*) dimension when it became amalgamated with the notion of *dominium*.[111] And *dominium* was based on an absolute entitlement to a *res*.[112] Rights talk is, then, property talk. Duty on the other hand attaches not to a *res* but to a person and thus is founded on the relationship between person and person. It is based on the *vinculum iuris* that acts as the basis of an *obligatio*.[113] In terms of structural relationships, the problem with identifying duty with right is that it reduces a three-dimensional model to two dimensions. It forces the *in rem* relationship between *persona* and *res* into the same dimension as the *in personam* bond between person and person and thus one loses the complexity of the historical model.

Such reductionism has its price. To say that P has a 'right' to £100 from D since D is under a contractual 'duty' to pay the debt to P is to assert that P has something approaching a 'property' right in the debt. P has a 'thing' (*res*) in the legal action itself. This 'thing' was recognised in Roman law itself and thus Gaius not only distinguishes between corporeal (*res corporalis*) and incorporeal property (*res incorporalis*),[114] but equally states that the latter includes obligations. Accordingly, even in Roman law owning and owing were confused, in that the *res* becomes something that is not just 'owed' but also 'owned'; the debt, as English law specifically admits, becomes a property right.[115] Ownership (right) and obligation (duty) become confused within the same plane and this has the effect of compressing ownership, obligation, right and duty as conceptual devices capable of clearly distinguishing property from obligations. Duty thus becomes a term incapable of expressing in itself a content. It may represent an absolute responsibility, as in the case of the seller of a defective product that causes damage to a purchaser, or it may express a form of unacceptable behaviour. This variability in meaning is well expressed by a commentator on the English law of tort:

> The manufacturer is responsible at common law for the condition of the ginger beer and the occupier is responsible by statute for the state of the premises: both are under a duty to take reasonable care. This equation is delusive, however, since the duties differ in their basis and in their extent. The manufacturer is responsible because he *does* make the thing dangerous, whereas the occupier is responsible because he *can* make the thing safe; the manufacturer's duty arises from his action, the occupier's from his capacity to act (he must because he can). And the extent of the duties differs. Unlike the manufacturer, the occupier is not just under a duty not to cause harm to people; he must prevent harm to them; he must mend the premises and tend the visitor. For example, he must protect the visitor against other visitors. Those other visitors of course owe a duty to everyone present or probably present, but that duty is only the standard one of not hurting them; they are not responsible save in so far as they make the place dangerous; the occupier must make it reasonably safe ...[116]

In a two-dimensional world 'duty' is unable to connect with things, with people and with legal actions at one and the same time and thus ends up as a 'simplistic formula'.[117] It cannot connect directly with factual reality. Like a 'right', a 'duty' is the creation of the mind and thus can give expression to a normative relationship without reference as such to a particular factual situation. However, it does differ from a right inasmuch as its historical foundation in *obligatio* has invested the whole term with much more of a behavioural aspect. Whereas a right-holder is entitled to revindicate the object of his right without reference to behaviour – thus a person can exercise a right 'for a good reason or a bad reason or no reason at all'[118] – a person under a duty is usually (but not always) adjudged in terms of his behaviour. Contracts are said to create rights. But the essence of the *vinculum iuris* is often to be found in the obligation of good faith or the duty not to abuse any contractual rights and this is one reason why contract, in the civilian systems, is said to be based on fault.[119] Thus right and duty cannot easily connect either with each other or with social reality. They usually need to be mediated through other terms or concepts.

Interests

Interests, in contrast to rights and duties, would appear to need no philosophical underpinning since they are empirically verifiable.[120] That is to say, they are social facts which are verifiable outside of any system of rational legal thought. To state that a person has an interest in something (a company for example), or that an enterprise has a commercial interest to protect, or that a public body acts in the public interest, is measurable against the social and economic goods in society. An interest is an economic or other social benefit or utility (from the Latin *utilitas*) attaching to an individual or a group which exists, seemingly, independently of the legal system. In civil law an interest has been distinguishable from a right (*ius*) since Roman times and so, for example, one finds the Roman jurist Gaius claiming that, while someone may have a *ius* to act in a particular way, it may nevertheless not be in his interest to do so.[121] And in modern continental law one who intentionally tries to enforce a right in a situation where he has no legitimate interest to do so may find himself liable, on the basis of an abuse of a right, in damages to anyone damaged as a result.[122]

'Interest' can also be seen as a major element in the construction of factual situations in law since it can attach to all three of the legal institutions in order to facilitate legal analysis. Take, first of all, persons (*personae*). They have interests and these are given expression as part of personality itself; accordingly, children have their own interests which can be used to trump those of others,[123] and all humans might be said to have interests that are both subjective (reputation, dignity and the like)[124] and objective.[125] Indeed, each person has his own mass of interests.[126] What makes them particularly valuable as a legal notion is that interest can become a means of giving expression to a 'person' who has not as yet been endowed with physical or legal existence. Thus one can talk of the interests of unborn children or even future generations; equally, one can use interest to endow a class of persons such as the family,[127] consumers or more fragmented groups with an interest, thus giving them a kind of legal personality.[128] Actual legal (corporate) persons have 'commercial interests' which can act as the object of legal protection and these commercial interests in turn help give greater 'empirical' definition to the corporate person itself.

Furthermore, the state itself can be seen as a 'person' with its own interest, and as a representative of the general or public interest. Accordingly, private interests are often contrasted with the general or the public interest. Thus *imprévision* in French contract law differs as between public and private law contracts since the courts must take account of the general interest when deciding a problem of public law.[129] Often cases can be made to turn on the conflict between public and private interests and when such a conflict arises the notion of an interest becomes a means of giving expression to the community *vis-à-vis* the individual.[130] Public interest can also be used to give expression to certain constitutional 'rights', or indeed as a reason for limiting such 'rights'.[131]

Interest can also attach to the *res*. Thus, in English land law, 'rights' in land belonging to another are expressed in terms of interests, and different kinds of losses can be analysed via different types of interest. For example, damages in English contract law are said to protect three different types of interest – expectation, reliance and restitution[132] – and in tort law some argue that the whole objective of this category can be reduced to protecting interests of one kind or another.[133] Interest can be seen as the empirical foundation of a 'right' and, although it cannot obviously be synonymous with such a normative concept, interest is often used as the basis for granting a remedy and thus erecting a right in private law.[134] In contrast, the distinction between (legitimate) interest and right lies, as we have already suggested, at the heart of the civilian principle of an abuse of a right. A person who has no interest whatsoever in enforcing a right may well be held liable to compensate anyone suffering damage from the enforcement. To say that property itself has interests is, perhaps, to abuse legal language; but where animals are concerned things may be different. Animals may have legally recognised interests.[135]

The notion of an 'interest' is also important in the law of actions, in that it is used to determine the standing of a legal subject (*persona*) in relation to the entitlement to bring a legal action. This is particularly important in public law where individuals can sue for judicial review only if they have a 'sufficient interest' in the matter,[136] and such a rule applies equally to private law in most civilian systems.[137] However, this standing question has become particularly acute when 'more and more frequently the complexity of modern societies generates situations in which a single human action can be beneficial or prejudicial to large numbers of people, thus making entirely inadequate the traditional scheme of litigation as merely a two-party affair'.[138] The law of actions is accordingly an area dealing with fundamental questions about access to justice. And the notion of an interest is a key notion which acts not only as a control device but as a defining focal point for giving expression to the function of legal claims and legal procedure.[139]

Rights and Interests

Despite the sharp distinction between a right and an interest, the two notions are nevertheless bound together in a number of important ways, First, interests have, since Roman times, been said to be the object of law itself. Thus Ulpian explained the distinction between public and private law on the basis that the former concerned itself with the public interest (*utilitas publica*) while the latter was a matter of the interests of individuals.[140] And more recently an English judge has talked in not dissimilar terms.[141] Rights and interests might be said therefore to represent, respectively, the science and object of science. Secondly, interests can act as a means of modifying existing rights. In family law, for example, the interests of children are paramount and this interest will, accordingly, modify any legal rights arising out of the relationship between the parents or out of parenthood itself.[142] The law of actions also responds to interests as much as rights. It may be that a person has an abstract right to a legal remedy, but if he has no legitimate interest in bringing the claim, he will be denied the action; *pas d'intérêt, pas d'action*.[143] Equally, there may be situations where a person has no right as such but may have a legal remedy founded upon an interest.[144] Thirdly, the idea of an interest has acted as the theoretical basis for the notion of a right itself. Thus, for Roscoe Pound, developing a theory of the German jurist Rudolf von Jhering, law exists to secure social interests and the idea of a legal right is simply the legal recognition of a particular social interest to be protected by the law.[145] This sociological analysis recalls the science and object of science dichotomy, but it goes further, in that it identifies each right with a particular interest and this identification is itself a matter of legal values. 'While philosophers are debating whether a scheme of values is possible,' wrote Pound, 'lawyers and courts have found a workable one which has proved as adequate to its tasks as any practical method in any practical activity.'[146]

Rights and interests are by no means inimical to positivism or to legal science. Indeed, if positive legal rules are seen as 'ought'-creating norms, then from the position of each individual legal person subject to such norms one viewpoint is undoubtedly that of obligation, or 'duty', of which the correlative is 'right'. If D is under a duty as a result of a legal rule (norm) to pay R £100, then R can be said to have a right to £100. And if every legally recognised interest is given the status of a right, the recognition process itself can no doubt be reduced to a positive structure of rules and (or) norms. Rights, in other words, are interests translated into obligation-creating positive rules. Nevertheless, the notion of a right or an interest can be used as a vehicle to extend the definition of law beyond one that just focuses on a system of positive rules. For rights and interests can be seen as having a conceptual independence from a system of rules since one can talk about rights and interests without having to talk about or imply rules. Rights and (or) interests can, for example, be regarded as things in themselves, invasion of which might give rise to a remedy (*ubi ius ibi remedium*). Thus rape and burglary can be seen as invasions in both a physical and a metaphysical sense. Alternatively, rights might be seen as resulting from the existence of a remedy (*ubi remedium ibi ius*) which itself arises only out of particular factual situations (*in causa ius esse positum*)[147] rather than out of rules. An action for possession, if granted, injects into the factual situation a 'right' (*ius possessionis*).

Rights and interests are important, then, to the legal theorist and legal epistemologist, in that they could locate law elsewhere than in a system of rules. For example, instead of asking whether the rules allow for the plaintiff to obtain a legal remedy such as an injunction, a court might ask if on the facts the plaintiff has a 'right' to a remedy. This would allow a decision to be made without recourse as such to any existing structure of rules. Accordingly, in one English case, Lord Denning MR said:

> The question ... becomes this: has the plaintiff a particular right which he is entitled to have protected? To this the answer which runs through all the cases is: a man who is carrying on a lawful trade or calling has a right to be protected from any unlawful interference with it ... It is a right which is in the nature of a right of property ...[148]

And he continued, this 'principle is capable of extension so as to apply not only to rights of property or rights in the nature of it, but to other rights or interests'.[149] In an earlier case, Lord Denning had also asserted:

> The judge said that he felt constrained by the law to refuse an injunction. But that is too narrow a view of the principles of law. He has overlooked the fundamental principle that, whenever a man has a right, the law should give a remedy. The Latin maxim is *ubi jus ibi remedium*. This principle enables us to step over the trip-wires of previous cases and to bring the law into accord with the needs of today ...[150]

A similar approach, as Lord Denning himself implies, can be taken with regard to an 'interest'. Does the 'public interest', or indeed the plaintiff's own 'commercial interest', dictate whether a remedy should issue? Certainly, there are cases to be found in the law reports where this kind of analysis occurs.[151] Rights and interests can be used, therefore, to reach beyond the narrow boundaries of positivism. They become, so to speak, pre-existing objects waiting to be rationalised by legal science and as such they are not the creations of positive legal rules even though they may *ex post facto* be rationalised in terms of a rule. Law becomes a language for understanding and controlling these 'objects'.

Property and Sovereignty

Rights, duties and interests are universal concepts inasmuch as they transcend any particular category of law. Nevertheless, the notion of a right is, historically, bound up with the Roman concept of private ownership (*dominium*) and this, to some extent at least, confines it to private law. In some civil law systems therefore, subjective rights are seen as based on the relationship between *persona* and *res*, whereas constitutional entitlements are viewed as arising out of 'legitimate interests' in turn determined by a quite different relationship.[152] This relationship in Roman law was *imperium*.

Imperium

In order to understand this notion of *imperium*, one has to return to the *persona*, *res* and *actiones* structure used by Gaius. This structure was in essence a model of private law and thus it was primarily concerned with the interests of private individuals as between themselves.[153] Roman law, as we shall see, also recognised a category of public law which was concerned with the interests of the state.[154] This idea of the state, although used in the Roman sources, is largely a post-Roman concept: that is to say, the notion of the state as an institution capable of being a focal point for legal relations (rules, rights, duties and interests) was never developed as such.[155] It is largely the work of the Post-glossators and Humanists (together with the political philosophers of the same period).[156] Nevertheless, the Roman jurists went far in constructing a number of institutions which acted as the forerunners of the modern state. For example, the institution of the *fiscus* (treasury) was used as a public *persona* capable, on the one hand, of owning and contracting and, on the other hand, of being endowed with privileges. These privileges allowed it to have a status and position in the institutional plan which was significantly different from that of private individuals.[157] Legal relations with the *fiscus* were accordingly of a special nature.[158]

The legal relation that underpinned the *fiscus* and other public bodies and offices in Roman law was *imperium*. This was the power of command and was found in its paradigmatic form in the hierarchical structure of the army. However, the emperor also had command over his subjects and, more directly, over his administrative officers; *imperium* equally expressed therefore a general governmental power (*potestas*).[159] This public power could be contrasted with the 'private' power of the *paterfamilias* over his property.[160] From a conceptual position, then, the distinction between the *ius publicum* and the *ius privatum* is that the former was concerned with power relations based upon *imperium* whereas the latter is founded upon *dominium*. Two immediate theoretical questions arise out of this *potestas* dichotomy. First, could *imperium* always trump *dominium*? And, secondly, how could the *imperium* of the emperor be justified? In Roman law itself there is little doubt that private ownership would yield to *imperium* and so, for example, one could not infringe upon a magistrate's power of command (*imperium*) by private agreement.[161] More generally, the private law could not be used to change the *ius publicum*.[162] With regard to the second question, the emperor's power of command, according to Ulpian, resulted from the *lex regia*; this was a transfer by the whole Roman population of their *imperium* and *potestas* to the emperor.[163]

This power of command was important for another reason as well. It lay at the basis of the emperor's power to legislate[164] and thus the whole notion of legislation itself was simply a means of issuing commands that had the status of law.[165] This command thesis is more problematic than it might first appear. If all legislation is ultimately founded upon *imperium* then it is arguable that all legislation is a matter of public law. Certainly, many great legislative interventions can be classified under public law, but when it comes to the civil codes there is something of a contradiction inasmuch as codes act as the foundation of private law. The paradox was to an extent solved by the positivists inasmuch as they attributed all law ultimately to the will of the king or legislator. Indeed the English 19th-century theorist John Austin specifically founded his theory of positivism on the idea that law was nothing less than a series of commands issued by a legislator.[166] Yet the older idea of private rights having their source in the *ius naturale* rather than in the will of the legislator has not actually disappeared. Conventions on human rights are specifically designed to act as sources of law beyond the reach of any national legislator.[167]

Dominium and *imperium* act, therefore, as concepts that represent the ultimate sources of legal *potestas*. If the power of the state is to be controlled then the obvious counterpoint is the idea of private ownership understood in its wider sense of the ultimate source of all private rights. Equally, if the power of the individual is to be curbed in the interests of the community then *imperium* is the obvious concept. In truth, of course, the dichotomy between the two notions is much more complex. In Roman law itself, whole aspects of private law were very much dependent directly or indirectly on *imperium*. For example, possession was protected by remedies directly based upon the magistrates' *imperium*.[168] Likewise, the law of status, part of the law of persons in the Gaian scheme, was a question of public law even if slavery itself was founded on the ownership of one person by another. Is commercial law, given the importance of the economy to the public interest, to be seen just in terms of ownership and contract? In the 17th century, commercial law was considered in France as part of public law[169] and today specialists in European Union law talk in terms of the constitutionalisation of private law.[170] Procedure is equally ambiguous.[171]

Dominium and Obligatio

The EU seems, then, to be founded upon a mixture of both *imperium* and *dominium* and on a closer inspection some of the inner regions of national private laws have a public law dimension. Each legislative intervention represents the power of *imperium*. However, the interrelationship between public and private law concepts is not the only conceptual ambiguity to be found in Western legal systems. One of the fundamental distinctions in the structural make-up of the codes themselves is the dichotomy between property and obligations. *Owning* is to be sharply distinguished from *owing*. Or, to put it another way, *dominium* is to be sharply distinguished from *obligatio*. In modern German law, the distinction has become so fundamental that it is a matter of legal science; real rights are to be strictly separated from personal rights.[172] In Roman law, however, the distinction was more ambiguous. Certainly, the Romans maintained a rigid distinction between real and personal actions and they never allowed property relations to become confused with personal obligations.[173] But in classifying both property and obligations under 'things' they also recognised that the law of obligations was an adjunct to the law of property. This ambiguity is important inasmuch as it indicates that there is nothing inevitable about the Roman scheme.[174]

When one moves into the second life of Roman law, the position becomes much more complex. The political structures of the Middle Ages, the period when Roman law was being rediscovered, did not think in terms of a sharp division between property and obligations or between the public and the private.[175] Feudalism was more realistic in some ways. It made a distinction between land and chattels, with the result that different legal categories developed which did not easily harmonise with the learned Roman law of the universities.[176] Indeed, *dominium* and *obligatio* were used as the basis for *imperium*.[177] The common lawyer is, of course, quite familiar with the complexities of feudalism, since this was the social and political context in which it developed. Accordingly, the common law is much more ambiguous about the Roman distinctions. However, even in Europe as a whole, the law of property is by no means as simple as is sometimes thought, and for several reasons.

First, the terms and notions to be found in the Roman sources have over the centuries been subjected to intense analysis and theoretical speculation. This analysis and speculation has of course refined the Roman concepts. Yet it has done more than this inasmuch as the history of the second life of Roman law is a history of differing intellectual methods and schemes of intelligibility. Ownership and obligations have therefore to be understood not just within an evermore structured and refined view of private law. They have to be appreciated within rather different theoretical conceptions of law itself. Secondly, the notion of property, particularly in more recent times, has not been static; new types of property have appeared and these new kinds of property have in their own ways contributed to further speculation about the nature of proprietary relationships. Thirdly, the common law has always maintained a property regime that is quite different from the one to be found in the Roman sources. This does not mean that common lawyers have not adopted some civilian ideas.[178] However, the distinction between law and equity in England has resulted in a more multidimensional system than is to be found in the codified countries. Developments have attached as much to the power of independent legal remedies as to coherent and refined notions of ownership and possession. The result is that property thinking probably provides one of the greatest obstacles to harmonisation of private law between the civil law and common law traditions.[179]

Roman and Feudal Concepts

The rediscovery of Roman law in the 11th century and its subsequent study over the following centuries was to have a major impact on the customary laws that were to be found in the societies of the late Middle Ages. These societies were, until the end of the 14th century, largely feudal in organisation, a political structure that was unknown to Roman law. Gradually, the customary law gave way to Romanisation.[180] However, in England the position was quite different. The customary legal system, consolidated by the Normans, was able to resist the learned Roman law, with the result that a quite separate legal mentality survived into the modern era.[181] The common law tradition is thus an independent one from the *ius civile* family on the continent. All the same, this historical dichotomy should not disguise the fact that the starting point for the modern civil law is, equally, the late Middle Ages rather than the Roman law of the Roman Empire.[182] It was the medieval lawyers, in particular the Post-glossators, who constructed the framework upon which modern legal and political theory in continental Europe is based.[183]

Of course, the Romans must be credited with providing the conceptual foundations and vocabulary upon which this framework was built. In particular, the notions of ownership (*dominium, proprietas*) and possession (*possessio*) were the two central features of the Roman law of property, and the sophisticated nature of Roman thinking is particularly evident in the ability to take legal thought to abstract levels. The dichotomy between tangible (*res corporales*) and intangible property (*res incorporales*), together with a range of other sophisticated ideas, facilitated the move from an agricultural model of law towards one capable of supporting a relatively advanced monetary and commercial economy. However, the Roman ideas to be found in the *Corpus Iuris Civilis* had little direct relevance to the feudal structures which actually dominated the society of the late Middle Ages. The rediscovered Roman law was the learned law largely confined until the 14th century to the law faculties, and feudal customary law was the reality outside of the universities.[184] This feudal law had a quite different view of property, in that the idea of an exclusive and absolute legal relationship between *persona* and *res* simply did not apply to the most important form of property in medieval society, namely land.[185] Several different people could have entitlements in a single piece of land. The medieval Roman lawyers tried to reconcile the feudal practice with the Roman notions of *dominium* and *iura in re* ('rights' in another's property) and this had the effect of reducing all entitlements in land to *iura*.[186] The Roman idea of a direct relationship between *persona* and *res corporalis* disappeared, in that all property entitlements, including *dominium*, became an entitlement to a 'right'.[187] As one French historian puts it:

> In the late Middle Ages, the words *proprietas, dominium* are always used by the scribes who were mechanically reproducing a dead Roman vocabulary; many are the texts which mention 'ownership'. But the word no longer meant the physical mastery of matter, but only the enjoyment of its interests ... 'Ownership' is no longer sovereignty, it is only, and pragmatically, the legitimate possibility to draw profit from land. It no longer is confused with the matter, it is only the exploitation of matter. Practice called it 'seisin', but right from the 13th century the jurists of Roman law erased this term from the vocabulary of property and replaced it with the Roman terms *proprietas* and *dominium* to mean a polymorphic appropriation technique which had no point in common with Roman ownership except the name.[188]

Nevertheless, the Glossators and Post-glossators, being scholars of Roman law, went to great lengths to distinguish *dominium* (the *ius domini*) from other property rights, the *iura in re*.[189] These rights, which could be granted to others by an owner, were, so the Glossators gleaned from the Roman texts, the right to use property belonging to another or the right to take the fruits. The Post-glossators arrived at the position where the *ius domini* must consist of the right to use, enjoy and dispose of a thing (*ius utendi, ius fruendi, ius abutendi*) in the most absolute manner.[190] Feudalism was, then, able to survive in outline in France up to the Revolution primarily because of the detailed theoretical work of the Roman lawyers; they Romanised the customary law. Their constructions accorded well with practice and they underpinned the landed classes with a legal foundation that was to allow them to continue until the 18th century.[191] At another level, however, the power of the feudal landowners was being drained by the strengthening power of the king. Roman ideas were proving more useful than those of the feudal lawyers, in that they promoted *imperium* and independent power.[192] *Quod principi placuit legis habet vigorem* (what pleases the prince has force of law).[193] The reduction of feudal (customary) law to writing and the extension of legislation favoured the Roman structures rather than the more local customary ideas. The political vocabulary was also developing along Roman lines; the notions of *respublica* and of *potestas* were leading inexorably towards an independent idea of the state which, although primarily concerned with public law, started to intervene in commercial and private law. The development of economic regulation went hand-in-hand with the first attempts at codification by Louis XIV's minister, Colbert.[194]

Political and legal philosophy itself was also changing. In the Roman world the idea of the individual as a political focal point found expression neither in public law nor in Latin.[195] In the 14th century, however, the philosopher William of Ockham, as we have already seen, is credited as being the catalyst for a revolution against the holistic view of the world. In posing questions about the existence of things (do men or forests exist as realities or do only individual humans and trees exist?) he, and like-minded thinkers, created an epistemological revolution in which universals were seen simply as names having no ontological (real) existence in the world. The starting point of all social and political thinking was no longer the *persona* and the *universitas* but the *individuum*.[196] When translated into legal thinking, *ius* (right) was a legal bond that attached to the individual. The individual had his natural right to own property since God had given man the power to acquire and dispose of goods on earth according to the modes dictated by natural reason.[197] Thus, with the decline of feudalism and the rise of individualism from the 16th century, the original Roman notion of *ownership* re-established itself as an absolute power (*potestas*) belonging to the individual.

However, ownership re-established itself, thanks to the Post-glossators, as a *ius* (right) and not, as in Roman law, a power relation in a physical thing separate from a *ius* in the thing.[198] Thus one arrives at the famous modern definition of ownership as 'the right to enjoy and to dispose of things in the most absolute manner'.[199] Thanks to the Roman jurists, there are in law both *res corporales* and *res incorporales*, but thanks to the Post-glossators, there are in law only *iura* (rights) which are *res incorporales*. The later civilians (Natural Lawyers) tried to escape from this feudal view by reintroducing the physical thing back into the law of property. Man is the master of his physical body and all his possessions and this, in turn, meant that each man had an exclusive power of a thing in his control and not just an entitlement to rights in property shared with others.[200] Modern writers are able to exploit this confusion by imposing upon the notion of a right (*ius*) the idea of an absolute power (*ius domini*) to something which can be conceived of as a 'thing', even if it is not actually physical.[201] This 'thing' having been conceived, it can, following the Romanist structure, be vindicated. The modern notion of a right (*droit subjectif*) is thus a concept constructed out of the Roman property relations. It is to apply the language of property to other areas of law. This can create difficulties when applied to the *in rem* and *in personam* dichotomy.

Things (res)

The codifications are all framed around institutions which, as we have seen, acted as the starting point of what is called the 'institutional system'. Law is about *persona, res* and *actiones*. *Res* can loosely be translated as 'thing' (although the Latin word is rather amorphous) and, like *persona*, represents another focal point around which legal propositions can be grouped. That is to say, things, like people, exist both in the real world and the legal world and thus *res* acts as a bridge between social fact and legal conceptualisation. 'Things' (*res*) also act as a counterpoint to 'person' (*persona*) and, accordingly, the law of things cannot be understood divorced from persons. *Persona* and *res* represent a legal structure upon which almost the whole of substantive private law is founded. Indeed, it has been noted that in the *Code civil* persons are dealt with only from the angle of potential subjects of the law of property.[202] That said, the law of things was, and arguably remains (in some systems at least), wedded to the law of actions; and so the distinction between a personal and a real action lies at the heart of the distinction between property and obligations.[203] Moreover, the varying structural patterns of these interrelationships are the key to the different comparative models. In civil law, ownership (*dominium*) is the paradigm relationship between person and thing,[204] but the feudal tradition of English law has resulted in a more complex picture where ownership as a relationship has much less practical importance than possession and its associated remedies.[205]

Res might be a difficult word to define or to translate, but within the institutional model it was, as we have already seen, a key institution, in that it had meaning in both the empirical and the legal worlds. As Gaius himself implied, tangible things (*res corporales*) are things that can be touched (*quae tangi possunt*), such as land, a man, clothes, gold and the like.[206] These things exist both in fact and in law. However, Gaius goes on to explain that *res* also encompasses intangible things (*res incorporales*) which exist only in law (*quae iure consistunt*);[207] here it is, in effect, the institutional system itself that is creating the *res*. A right to a debt is a *res* – a form of property – even though the legal asset consists only of an entitlement to a legal action (*actio in personam*). This idea of debt as a *res* is also to be found in English private law. Appropriately, a debt is termed a 'chose in action' which reflects the Roman law idea that the relationship is as much between *persona* and *actio* as between person and thing. A chose in action, in turn, is a form of property.[208] In Roman law, however, a debt might have been a *res* but it was not something that could be claimed directly through an *actio in rem*. It was a personal claim that could be recovered only through an action directed at the debtor. English law, in contrast, has not been so formal. The Court of Chancery has allowed trustees and beneficiaries to trace wrongfully appropriated money into the bank account of all but the bona fide purchaser for value;[209] and this idea of a right *in rem* to a debt has been adopted by the common law. In cases of unjustified enrichment, a common law claim in debt, in the absence of a contractual obligation, can be founded upon the proprietary relationship between creditor and debt.[210]

In fact, *res* has always been interpreted widely by the courts of equity. A deliberate interference with the plaintiff's property will be restrained by an injunction and for this purpose 'property' has been held to include a whole range of intangible 'things', including a live musical performance.[211] In effect, it is sometimes difficult to distinguish between 'property' and 'rights' in some of these injunction cases and this results in a situation where, from a law of remedies point of view, it is the injunction rather than the *res* itself which is the defining vehicle.[212] In some ways this is reminiscent of the Roman method inasmuch as it was the *actio in rem* rather than *dominium* which determined property rights.[213] But the Romans nevertheless found it difficult to escape from the idea that property relations were based upon a relationship between *persona* and *res* and they were reluctant to venture beyond a fairly traditional view of things. The paradigm *res* was always physical.[214]

Corporeal and Incorporeal Property

This paradigm of ownership of a physical thing might be said to be the starting point of the civilian law of property.[215] Nevertheless, despite its conceptual simplicity, the Roman notion of *dominium*, particularly when related to other legal notions, can be problematic. The Romans did not, it seems, conceive of ownership as a right (*ius*), but as a direct power relationship with a physical thing (*res incorporalis*) and thus the thing itself became, so to speak, confused with the notion of ownership.[216] The action to recover a physical thing, the *actio in rem*, was, as the name suggests, originally an action against the thing itself and thus the name of the defendant was not mentioned in the action.[217] Furthermore, the thing itself (or something representing it) had to be in court.[218] If D took wrongful possession of P's chalice and would not return it to P, the latter would, in effect, bring an action against the chalice itself. If the judge found P to be the owner he had to order the chalice to be handed back to P.[219] The power of *dominium* was thus located in the 'duty' of the judge to order repossession. Such a law of actions 'duty' could then be extended to a thing of which the plaintiff was not the actual owner.[220] In this situation the power (*potestas*) of ownership was in effect being extended simply by recognising that the plaintiff could bring an action against the *res*. The Romans were getting very close to the idea that ownership was a 'right' (power) over a thing.

With regard to lesser property rights, for example a right to quarry on someone else's land, the theoretical position was ambiguous.[221] Such 'rights' were, on the one hand, legal relations between *persona* and *res* and thus there had to be a tangible physical object.[222] On the other hand, they were also *res incorporales* and thus only existed in law as, so to speak, a 'right' (*ius in re*, as the later civilians called it).[223] Equally, it is almost impossible to envisage this kind of intangible thing without a *persona* and so the object of such a property right is as much the relationship (*ius*) between *persona* and *res* as the *res* to which the *ius* attaches. A *décalage* therefore begins to emerge between the ownership of physical things (*res corporales*) and the ownership of intangible things (*res incorporales*).

Matters became more complicated in the later civil law when the medieval Roman lawyers amalgamated *ius* with *dominium*: ownership then became a right (*ius*) and a kind of *res incorporalis* in itself.[224] In order to avoid this confusion, the medieval Romanists concluded that ownership was to be found in the physical thing, whereas all other real rights were *res incorporales*; one talked of 'my thing' as opposed to 'my right'.[225] One arrives at a situation, bearing in mind that 'goods' (*bona*) are 'things' (*res*) which have been appropriated by a person (*persona*),[226] where 'goods are things, but things are goods only by the rights of which the things form the object; thus it is the rights which are in reality the goods'.[227] All goods are goods only because they are rights. One can then reverse the situation in saying that all rights are goods of a sort (a right *to* something). But the problem with this analysis is that there are, according to the structure of the codes, rights which are not property rights, that is to say rights which are not goods. A contractual right is, for example, a right against some other person; it is a right that is *in personam*.[228] That is to say, it is a right whose object is another person (*persona*) rather than a thing (*res*). The *Code civil*, like the *Institutes* of Gaius, is, however, ambiguous because, although it does distinguish between property and obligation rights, it places the law of obligations (personal rather than real rights) under the general heading of 'things'. This suggests that behind every right there is in fact a 'thing'. However, at the same time, the code retains the Roman notion that ownership devours the *res*; ownership (*la propriété*) is the thing itself.[229] Theorists on the continent are still trying to escape from this paradox.[230] Is ownership simply a right or is it something more?

If it is only a right, this has the effect of reducing it to the level of all rights. It becomes a patrimonial right like any other right. Now, if contractual rights are extended through the gradual abolition of the relative effect of contractual rights (the rule of privity of contract, as English lawyers would call it) this will have the effect of endowing them with an *in rem* flavour. That is to say, they will become effective against third parties. Contractual rights become more like rights good against the whole world. This may not actually destroy the distinction between owing and owning, but it certainly weakens the boundary inasmuch as it interferes with the symmetrical dichotomy between relations between person and person (personal rights) and relations between person and thing (real rights).

Vindication

The Romans themselves were little interested in theorising at an abstract level about the distinction between property and obligations. They, seemingly, provided no definition of *dominium* and gave legal expression to the idea only through the law of actions.[231] It was the *actio in rem* which functioned as the vehicle for ownership and other real rights (*iura in re aliena*) and these claims were alternatively called vindication actions (*rei vindicatio*). They were about asserting a relationship directly against a thing and thus they attached to the thing itself, with the result that, once the thing disappeared, so did the *vindicatio*.[232] Of course, in order to bring the *actio in rem*, the plaintiff had to show that he was either the owner or had some *ius* in the thing;[233] and thus, to this extent, it could be said that the remedy was founded upon a legal 'right'. But title was often tested via the question of who had the *vindicatio* remedy.[234] In contrast, it was the *actio in personam* that gave expression to an obligation relationship, although an obligation was defined by Justinian as a legal chain (*vinculum iuris*) binding two people to perform something.[235] As Gaius observed, one would not use an *actio in personam* to recover one's property 'for what is ours cannot be conveyed to us'.[236] Property 'rights' thus tended to be expressed as matters attaching to the *actio* (and then to the *res* itself) and not as substantive matters concerning ownership.

In the later civil law, when categories were no longer being defined in terms of actions, the idea of a vindication remedy was nevertheless retained. Owners deserved the full protection of the law and they ought thus to be able to claim physical restitution of the things which they owned.[237] In the modern civilian systems, then, a distinction is still made at the level of legal remedies between real and personal actions. Real rights are expressed through the idea that one is asserting a right in a thing rather than against a person and this allows a plaintiff owner in theory to follow (trace) his thing into the hands of others.[238] It is the *res* and not the *persona* that is the subject matter of the remedy and the right.[239] All the same, such a structure, it should be noted, continues to emphasise the distinction between physical things and real rights, since the vindication action presumes the existence of a thing. The *actio in rem* has by definition the need for a *res* and thus was developed in relation to *res corporales*. It can extend to certain types of *res incorporales*, but only where there is some kind of 'thing' that can support the conceptual structure.

Possession

The *rei vindicatio* was a remedy allowing a dispossessed owner to recover possession of his thing. At first sight, therefore, it might appear that the *actio in rem* was a remedy protecting both the legal relation with a thing and the factual relation. The medieval jurists discovered, however, that the two kinds of relationship were sharply distinguished in Roman law. Possession was protected by its own set of quite separate public law (*imperium*) remedies called 'interdicts'. And it was a relationship with a thing that endowed the possessor – even the unworthy possessor – with certain 'rights' *in rem*.[240] As the Roman sources themselves (rather misleadingly) state, possession has nothing in common with ownership.[241] One can be owner without possessing and one can possess without owning.

The distinction was originally seen as being one of fact and law.[242] Possession gave expression to factual detention of a thing[243] – thus there could only ever be one possessor at any given moment[244] – whereas ownership gave expression to a legal relation with the *res*. However, the moment that possession itself was given its own separate regime of protection in the law of actions, possession as a concept no longer expressed a pure situation of fact. Possession became a more subtle notion.[245] Thus someone who was ejected from possession was still considered to be in possession since he could recover the *res* through the interdict remedies (*interdicta*).[246] Moreover, with respect to the possession of an inheritance that might contain no corporeal property, one could talk of legal rather than factual possession.[247] As well as expressing a situation of fact, it was also, then, a notion giving expression to a legal relationship between *persona* and *res*. Person A, although not owner of a thing, might nevertheless have a better 'right' to possess (*ius possessionis*) it than person B and could seek a possessory remedy giving expression to this 'right'.

In addition to this ambiguity, actually defining possession has not been easy and has given rise to much controversy and literature over the centuries.[248] In Roman law, possession was distinguished from *detentio* which meant that the mere transfer of a *res* under, say, a contract of deposit would not pass possession.[249] At the level of definition, one could not possess without both physical control (*corpus*) and mental intent (*animus*) to control,[250] and so Roman possession continued to emphasise the distinction between *res corporales* and *res incorporales*. This distinction became blurred when the later civilians started to see ownership (*dominium*) as a right (*ius*); what one possessed was a right (*ius*) and what one exercised was a right (to possession).[251] If the *actio in rem* was an action giving the owner a right to possession (*ius possessionis*), what kind of right was being protected by an interdict? Roman law provided some help in answering this question, since the sources stated clearly that in cases of disputed ownership the possessor was in the stronger position.[252] Possession and possessory remedies could thus be seen as some kind of procedural prelude to a *vindicatio* action.[253] Another way of viewing the possessory interdicts is through the public–private divide; the protection of possession can be seen as a series of public law remedies designed to keep the peace and to discourage self-help.[254] It is an example of public law protecting private interests for the sake of the general interest.

The problem for the later civilians, however, is that these Roman techniques did not accord with the feudal structure of the late Middle Ages. Land was possessed rather than owned in the Roman sense. Remedies protecting 'possession' could effectively be seen as protecting actual property 'rights'. Each 'right' in its turn could be seen as a form of *dominium*.[255] Possession, in other words, acquired the capacity to become a complex and subtle legal relation in itself. With the decline of feudalism and the ascendancy of Roman law throughout Europe, the emphasis was once again on the sharp distinction between *dominium* and *possessio*. However, the confusion between *ius possessionis* and the object of such a *ius*, namely the possibility of possessing a right (*ius*), was ingrained in legal thought.[256] One could, it seems, have a right to possess (*ius possessionis*), that is to say a *ius in re*. All rights are, in this scheme of thought, capable of being possessed. Yet modern French law actually defines possession as 'the detention or the enjoyment of a *thing or a right* that we hold or that we exercise ourselves or through another who holds it or exercises it in our name'.[257] This seems to be continuing the distinction between physical property and rights.[258]

In fact, one of the main functions of possession is to confer ownership either through a long period of uninterrupted possession[259] or through the appearance of being an owner *vis-à-vis* a third party bona fide purchaser for value.[260] In truth, then, possession does, after all, have important connections both with ownership and with physical objects (for example, consumer goods). This has an impact upon the theory of possession. Is possession simply an adjunct of the law of ownership or is it an independent notion with its own theoretical and social basis? No doubt both theories have their relevance, but two points in particular can be noted. First, possession acts as an essential bridge between the worlds of social fact and legal relation; accordingly, possession as a legal notion has the capacity of turning raw fact (long possession) into legal title (ownership by prescription).[261] Secondly, the distinction between possession and ownership remains rooted as much in the law of actions as in legal theory. Possessory remedies, even in the modern civil law, are distinct both from revindication claims and from personal actions.[262]

Possession therefore assumes an interesting conceptual status. It started life as a descriptive notion but became increasingly normative as it attracted its own remedies; this resulted in possession acquiring the status of a right (*ius*). Now, in relation to the concept of a right, it has a tendency to retain its descriptive identity. It is a situation of fact that ought to be maintained by public law remedies probably designed to ensure the keeping of the peace. However, the moment that one brings together the law of actions and possession under the rubric of a 'right', complexity sets in around the notion of the right itself. Is it a right to the *res*? Is it an entitlement to an abstract 'thing' (*ius*), that is to say a 'right' detached from the *res*? Or is possession itself a relationship now endowed with a normative dimension? This may all seem academic, if not scholastic,[263] yet it represents a confusion of ideas that itself is a cause of serious complexity at the heart of 'rights' talk. In the area of time-share apartments, does one own a right to possession for a limited period every year? And can one possess the right to possession? If D takes possession of an apartment during the period when P has his or her exclusive possession, has D taken possession of the *res* or of the *ius*?

Universals

The Roman emphasis on the physical thing gave rise to another problem.[264] What exactly was owned and (or) possessed where the physical thing consisted of, or contained, other things? If one owned a house did one own, as well, all the things in the house? If one possessed a library or a flock, what exactly did one possess: the thing as a whole or its individual parts? The Romans recognised the problem and so distinguished between three types of physical things (*corpora*): a single unitary thing such as a branch or stone; a constructed thing such as a house or a ship; and a thing consisting of individual things such as a flock or a legion.[265] The problem was more complex where *res corporales* became mixed with *res incorporales* within a single mass which itself was viewed as an independent 'thing'. That is to say, the two types of property formed part of a person's 'goods' (*bona*)[266] which in turn was seen as an asset which could be valued in terms of money[267] and described as a person's patrimony (*patrimonium*).[268] In Roman law the classic example of such a universality was the estate of a dead person (*hereditas*); this was a distinct 'thing' (*universitas*) protected by its own *actio in rem* which would be applicable even with respect to the personal obligations contained in the estate.[269] A marriage dowry and slave's *peculium* were conceived of in a similar way: each was a *universitas*, a kind of mini patrimony (*patrimonium pusillum*).[270]

This form of abstract thinking was to prove fundamental to commercial property law, in that it established the idea, not just of a general asset or 'thing' made up of other things, but of a patrimony that remained constant while the individual things within it came and went. The Romans drew an analogy with a boat or a legion where every plank or every soldier changes over a long period but one still had the same 'thing',[271] since one thing could be substituted (subrogated) for another.[272] The commercial aspect to this conceptual structure becomes clearer when one views a slave and his *peculium* as an independent 'company' with an independent patrimony. One is getting very close to the idea of an independent trading patrimony which can be born, grow and die,[273] and which provided a limited liability for the master.[274] The notion of a patrimony became even more commercially creative when associated with a *universitas personarum*, that is to say a group of persons viewed as a single *persona*. Colleges and towns, for example, were treated as if they were a single person in the legal plan and thus could sue and be sued as an entity.[275] The medieval jurists developed these Roman ideas into a *corpus fictum* since, as we have mentioned, universals did not exist according to the late medieval philosophers; what existed were only the individual things. Thus the separation between the *universitas* and the individual things was complete: things could come and go with ease, but the *universitas* would remain the same. When the same intellectual thinking was applied to groups of people, the medieval jurists developed, to accompany the *universitas rerum*, a *persona ficta*; the elements of the modern commercial trading and property company were now becoming even clearer.[276]

Subrogation

The structural idea that one *res* can be substituted for another within a *universitas rerum* can also be applied to the notion of a *res* itself. That is to say, if a thing is envisaged not as a physical object but as an intangible idea (*res incorporalis*) there is no reason in principle why one physical thing cannot be substituted for another. Such substitution need not destroy the existing *persona* and *res* proprietary relationship. For example, O is the owner of a gold chalice which he swaps for an ornate silver one of similar value: could it not be envisaged that the actual legal relationship between O and 'chalice' remains unchanged? That is to say, can the idea of a 'chalice' be divorced from the physical object? In a commercial context such a possibility has very real advantages since, for example, it means that a creditor can take out a real security right (*in rem*) over a commercial asset without immobilising the asset itself. A business can continue to trade while its creditors continue to enjoy rights *in rem* over the stock-in-trade. The Romans themselves never reached this level of sophistication and the actual development of real subrogation was the work of the medieval Roman lawyers who formulated the maxim *res succedit pretio et pretium rei* (the thing succeeds the price and the price the thing).[277] However, Roman law certainly provided the conceptual building blocks for such ideas.[278] The original contribution of the Post-glossators was to hold that the second *res* not only replaced the first but also took on its nature: *subrogatum capit naturam subrogati*.[279]

By way of analogy, a similar substitution can be made at the other end of the proprietary relationship, so to speak. One *persona* can be substituted for another. If one person pays a debt secured by a right *in rem* on behalf of another person, it is conceptually possible to allow the person who has paid off the creditor to be subrogated to the relationship *in rem*. Such a substitution will have the effect of giving the person who has paid off the debt the security enjoyed by the original creditor. This type of subrogation was originally based upon a contract and thus there had to be an *in personam* relationship between the original debtor and the payer stipulating that the latter would take over the security.[280] Later civilians allowed such a substitution by operation of law.[281] Personal subrogation thus became an important personal right outside of the law of contract.

Subrogation, particularly real subrogation, is, however, more complex than it might at first seem, since it raises the question of what is being revindicated. Is it the physical *res* itself or is it the right, the *res incorporalis*? Such a question comes close to undermining the whole dichotomy between rights *in rem* and *in personam*, in that, the moment one says that it is the *res incorporalis* (the right to security) that is being revindicated, one is coming close to allowing a real action for the debt itself.[282] Real subrogation, when applied to a sum of money that has replaced a piece of property in a patrimony, becomes in effect an *actio in rem* for a debt. One theory, in other words, undermines another.

The Conceptual Success of the Codes

Such a theoretical contradiction illustrates how the internal structure of modern continental private law is, on closer examination, rather more complex than the general categories of persons, things and obligations might at first suggest. Ideas that were basically rather straightforward in Roman law itself became distorted through the theoretical contortions of the later civilians. These civilians were keen not only to adapt Roman structures to the quite different social conditions of the late Middle Ages, but to discover the supposed truths hidden beneath the institutions of the classical world. One major structural distortion was the movement away from the law of actions; for the *actio* actually provided the basic institution by which the Roman scheme made sense. Once one tried to explain *dominium, possessio, obligatio* and *iura in re* uniquely through the substantive idea of a *ius* itself, problems were bound to occur, since the theorists were investing the universal notion of *ius* with the *dominium* idea of power (*potestas*). All rights became things to be revindicated.

Matters were made even more complex when the word *ius* (right) was injected with a more subjective meaning by the Enlightenment and post-Enlightenment philosophers. Attempts to analyse institutional relationships like possession in terms of subjective right were bound to cause theoretical difficulties and they continue to do so.[283] For the subjective right – itself traceable back, as we have mentioned, to the merging of *ius* with *dominium*[284] – had transcended the law of property to become a general normative concept applicable throughout private law. In other words, all law had become 'property' law, since all law concerned 'rights' (*iura*) and all rights were founded ultimately on the notion of *dominium*.

Nevertheless, the structural contribution of both Roman law and the modern Romanists to the internal plan of private law must never be underestimated. It is not so much the rules as the institutional structure that is important. The distinctions between ownership and possession, between property and obligations, between the universal and the singular, between rights and remedies and so on are part of a structural framework. And this structural framework is vital for understanding not just the organisation of legal rules and principles but also, and perhaps more importantly, the organisation of facts. Property, obligations and rights are notions for understanding the social world and it was the civilians that sought to impose this world-view on a non-Roman Europe. The codes and their structure are a measure of their success.[285]

Notes

1 Granger (1995, p. 111).
2 Villa (1990, p. 84).
3 Bergel (1999, p. 178).
4 Ibid.
5 Ibid., pp. 178–80.
6 See, for example, Sale of Goods Act 1979, s. 14.
7 Justinian, *Constitutio Deo Auctore* 11; *Constitutio Omnen* pr.
8 For a relatively recent and new translation, see Gordon and Robinson (1988).
9 For relatively recent and new translations, see Thomas (1975); Birks and McLeod (1987).
10 See, generally, Honoré (1962).
11 See, generally, Samuel (1994).
12 Stein (1988, pp. 73–82).
13 Stein (1983, p. 156).
14 G.1.8; J.1.2.12; D.1.5.1.
15 Stein (1983, pp. 157–8).
16 Jolowicz (1957, p. 71).
17 See, for example, H.F. Jolowicz (1957, pp. 61–81).
18 Ibid., p. 69.
19 Ibid., p. 73.
20 Ibid., pp. 75ff.
21 See, generally, Samuel (2001). And see Arbitration Act 1996, s. 48.
22 Stein (1983, p. 158).
23 See NCPC, arts 12, 30–31.
24 Watson (1994, p. 5).
25 Cf. Bergel (1999, p. 178).
26 See, generally, Van Warmelo (1983).

27 See D.22.6.2.
28 See, generally, D.50.17.
29 Kelley (1990, p. 49).
30 D.1.1.10pr.
31 D.6.1.9.
32 Bergel (1999, p. 178).
33 Kelley (1990, p. 49).
34 Ellul (1982a, pp. 17–28).
35 See, for example, Stein (1984).
36 Ellul (1982a, p. 27).
37 Ellul (1984, pp. 480–81). And see generally Duff (1938).
38 But note the curious position of a trade union in English law: it can bring or defend an *actio* and it can contract, but statute decrees that it is not a body corporate: Trade Union and Labour Relations (Consolidation) Act 1992, s. 10. It is described as having 'quasi-corporate status'.
39 D.50.16.16.
40 With respect to an English trade union, its property has to be owned by trustees: Trade Union and Labour Relations (Consolidation) Act 1992, s. 12.
41 Ellul (1984, pp. 481–4). And see, generally, Patault (1989).
42 G.2.14.
43 See, for example, Ginossar (1960).
44 G.4.2–4.
45 D.44.7.3pr.
46 G.2.14.
47 This point seems to have been appreciated by Ulpian (D.1.3.41).
48 D.50.16.208.
49 See, generally, Villey (1975) and Tuck (1979) but cf. Tierney (1997).
50 D.1.4.1.
51 Samuel (1994, pp. 40–42).
52 D.1.1.7.
53 G.1.5.
54 De Ste-Croix (1981, pp. 391, 399).
55 D.14.2.9.
56 D.41.2.2.
57 D.4.3.15.1.
58 D.50.16.16. But cf. Trade Union and Labour Relations (Consolidation) Act 1992, s. 10.
59 Ellul (1982a, p. 27).
60 D.1.4.1.
61 C.7.37.3.
62 Ullmann (1975b, p. 218).
63 Tierney (1982, pp. 42, 43, 44).
64 Ellul (1982a, pp. 344–9). And see, generally, Ullmann (1975b).
65 Ellul (1982a, p. 345).
66 Ibid., p. 349.
67 Ibid., pp. 345–6.
68 Ullmann (1975a, p. 31).
69 Kelly (1992, pp. 385, 386).

70 Lefebvre-Teillard (1996, pp. 48–50).
71 In particular the torts of trespass to the person and defamation; but see also *Khorasandjian* v. *Bush* [1993] QB 727.
72 *Ex parte Island Records* [1978] Ch 122.
73 D.1.5.2.
74 See, generally, Foucault (1966, pp. 137–76).
75 Berman (1983, p. 139).
76 Laurioux and Moulinier (1998, p. 92).
77 Villey (1975, pp. 533–6).
78 On which see, generally, Stein (1988, pp. 73–82).
79 Imbert (1996, pp. 68–9).
80 See, generally, Kelley (1990).
81 Kelley (1984, p. 128).
82 See, for example, Leroux and Marciano (1998, pp. 15–18).
83 Dubouchet (1990, pp. 144–5).
84 See, for example, CC, art. 1382.
85 See, for example, BGB § 823.
86 See, for example, *Caparo Industries plc* v. *Dickman* [1990] 2 AC 605.
87 See, for example, *Blackpool & Fylde Aero Club Ltd* v. *Blackpool BC* [1990] 1 WLR 1195.
88 See, for example, CC, art. 1384.
89 See, for example, Swiss Code of Obligations, art. 62.
90 Jones (1940, pp. 69–75).
91 Dworkin (1977, p. 85).
92 Dworkin (1977, pp. 82–8).
93 For the history of the notion of a 'right' (*ius*), see Villey (1975), Tuck (1979), Tierney (1997).
94 G.2.14.
95 Jolowicz (1957, pp. 61–81).
96 D.1.5.2.
97 D.1.3.41. See also D.1.1.11–12.
98 Leca (2000, p. 233). But note now Tierney's view on the importance of Ockham: Tierney (1997).
99 NBW Book 3.
100 See, for example, *Moorgate Mercantile Ltd* v. *Twitchings* [1977] AC 890.
101 The term right (*droit subjectif*) is developed from the Roman law term *ius*. In Roman law itself *ius* did not mean 'right' in the modern sense; it meant, among other things (D.1.1.11), a legal connection (D.1.1.12). Originally, it gave expression to an objective legal relation flowing between two people or between a person and a thing. However, such a relation came, in late Roman law, to give expression to substantive 'rights' in the sense of entitlements at the level of the law of actions. *Actio autem nihil aliud est, quam jus persequendi judicio, quod sibi debetur* (J.4.6pr; D.44.7.51). This is clearly a major development, but *ius* was never seen as a form of *potestas* (power) by the Roman jurists (D.1.1.11). Power was, instead, to be found in the two key concepts of *dominium* (ownership) and *imperium* (sovereignty) (D.50.16.215). Now the Romans never identified *dominium* with *ius*; this was a development brought about by the later civilians (see Tuck, 1979 but cf. Tierney, 1997). Thus the Post-glossators (13th–14th centuries) in attempting

to Romanise feudal relations with land ended up by seeing *dominium* as a form of *ius*. Ownership became a kind of 'super real right' with the implication that all other *iura* were lesser, but still powerful, 'rights'; in other words, *iura* (rights) had become powers which all persons had in relation to things (*res*) (Zenati and Revet, 1997, p. 134). This was an important development since, not only was *dominium* a power relation in itself, but the power was given expression in law through a *vindicatio* claim, the paradigm *actio in rem*. Once P had established that he was owner of a thing in the wrongful possession of another, the judge had to order the thing to be redelivered to P (D.6.1.9). *Ius* thus became infected with this ability to *vindicate* something. This 'something' (*res*) was also capable of abstraction, since the Romans themselves had recognised intangible things as forms of property (*res incorporales*). The medieval lawyers accordingly provided the structural foundation in law for the development of *ius* as a power relation, as a legal relation giving expression to vindicate a claim for a rarefied 'thing'. Rights are thus property talk.

102 Dworkin (1985), extracted in Lloyd and Freeman (1994, p. 434).

103 See Hoffmann LJ in *R* v. *Central Television plc* [1994] 3 WLR 20.

104 See, for example, *Foskett* v. *McKeown* [2001] 1 AC 102.

105 Samuel (1987).

106 Human Rights Act 1998.

107 See, for example, *Camelot Group plc* v. *Centaur Communications Ltd* [1999] QB 124; *Ashworth Hospital Authority* v. *MGN Ltd* [2001] 1 WLR 515.

108 *In re K (A Child)* [2001] 2 WLR 1141, 1175 per Judge LJ.

109 Hohfeld (1919, p. 36).

110 Ibid., p. 38.

111 See, generally, Villey (1975, pp. 656–7).

112 See, for example, D.6.1.9.

113 J.3.13pr.

114 G.2.12–14.

115 Law of Property Act 1925, s. 205(1)(xx).

116 Weir (2000, p. 38).

117 Ibid.

118 Pearson LJ in *Chapman* v. *Honig* [1963] 2 QB 502, 520.

119 Treitel (1988, para. 9).

120 On the notion of an interest, see Ost (1990).

121 D.1.6.2.

122 Ost (1990, pp. 139–50).

123 See, for example, CC, art. 388–2; *In re L (A Child)* [2001] 2 WLR 339.

124 See, for example, CC, art. 16–3.

125 See, for example, *Airedale NHS Trust* v. *Bland* [1993] AC 789; *In re S* [1995] 3 WLR 78.

126 See, for example, CC, arts 117, 232.

127 See, for example, CC, arts 220–1, 264–1.

128 Jolowicz (1983).

129 CE 30.3.1916; D.1916.3.25.

130 See, for example, *Miller* v. *Jackson* [1977] QB 966, 981–2.

131 See, for example, *Camelot Group plc* v. *Centaur Communications Ltd* [1999] QB 124.

132 *Surrey CC* v. *Bredero Homes Ltd* [1993] 1 WLR 1361, 1369.
133 See, for example, Cane (1996).
134 Samuel (2001, pp. 87–9, 117–22).
135 See, for example, Animals (Scientific Procedures) Act 1986, s. 5(3)(c).
136 Supreme Court Act 1981, s. 31(3).
137 See NCPC, art. 31; CC, art. 184.
138 Cappelletti (1989, p. 271).
139 See, for example, Control of Misleading Advertisements Regulations 1988, reg. 6(1), (3).
140 D.1.1.1.2.
141 Glidewell LJ in *R* v. *Education Secretary, Ex p. Avon CC* [1991] 1 QB 558, 561.
142 See, for example, CC, art. 287; *In re L (A Child)* [2001] 2 WLR 339.
143 See, for example, *Nouveau code de procédure civile*, art. 31; Supreme Court Act 1981, s. 31(3).
144 See, for example, *American Cyanamid Co* v. *Ethicon Ltd* [1975] AC 396; *Jackson* v. *Horizon Holidays Ltd* [1975] 1 WLR 1468.
145 Ionescu (1978, p. 143).
146 Pound (1959, pp. 5–373); for a short summary see Jolowicz (1963, pp. 175–9).
147 D.9.2.52.2.
148 *Ex parte Island Records* [1978] Ch 122, 136.
149 Ibid., p. 137.
150 *Hill* v. *CA Parsons & Co* [1972] Ch 305, 316.
151 See, for example, Lord Denning's judgment in *Miller* v. *Jackson* [1977] QB 966.
152 Certoma (1985, pp. 20–24).
153 Bell (2001, p. 77).
154 D.1.1.1.2.
155 But cf. Leca (2000, pp. 153–61).
156 Van Caenegem (1995, pp. 72–107); Tierney (1982).
157 Mestre (1985, pp. 106–8).
158 D.49.14.28.
159 D.2.1.3.
160 Lefebvre-Teillard (1996, pp. 99–100).
161 D.2.14.7.14.
162 D.2.14.38.
163 D.1.4.1.
164 D.1.4.1.1.
165 D.1.3.7.
166 For a useful overview, see Jolowicz (1963, pp. 15–27, 106–18).
167 Although this does not mean that countries adopting the convention into their legal systems will allow it to trump the power of the legislator: see Human Rights Act 1998, s. 4; *In re K* [2001] 2 WLR 1141, 1172–3.
168 Borkowski (1997, pp. 168–9).
169 Hilaire (1986, pp. 59–69).
170 Joerges (1998).
171 Barbiéri (1995, pp. 9–10).
172 Van der Merwe and De Waal (1993, no. 14).

173 D.44.7.3pr.
174 Jolowicz (1957, pp. 61–2).
175 Lévy (1972, pp. 35–6).
176 Ibid., pp. 44–6.
177 Ullmann (1975b, p. 216); Van Caenegem (1995, p. 77).
178 See, for example, Sale of Goods Act 1979, ss. 16–18.
179 Samuel (1999a, 1999b).
180 Stein (1984, pp. 77–9); Van Caenegem (1992, pp. 35–8).
181 Van Caenegem (1988, pp. 88–93).
182 See, generally, Berman (1983); Leca (2000, pp. 203–20).
183 See, generally, Ullmann (1975b).
184 There was also political opposition to Romanisation (Van Caenegem, 1992, pp. 80–83).
185 Patault (1989, pp. 21–3).
186 Zenati and Revet (1997, pp. 133–5, 245–6).
187 'If Gaius had known of customary law seisin he would have classed it under incorporeal things, *jura*' (Patault, 1989, p. 22).
188 Patault (1989, p. 19).
189 Ourliac and De Malafosse (1971, pp. 156–62).
190 Patault (1989, pp. 110–11).
191 Ourliac and De Malafosse (1971, p. 159).
192 Legohérel (1994, pp. 48–63).
193 D.1.4.1pr.
194 Hilaire (1986, p. 16).
195 Laurent (1993, p. 19).
196 Ibid., pp. 21–4; but see Tierney (1997).
197 Ibid., p. 24.
198 D.39.2.19.
199 CC, art. 544.
200 Patault (1989, pp. 142–3).
201 Villey (1975, pp. 671–2).
202 Halpérin (1996, p. 25).
203 G.4.4.
204 CC, art. 544.
205 *Waverley BC* v. *Fletcher* [1996] QB 334.
206 G.2.13.
207 G.2.14.
208 Law of Property Act 1925, s. 205(1)(xx).
209 Lawson (1980, pp. 147–60).
210 *Lipkin Gorman* v. *Karpnale Ltd* [1991] 2 AC 548.
211 *Ex parte Island Records* [1978] Ch 122.
212 *Kingdom of Spain* v. *Christie, Mason & Woods Ltd* [1986] 1 WLR 1120.
213 See, for example, D.6.3.1.1.
214 This view has been bequeathed to German law: Van de Merwe and De Waal (1993, no. 14).
215 Van de Merwe and De Waal (1993, no. 103).
216 Patault (1989, pp. 17–18); Zenati and Revet (1997, pp. 133–5).
217 Buckland (1963, p. 677).
218 G.4.16–17.

219 D.6.1.9.
220 See D.6.3.1.1.
221 Van de Merwe and De Waal (1993, nos 42–3).
222 D.7.1.2 (*ius in corpore*).
223 *Usus fructus est ius alienis rebus utendi fruendi* (D.7.1.1). See also D.39.2.19pr.
224 See, generally, Villey (1975, pp. 381–2, 672).
225 Zenati and Revet (1997, pp. 58–9).
226 Cf. D.50.16.49.
227 Zenati and Revet (1997, p. 19).
228 Van de Merwe and De Waal (1993, no. 43).
229 See, for example, CC, art. 644.
230 Zenati and Revet (1997, pp. 133–42).
231 See in particular D.6.3.1.1.
232 J.2.1.26; D.5.3.16.8. Note also that the *actio in rem* could not be used to enforce the return of consumable goods (which included money: D.7.5.5.1) since ownership in these goods passed on delivery; restitution could be enforced only through the law of obligations (G.3.90).
233 D.7.6.5pr.
234 See, for example, D.39.6.29.
235 J.3.13pr.
236 G.4.4.
237 Zenati and Revet (1997, pp. 201–30).
238 Cf. CC, art. 2279.
239 See, for example, CC, art. 644.
240 D.41.2.53; D.43.17.2.
241 D.41.2.12.1.
242 Van de Merwe and De Waal (1993, no. 53).
243 *Possessio plurimum facti habet* (D.4.6.19).
244 D.41.2.3.5.
245 Van de Merwe and De Waal (1993, no. 53).
246 D.41.2.17.
247 D.37.1.3.1.
248 Definition may in truth be impossible (Van de Merwe and De Waal, 1993, no. 63).
249 D.16.3.17.1; D.41.2.3.18.
250 D.41.2.3.1.
251 Van de Merwe and De Waal (1993, no. 53).
252 D.50.17.128pr.
253 D.41.2.35.
254 See, for example, D.43.16.1.1.
255 Ourliac and De Malafosse (1971, p. 240).
256 Van de Merwe and De Waal (1993, no. 53).
257 CC, art. 2228, emphasis added.
258 Zenati and Revet (1997, p. 336).
259 CC, art. 2229.
260 CC, art. 2279.
261 Borowski (1997, pp. 162–3).
262 CC, art. 2283; NCPC, art. 1265.

263 Van de Merwe and De Waal (1993, no. 53).
264 Ibid., no. 30.
265 D.41.3.30pr.
266 D.50.16.49.
267 D.50.16.5.
268 D.27.1.30.1.
269 D.5.3.25.18.
270 D.15.1.5.3.
271 D.5.1.76.
272 D.15.1.32.1.
273 D.15.1.40.
274 D.15.1.41.
275 D.50.16.16.
276 Ourliac and De Malafosse (1971, pp. 63–6).
277 Zenati and Revet (1997, pp. 107–8).
278 See, for example, D.4.2.18.
279 Zenati and Revet (1997, p. 108).
280 C.8.19.1.
281 Ourliac and De Malafosse (1969, pp. 241–2).
282 Zenati and Revet (1997, p. 223).
283 Ibid., p. 337.
284 Tuck (1979, pp. 5–31).
285 Bell (2001, p. 77).

5 Facts and Law

The relationship between law and fact is at the heart of this enquiry. The role of institutions and concepts, as we have seen in the last chapter, is central to an epistemological and methodological investigation of law, in that they act as bridges between the worlds of law and social fact. Equally, legal categories, which will be examined in the following chapter, mediate between a factual situation and the law applicable. Indeed a final chapter (Chapter 8) will look more generally at the whole relationship between social science and social phenomena. However, what makes the relationship between law and fact so complex is that much will depend upon how one envisages not just law but facts themselves.[1] Is law a science in the natural science sense of explaining and predicting social phenomena? Or is it just a body of norms or rules ('ought' propositions) which apply themselves – or have to be applied – to particular social situations? And how do such rules get applied to facts? With regard to the facts themselves, do such facts arise independently, or relatively independently, of law or are they fully, or in part, constructed by legal discourse itself? And, indeed, what is a fact? Is it, for example, a fact that forests exist or is 'forest' simply a name and that only trees exist? It has been suggested in previous chapters that facts are at least in part constructed through legal institutions, since the object of legal science is not a set of social facts arising independently of the science. Law, like the natural sciences, constructs schemes or models of facts. However, little 'empirical' evidence has so far been produced to support this thesis and so the purpose of this chapter is to investigate facts from, so to speak, the inside.

Facts and the Rule Model

If knowledge of law is envisaged as propositional knowledge – that is to say, as a matter of rules, principles and (or) norms – then this suggests that facts are independent, or relatively independent, of this body of knowledge. One talks of rules existing as a distinct body even if this distinct body is in turn envisaged as a social fact itself.[2] This is not to suggest, of course, that rule theorists deny any close link between law and society. Often it is quite the opposite; law is envisaged as arising out of social fact.[3] Yet the point that needs stressing is that the rule model envisages law as text (written or even unwritten general principles) and thus the role of the lawyer is one of applying these texts – these rules and principles – to factual situations.

Rules and the Syllogism

How does such an application occur? The traditional thesis that accompanies the rule model is that legal method is the process of applying rules to facts and the way this is achieved is, as we have seen in an earlier chapter, through the device of the syllogism. In French law, for example, the role of the *Cour de cassation* is, according to traditional theory, simply to apply rules:

> In order to understand the very particular role of the *Cour de cassation* it is necessary to start from this idea that every judicial decision is the conclusion from a syllogism habitually called the '*legal syllogism*'. The major premise is the rule of law, the minor the mass of facts which condition the application of this rule: the conclusion which flows from them is then the judgment.[4]

This approach is rooted, as we have seen, in the cultural history of the civil law. The method resulted from the knowledge revolution that occurred during the Enlightenment, when professors trained in both law and mathematics believed that the latter discipline held the key to the former. These professors developed systems which 'consisted of ignoring anything observable or inducible from observation, and presented natural law down to its finest details as a matter of strict deduction from higher axioms, with all the severity of geometrical proof'.[5] The *mos geometricus* was to establish the syllogism as the methodological means of relating law to fact, fact itself having been reduced to a logical premise.[6]

The common law tradition was in many important ways very different. It is not a history of university-trained jurists developing their systems and, through their students, secreting them into legal practice. Nevertheless, the civil law thinking was not without some influence and the rule model was firmly established in England by influential legal theorists such as Blackstone and John Austin.[7] The result is that the rule model is still the dominant model in the modern common law. In turn, this implies the syllogism. Thus, according to Lord Simon of Glaisdale:

> A judicial decision will often be reached by a process of reasoning which can be reduced into a sort of complex syllogism, with the major premise consisting of a pre-existing rule of law (either statutory or judge-made) and with the minor premise consisting of the material facts of the case under immediate consideration. The conclusion is the decision of the case, which may or may not establish new law – in the vast majority of cases it will be merely the application of existing law to the facts judicially ascertained.[8]

However, the 'complex syllogism' does, seemingly, differ from the legal syllogism used by the French lawyers, in that the facts of precedents have to be accommodated within the premises. This adds a new reasoning dimension, as Lord Simon recognised:

> Where the decision does constitute new law, this may or may not be expressly stated as a proposition of law: frequently the new law will appear only from subsequent comparison of, on the one hand, the material facts inherent in the major premise with, on the other, the material facts which constitute the minor premise. As a result of this comparison it will often be apparent that a rule has been extended by an analogy expressed or implied.[9]

Lord Simon went on to illustrate the role of analogy with an example from the law of tort:

> I take as an example ... *National Telephone Co* v. *Baker* [1893] 2 Ch 186. Major premise: the rule in *Rylands* v. *Fletcher* (1866) LR 1 Exch 265, (1868) LR 3 HL 330. Minor premise: the defendant brought and stored electricity on his land for his own purpose; it escaped from the land; in so doing it injured the plaintiff's property. Conclusion: the defendant is liable in damages to the plaintiff (or would have been but for statutory protection). Analysis shows that the conclusion establishes a rule of law, which may be stated as 'for the purpose of the rule in *Rylands* v. *Fletcher* electricity is analogous to water' or 'electricity is within the rule in *Rylands* v. *Fletcher*'. That conclusion is now available as the major premise in the next case, in which some substance may be in question which in this context is not perhaps clearly analogous to water but is clearly analogous to electricity. In this way, legal luminaries are constituted which guide the wayfarer across uncharted ways.[10]

Lord Simon's analysis might look logical enough. That is to say, it gives the impression that the conclusion that an escape of electricity gives rise prima facie to liability results from the logical application of the rule in *Rylands* v. *Fletcher* to the facts. Moreover, it is possible to claim an apparent inference in Lord Simon's example once one treats both water and electricity as 'things' brought onto land which escape. For Blackburn J's rule stated 'that the true rule of law is, that the person who for his own purposes brings on his lands and collects and keeps there *anything* likely to do mischief if it escapes, must keep it in at his peril, and, if he does not do so, is prima facie answerable for all the damage which is the natural consequence of its escape'.[11] However, the inference as a deductive method functioning without reference to empirical experience or other exterior source is an illusion. And what is valuable about Lord Simon's analysis is that it indicates how the reference to a world beyond the rule model functions. It is a question of analogy which, in turn, is a matter of image (non-symbolic knowledge) rather than proposition. The person who brings on to his land and keeps there electricity is prima facie liable for its escape because electricity is *analogous* to water, and water was the main factual focal point in *Rylands* itself. But why is electricity analogous to water? What universal proposition dictates that it should be so? In arriving at the conclusion that electricity is within the proposition of law dictated by precedent, the reasoning has gone outside the formal model of rules. It has gone beyond the syllogism. It is not therefore inferred from the rule model itself. In order to understand the reason why a person may be liable in the law of tort for keeping electricity which has escaped and done damage, one will need to have knowledge beyond the rules of the law of tort. One will need to know something about the factual relationship between water and electricity.

Language and Interpretation (Ars Hermeneutica)

One response to this thesis might be to say that, while it is true that the reasoning has gone beyond the syllogism, it has not gone beyond the rules, since rules are expressed in language and whether or not electricity is within the rule is simply a matter of interpretation. Does the word 'anything' in Blackburn J's rule include electricity? This interpretation thesis is extremely powerful and influential and has largely displaced, in the civil law world, the deductive inference approach. The application of the legal rule (an empirical fact) is, according to some theorists, achieved through the medium of a norm (a metaphysical 'ought') and in order to discover the relevant norm within a factual situation an interpretation of the text (rule) in relation to the facts is required. Interpretation is application through the concretisation of the legal norm to the circumstances of each case.[12] The process has been well described by Bengoetxea (who does not himself adhere to the theory). Legal interpretation 'becomes the process through which a legal provision (a text) is transformed into a norm by means of the ascription of meaning'; and it 'follows that there are no norms before interpretation, only texts or provisions which will tendentially become norms once a given meaning is concretized for them'.[13] The process is not one of *ars mathematica* but of *ars hemeneutica*. In order to apply the rule in *Rylands* to a situation of escaping electricity, one interprets the norm in relation to the facts and it is the interpretation itself which determines the conclusion. Interpretation of language, and the norm within it, is the technique by which it is applied to a factual situation.

The theory of interpretation is, as we have seen, extremely important for both civil law and common law. In the civil law, with its emphasis on statutory texts, the relevance is evident; case law *is* statutory interpretation. However, it would be an error to think that statutory interpretation is a secondary activity in the common law; nine out of ten appeal cases concern the meaning of words in a statute or regulation,[14] and even those cases involving precedents could well be seen as interpretation cases. Many commercial problems involve the interpretation of written contracts and it is theoretically feasible, as has been seen, to reduce the *ratio decidendi* to a rule in need of interpretation. Much legal method can, therefore, seemingly be reduced to interpretation. Indeed, according to Ronald Dworkin, law itself is no more nor less than interpretation; law is an interpretative concept.[15] The point to notice about this focusing on interpretation as the key to legal conclusions is that it reinforces the rule model of legal knowledge. The starting point for law is a body of linguistic propositions (rules and principles) which cause difficulty only because language is ambiguous. Adjudication is, according to this view, a matter of resolving the ambiguities within the language knowledge system. Certainly, a philosopher such as Dworkin is going further, in that he puts the emphasis as much upon the interpretative process itself as on the rules and principles. But even for Dworkin legal reasoning is about rights and rights are defined in terms of rules and principles.[16]

But what is meant by interpretation and how does it relate to legal method in general? The answer to this question is by no means simple, if only because, to appreciate interpretation as a scheme of intelligence, it needs to be placed in the context of a whole range of schemes used in social science (see Chapter 8). Interpretation, or the hermeneutical scheme of intelligence, can thus be compared with the causal, the structural, the systems and (or) the dialectical schemes.[17] An interpretative, or hermeneutical (*ars hermeneutica*), approach is one where knowledge consists in the combination of two 'realities', the signifier and the signified. The signifier is usually a form of symbolic knowledge, that is to say a set of mathematical signs or a natural language, which expresses a further form of knowledge (norms) which lies beyond the signifier but is fully expressed by the signifier. The job of the interpreter is to tease out of the signifier, out of the symbolic knowledge (language), this further knowledge element (norm).

In comparison with the syllogism, where if A=B and B=C then necessarily A=C, the hermeneutical scheme involves an active role of a mediator (interpreter) in the process of deciding if A=C. Being given that A=B, whether A=C depends upon whether B incorporates C. However, this can be answered not only in combining A with B and B with C, but in treating A+B as a single element of knowledge.[18] Now, with respect to law, the signifier (A incorporating B) will normally be a legal text such as a statutory provision or a case law principle and the signified (B, perhaps or perhaps not incorporating C) will be the factual world expressed by the textual provision. The job of the interpreter will be to tease out of the text the depths of knowledge beyond the mere surface appearance. Thus the rule in *Rylands* v. *Fletcher* can be described as A+B where A is the actual rule as expressed by Blackburn J and B is the water which formed the main factual object in the precedent. C is the electricity which forms the factual object in the case before the court. Does A(+B)=C?

According to the hermeneutical scheme the emphasis, in answering this question, is normally on A inasmuch as A represents the text and the job of the interpreter is to interpret the text. Indeed, even B, the water, becomes a part of A in being reduced to a rule, as Lord Simon observed. He says that, for the purposes of the rule in *Rylands* v. *Fletcher*, there is a sub-rule that 'anything' includes water. The text represents the knowledge (and thus to have knowledge of law is to have knowledge of legal texts). This is not to say, of course, that such an interpreter is necessarily confined to a single text; reference may well be made to other texts, perhaps even to propositions that lie outside of law. But it is the text which forms the immediate and manifest object of knowledge and it is the interpreter who is the means of application. With the failure of the *mos geometricus* logical scheme of intelligence, the hermeneutical approach has an obvious attraction for the civil law tradition. The codes and texts remain the foundation of legal knowledge, only the methodology has changed. Does the norm behind the text encompass the facts of the concrete case?

The law reports in modern civil law bear witness to this change of method. Take, for example, the following problem which, by chance, has arisen at identical times in both France and England. The tenant of premises dies, having lived within a stable homosexual relationship for many years: can the surviving partner claim, under legislation, that the tenancy be transferred to him? A French legislative text lays down that 'at the time of the death of the tenant, the contract of lease passes (...) to the established partner (*concubin notoire*) who was living with him or her for more than a year at the date of the death'. The advocate general, in the report delivered to the *Cour de cassation*, is quite clear in its methodology:

> At the end of this study, I conclude that, on this pure legal question, the decision of the Paris Court of Appeal has given a too restrictive definition to the term '*concubin notoire*' in art. 14 of the law of 6 July by adding a condition which does not feature in it. This interpretation does not correspond any longer to the state of our society, to the orientation of our law which has created a right to accommodation, and to the wishes of Parliament since the problem would not have arisen if art. 62 of the law of 27 January 1993 had not been invalidated by the *Conseil constitutionnel* for a simple reason of parliamentary procedure and not on the substantive question that you are going to decide.

And the advocate general concluded: 'Without waiting for an eventual intervention of the legislature, the simple interpretation of the law will allow you to adapt your case law to the actual social reality. I am then for the quashing of the referred decision.'[19] In fact, the supreme court itself rejected the advocate general's view, and in the time-honoured form of the syllogism.[20] But it is clear from the whole approach of the advocate general that law is not a question of mathematical logic; the approach is one that is closer to Dworkin. Of course, Dworkin is nowhere mentioned by the French jurists. However, in the English version of this problem, there is a reference to his work in the court of appeal. In his dissenting judgment, Ward LJ says:

> the words of this Act must be given their contemporary meaning. Professor Ronald Dworkin expressed the point well in *Law's Empire* (1986), p. 348, when he said: '[The judge] interprets not just the statute's text but its life, the process that begins before it becomes law and extends far beyond that moment ... [the judge's] interpretation changes as the story develops.' Since families are dynamic, the statutory interpretation must equally reflect the motive forces, physical or moral, affecting behaviour and change in domestic organisation. On reading Professor Zimmermann's article, 'Statutes and the Common Law: A Continental Perspective' [1997] C.L.J. 315, 323, I realise, with some apprehension (but with some pleasure at the recollection of it) how close I am to a return to Celsus, The Digest of Justinian, D.1,3,17, whose rule of interpretation was, 'Scire leges non hoc est verba earum tenere, sed vim ac potestatem': to know the laws is not a matter of sticking to their words, but of grasping their force and tendency ...[21]

Interpretation theory has, however, brought to the surface some questions that inference theory suppressed. Is an interpreter free, at least where the text is ambiguous, to interpret a text in any way he or she cares? Do judges have complete discretion as to whether to interpret and to apply the rule in *Rylands* v. *Fletcher* to an escape of electricity? And what determines, cognitively speaking, the answer to the question whether a term is to be interpreted one way or another? Dworkin's reply is that judges do not have such discretion since there is a 'right' answer to all hard cases. Other theorists dispute this. Nevertheless, what all of the new hermeneuticians share is the idea of a structured reasoning model behind the language of the text which the legal reasoner must access when deciding cases. The question, however, is whether such a model ought to be located at the level of facts rather than rules. Should, as Ivainer suggests, the judge be interpreting facts rather than texts?[22]

Rules and Facts

Now, in order to relate to factual situations, rules must contain within them the means by which one can move from pure norm (the world of 'ought') to the world of social fact. Thus, in Blackburn J's rule in *Rylands* v. *Fletcher*, one key term was 'anything'. This was the term that linked the rule to water and to electricity. Rules, in other words, need to be framed around terms which have meaning both in the normative world of 'ought', abstracted from reality, and the empirical world of social fact. Indeed, this is essential for the legal syllogism; for if there is no connection between the major premise (universal rule) and minor premise (description of fact) there can be no feasible conclusion. Moreover, the connecting terms have to be understood in the context of their own particular reference systems, otherwise the syllogism itself, or at least the conclusion, becomes distorted, as the medieval logicians discovered. Thus care must be taken with words such as 'escapes' in the Blackburn rule. Such a word again acts as a bridge between the 'ought' and the 'is' premises, but it can function within two different contexts. If a prisoner 'escapes' from his cell, has he 'escaped' from prison? In one leading case on the rule in *Rylands* v. *Fletcher*, a plaintiff injured by an explosion while actually on the land of the defendants was held to fall outside of the rule since there had been no 'escape'.[23] Was this decision a matter of envisaging facts or interpreting the word 'escape'? In a sense one might say it was both. The idea of escape presupposes boundaries, and what the judges did was to search within the facts for an identifiable boundary. Presumably, had she been standing one foot outside of the front gate, she would prima facie have been within the rule.

Rules therefore delimit facts. They describe areas and boundaries. One should not, of course, be surprised by this since the whole objective of law is to define and delimit 'oughts' to particular areas of social action and inaction. But this idea of delimiting and defining does introduce into rules an aspect which will take one beyond the rule itself. Before rules can be formulated, they must have been envisaged or experienced within the world of fact. When regularity is detected, this regularity can be induced out of the fact to become a 'law'. Now, this idea of description and induction is fundamental to the natural sciences. In the sciences induction has been described as a process whereby one goes from one degree of rationality to another.[24] One starts out from facts organised in a certain manner and according to a certain structure to arrive at another, and new, organising category and structure. Induction is an active process through which the scientific mind goes from an inferior degree of organisation to a superior degree in terms of abstraction; and this whole process of itself generates the new categories and the new structures. There is no such thing as static rationality in the sciences. Is this true of legal science as well? Again, this can only be tested by getting beyond the rules. And, like the early scientist, one should start with the facts.

Moving beyond the Rules

In moving beyond the rules it is necessary, at first, to put aside one's knowledge models of law. It is, at this stage, important to try to think of facts as facts. This, admittedly, is almost impossible, particularly as legal rules and concepts have already been extensively discussed. Moreover, there is no such thing as brute fact. All the same, there are facts and facts; there are those that can be directly imagined and those that can only be described through names.

Donoghue v. *Stevenson*

Take the facts of the famous decision of *Donoghue* v. *Stevenson*.[25] They are a useful starting point for reflection since they are, on the one hand, simple and, on the other, creative. Mrs Donoghue alleged that she had gone to a café with a friend and that the latter had purchased for her a bottle of Stevenson's ginger-beer and an ice-cream. She claimed that she had poured half of the beer from the opaque bottle onto her ice-cream and had started to consume the whole concoction. Then, while she was pouring out the rest of the ginger-beer, a decomposed snail floated out, the sight of which caused her to suffer severe nervous shock and subsequent gastro-enteritis.

What is the lawyer to make of these facts? The difficulty for the law student is that they are often encountered for the first time within a particular legal subject, the law of tort. This has the effect, in itself, of injecting a normative dimension: these facts must be the subject of a rule, otherwise they would not be raised within the area of law under study. It may be useful, however, to try to regress. Imagine a jurist well trained in, say, remedies and procedure, but whose grasp on the substantive rules of criminal, contract, tort and property law has evaporated. Such a jurist might well start his or her analysis at the one place which a legal system itself would seemingly deem the most relevant. What is the complaint? This is both obvious and not so obvious. The obvious starting point might well be Mrs Donoghue, who has suffered nervous shock and gastro-enteritis. But, on the bare facts given, this need not necessarily be the case. Mrs Donoghue might well not wish to pursue the matter; yet her friend, annoyed by the incident, might. Is there anything that the friend can do in terms of legal redress? The answer here might depend, first of all, upon what kind of redress the friend would wish to seek. He or she might wish to seek compensation or might wish to see the person running the café and (or) the manufacturer of the ginger-beer prosecuted for supplying drink unfit for human consumption.

The facts disclose, then, two main possibilities in terms of the type of legal action that can be wielded against the suppliers of the wayward ginger-beer. The first possibility is a claim by one private person, either Mrs Donoghue or the friend (if not both), against another person, the person running the café or the manufacturer. It will be necessary here to look at what types of action the law offers the private citizen in these circumstances and what normative rules and principles govern the action. The second possibility is a prosecution which, as a general rule, is brought not by a private citizen (although this is not impossible in some legal systems) but by a public person or body.

This analysis may seem obvious enough. Yet it is worth reflecting exactly on what has been achieved so far in terms of analysis at the level of the facts themselves. The various individual persons and possible public bodies have been identified and put into a structural relationship not just with each other, but with the bottle of ginger-beer and the snail. Descriptive terms such as 'supply' and 'nervous shock' have been noted, along with the possibility of 'annoyance'. A distinction has been made between various types of legal actions. Of course, this exercise is not untainted by law and legal rules. Much of the analysis makes sense only within the framework of an existing system of courts which distinguishes between private and public actions and which thinks in terms of legal actions. But these legal aspects are descriptive inasmuch as it is possible to talk of the real existence of the civil courts and the criminal courts. One can talk of nervous shock, or gastro-enteritis, outside of legal discourse, just as one can use terms such as 'supply' and 'running (or similar expression) a café' in a non-legal context. One is preparing facts for the law, although as yet there is nothing normative, save the feeling on the part of Mrs Donoghue and (or) her friend that they 'ought' not to have been supplied with a defective bottle of ginger-beer.

Comparing Facts

Before proceeding any further with the ginger-beer facts, it might be useful to reflect on a second set of facts. The second set comes from a case almost as well known as the snail in the ginger-beer bottle affair. In *Grant* v. *Australian Knitting Mills*,[26] Mr Grant was injured when he put on a new pair of underpants which contained an excess of a particular chemical used in the manufacturing process but which was harmful to humans. Mr Grant, who had purchased the pants from John Martin & Co, who in turn had obtained them from the manufacturers, the Australian Knitting Mills Ltd., suffered acute dermatitis as a result of wearing the infected garment.

Again, what should the lawyer make of these facts? A similar analysis of the various persons in relation to the underpants can be made; and the medical complaint is clearly identifiable. However, in analysing the facts, it might be valuable to assume that the jurist has a knowledge of the facts of *Donoghue* v. *Stevenson*. Can they be compared? Several differences emerge immediately. For a start, unlike Mrs Donoghue, Mr Grant purchased the pants himself. Furthermore, there is a difference between pants and ginger-beer: if a person goes to a bar or a restaurant and orders a bottle of ginger-beer and is served with a pair of underpants, that person is likely to be, to say the least, surprised. On the other hand, it has to be said that a person might not be surprised to observe a customer returning a pair of underpants to a supermarket or chain store and emerging with a bottle of ginger-beer. Then there is a difference between the harm suffered by Mrs Donoghue and by Mr Grant; in the latter situation, it is possible to observe directly the dermatitis, whereas it is not so easy, perhaps impossible, to observe directly the effects of mental shock (although gastro-enteritis is physical enough). This is not to suggest that dermatitis is necessarily a more serious condition than nervous shock. The point is simply one of how easy it is actually to measure and assess the two conditions.

Ginger-beer and pants are not the only things that can cause injury. A man and wife go to a restaurant for a pleasant lunch and the husband pays the bill; but it subsequently turns out to be a rather unpleasant experience when the wife suffers food poisoning from the whitebait hors d'œuvre. How might these facts compare with those in *Donoghue*? The person who purchased the whitebait was certainly more than a mere friend of the person suffering the injury, and the incident took place in a restaurant rather than a bar.

Take two further sets of facts. Two people go into a supermarket to do their shopping. The first person, while walking around the store, slips up on some spilt yoghurt and fractures her ankle. She hobbles off home but subsequently returns, some three weeks later, to do some more shopping and notices some spilt orange-juice. She decides to observe how long it takes supermarket staff to clean up the mess and notes that after a quarter of an hour the spillage is still there. The second person did her shopping and went to the checkout where the cashier took out of the supermarket basket a bottle of lemonade. While waiting for the price of the lemonade to be registered, the shopper transferred it to her own bag, where it knocked lightly against another item and exploded, injuring the shopper in the eye. What can be made of these facts? In the case of the spilt yoghurt it can certainly be said that the yoghurt was the immediate cause of the shopper's injury. Yet it might also be said that the accident was caused by the supermarket staff's failure to clear up the mess promptly. What cannot be said, however, is that the yoghurt had been 'supplied' to the shopper. But is this true with regard to the accident involving the exploding bottle of lemonade? Had the bottle of drink been 'supplied' to the customer? Again, it can be said that the immediate cause of the eye injury was the exploding bottle. Yet imagine that the supermarket manager was asked by head-office to draw up a full report on the accident: would the manager be satisfied with the explanation that it simply exploded? Would there not be an investigation as to why it exploded? Had it been stored near a radiator? Was it part of a batch which had contained other bottles which had exploded? Was the bottle faulty?

No doubt there are further questions that can be posed. However, a number of relationships between supermarket, employees, shoppers, yoghurt and lemonade can be constructed. There is the relationship between the supermarket and its premises; the relationship between supermarket premises and the shoppers; the relationship between the supermarket and the goods that it sells; the relationship between shoppers and the goods that they wish to buy; and the relationship between the supermarket as employer and its cashiers, cleaners and other staff. In addition, there is the relationship between the supermarket and its suppliers. Moreover, if the supermarket advertises itself in the media, one might talk of a relationship between the supermarket and the population at large. Finally, with respect to both the restaurant and the supermarket, there is the relationship with the public service officials (food inspectors, firemen and the like) who might well visit the premises of both commercial businesses to carry out inspections.

Facts and Words

A next step that can be taken in analysing these facts is to put all of them together in order to see what kind of information may be obtained from such an exercise. Are there common features between all the sets of facts, as well as important differences? One might start with common features. Yet at what level is this to take place? The common features can all be described by descriptive words, but can they all be imagined in some single unitary picture? At the level of words, one can find the terms of 'injury' and 'product' which will describe the complaints and the things that immediately caused them in all of the situations. But what if one wants to translate these facts into images? The difficulty for the artist is this. While he or she could paint a bar, restaurant, shop and supermarket as individual scenes, could a general image capturing all of these incidents be executed? No doubt a photograph of one of the latest out-of-town supermarkets could contain in one image all of these scenes, and thus it is now possible to conceive of all these accidents taking place within the borders of a single photograph or painting. And the artist might care to call her work the 'Perils of a Consumer Society'. The bringing together of all the images does then suggest a common image of a 'consumer', that is to say a mass of people buying goods and services, and suffering accidents, under a single roof. The individual images help create the new image of a 'consumer'. Such an image will no doubt be reinforced by the images of media advertising, the idea of people being encouraged to 'consume' products.

However, it is also important to keep in mind the individual images. One simply cannot go into a shop or a restaurant and order a 'product', just as one cannot go to the doctor and say that one has suffered an 'injury'. The doctor will need to know whether it is nervous shock, a skin disease, a bad stomach and so on. Of course, the comedian or the surrealist could benefit from the intermixing of the images: one can imagine some kind of surreal sketch involving a man in a restaurant ordering whitebait and being served with a pair of underpants. But one cannot imagine a 'product' or an 'injury' as things in themselves. There has been a movement from things to words.

All of this may seem obvious, yet the dichotomy between facts and words is a useful reminder of how the perception of descriptive facts is never as straightforwardly descriptive as it might at first seem. To talk of ginger-beer, underpants, yoghurt and dermatitis, on the one hand, and products and injury, on the other, is to talk descriptively. But behind the two levels of description lies the old problem of universals and entities. While few would doubt that bottles of ginger-beer and underpants actually exist, can the same be said of 'products'? The effect of the nominalist revolution was profound, in that it created a dichotomy between what was perceived to exist in the world of fact and what constituted the structures of knowledge. The *res et intellectus* (reality and mind) became separate starting points for constructing a 'true' descriptive view of the world. And this separation has in turn given rise, not just in law but in all of the sciences, to a situation where there exists a whole range of true statements, each with very different values.[27]

Thinking about facts, even in the most obvious ways, is thus a vital aspect of legal knowledge. In a café the distinction between a bottle of ginger-beer and a pair of underpants has a truth value that is undeniable, but only in the context of the time and place. In the supermarket or chain store the truth value of the distinction is no longer so evident and indeed, for the purposes of stocktaking or for the awarding of reward points to a customer on a purchase, the similarity between the two products is the more evident truism. The *décalage* between things and words is thus a fundamental aspect of legal knowledge. The words of law are fixed and immutable and that is why they can seemingly be grasped by the mind and transmitted in books. The facts of the law are quite a different matter. They are not fixed, since the dimensions of time and place are a fundamental part of how they are to be perceived at any given moment.

The words versus things question is, accordingly, important for legal method for several reasons. First, when it comes to identifying and classifying the elements in legal analysis and reasoning, it is important to know what these elements are. Is law, on the one hand, about ginger-beer, underpants, yoghurts, lemonade, new cars, second-hand cars, boats, holidays, mink stoles and so on; and, on the other hand, about shoppers, holiday-makers, pub-goers, second-hand car dealers, property owners and others? Or is it about products, services, injury, consumers, manufacturers, *personae* and other terms which, while remaining descriptive, cannot directly be translated into an image capable of being precisely captured on a photograph (since they are in effect universals). If the latter, does this mean that law is about words rather than things?

A second reason why the rule or facts knowledge question is important is that, even if the emphasis is to be put on the rules, there has to be a bridge between the world of social fact (ginger-beer, underpants, shoppers and so on) and the world of language propositions. How are rules framed? What are the elements around which they are constructed? The examples discussed so far have gone some way in indicating that the more abstract one becomes in the language employed – for example 'product' instead of 'yoghurt' – the more one loses in detail. This of course is evident in itself. But the word 'anything' in the rule in *Rylands* v. *Fletcher* cannot serve as the basis of a reasoning process it itself. It has to connect with water, electricity, explosive shells and the like, and it is this connection which needs investigation. Is it a question of analogy between past specific things that have caused damage and the specific thing now before the court? Or is there some metaphysical element within the word 'anything' – an element which needs to be teased out of it – which determines whether the thing before the court falls within the rule? Similar questions can be posed about a term such as 'person', 'partner' (*concubin notoire*) or 'family'. Indeed, with respect to corporate persons or families, how are these to be envisaged? Are they to be envisaged in terms of a group of individuals acting together within a single building or whatever or through the use of some metaphorical (analogical) image such as the human body? How is such knowledge within words to be represented?

A third reason why the rule or facts knowledge question is vital is that the relationship between facts themselves is in need of analysis and reflection. How should the relationship between Mrs Donoghue and the café proprietor or the manufacturer be expressed? What are the important relationships in the example of the shopper who breaks her ankle as a result of spilt yoghurt? Is it a matter of shopper and yoghurt; customer and supermarket; consumer and safety system; or what? And how does one arrive at the relevant relationship? In addition to the relationships, there are also the elements that go to make up an event or a series of events and the causal relations that link them. Is a catastrophe to be viewed as a single event or as a series of smaller independent, if causally related, events? If one buys land with building attached, is the land to be considered as a separate *res* from the building in respect of the causal events that give rise to economic profits and losses? Can cases be criticised because they focus on one factual relationship rather than another? Can the relationships be tested by hypothetically altering or changing the facts? Are facts, one might say, constructed from within? Each time one arrives at a certain level of reflection on reasoning and method, one sees reappearing the old metaphysical dichotomy between the universalists and the nominalists. This is the fundamental dichotomy between words (names) and things (reality).[28] It is, therefore, the key, or one key, to the world beyond the rules.

Facts as Images

One epistemological theme that has begun to emerge in greater detail is the notion of facts as images. These images are non-symbolic knowledge inasmuch as they cannot adequately be captured by words; or, put another way, some universal terms such as 'product' cannot directly be translated into an image. A rule about a 'product' thus loses, in terms of complexity, a whole dimension of meaning. Yet images are vital in the knowledge sense in that they can create a pattern of facts which can in themselves determine solutions. For example, once electricity is seen as something 'fluid', like water, the easier it is to conclude that the escape of electricity is analogous to the escape of water. Both, one could easily assume, should be governed by the same rule.

Methodology and the Practitioner

Does any of the descriptive analysis discussed so far matter to the practitioner? Arguably the answer is that it does. At a practical level, the analysis of facts is useful inasmuch as it acts as an entry point for the lawyer to problem solving. In addition, at the cognitive level, it can be vital in the process of decision making and in the way one links words to things. Take the following example. A client complains that he has purchased a house in reliance upon a statement by the seller that the building had not been the subject of any subsidence. The statement was false, but, because the client was unable to afford the cost of the structural repairs needed to bring the building up to the state he was led to believe it was in, he applied for, and obtained, planning permission. This planning permission allowed him to resell the land at a profit that exceeded the cost of repairing the building. Can he sue the sellers for damages for the cost of remedying the defective building or has the profit received on the resale of the land wiped out the loss?

The answer to this question cannot be found within the legal rule that governs the situation. The rule is clear enough. It states that the 'basic principle applicable in assessing damages is that there must be measured the sum of money which would put the innocent party in the same position as he would have been in if the contract had been performed or if he had not sustained the wrong'.[29] But it simply does not contain the complex factual information needed to decide if the client has purchased a *res* (object or thing) that is worth less than he was induced to pay by the false statement. The answer to the problem can be found only at the level of fact. Is one talking of a single *res*, namely land plus house, or is one talking of a series of separate objects, that is to say the defective building, the land and the planning permission? If one were to take a 'universalist' view of the *res*, then it could be envisaged as acting as the focus for both the loss and the profit. A 'nominalist' image, in contrast, would result in a separation between the object of loss (house) and the object of profit (land). When this actual problem found itself in the court of appeal, Mustill LJ concluded that 'when the plaintiffs unlocked the development value of their land they did so for their own benefit, and not as part of a continuous transaction of which the purchase of land and bungalow was the inception'.[30] Mustill LJ had effectively constructed the facts from within to produce two separate events. The purchase of the house was to be seen as a separate event from the pursuit of a legitimate profit, even although both acts involved the same *res* (the land).

The idea that facts can be constructed from within might look a little curious at first sight. The traditional rule-oriented view of law is that facts arrive 'cold', so to speak, and it is for the lawyer to analyse them in terms of the relevant rule, or rules, applicable. However, facts, as has been seen, involve relationships between the elements that make them up and these elements are open to manipulation. Take two sets of facts discussed earlier: Mrs Donoghue and the unfortunate bottle of ginger-beer, and the wife poisoned by the whitebait lunch. In both cases it was not the person actually injured by the food who paid the bill. In *Donoghue* v. *Stevenson*[31] this was a vital aspect in the construction of the relevant relationships. Yet, in the restaurant case of the wife who suffered food poisoning, the judge put stress on the relationship between the wife and the restaurant.[32] Is there really that much difference between a bar and a restaurant?

The point can be tested. Imagine that in a restaurant a man orders for a woman a meal, the woman and the restaurant both being under the impression that he is going to pay the bill. In fact, after they are both half-way through the meal, the man excuses himself and disappears into the night. Will the woman have to pay for the meals? It is feasible to imagine, leaving aside the actual legal situation, that she will not have to pay for the man's meal, but, having eaten half of her own food, would feel under a social obligation to pay for her food. In fact, according to the decision in *Lockett* v. *Charles*,[33] she would have to pay for her own meal since there existed an independent contractual relationship between wife and restaurant. Imagine, now, an analogous situation, in a bar with respect to two bottles of ginger-beer. If the woman had drunk half of her beer, would she not feel under a social obligation to pay for her drink? Could she leave without paying? The actual decision in *Donoghue* suggests that she does not have to pay the price of the beer, even if it had no snail and was delicious, since she had no contract with the bar and, presumably, gave no restitutionary implied undertaking to pay (a fact capable of being constructed?).[34] Yet are not the two relationships analogous at the level of fact if not law? Or, put another way, is it not possible to construct a similarity? The point that emerges from the hypothetical situations in bar and restaurant is that decisions can flow from the way situations are imagined.

Researching Analogies

Factual images are also fundamental in analogy. A ship heavily laden with a cargo of crude oil founders on a sandbank and in order to protect the lives of the crew the captain orders that the oil be discharged into the sea. The oil some time later is washed up on the beaches of a local holiday resort and the council spend much time, energy and money in clearing up the mess. Imagine that an employee of the council is looking through the facts of old cases to find an analogy with what has happened. The employee finds some old cases involving, not ships, but horse-drawn transport and, in the first case, he discovers a situation where the owner of a house has had his front wall, adjoining the roadway, severely damaged by a coach and horses crashing into it. In another case he discovers that the owner of a café has suffered loss of business, plus increased gas light bills, as a result of a neighbouring transport firm having left its horses on the road outside the café, where they blocked the daylight, and the smell from their droppings and urine overpowered the customers. Which situation, the council employee asks herself, is the closer analogy to the problem of the stricken ship and dirty beach? Is it helpful to think in terms of 'pollution'? What kind of image does pollution conjure up? Or should one be thinking more in terms of damage to an adjoining beach?

There are further analogies to be researched. When looking at what caused the polluted beach a number of possibilities present themselves. First, there is the captain. He ordered the oil to be discharged and so could be seen as the immediate human cause of the oil ending up on the beach. Yet he ordered the discharge to save lives. However, in response to that, it might be asked how the ship ended up on the sandbank in the first place. Then there is the ship. Who owned the ship and ordered it to sea with a cargo of crude oil? What condition was it in when it left port? If it left in poor condition, was this because a firm of ship repairers had not done its job properly? Or had a ship's inspector failed to detect, say, the poor condition of its steering system? Then there is the owner of the ship. How should its relationship with the ship be described? Is it, for example, analogous to the relationship of the owner of an animal and the animal itself? If so, what type of animal might present a relevant image? For example, if an owner takes a vicious dog into the park and the dog bites another park user, what is the cause of this injury? Is it simply caused by the dog, or can one say that it was caused by the owner taking a vicious thing into the park in the first place? Or is it more like the relationship between the owner of a car and his or her vehicle? If a car injures a passer-by or another road user, how is this to be assessed in terms of causation? Is the person injured because of the actual driving of the driver or the activity of taking a car onto the road? Alternatively, it might be asked whether the idea of a relationship between owner and his or her thing is the wrong image. Perhaps one should be envisaging the relationship between the owner of the ship and the captain. Was this an image of an employee doing a job for the employer? Is it the image of an individual just not up to the job? Or, indeed, is it quite the opposite: is it an image of an employee thinking quickly and putting the lives of humans before anything else? Finally, one might turn towards the elements. Was the whole episode the result of rough seas and tides washing the cargo onto the beach? Was this an 'Act of God' to be attributed to the weather and the seas?

What analogies are chosen can in turn depend upon how one sees the pattern of events. In the polluted beach example, if one concentrates only upon the act of the captain in discharging the oil, the image is likely to be one focusing only upon his behaviour in the immediate circumstances. Was it a reasonable act in the circumstances? However, if the viewer were to stand back and look at the bigger picture, so to speak, a different pattern of events comes into view. How did the ship get into this predicament in the first place? The picture is no longer one of captain's act and polluted beach. It now brings into the frame the owner of the ship itself. Did the owners put to sea a ship that was not really fit to carry a large and environmentally dangerous cargo? Might not the owners be part of the bigger causal picture? Might not the correct analogy be with similar types of *activities* as opposed to analogies about *acts*?

Envisaging Loss

How one sees the world can, then, determine the kind of questions asked. Is one viewing an event or a series of events? Events in this context can have a variety of subtleties. They can concern the easily imaginable situation (and thus a favourite topic for filmmakers) such as the tragedy of a sinking ship. Equally, however, they can take a more subtle form. In *Lazenby Garages Ltd* v. *Wright,*[35] Lord Denning MR outlined the following situation:

> Mr. Wright works on the land. On 19th February 1974 he went to the showrooms of motor dealers called Lazenby Garages Ltd. He saw some second-hand cars there. He agreed to buy a BMW 2002. He signed a contract to pay £1,670 for it. It was to be delivered to him on 1st March 1974. He went back home to his wife and told her about it. She persuaded him not to buy it. So next day he went back to the garage and said he would not have it after all. They kept it there offering it for resale. Two months later on 23rd April 1974 they resold it for £1,770, that is for £100 more than Mr. Wright was going to pay.[36]

Lord Denning then described what happened after the return of the car:

> Notwithstanding this advantageous resale, the garage sued Mr. Wright for damages. They produced evidence that they had themselves bought the car second-hand on 14th February 1974, that is five days before Mr. Wright had come in and agreed to buy it. They said that they had bought it for £1,325. He had agreed to buy it from them for £1,670. So they had lost £345 and they claimed that sum as damages.[37]

And he continued:

> In answer Mr. Wright said: 'You haven't lost anything; you've sold it for a higher price.' The garage people said that they were dealers in second-hand cars; that they had had a number of cars of this sort of age and type, BMW 2002s; and that they had lost the sale of another car. They said that, if Mr. Wright had taken this car, they would have been able to sell one of those other cars to the purchaser. So they had sold one car less and were entitled to profit accordingly.[38]

Lord Denning then analysed the situation as it appeared to him. The cases indicated that, with respect to the sale of new cars, the situation is as follows. If they are all exactly of the same kind, and the dealers can prove that they sold one car less than they otherwise would have done, they would be entitled to damages amounting to their loss of profit on the one car. However, second-hand were entirely different. Each is different from the next, even when it is the same make. And he concluded:

> In the circumstances the cases about new cars do not apply ... The measure of damages is the estimated loss directly and naturally resulting in the ordinary course of events from the buyer's breach of contract. That throws us back to the test of what could reasonably be expected to be in the contemplation of the parties as a natural consequence of the breach. The buyer in this case could not have contemplated that the dealer would sell one car less. At most he would

> contemplate that, if they resold this very car at a lower price, they would suffer by reason of that lower price and should recover the difference. But if they resold this very car at a higher price, they would suffer no loss. Seeing that these plaintiffs resold this car for £100 more than the sale to Mr. Wright, they clearly suffered no damage at all.[39]

This conclusion results from the way Lord Denning viewed the world (at least in respect of these facts). Each sale of a second-hand car is a unique event and must be judged within the framework of that uniqueness. The picture is not to be expanded into the event of selling cars as an activity with each failed sale being viewed as a loss. In other words, what amounts to 'loss', in contrast to immediate physical damage to property or injury to a person, is, or can be, a matter of construction of the facts themselves.

This point about loss is worth developing since, while one can register in terms of imagery physical damage and personal injury – the artist or photographer can paint or photograph car crashes, ships on the rocks and the like – loss is a different question. It can only be caught, in terms of image, indirectly on canvas or paper. In terms of figures, it can of course be depicted in the double-entry balance sheet; but this kind of image carries little pictorial force. Now some types of loss are easy enough to register in the mind, if not on canvas: the theft of a valuable and much loved family heirloom or a stock-market crash is easy enough to imagine. But is this true of a failure to win a valuable prize or to inherit a nice house? Harder still is the 'loss' which arises from the failure to earn a profit because of some intervening event. Indeed, even where there has been physical damage, the moment one tries to evaluate the damage in terms of money, problems of factual description can arise.

The case of *Spartan Steel & Alloys* v. *Martin & Co (Contractors) Ltd*,[40] although relatively straightforward in its facts, begins to provide an insight into this difficulty. The defendants were digging up the road when they cut through a cable that supplied electricity to the plaintiffs' metal factory. The source of heat was cut off for some fourteen or fifteen hours and this resulted in metal solidifying in the furnaces. The factory owners sued the road contractors for compensation and they described their damage under three heads. They claimed compensation for: (i) damage to the metal which solidified in the furnaces; (ii) the loss of profit on the ruined metal in the furnaces; and (iii) the loss of profit on four other melting operations that they could have carried out if the electricity had not been off. When viewed from the position of an accountant, these three heads were no doubt simply the parts of a single 'event'. That is to say, the event of the power cut-off and the economic consequences that ensued are all one and the same fact.

Nevertheless, as we have seen, the photographer would have much greater difficulty in capturing all the damage as a single event. Certainly, the damaged metal could, perhaps, be recorded. But the loss of production would have to be registered as a separate event. Lawyers achieved this by dividing up 'damage' into different 'interests' and counsel for the defendants argued that they were not liable for head (iii) on the ground that it was a pure economic interest not protected by the tort of negligence.

Counsel for the plaintiffs, accepting in part this 'interests' image of the world, nevertheless tried to suggest an alternative approach. He argued that, where there was some actual physical damage, all the subsequent loss of profits could be claimed as 'parasitic damages'. The idea behind this type of claim is that an interest not normally protected in itself can be compensated when attached to an established wrong which invades some protected interest. Thus, although the loss of a chance to make a profit is not normally a protected interest in the tort of negligence, when attached to some other protected interest such as physical damage, it will become the object of compensation. Lord Denning's response to this argument was again in terms of imagery. But this time the image, accurate or not, was, to say the least, more powerful:

> I do not like this doctrine of 'parasitic damages'. I do not like the very word 'parasite'. A 'parasite' is one who is a useless hanger-on sucking the substance out of others. 'Parasitic' is the adjective derived from it. It is a term of abuse. It is an opprobrious epithet. The phrase 'parasitic damages' conveys to my mind the idea of damages which ought not in justice to be awarded, but which somehow or other have been allowed to get through by hanging on to others. If such be the concept underlying the doctrine, then the sooner it is got rid of the better.[41]

The plaintiffs' argument was rejected, not by focusing on the loss itself, but by attacking the image used by counsel to justify the remedy. It was an argument designed to create an impression beyond the rule itself. Such an impression can, of course, be dismissed as unscientific, if not irrational. Yet, while its metaphorical force is perhaps more vivid than one has normally come to expect in judicial reasoning, such force should not be permitted to eclipse the importance of the non-symbolic forms of cognitive processes at work. The images created by analogies and metaphors are part of the process of thinking about facts and what is so striking about these images is the way they can determine decisions. Some might talk in terms of how such images influence the interpretation of rules. It might be more useful to talk in terms of how descriptive analysis is itself part of the decision-making process.

None of this is to claim that the elements in this empirical construction, or reconstruction, of factual images will always be so easy. What is the situation in more mundane disputes over words or phrases? Several possibilities present themselves. The first is to transform the mundane into the vivid through the use of analogy and (or) metaphor. A good recent example of this is to be found in *Banque Bruxelles Lambert SA* v. *Eagle Star Insurance*.[42] The basic question to be decided in these consolidated appeals was stated by Lord Hoffmann, who delivered the judgment of the House, at the beginning of his judgment. 'What,' he said, 'is the extent of the liability of a valuer who has provided the lender with a negligent overvaluation of the property offered as security for the loan?'[43] The court of appeal[44] had treated this question as a matter of damages rather than actual liability, but Lord Hoffmann thought that this was the wrong place to begin. It was a matter of duty that in turn was to be measured by the kind of loss sustained. The kind of loss question was, in its turn, to be analysed, where the duty was contractual, not just by the reasonable contemplation test but by causation. And rules 'which make the wrongdoer liable for all the consequences of his wrongful conduct are exceptional and need to be justified by some special policy'.[45] In other words, it was not just a question of liability and damage as such; each item of damage had to be justified in its own right as being factually caused by the breach of duty and justified by recourse to policy. In order to justify this nominalist approach, Lord Hoffmann employed a vivid analogy which was to act as the main reference point of his judgment:

> I can illustrate the difference between the ordinary principle and that adopted by the Court of Appeal by an example. A mountaineer about to undertake a difficult climb is concerned about the fitness of his knee. He goes to a doctor who negligently makes a superficial examination and pronounces the knee fit. The climber goes on the expedition, which he would not have undertaken if the doctor had told him the true state of his knee. He suffers an injury which is an entirely foreseeable consequence of mountaineering but has nothing to do with his knee.[46]

The role of this vivid 'picture' is to justify the separation between different heads of losses flowing from the breach of duty. It is not a matter of rules as such since the rules are determined more by how one sees the facts (damage) than how one analyses and applies to the damage a pre-existing model of principles. Certainly, one can construct a pre-existing model. Thus one could say that causation in the law of obligations functions at four different levels – actionability, factual causation, legal causation (remoteness) and damages (quantum)[47] – and that what the House of Lords was doing was to shift the level from damages to factual causation. Yet this model, although capable of being described by rules, cannot be governed by them, as Lord Hoffmann's reasoning indicates. As he says, there is no reason in principle why the causation question should not function at the level of quantum of damages. According to him, 'it would, for example, be perfectly intelligible to have a rule by which an unlicensed driver was responsible for all the consequences of his having driven, even if they were unconnected with his not having a licence'.[48] To escape this damages level Lord Hoffmann had to leave the world of rules and have recourse to feeling:

> Your Lordships might, I would suggest, think that there was something wrong with a principle which, in the example which I have given, produced the result that the doctor was liable. What is the reason for this feeling? I think that the Court of Appeal's principle offends common sense because it makes the doctor responsible for consequences which, though in general terms foreseeable, do not appear to have a sufficient causal connection with the subject matter of the duty. The doctor was asked for information on only one of the considerations which might affect the safety of the mountaineer on the expedition. There seems no reason of policy which requires that the negligence of the doctor should require the transfer to him of all the foreseeable risks of the expedition.[49]

The force of the argument depends, then, on the analogy of image between a doctor and a valuer. And it is difficult to talk in terms of valid and invalid images since the debate simply reduces itself to the problem of images and how one sees the world. Perhaps the real difficulty from a methodology point of view is that, while the doctor and the valuer are both professionals, the House of Lords has on other occasions rejected such analogies. In a medical negligence case, comparison with other professionals has been deemed unacceptable since doctors and surgeons give rise to special policy problems.[50] Professionals, one might say, are analogous to products, that is to say ginger-beer and underpants. Sometimes they can be united as a single group under the term 'professional liability', just as ginger-beer and underpants can be united under 'product liability'. At other times one abandons the universal term for the individual part. Doctors and accountants are as different as, say, ginger-beer and underpants.

Categorising Facts

Facts not only need to be envisaged, they need also to be categorised. This will be true whatever the level of abstraction in operation regarding the legal rules and precedents. Highly descriptive rules functioning at a very low level of abstraction can be applied only to those specific things or specific persons around which the rule is formulated and this will require, however unconscious the process, a categorisation of the facts. A rule about 'a dog' can only apply to those things which qualify as 'dogs',[51] just as a rule about 'a firearm' can only apply to those things which qualify as 'firearms'. Certainly, there may be occasions of doubt. Does a pet wolf or fox fall within the meaning of 'dog'? Does a crossbow fall within the meaning of 'firearm'? But the point to be stressed here is that legal reasoning in these ambiguous cases will largely be a question of taxonomy. Classification is legal method.[52]

Classifying the Harm

Take once again the facts of *Donoghue* v. *Stevenson*. The first matter that the legal classifier might wish to focus on is the nature of the complaint. There are several possibilities, depending upon the person seeking a legal remedy. Mrs Donoghue's nervous shock (leaving aside the gastro-enteritis) is an obvious cause for complaint, but the local consumer protection officer might well be seeking to take the café proprietor and (or) the manufacturer to court for selling food that is unfit for consumption and indeed dangerous.[53] In Mrs Donoghue's case, the complaint is classifiable not only under 'damage' but also under 'injury' and thus requires two labels, so to speak. However, the nervous shock is a special kind of injury inasmuch as it cannot be seen in quite the same way as a broken arm or cut leg. This may set it apart from the more observable injuries, in that it may require specialist evidence.[54] The nature of the injury, in other words, will need to be categorised. The consumer protection officer will have a quite different complaint. He or she will be complaining not about the injury – although no doubt this will be an important piece of evidence – but about the actual thing itself. Such a product, capable of being a danger to health, ought, from the viewpoint of the consumer protection official, not to be on the market. The purpose behind the consumer protection officer's legal action will be to protect the public through an action aimed at deterring such a situation.[55]

Classifying the Actors

The next elements for classification are the various persons involved. Mrs Donoghue has been identified as victim and her damage classified accordingly. But her situation and standing need to be categorised, in that this will help determine and define her relationship with other elements in the facts. Now much has already been written by others on various categories that are irrelevant for the legal taxonomist: the fact that she is a woman and has a particular colour of hair or skin is of little or no interest to the lawyer.[56] However, it is with respect to these relevant and irrelevant categories that one has to bring into play knowledge of the law. It is no longer feasible even to try to analyse the facts in some kind of neutral way by a lawyer standing apart from any particular specialism. Nevertheless, it is still important to reflect on the general classification aspects of any legal set of facts, since such reflection can reveal how classification decisions often take place almost unconsciously. For example, if the legal system discriminated against persons on the ground of race or religion, any lawyer prepared to work within such a society would have to bring into play classification categories that are irrelevant to most Western liberal democratic societies. In such a society the colour of the plaintiff's skin or her particular religion might be of the utmost relevance in relation to access to the courts. Indeed, in a legal system that discriminated against women or recognised slavery, characteristics to be found in Roman law,[57] it would be important, for example, to classify Mrs Donoghue as a free person or slave. Even in English law, before universal suffrage, the sex of a person was vital in disputes about the right to vote.[58]

Status is not, however, irrelevant to Mrs Donoghue. The fact that she consumed the ginger-beer endows her with the status of consumer and this is a classification category of importance in private law.[59] Equally, the fact that she did not buy the ginger-beer herself puts her into a class that is treated separately from those who actually purchase.[60] The status of the other actors involved in the drama is also important. The fact that the seller of the beer to Mrs Donoghue's friend is a café proprietor is of relevance since a private supply by one neighbour to another is treated differently than the supply in the course of a business.[61] The fact that the supplier of the ginger-beer to the café is the manufacturer of the product, and not, say, its importer, needs to be noted as well.[62]

Classifying the Things

The status of the various persons cannot, however, be treated in isolation from the other mediating elements in the facts. The classification of the ginger-beer as food rather than an item of furniture or work of art defines the standing of the various suppliers. And the actual type of bottle and its label will have an impact upon the purchaser and consumer. If the bottle had been clear (it was in fact opaque) this could have been of importance, since one could claim that the consumer ought to have been aware of its defective state. As Tony Weir once indicated, the label needs to be categorised as well; had it read 'Ginger-Beer with Decomposed Snail', this may well have been a vital fact.[63] Accordingly, the lawyer needs to categorise the things in play at the same moment that he or she is classifying the persons and actions.

This last point becomes more evident if one replaces ginger-beer with, say, a painting. A gallery that sells paintings can be equated with a shop that sells ginger-beer, in that both sell 'products'. Yet is the standing of the gallery *vis-à-vis* its products the same as that of a retailer in respect of food and drink? This standing is to an important extent determined by the nature of the product sold and the inherent capabilities of the product to cause particular kinds of harm. Unlike food and drink, which have the capability of causing physical illness and death (as the e-coli and BSE tragedies only too vividly illustrate), the main inherent danger with works of art is that they could turn out to be bad financial investments. Thus the standing or status of a seller is also determined by the relationship between seller and buyer. Purchasers of paintings may well belong to a different class than consumers in the usual sense of the term since they may, to a greater or lesser extent, be professionals themselves.[64] The mere supply of products is not, therefore, a sufficient factual category when it comes to classifying facts. One has to think about the products themselves. Food, works of art, cars and so on have differing capabilities when it comes to the kinds of harm they can cause. These differing capabilities can even occur within a single type of product. A consumer purchases some meat and eats it undercooked. If the consumer becomes ill as a result of the meat it would, as a matter of commonsense, be important to know if the meat was lamb, beef, chicken or pork, since most people know that it is unsafe to eat undercooked pork.[65] It may even be important to put chicken in the same category as pork, since in recent years it has become evident that raw chicken can be dangerous. In contrast, the internal sub-category of, say, clothes seems less urgent, since socks are unlikely to be any more or less dangerous than underpants.

Categorisation and Institutions

Categorisation of facts is thus a matter of starting off at the level of mediating terms. Persons, things, actions and damage are, since Roman times, the primary categories. But these categories interrelate to produce other sub-categories which can be just as important. Thus things must be juxtaposed to damage in order to elicit the inherent capabilities of any particular thing to cause harm. In turn, this harm needs to be related to the category of persons so as to reveal the standing and status of particular parties towards each other and towards the relevant things in any litigation set of facts. It would no doubt be false to say that this categorisation exercise can be undertaken without a broad knowledge of relevant and irrelevant legal categories. Nevertheless, categorisation of facts is an exercise that can be undertaken before one need consciously apply any relevant legal rules. It is an exercise that stimulates the legal mind into positive action.

Statutory Texts and Factual Images

Many of the examples looked at so far have been cases that have a direct relationship with facts inasmuch as they have involved case law rules. Such rules have themselves arisen out of factual situations and thus have a direct connection with the solution of a particular and concrete case. Indeed, the rule of precedent dictates that the factual situation of the precedent must continue to play a role in the determination of all future solutions. Cases involving statutes are different. Here the dispute is not so much connected with a previous factual situation and its relation to the one in hand. It is related directly to a linguistic proposition set down in a text. Such cases are collected together under the general heading of 'statutory interpretation' and this heading implies that the method to be adopted is one of interpretation of language. Also included under this heading are some interpretation of contract cases where the approach and method are very similar.[66] The scheme of intelligibility seems by necessity to be hermeneutical (cf. Chapter 8), yet arguably this is misleading. The role of the image in relation to the facts is as important in statutory interpretation cases as it is in problems based on precedent.

Isomorphs and Rules

It has already been seen from the examples above that, if one treats a written rule as the foundation upon which one builds knowledge about legal reasoning, there will often be a significant loss of information. For the linguistic proposition cannot in itself ever contain information about the imagery which surrounds the actual application process to the facts. One example is the statutory rule relating to the measure of damages applied in the *Lazenby Garages* case. This case involved Lord Denning who, as we have seen, was perhaps a judge who used particularly florid arguments on occasions. Yet other judges often reason in a similar, if less striking, vein. For example, *Young* v. *Sun Alliance and London Insurance Ltd*[67] involved Lawton LJ, a judge who on the whole wrote in a style somewhat different to that of Lord Denning. In this case he had to decide if three inches of water covering the whole of the plaintiff's lavatory floor amounted to a 'flood' for the purposes of an insurance policy. 'This appeal,' he said, 'raises a semantic problem which has troubled many philosophers for centuries, and it can, I think, be expressed in the aphorism that an elephant is "difficult to define but easy to recognise".' Accordingly, although Lawton LJ had great difficulty in actually defining the word 'flood', he had 'no difficulty in looking at the evidence in this case and coming to the conclusion ... that the water in the lavatory was not a flood within the meaning of ... this policy'.[68]

Despite the difficulties of defining an elephant, pictures can, to an extent, be translated into language and language can be translated into pictures. Novels, to put it more simply, can be made into films and films can be reduced to novels. The aim of rules could, then, be said to be to translate factual situations into language with the purpose of using the language to provide the normative dimension. Legal reasoning thus becomes a question of comparing isomorphies: that is to say, of comparing formal patterns. Where the facts of a case clearly fall within the factual situation envisaged within the rule there is a situation of 'isomorphy' with the result that a legal reasoner can apply the rule in an unreflective way.[69] In the *Young* situation, if the whole of the insured's land had been submerged under three inches of water as a result of a river overflowing its banks, most legal reasoners would probably say that the insurance company must pay out. The factual isomorphy contained in the insurance policy clause (the rule) would have matched that of the situation which occurred in fact. Yet does it follow from this that one can conclude that knowledge of legal method must start out from knowledge of law as a body of rules?

Certainly, it is tempting to say that rules can orientate. But rules that are excessively detailed in the pictures, or operative facts, that they try to capture, are likely to end up as self-defeating. In addition, there remains the methodological issue of actually applying the isomorphies. Why is it that legal reasoners can conclude unreflectively that the river flood falls within the clause of the policy, whereas in other statutory interpretation cases they cannot? One answer to this question may be that some textual rules are so complex that confusing images emerge. For example, in section 2(2) of the Animals Act 1971 the following is stated:

> (2) Where damage is caused by an animal which does not belong to a dangerous species, a keeper of the animal is liable for the damage, except as otherwise provided by this Act, if

> (a) the damage is of a kind which the animal, unless restrained, was likely to cause or which, if caused by the animal, was likely to be severe; and
> (b) the likelihood of the damage or of its being severe was due to characteristics of the animal which are not normally found in animals of the same species or are not normally so found except at particular times or in particular circumstances; and
> (c) those characteristics were known to that keeper or were at any time known to a person who at that time had charge of the animal as that keeper's servant or, where that keeper is the head of a household, were known to another keeper of the animal who is a member of that household and under the age of 16.

What kind of isomorphy does this proposition contain? Will the keeper of a cat be liable if it eats a neighbour's canary? Will the keeper of a bull mastiff dog be liable if it attacks a passing child in the street? Cats have the well-known characteristic of eating birds and it would seem that the owner would not be liable if it indulged itself in the predictable way. But can one be sure?[70] In order to apply the rule to the facts the reasoner needs to have a clear picture of the operative images contained in the rule. Now, such images may well be found in the reports and debates leading up to the passing of the legislation. It may be that the section was not intended to impose strict liability on the keepers of domestic animals for the typical damage they might cause, such as harming a neighbour's flowerbed or eating his pet canary. These were risks that were to be transferred only via the fault principle.[71] Yet the point to be stressed is that the application process is one that takes place at the level of the isomorphy and not the linguistic rule.

This point can be illustrated by the example of the bull mastiff taken from the case of *Curtis* v. *Betts*.[72] The keeper of the dog will escape liability under the section 'if, on the particular facts, the likelihood of damage was attributable to potentially dangerous characteristics of the animal which are normally found in animals of the same species'.[73] If, therefore, a bull mastiff attacks a child in the street in a situation where the keeper was not at fault, it is necessary to investigate the relevant characteristics of this particular dog. The emphasis, in other words, is not on the rule as such – save inasmuch as the rule contains an image about the characteristics of domestic animals – but on the actual character of the animal. The case reads as if it is a trial of Max, the bull mastiff, and as such it is difficult to see this area of law as governed by some statutory principle, knowledge of which will enlighten jurists. The required knowledge for dealing with these kinds of cases is to be found only in detailed works on the characters of individual species of domestic animals.

Even if the rule had been much less complex, there would still be the problem of how one gets from rule to result. The *Code civil* has a single principle, article 1385, dealing with damage caused by animals. It states: 'The owner or user of an animal, while it is in his service, is liable for the damage that the animal has caused whether it was under his control or whether it had strayed or escaped.' A donkey, while being driven by its owner up a public path, is startled by a passing car and knocks against a wall, dislodging a stone. If the stone fell on, and injured, a person asleep behind the wall, will the owner of the donkey be strictly liable for the injury under article 1385? No doubt a lawyer could find reasons both for and against liability.[74] Yet the knowledge point to be stressed is that the rule itself simply does not contain the answer. The answer, as the Roman jurist would have said, can be found only in the circumstances of the case. How are these events to be 'interpreted' (or more accurately 'constructed')? Is a distinction to be drawn between direct and indirect damage? Is a donkey to be differentiated from a stone? French judges, like Roman and English lawyers, will need to think in pictures and such thinking will, in its turn, depend upon how one sees the world. How are events like an accident to be viewed and analysed? To answer these questions one must look beyond the rules. One starts with the facts and, as we have seen, one can do much with them before actually turning to the rules.

The Imagined Bystander

The case of the bull mastiff involved an examination of the characteristics of the animal itself. An alternative method is to adopt the imagined dialogue of a bystander. For example, in *W* v. *L (mental health patient)*,[75] the court of appeal had to decide the meaning of 'mental illness' within section 26(2)(a)(i) of the Mental Health Act, 1959. Lawton LJ, after observing that the Act itself contained no definition of the term, stated that they were to be approached as ordinary words of the English language having no particular medical or legal significance. In order to construe them one should have reference to the way ordinary sensible people would construe them. This would involve the following test: 'what would the ordinary sensible person have said about the patient's condition in this case if he had been informed of his behaviour to the dogs, the cat and his wife?' According to Lawton LJ, the response would be: "'Well, the fellow is obviously mentally ill.'"[76]

Now the facts of this case were particularly sad, as Lord Denning MR pointed out, in that the patient's behaviour towards his wife and the family pets had been both vivid and horrifying. Moreover, the term 'mental illness' itself is one that tends towards the vivid.

Consequently, the resorting to mental imagery was perhaps unavoidable. Yet the technique employed by Lawton LJ (the use of the ordinary sensible person as the vehicle for interpretation) was on the one hand a not untypical statutory interpretation device when dealing with so-called ordinary words. On the other hand, it was nothing less than a means of painting a picture in the sense that he moved from the facts (the behaviour of the patient) to the law (mental illness) through the construction of an image of which the main characteristic was its vividness. The isomorphy contained in the rule may have been opaque, but the isomorphy in the facts was not, and the 'ordinary sensible person' became the means by which this isomorphy could be channelled from the particular to the seemingly abstract major premise.[77]

Comparing Images: Attorney-General v. Howard United Reformed Church

Another possibility is to have recourse to a mixture of visual approaches. Take, for example, *Attorney-General* v. *Trustees of the Howard United Reformed Church*.[78] This was a relator action on behalf of a local authority for a declaration that a particular church was not 'an ecclesiastical building' in respect of town planning legislation. The technique suggested by counsel was that of the objective observer. In the words of Willis J:

> A test suggested by counsel for the plaintiff is that of the officious bystander: standing at the back of the building he would say, says counsel for the plaintiff, 'This is a disused school', while standing at the front outside, he would say 'this is an ecclesiastical building', but on going in and seeing the conditions he would say 'I was wrong, it was but is no longer an ecclesiastical building'.[79]

Willis J went on to say that he found this approach helpful in the absence of any other guide. However, the problem facing counsel for the plaintiff was that the image of a disused church was to some extent threatened by the fact that it continued occasionally to be used by the elders for their meetings and that these meetings were preceded by prayers. Carol services were also held during the Christmas period. Yet counsel for the defendant had, equally, to contend with an image which was not necessarily helpful; this was the image of a building which for much of the time was used only for social activities.

Counsel for the defendant accordingly tried to create a picture of a congregation involved in social activities whose aim was to encourage 'fellowship within the church'.[80] Indeed, it was even suggested on behalf of the defendant that the fielding of a cricket team was an activity of fellowship which amounted to an ecclesiastical purpose.[81] In effect, then, the case appeared to come down to a comparison of images. On the one hand, there was the image of a disused building whose churchlike activities belonged to a past age; on the other hand, there was the image of a fellowship of people bound together by social activities. In dealing with this factual ambiguity, Willis J did not as such choose one image over another. What he did was to add his own analysis of the defendant's image whereby he accepted that, if the activities could be described as ecclesiastical, then the building could still be said to be in ecclesiastical use. However, the activities themselves could be analysed factually into the ecclesiastical and the social and, once this had been done, the image of the activities actually taking place within the building took on the image that did not accord with the one advanced by the defendant.

The court of appeal reversed this decision of Willis J.[82] Lord Denning MR agreed in part with the conclusion reached by the first instance judge: no one could regard church bazaars and coffee mornings as ecclesiastical purposes. However, the building itself had such an attribute since it was designed and built as a church and, crucially, it 'looks like a church'. Even if 'it should fall into disuse, it would still remain an "ecclesiastical building"', which would cease only if it was 'put to some secular purpose, such as storing records or as a museum'.[83] The quality of being 'ecclesiastical', for the then Master of the Rolls, thus attached to the image of a building and it would require some positive act of non-ecclesiastical use to destroy this image. Stephenson LJ and Lawton LJ also agreed that social gatherings and the like were not enough to make the building ecclesiastical; but the monthly church meetings and the carol services were sufficient to allow the building to retain its character. Earlier in his judgment, Stephenson LJ had used a striking image in order to reject the argument that mere ownership by an ecclesiastical organisation was enough to endow a building with an ecclesiastical character: 'if it were, a brothel owned by the Church Commissioners would be an ecclesiastical building'.[84]

Lawton LJ thought that a distinction should be drawn between social gatherings and activities 'connected with the worship of God'.[85] Churches have many activities and if there were any activities which had some direct connection with the worship of God then this would suffice to continue to give a building its ecclesiastical character. Lawton LJ, like the other judges, also had recourse to various images in order to give support to what would be his conclusion. In particular, he described in some detail the cathedrals run by Benedictine monks before the Reformation:

> Each cathedral had its chapter house, sleeping accommodation for the monks, a refectory brewhouse and a kitchen. The buildings in which administration, sleeping and eating were carried on could properly have been described as ecclesiastical because they were necessary adjuncts to the celebrating of mass and the singing of office in the cathedral. But in addition most of these cathedrals had schools attached to them and their chapters owned farms situated over wide areas which supplied the monks with food and the cathedrals with revenue. The school if in buildings apart from the cathedral and monastery, and farm buildings could not, in my opinion, have properly been described as ecclesiastical buildings as they were not adjuncts to worship.[86]

The House of Lords restored the decision of Willis J.[87] Lord Cross, who delivered the only substantive speech, agreed with the court of appeal that the disused building was still an ecclesiastical building. However, the vagueness of the phrase 'ecclesiastical purposes' was in itself enough to indicate that the wrong approach had been adopted with regard to the statute. If the trustees of an ecclesiastical building were to stop using it for ecclesiastical purposes, said Lord Cross, before they had decided to demolish it and then later decided to demolish it while it was unused, they would have to obtain listed building consent. But if they decided to demolish it while they were still holding services in it 'and go on using it for ecclesiastical purposes until the "bulldozers" make its continued use for such purposes impractical they do not require "listed building" consent'. This, concluded Lord Cross, would be a ridiculous distinction.[88] The law lord had, earlier, also shifted attention off the building itself and onto the intention of the trustees to demolish the church. 'If a stranger who saw the church being demolished,' Lord Cross said, 'were to ask, "Why is the building not being used as a church?" he would hardly think "Because the works of demolition which you see in progress make such use impracticable" a satisfactory answer.'[89] This was not, it would finally seem, a case about a building at all, but one about the intention of owners.

In terms of a rule it is no doubt possible to say that Willis J was refusing to interpret the word 'ecclesiastical' very widely whereas the court of appeal were more generous. But the reasoning process by which the judges arrived at their respective interpretations is much more a matter of isomorphic imagery than of semantic interpretation and syllogistic logic. Counsel and judges participated in exercises of construction within the facts. And while it is perfectly reasonable to argue that the imagery contained in the word 'ecclesiastical' determined the broad types of factual pictures in play, it would be misleading to say that the rule contained, or could ever contain, the kind of information to be found in the reasoning of all of the counsel and all of the judges. Indeed, this is particularly evident when one adds the decision of the House of Lords, which changed the whole dimension of the image in the way it took attention off the building (*res*) and onto the intention of a person (*persona*). This particular shift took place within the facts and was not of itself pre-ordained in the statutory rule. In fact, there is nothing in the statutory rule to suggest that the various images of cricket, monks, bulldozers and passers-by watching a building being demolished might have a relevance. All these images were in the minds of the reasoner rather than the rule.

Attorney-General v. *Howard United Reformed Church* is, evidently, a case that found itself before the courts because of the existence of a clear and immutable rule in the sense of a densely written text. To that extent it is substantively and methodologically a statutory interpretation case. But the rule, as useful as it might be in locating the legal issue within the general legal system (planning law, for example), is not as such the cause of the decision. The differences of conclusion between the various courts is indicative of the inability of the written proposition to contain much more than superficial information. The decision as to whether the building was an ecclesiastical building depended upon the construction of images whose possibilities and permutations were quite considerable. The building could be related to the persons who were continuing to use it, or to other buildings conjured up from history. Equally, it could be linked to the imaginary bystander and a dialogue created to reinforce the image desired. The point to be stressed, again, is that legal reasoning cannot be conceived either as an activity tied to words or as a process of syllogistic inference. Statutory interpretation is a matter of constructing and reconstructing facts and requires a cognitive dimension beyond the rules.

Framing the Image

If one returns to the facts of the discharged oil that polluted the beach, it has already been suggested that one can focus on the facts in one of two ways. Either one can look at the act of the captain *vis-à-vis* the discharged oil and the distressed ship or at the wider picture of a proprietor sending out his ships and cargoes. In this latter image the focus of attention is likely to be the activity of the control of things. Just how the two different images can lead to different analogies and different conclusions has been analysed in detail elsewhere.[90] But what is worth repeating with respect to the various decisions in *Esso Petroleum Ltd* v. *Southport Corporation*[91] is the subtlety with which Denning LJ used the tort of public nuisance to create a different picture that went back in time. In bringing into the frame, so to speak, the whole activity of putting to sea a tanker laden with oil, he created a pattern of elements that changed the nature of the normative structure. He not only made the trial judge's analogy between a car and a ship redundant, but his broader frame also gave rise of itself to a different normative situation. The question was no longer one about the act of a captain in an emergency, but the activity of a transporter of environmentally harmful material.

Now this affair was, of course, not a statutory interpretation case. Indeed, it might be thought that this pictorial approach is a result of the peculiar nature of the cause of action approach to liability which is often seen as a hangover from the forms of action. This was a system of 'typical fact-situations' where 'to discover whether you had a remedy you matched the facts of your case against the type or template offered by the law'.[92] In fact, the two different pictures are just as relevant for cases involving legal texts since they can be discerned in the structures which underpin the highly abstract propositions in the French *Code civil*. The two provisions are:

> 1382 Any act whatsoever of a man, which causes damage to another, obliges the person by whose fault the damage has occurred, to make compensation.
>
> 1384 One is liable not only for damage that one has caused by one's own act, but also for that caused by the act of any person for whom one must answer, or for things under one's control.

The pictures are by no means very vivid and they represent more of a structure than a detailed photograph. Nevertheless, an act and its effect upon another individual (article 1382) is different from the idea of a relationship between an individual and a thing (article 1384) in that the emphasis is no longer on the act but on the relationship of control. Denning LJ, in the eyes of a French private lawyer, was no doubt shifting attention off article 1382 (liability for acts) and onto 1384 (liability for activities). What is interesting about such a shift is what it tells us about imagery operating at an abstract level. That one can talk in such terms is of course to leave the descriptive world of detail – a world of ginger-beer, underpants, oil tankers, captains and the like – but it is not to leave the world of fact. Thinking about facts involves thinking about the relationships and connections between the various elements within a set of facts. It is a question of level of abstraction. Nevertheless, the very abstraction of the French rules brings its own problems, in that a provision like article 1384 cannot easily connect with the images of particular factual situations. In emphasising the relationship between person and thing it is unable to distinguish between various types of things.

Of course, the method by which Denning LJ achieved this change of picture in *Southport* was through the application of different causes of action. The judge ran through trespass, private nuisance and public nuisance before he was able to find a cause that fitted the factual situation. He then used the burden of proof requirement that attached to public nuisance to expand the picture and this allowed him to include within the frame Esso itself. In the words of Denning LJ:

> The defendants seek to justify themselves by saying that it was necessary for them to discharge the oil because their ship was in danger. She had been driven by rough seas on to the revetment wall, and it was necessary to discharge the oil in order to get her off. If she had not done so, lives might have been lost. This is, no doubt, true at that stage in the story, but the question is, how came she to get upon the wall? If it was her own fault, then her justification fails, because no one can avail himself of a necessity produced by his own default. Where does the legal burden rest in this respect? Must the Southport Corporation prove that the ship was at fault in getting on to the wall, or must the ship prove that she herself was not at fault? In my opinion the burden is on the ship. She does not justify herself in law by necessity alone, but only by unavoidable necessity, and the burden is on her to show it was unavoidable.[93]

In the picture presented by the trial judge, Esso remained outside of the frame inasmuch as its liability was entirely dependent upon whether the act of the captain amounted to a tort or not. It was simply a question of vicarious liability whereby the employer is held responsible only indirectly.[94] Indeed, in order to reinstate the decision of the trial judge, the House of Lords was forced to restrict, once again, the frame, which they did at the level of procedure. Thus Lord Radcliffe asserted the case ought to be decided in accordance with the pleadings. And he continued:

> If it is, I am of opinion, as was the trial judge, that the respondents failed to establish any claim to relief that was valid in law. If it is not, we might do better justice to the respondents – I cannot tell, since the evidence is incomplete – but I am certain that we should do worse justice to the appellants, since in my view they were entitled to conduct the case and confine their evidence in reliance upon the further and better particulars of the statement of claim which had been delivered by the respondents.[95]

As he appears to admit, to restrict the case at the level of procedure might well do some injustice to the plaintiff. Had the plaintiffs pleaded the case on a direct non-delegable duty between Esso and themselves, the outcome could have been different. Now the importance of course with Lord Radcliffe's assertion is that the case can be explained in terms of rules of procedure. The plaintiffs failed because they did not adhere properly to the rules of pleading. Yet what is important from a cognitive point of view is the way the case was decided on a factual image that was defined by the dimension of the frame. In failing, at the outset, to construct and to frame the facts in a particular kind of way, the plaintiffs undermined the strength of their own case.

Such an exercise, as the *Code civil* suggests, might be equally relevant where the law applicable is contained in a text. Two different texts might be providing independent frames for encapsulating factual situations differently. Accordingly, the solution finally arrived at is not so much the result of a particular *interpretation* of a statute; it flows from the way the image is structured and framed.

Res (Imago) Ipsa Loquitur

Another way of approaching the dichotomy between articles 1382 and 1384 is at the level of procedure. Where damage is caused by an object under the control of another, this gives rise to a presumption of fault and causation. The 'thing' speaks for itself. Such a theory has been formally abandoned in France inasmuch as article 1384 is independent of article 1382 and lays down a substantive rule of strict liability.[96] Yet the interrelationship between burden of proof and strict liability can still cause problems. In English law, as Denning LJ expressly recognised in *Esso*, the essential difference between negligence (fault liability) and public nuisance (strict liability) is one of evidence more than substance:

> (4) *Burden of proof.* One of the principal differences between an action for a public nuisance and an action for negligence is the burden of proof. In an action for a public nuisance, once the nuisance is proved and the defendant is shown to have caused it, then the legal burden is shifted on to the defendant to justify or excuse himself. If he fails to do so, he is held liable, whereas in an action for negligence the legal burden in most cases remains throughout on the plaintiff. In negligence, the plaintiff may gain much help from provisional presumptions like the doctrine of *res ipsa loquitur*, but, nevertheless, at the end of the case the judge must ask himself whether the legal burden is discharged. If the matter is left evenly in the balance, the plaintiff fails. But in public nuisance, as in trespass, the legal burden shifts to the defendant, and it is not sufficient for him to leave the matter in doubt. He must plead and prove a sufficient justification or excuse.

From the position of cognitive analysis, then, the point that needs to be made is that burden of proof becomes the means for widening or narrowing the dimension of the frame. D drives into P's front wall: what must P show in order to be able to claim damages from D (or D's insurance company)? The general principle is clear enough: the plaintiff must prove that the defendant's act was the cause of his damage. However, if one can widen the frame, so to speak, to encompass a series of events culminating in the crash then one can move from the act to the activity. Such a crash, it could be argued, does not happen within the context of the relationship between person and thing (car) unless there was negligence and thus the onus is on D to advance an alternative explanation. But what if D claims that the crash could have happened as a result of a defect in his car? It is in this situation, as the *Esso* case illustrates, that the widening of the frame becomes particularly important because the emphasis will then shift onto the longer-term relationship between driver and car. Was the car regularly serviced? Was the defect of a kind of which the owner or driver ought to have been aware?

Just how effective this change in the frame of the image can be is illustrated by the *res ipsa loquitur* cases. The brakes fail on a lorry and it careers down a hill, killing the plaintiff's husband. What must the plaintiff prove in order to obtain damages? Can the owners of the lorry escape liability by showing that the brakes failed because of a defect undiscoverable by the use of reasonable care? If one concentrates only on the act of the driver and the owner, it could be difficult to pinpoint any negligence, especially if the owners can prove that the defective brake was visually inspected once a week. In other words, if one takes a narrow view of the facts, it is easy to come to the conclusion that there was no negligence.

However, if one extends the frame, the image can change quite dramatically as the speech of Lord Donovan, one of the majority in *Henderson* v. *HE Jenkins & Sons Ltd*[97] indicates. Lord Donovan stated, first of all, that the defendants 'proved that the pipe in question was visually inspected *in situ* once a week; that the brake pedal was on these occasions depressed to check for leaks from the pipe and none seen; that nothing more than such visual inspection of the pipe was required by Ministry of Transport rules or the maker's advice'.[98] He then continued:

> Yet the kind of load this lorry had been carrying in the past was something which had to be known in order to assess the measure of the duty of reasonable care resting on the [defendants]. For the corrosion of the pipe was caused by some chemical agent. Had the lorry, therefore, been carrying chemicals of any kind? Or had it operated under conditions where salt (also a corrosive agent) might

> come in contact with the pipe? Or had it at some time been adapted for carrying cattle and done so? If any of these things were the case then clearly visual inspection of the pipe *in situ* would not have been enough. It should have been removed at intervals so that the whole of it, and not merely part of it, could be examined.[99]

And he concluded:

> It was, therefore, incumbent on the [defendants], if they were to sustain their plea of latent defect undiscoverable by the exercise of ordinary care, to prove where the vehicle had been and what it had been carrying whilst in their service and in what conditions it had operated. Only then could the standard of reasonable care be ascertained, and their conduct measured against it.[100]

Lord Donovan was evidently engaging in a similar exercise to the one undertaken by Denning LJ in *Esso* v. *Southport*. Nevertheless, he opens the frame of reference, not through the application of an alternative cause of action, but through the normative relationship of 'duty'. The assessment of the content of the lorry owner's duty was not to be measured by reference to the act of examining the brakes *in situ* as required by government rules. Measured by that standard, the factual image is clearly one of reasonable behaviour. Instead, the content of the duty was to be measured against the wider historical and geographical picture. This new image was entirely different, in that it brings into the frame not just the relationship between owner and lorry, but the further relationships between owner and goods and owner and location. In turn this creates an image of a social responsibility between person and thing that goes beyond mere adherence to government regulations. In other words, the more complex the factual relationships attaching to the lorry owner, the more complex the duty.

The common denominator, then, between Denning LJ and Lord Donovan is not to be found in the words of the law. They both adopted different legal tools. Instead, it is to be found in the construction of the facts. What both the judges did was to widen the image by changing the frame of the picture. They pushed the frame of reference back into the past so as to produce a much richer canvas and this allowed them to create a normative situation that was more subtle than the one adopted at first instance in each of the cases. Such an exercise can be captured by words inasmuch as the *Code civil* is able to create at the level of abstract principle a dichotomy between liability for acts and liability for things. However, neither of the two French provisions is able to encompass within their language the richness of the factual relations that are to be found surrounding any litigation problem. This is why the emphasis in this area of French private law is, in reality, on the case law rather than the code.[101] Indeed, one French textbook comments that the case law surrounding article 1384 is complex, technical and uncertain. And it suffers from trying to submit a bottle of fizzy drink, a needle, a horse, a lift, a boat, a tree, a stair rod, a ski, a television set and the like to a single rule.[102] This is not to say that French obligations lawyers have much to learn from the English law of tort. The point to be made is simply that knowledge of law does not reside exclusively at the level of words. Statutory interpretation is not 'interpretation' in the strict sense of the term. It is, as with reasoning from precedent, about *constructing* images.

Notes

1 See, generally, Bergel (1999, pp. 153–69).
2 Ibid., p. 154.
3 Ibid., pp. 154–5.
4 Perrot (2000, para. 215).
5 Wieacker (1995, p. 254).
6 Dubouchet (1990, pp. 106–10).
7 Lobban (1991, pp. 34–46, 234–44).
8 *FA & AB Ltd* v. *Lupton* ([1972] AC 634, 658–9).
9 At p. 659.
10 Ibid.
11 (1866) LR 1 Ex 265, 279, emphasis added.
12 Müller (1996, pp. 106–7).
13 Bengoetxea (1993, p. 95).
14 Zander (1999, p. 107).
15 Dworkin (1986, pp. 87, 410).
16 Dworkin (1977, p. 85).
17 See, generally, Berthelot (1990, pp. 43–85). For a summary, see Granger (1995, pp. 90–92).
18 Berthelot (1990, p. 73).
19 Cass.civ.3e.17.12.1997, D.1998.111 note Aubert.
20 'But whereas having held, in good law, that the partnership (*concubinage*) could result only from an established and stable relationship having the appearance of marriage, that is to say between a man and a woman, the Court of Appeal has neither violated article 26 of the International Pact on civil and political rights nor article 8, paragraph 1, of the European Convention safeguarding the human rights and fundamental liberties; it follows from this that the motion has no basis. For these reasons, reject.'
21 *Fitzpatrick* v. *Sterling Housing Association* [1998] Ch 304, 336. The House of Lords reversed the court of appeal's decision, thus validating Ward LJ's dissenting judgment: [2000] 1 AC 27.
22 Ivainer (1988, pp. 22–4, 84–6).
23 *Read* v. *J Lyons & Co* [1947] AC 156.

24 Blanché (1975, p. 152).
25 [1932] AC 562.
26 [1936] AC 85.
27 Atias (1994, pp. 111–12).
28 Blanché (1983, p. 20).
29 Peter Gibson LJ in *Gardner* v. *Marsh & Parsons* [1997] 1 WLR 489, 505.
30 *Hussey* v. *Eels* [1990] 2 QB 227, 241.
31 [1932] AC 562.
32 *Lockett* v. *A & M Charles Ltd* [1938] 4 All ER 170.
33 [1938] 4 All ER 170.
34 Cf. *Sumpter* v. *Hedges* [1898] 1 QB 673.
35 [1976] 1 WLR 459.
36 At p. 461.
37 At pp. 461–2.
38 At p. 462.
39 Ibid.
40 [1973] QB 27.
41 At p. 35.
42 [1997] AC 191.
43 At p. 210.
44 [1995] QB 375.
45 [1997] AC 213.
46 Ibid.
47 Samuel (2001, pp. 215–38).
48 Ibid., p. 212.
49 Ibid., p. 214.
50 *Sidaway* v. *Governors of Bethlem Royal Hospital* [1985] AC 871, 884.
51 Animals Act 1971, s. 3.
52 Izorche (2001, pp. 29–76).
53 See now the Consumer Protection Act 1987 and Food Safety Act 1990.
54 See, generally, *Alcock* v. *Chief Constable of South Yorkshire* [1992] 1 AC 310.
55 But cf. *Smedleys Ltd* v. *Breed* [1974] AC 839.
56 See, for example, Llewellyn (1951, p. 48).
57 See, for example, D.2.13.12.
58 See, for example, *Nairn* v. *University of St Andrews* [1909] AC 147.
59 See, for example, Unfair Terms in Consumer Contracts Regulations 1999.
60 See, for example, *Jackson* v. *Horizon Holidays Ltd* [1975] 1 WLR 1468.
61 Sale of Goods Act 1979, s. 14(2), (3).
62 Consumer Protection Act 1987, s. 2(2)(c).
63 Weir (1967, p. 19).
64 See, for example, *Harlington & Leinster Enterprises Ltd* v. *Christopher Hull Fine Art Ltd* [1991] 1 QB 564.
65 See *Heil* v. *Hedges* [1951] 1 TLR 512.
66 See, for example, *Staffordshire AHA* v. *South Staffs Waterworks* [1978] 1 WLR 1387.
67 [1976] 3 All ER 561.
68 At p. 563.

69 Bengoetxea (1993, p. 186).

70 It appears that Lord Denning had second thoughts about this question in *Cummings* v. *Granger* [1977] QB 397: see the Law Report in *The Times*, 28 May 1976.

71 *Cummings* v. *Granger* [1977] QB 397.

72 [1990] 1 WLR 459.

73 Slade LJ [1990] 1 WLR 459, 464.

74 Cf. Cass.civ.27.10.1885; S.86.1.33.

75 [1973] 3 All ER 884.

76 At p. 890.

77 A variant of the imagined bystander is the imagined conversation: see, for example, Lord Denning MR in *Re Rowland* [1963] Ch 1, 11; discussed by Samuel (1994, pp. 149–51). Note also the recent approach of Sir Christopher Staughton: 'Left to myself and guided only by the ordinary English meaning of words, I would say that a person is not habitually resident here on the day when she arrives, even if she takes up residence voluntarily and for settled purposes. "Habitually", to my mind, describes residence which has already achieved a degree of continuity. I can illustrate that by this imaginary conversation: *Q*. Do you habitually go to church on Sunday? *A*. Yes, I went for the first time yesterday. That does not make sense to me' (*Nessa* v. *Chief Adjudication Officer* [1998] 2 All ER 728, 731). Note also the examples given by Morritt LJ at p. 742.

78 [1973] 3 All ER 878 (QBD); [1974] 3 All ER 273 (CA); [1975] 2 All ER 337 (HL).

79 [1973] 3 All ER 878, at p. 881.

80 At p. 882.

81 See p. 883.

82 [1974] 3 All ER 273.

83 At p. 276.

84 At p. 278.

85 At p. 281.

86 Ibid.

87 [1975] 2 All ER 337.

88 At p. 346.

89 Ibid.

90 Samuel (1994, pp. 199–200; 2001, pp. 27–30).

91 [1953] 3 WLR 773 (QBD); [1954] 2 QB 182 (CA); [1956] AC 218 (HL).

92 Weir (1974, p. 16).

93 [1954] 2 QB 182, 197–8.

94 Samuel (2001, pp. 461–4).

95 [1956] AC 218, 241.

96 See, for example, Cass.civ.19.2.1997; JCP.1997.II.22848.

97 [1970] AC 282.

98 At p. 299.

99 Ibid.

100 At p. 300.

101 Malaurie and Aynès (1999, nos 29, 188).

102 Ibid., no. 188.

6 Taxonomy in Law

It has already been seen in the last chapter that facts need to be classified. But making sense of facts beyond the individual case involves schemes of intelligibility that will organise these facts according to a 'scientific' discourse that itself will be organised into conceptual categories. Knowledge is inconceivable without organisation and organisation is inconceivable without classification.[1] The history of the natural sciences is largely a history of classification and categorisation of objects allowing for the induction of new higher-level categories in turn acting as the basis for conceptual and propositional constructions.[2] The knowledge (epistemological) value of such schemes is that they act both as a means of reductionism and as a method of constructing a model of reality. Knowledge is reduced to manageable propositions ('laws') or abstract conceptual categories ('animal', 'vegetable' and 'mineral') while at the same time functioning as a structure capable of describing, explaining and predicting.

Classification and Knowledge

Categories have a fundamental role to play in the production of knowledge inasmuch as they act, not just as a means of access from the empirical world to the world of science and vice versa: they act also as objects of knowledge in themselves. Theories can thus attach to categories, while categories can insert themselves into reality to become an essential part of its description. 'The historian of science must take ideas as facts,' wrote Bachelard, but 'the epistemologist must take facts as ideas.'[3] Categories, in the natural sciences or in law, are knowledge ideas inserted within a structure or system which itself represents an idea. This suggests of course that categories are part of the *intellectus* rather than the *res*, but this is not so. Categories are part of the relationship itself between *les mots et les choses*.

The ease with which categories can become assimilated into knowledge rendering them, like the foundations of some great building, almost invisible to the casual onlooker is startlingly illustrated by Foucault. In the preface to his work on the history of the sciences, Foucault recalls the effect of reading Borges's mythical Chinese encyclopedia where the animal kingdom is divided up into a range of exotic categories. These categories, set out in alphabetical order, divide animals into, for example, 'a) belonging to the emperor ... f) fabulous ... h) included in the present classification, i) which act as if mad, j) countless, k) drawn with a fine brush of camel's hair', and so on.[4] Foucault asks just what makes this scheme of categories so exquisite yet so conceptually impossible. His response is to highlight the 'dangerous intermixing' of fantastic and empirical categories which in no way insert themselves into the actual world of animals. There are neither ugly monsters nor dragons with red-hot breath; the monstrosity neither alters nor modifies a living body nor does it contain any strange power. Foucault writes:

> It is not the 'fabulous' animals which are impossible, since they are designed as such, but the narrow distance according to which they are juxtaposed to stray dogs or to animals which from afar look like flies. What transgresses all imagination, all possible thought, is simply the alphabetical series (a, b, c, d) which ties each category to all the others.[5]

What is impossible, continues Foucault, is not the proximity of the things: 'it is the site itself where they might intermingle as neighbours'. Where can they meet 'except in the intangible voice which pronounces their enumeration, except on the page of the transcript?' They can juxtapose themselves only in the non-existent place that is language; yet 'this language, in deploying the categories, opens only a space which is unthinkable'. Moreover, in employing the central category of animals 'included in the present classification', Foucault makes the point that Borges is ensuring, through the use of a well-known paradox, the ruination of the classification scheme. For one will never succeed in defining as between each of the categories and the scheme which unites them any stable relationship of category and content. If all the classified animals without exception are housed in one of the categories, what of the animals which are not in the scheme? In what kind of space do they reside? The possibility itself is there to imagine, since Borges teases the reader with the order of the alphabet, yet the categories themselves are impossible. And they are impossible either as empirical or as imaginary categories. One can think, thanks to the alphabetical ordering, only of an unimaginable space.[6]

What the alphabetical scheme of classification seems to indicate, therefore, is a 'totality of the words of a language so juxtaposed in order to say precisely nothing'.[7] There is no internal logic or coherence save in respect of the words themselves. Classification, then, is important as a rational (*ratio*) or knowledge (*scientia*) process in itself. Categories, once established, become objects of knowledge in themselves and attract their own theoretical speculation. Yet it is not just the categories; it is equally the structure, scheme or system that binds them (*cohaerere*) that acts as the means by which an object or phenomenon is explained and manipulated. In the natural sciences categories such as 'mammal' or 'vertebrate' are dependent upon the existence of certain empirical qualities that determine which animals will fall within the classification and which will not. Such categorisation is vital for the deductive method in the sciences; classifying an organism as a 'virus' or a 'bacterium' will determine whether or not a doctor should prescribe antibiotics.

In the arts and social sciences, in contrast, categories are often more fluid. Indeed, their role is usually rather different. In the human sciences, categories have a much greater theoretical dimension inasmuch as their function is not restricted to describing an empirical object in terms of clearly identifiable qualities. Categories often have a normative theoretical function which imbues the object categorised with qualities that attach more to the category than to the object as an empirical reality. Of course, to describe a specific animal as a 'vertebrate' imbues the animal with certain qualities; but those qualities can be verified empirically. An animal either has a backbone or it does not. To locate a painting within the category of 'impressionist' implies that the work will display certain features and qualities. Now these qualities can to an extent be verified independently of the category. But the qualities are much more fluid and they have their source more in the theoretical discourse within which the category of 'impressionism' gains its meaning. A single painting can belong to more than one category at one and the same time, or it can display qualities that, depending on the point of view of the classifier, might or might not locate it in the category of 'impressionism'. In addition, the whole system in which 'impressionism' gains it meaning is open to debate.

Facts, then, are often capable of being classified in a whole range of alternative ways, depending upon which element is used as the focal point of classification. However, categories themselves need to be classified. Cumulative categories, which are categories in which something belonging to more than one category can be classed (for example 'accountant' and 'Catholic'), are to be contrasted with alternative categories, which are mutually exclusive categories (for example, 'man' or 'woman', 'bacterium' or 'virus').[8] It is not therefore mutually exclusive to classify someone as an accountant and a Catholic. It is mutually exclusive to categorise an organism as a virus and a bacterium. Genus also needs to be differentiated from species (all tigers are animals but not all animals are tigers). More specifically, equivalent categories must be differentiated from hierarchical categories; thus to contrast humans with animals is no doubt an everyday exercise in ordinary discourse, but it is still to make a category mistake.

In addition to distinguishing between categories as a matter of form, there are substantive differences to be made between the 'describers' that give each category its reason for being.[9] In many of the natural sciences these 'describers', as has been suggested already, are objective in that the categorisation is being made with reference to empirical fact.[10] To classify a thing as liquid or solid or an animal as vertebrate or invertebrate is to reflect a factual reality. These categories are relatively uncontroversial (in Western thinking at least) and belong to systems that are stable and considered complete as knowledge models. There may be controversy over the classification of some poorly understood disease or various phenomena in astrophysics, but most of the categories used by scientists to describe the objective world are accepted as axiomatic. However, as Oléron points out, in a great many cases outside the sciences, the 'describers' are blurred and involve an estimation that can itself be a matter of argument.[11] This is even truer when categories have values as their 'describers'. To classify an act as 'sinful' or 'unnatural' is to attach a connotation that will of itself provoke a positive or negative reaction and thus these categories are often employed by public speakers and politicians. In these situations, however, care must be taken to distinguish classification as a method from reasoning or arguing by analogy. To argue that electricity is analogous to water is not strictly to categorise the two things within a single class. Yet it is to imply that there is an objective describer that links the two things and this describer could then become the foundation for a higher-level category that would encompass both water and electricity (for example, the category of 'fluid').

Legal Classification

When one turns to law, classification, as we have already suggested in the previous chapter, is one fundamental legal skill in the analysis and sorting of facts. However, it is evident from a case like *Donoghue* v. *Stevenson* that facts can be classified in a number of quite different ways, depending upon the 'describer' used. The facts could be classified according to the relationships flowing between the parties, the damage suffered, the status of the parties or the nature of the thing that does the damage. Another way of classifying the facts is in relation to a 'describer' that is dictated as much by the discourse of law as by any objective reality. For example, the case could be categorised according to the nature of the interests in issue; in turn these interests could imply a certain category of plaintiff, such as 'consumer'. Classification is equally essential with respect to legal rules and legal concepts. Different categories of law reflect different normative 'describers', these 'describers' in turn finding expression through different kinds of legal concepts.[12] Contractual rights are to be differentiated from proprietary rights; tort duties from equitable obligations.

Taxonomy and Legal Science

The epistemologist will not of course be surprised by this central role of classification. The history of legal thought, at least within the civilian tradition, is a history of *scientia iuris*. And since the whole notion of a rational science implies systematisation, classification and conceptualisation, this history of law, like the history of science, is likely to be one in which the development of a genealogy of categories is of major importance. Logical deduction, the assumed method of the Natural Lawyers and the Positivists, requires secure categories. Of course the problem with social facts is that they never lend themselves to any single scheme of carefully constructed categories. Instead, they are continually open to a multitude of categorisation possibilities which in turn bring to bear on the facts differing schematic possibilities in the scientific sense.[13] Accordingly, a unitary classification scheme of mutually exclusive categories acting as the basis of a model from which solutions can be inferred simply as a result of the logic of the taxonomy is a kind of Holy Grail that generations of jurists have pursued and, indeed, are still pursuing.[14] Yet it is evident, particularly within the common law tradition, that legal reasoning is not founded in some inferential model. Consequently, it is worth recalling, once again, the words of Professor Bergel:

> Every legal system aims to extend to all persons within its rule the security they need and, to achieve this, must allow each person to have knowledge in advance of the rule to which he will be subjected. This presupposes a sufficient stability of rules and an internal coherence of the system, based upon a specific organisation of relations between the elements which compose it, so that each of these elements is dependent on others ...[15]

However, as he goes on to point out, 'the reduction of law to equations is a myth' because it 'comes up against insurmountable difficulties of method and against the objectives of every legal system'. For the 'law is full of departures from logical solutions deduced from an axiom' and these 'exceptions result from other preoccupations, other principles and other axioms of which the sheer number, the complication and the differing intensity make impossible an expression of positive law in mathematical form'.[16]

Where legal categories have been of major importance, however, is with regard to the development of theoretical ideas underpinning positive law. Legal categories such as 'contract', 'tort' and 'crime' have all, for example, been the objects of intense theoretical writing and this theoretical literature has in turn had important influences in shaping directly or indirectly the functioning of the legal reasoning within each category.[17] What is meant by the term 'tort' and what are its aims and purposes? Indeed, in the case of 'restitution' in English law, the whole development of the subject over the past thirty years has been driven by a literature concerned as much with the category as with its contents. And an important side-effect of the restitution debate is that it has led one participant to try to re-emphasise the importance of classification in law. Taxonomy, asserts Peter Birks, is the essential rational basis for all legal thought.[18] Professor Birks, as we have already seen, has attacked English legal reasoning on the basis that it exhibits a lack of rigour when it comes to legal taxonomy, and he advocates – or seems to be advocating – that common lawyers have much to learn from the civilians. In particular, he asserts that the *Institutes* of Justinian provide the basic map of the law.[19] Now, few civilians would dispute this map since its structure is imprinted on every modern European code. Thus Birks is undoubtedly correct in implying that any serious investigation of taxonomy in law must start with the Romans. What one can legitimately ask, however, is whether such a taxonomical scheme has the same objective validity as the schemes that underpin a natural science like zoology. Or, put another way, are the objective 'describers' that underpin the civilian scheme rooted in social fact or social values?

Classification in Roman Law

Taxonomy in law starts, then, with the Romans, inasmuch as the structure of all the modern codes is based to a greater or lesser extent upon what is called the institutional system of Roman law.[20] The system developed by Gaius, and adopted by Justinian, focused, as we have seen in Chapter 4, on the three institutions of *persona, res* and *actio*.[21] These three institutions, it must be said, have a solid empirical basis inasmuch as people, things and social disputes exist as objects in social reality; accordingly, they act as a good starting point as describers for legal categories. Gaius thus subdivides 'law' into the three generic categories of the law of persons, law of things and law of actions. However, the scheme is wanting in two major respects. First, 'law' for the purposes of the *Institutes* is not law as a whole, but just private law. As Justinian makes clear, the great *summa divisio*, which inserts itself between law and private law, is the division between public and private law.[22] According to the late classical jurist Ulpian, the distinction reflects a difference of interests (*utilitates*). The *ius publicum* was an area of law concerned with the interests of the state, whereas the *ius privatum* dealt with the interests of individuals.[23] Secondly, although the scheme has empirical objects (the institutions of *persona, res* and *actio*) acting as the describers of each category, these institutions ended up by transcending the actual empirical objects. This development effected a shift from the describer to the category; persons and things became categories that created their own objects. Classification in law thus became an exercise subtly different from taxonomy in the natural sciences.

Public Law

The Romans may have established the category of public law and given it a describer, but they failed to provide much structural substance. The two main subdivisions of constitutional and administrative law are products of the later canonists and civilians. These later lawyers used the category of the *ius publicum* to give expression to royal (state) power (*potestas*) which in Roman law had been encapsulated by the term *imperium*.[24] This public power was to be contrasted with the private power of individuals given expression by the word *dominium*.[25] Another describer, then, for the categories of public and private law are these two different kinds of *potestas*. A third object of the category of public law is the public law *actio*. Again Roman law itself was ambiguous, the *actio popularis* spanning the borderland between public and private law.[26] However, the late-medieval canon lawyers started to fashion specific procedures by which an interested party could appeal against an administrative decision.[27] At first, these procedures were indistinguishable from an appeal against a judicial decision and thus administrative remedies and the ordinary appeal procedure have a common history. Later, the appeal procedure against judicial decisions became a separate process from the *recours pour excès de pouvoir*. The first became part of civil procedure, not normally seen as public law, while the latter formed the subject matter of administrative law.

Administrative law is, accordingly, concerned with the actual exercise of power by government organs and officials. As such, the focal point of this category is not the actual harm caused to a citizen as a result of the exercise of the power, but the decision of the organ or official. Administrative law is concerned with the legality of such a decision. If the decision turns out to have had no legal basis or was otherwise abusive (a term construed quite widely), an administrative court, in addition to declaring the administrative decision void, normally has the power to award compensation (at least in the civil law tradition). The language used in such cases is not so much one of rights; the harmed citizen is said to have had his or her legitimate interest invaded by the abusive state act.[28] Such interests evidently recall Ulpian's original 'describer'. But administrative law as a category is not often actually analysed in terms of particular interests. The focal point is the decision and the circumstances surrounding it, together with the remedy pursued by the interested party.

Constitutional law, the other sub-category of public law, has as its main object the constitution. In civilian countries this is normally a written document setting out the rules relevant to the form of the state, the structure of its government and the powers of the various organs of government. As a category in itself, constitutional law is the product of a long and rich history whose foundations are primarily in the work of the Post-glossators and the Canonists.[29] However, as Tierney insists, it is not really possible to understand the growth of constitutional law in the West 'unless we consider constantly, side by side, ecclesiology and political theory, ideas about the church and ideas about the state'.[30] The church as an organisation provided an administrative structure within which competing ideas from Roman law, canon law, political theory and theology were constantly in play from the late Middle Ages onwards.[31] As a category, constitutional law is, then, both a product of history and a framework for political theory. It is Roman in origin inasmuch as it developed within the category of the *ius publicum* and utilised Roman legal concepts, many often taken from the *ius privatum*. But it is modern in its idea of a state based on the rule of law and ideas of individualism and democracy.[32] Constitutional law is thus closely bound up with the whole notion of law itself and, in particular, its sources. One can legitimately say, therefore, that all interpretation of written law – of legislation – is a constitutional matter. However, most civilian systems have in effect delineated a specific domain of constitutional law through the creation of constitutional courts.[33] If administrative law is about controlling the actual workings of governmental power, constitutional law is about controlling the activities of the lawmakers themselves.

Constitutional and administrative law are not the only sub-categories of public law. Fiscal law is usually seen as an independent subdivision and such a category is given greater definition when subject to a specialised jurisdiction with its own particular court.[34] Some might go further and see economic law as a sub-category of public law. Such a category has as its basis all the rules allowing the state to intervene in the economic life of the country in order to regulate it.[35] However, other jurists consider this category as transcending the public–private divide to form an independent area of the law.[36] Economic law 'is not a new subject area in the material sense, but a new way of seeing vis-à-vis the traditional subjects'. In this sense it is like 'comparative law', that is to say a 'categorisation of the law'; 'it is the law envisaged from the viewpoint of its economic consequences'.[37]

Criminal Law

A more general and better-known subdivision of public law is criminal law. This is logically part of public law, since criminal prosecutions are based on the relationship between the individual and the state.[38] It is, in general, the state which investigates crimes and prosecutes alleged offenders. However, the separation between criminal and private law is complicated for two interconnected reasons: first, because in Roman law itself, despite the clear distinction between *ius publicum* and *ius privatum*, the notion of a criminal law was by no means clearly discernible as a distinct and separate category of law. Certainly, there were criminal procedures which were based on the governmental power (*imperium*) and there were legal actions which could be described as *delicta publica*.[39] However, these procedures were largely discretionary, having been delegated from the emperor,[40] and the distinction between *delicta privata* and *delicta publica* was by no means clearly made. Thus private delicts continued to perform the role of punishing a defendant as well as compensating a plaintiff.[41] Equally, the facts which constituted crimes such as theft were also the basis for an important delictual remedy (*actio furti*) in private law.[42] Nevertheless, the outlines of a modern system of criminal law are to be found in the Roman sources. Notions of proof, criminal responsibility and inquisitorial procedures are developed to quite a sophisticated level and certain ideas exhibit a clear philosophy of criminal law, thus laying the foundations for a distinction between criminal and private law.[43]

The second complication results from the fact that in modern French law criminal law is technically attached to private law.[44] This does not mean that there are not separate courts in France for criminal prosecutions or that a distinction is not made between compensation and punishment or between public and private power. Moreover, the separation is clearly made at the level of substantive law, in that there is a criminal code quite distinct from the civil code. However, because of the historical confusion between public and private delicts and the fact that criminal law protects private as well as public interests, the subject fell outside the *ius publicum*. Consequently, according to this logic, it had to fall within the *ius privatum*. One might add that in one respect there is a very real connection between private and criminal law. *L'action civile* allows a victim who has suffered damage to use the criminal process to obtain full compensation as if one was using the private law courts.[45] This connection is, in theory, one that functions only at the level of procedure; yet it has led to differences of substance in the case law between the various divisions of the *Cour de cassation*.

Law of Persons

When one turns to private law and its individual parts, the starting point of the institutional system was the person, for, as the Roman sources themselves state, all law was constituted for the sake of man.[46] The Latin term *persona* has a long and complicated history, ending up as a technical legal term representing the capacity of a legal subject to be the bearer of legal rights and duties. In Roman law itself, *persona* was never, as such, the focal point of any general theory or specific definition (that was never the Roman way); but the basic elements for the institution of the legal subject are to be found in the Roman sources. In particular, the foundations were laid for the legal person. The classical jurists realised that towns and some other groups, in being able to bring and defend claims, were in effect like individual humans and indeed were legal subjects quite independent of the human subjects which made up the group (*universitas*).[47] What is owed to the corporation is not owed to the individuals and what the corporation owes the individuals do not owe.[48]

The extension of legal personality beyond the individual human being might arguably be seen as one of the most important contributions of Roman legal thought to the modern commercial world, although its actual modern development owes more to the later civilians than to the Roman jurists themselves.[49] Nevertheless, it was the Roman institutional system that established the basic epistemological structure. The jurists, as we have seen (Chapter 4), went far in appreciating that, the moment one says that a town itself has possession or ownership of a particular piece of property and is entitled to bring an action to recover the thing, one is, in effect, endowing the town with legal personality.[50] Other texts reinforced, indirectly, this idea of legal personality.[51] For example, the Roman jurists discussed the problem of the relationship between an office and the human person who occupied it.[52] What would be the position if two or more humans occupied a single office: would one still talk in terms of the office as a single institution? In responding positively to this question, the jurists displayed a sophisticated awareness of the distinction between office (legal person) and individuals.

The medieval civilians (Post-glossators) and Canonists, working out the legal position of churches and monasteries in relation to their property, developed these Roman ideas even further. They gradually moved towards the idea of a fictitious person (*persona ficta*).[53] Such a creation did not at that time fully accord with full legal capacity, mainly because the Roman contract of *societas* (partnership) was resolute in its individualism; any legal group other than the Roman state tended to be viewed as a conspiracy.[54] However, the law merchant was much less hesitant. In bringing together the contract of *societas* with the idea of legal personality, commercial law made one of its most important contributions to legal thought.[55] Nevertheless, the Roman political distrust of corporations was to survive well into the modern era and this is one reason why the *Code civil* is ambiguous about the place and relevance of legal persons.[56] The codification implicitly recognised the legal personality of the commercial corporation but did not formally lay down its principle.[57]

Several characteristics are particularly important with respect to the development of legal personality. First, there is the idea that a legal person, as a separate legal subject, will have its own patrimony; the assets of the individuals who make up the corporation are thus separated from the business assets of the commercial undertaking. This endows the modern corporation (company) law with a certain complexity and ambiguity, since it becomes intertwined with the law of property. Secondly, the legal person will be deemed a legal subject capable of contracting and thus legal relations between employer and employees are kept quite separate from any relations with those that run the company. Indeed, the directors and managers themselves will be bound to the company by a contract of employment and this contractual relationship will be independent of any proprietary links. Again, this adds complexity, in that corporation law has an impact upon the law of obligations and the law of obligations, in turn, influences corporation law. Thirdly, the legal person will not be legally affected by the death of the human persons that constitute the group endowed with legal personality; a company is thus freed from the human condition of mortality. The legal person is, then, a conceptual creation through which human persons can pass but whose existence is by no means legally dependent upon them. It is the owner and possessor of its own property which in effect means that commerce can function in a world of 'independent' patrimonies. Legal personality is, accordingly, a category quite separate from the law of property and the law of obligations. But as a category its borders have become increasingly fluid.

The Romans also established the idea of legal status (*de statu hominum*). The distinction between slave and free person was the most fundamental division, but there were other classes of person whose legal position resulted simply from belonging to that particular class.[58] One problem with the actual Roman law of persons is that it is not always easy to distinguish between personality and status. Was a slave a person without legal personality or was the slave's legal position a matter of status? A free person who became a slave was sometimes said to have lost his or her personality by way of 'civil death'.[59] Yet, remaining a living human being, the slave continued to act as a focal point for legal rules, some of which could not be explained simply by treating the slave as property. Such lack of clarity did not seem to have concerned the Roman jurists, who were more interested in analysing factual problems than propounding theories. All the same, categories such as the one between slaves and freemen were to bequeath the general idea of status categories. As an English judge has put it, status is 'the condition of belonging to a class in society to which the law ascribes peculiar rights and duties, capacities and incapacities'.[60]

In modern civil law, therefore, the law of persons can be divided into two broad areas, legal personality and status. The former is concerned with the nature and definition of the legal subject (for example, children in the womb, companies, associations), while the latter deals with the legal standing of particular legal subjects *vis-à-vis* each other, the state (children, citizens, aliens and so on) and the courts themselves (*locus standi*). If the human (*homo*) is the starting point for legal thought, it should by no means be assumed that all human beings, even in modern law, automatically have legal personality. Unborn children present particular problems, in that they have interests but not personality;[61] and the death of a human does not always extinguish the right to sue.[62] The life and death of a human being is not necessarily synonymous with the life and death of the human's legal personality.[63] The law of persons also acts as a definitional category for certain kinds of personal interests. These interests are now being recognised as rights independent of the law of things, with the result that areas such as privacy and dignity are seen as having their foundation, not in the law of property or obligations, but in the law of persons.[64] Some might go further and locate the whole idea of human rights within the law of persons, which would be one reason why such rights are regarded as inalienable; others insist upon distinguishing human rights from human dignity.[65]

Law of Things

Just as *persona* acted as the basis for a law of persons, so *res* acted as the foundation in the institutional scheme for a law of things. This category, in the Gaian scheme, must not be confused with the modern 'law of property', which is based upon rights in things (*iura in rem*). For, in the *Institutes* the law of things consisted of 'things' in their widest sense and this included a category which is today contrasted with the law of property, that is to say the obligations.[66] Obligations were a form of intangible 'thing' (*res incorporalis*).[67] In the modern codes these sub-categories of property and obligations were to be elevated into generic categories, each category containing two fundamentally different kinds of right. Property rights (*iura in re*) are quite different from personal rights (*iura in personam*).[68] In other words, the later civilians sharply distinguish, at the level of legal systematics, between owning and owing. Nevertheless, the modern civil law has retained the remedial distinction: a revindication claim for a thing is quite a different kind of claim from personal action for damages.[69] One might note, also, that in the *Code civil* the law of obligations still forms part of the law of property, in that obligations are classified alongside succession and gifts in Book III entitled *Des différentes manières dont on acquiert la propriété*. In the *Código civil* obligations are elevated into their own Book IV under the title of *De las obligaciones y contractos*. It is the BGB that makes a fundamental distinction between the two.

Another way of viewing the law of things is exclusively in relation to the person. The mass of things, tangible (*res corporales*) and intangible (*res incorporales*),[70] that each natural or legal person has can be viewed as a legal entity in itself (*universitas rerum*) and this entity has attracted the name patrimony from the Roman law term *patrimonium* (cf. Chapter 4). The mass of assets and liabilities can, in other words, be seen as an independent *res* in itself, just as a mass of human beings (*universitas personarum*) can be viewed as an independent *persona*. The Romans themselves did not develop any kind of general theory with regard to patrimony, but they certainly established some of its foundational ideas, which were to be built upon by the later civilians. In particular, they developed the idea of a mass of individual tangible and intangible things as an entity in itself capable of being protected by its own legal remedy.[71] In modern French law every legal subject has his, her or its own patrimony and each *persona* can have only one patrimony. Such a *res* cannot itself be alienated (although it can pass on the death of the subject by way of succession), only the goods and money in the patrimony can come and go.[72] In turn, every legal patrimony has to have its own legal subject, since independent patrimonies cannot in theory exist in

France;[73] in practice, of course, separate and 'independent' patrimonies can be established in the world of commerce through the use of legal personality. The New Dutch Code has gone a step further in respect of the notion of a patrimony. It has specifically incorporated it as part of its system, in that Book III is concerned only with patrimonial rights, and thus one finds in a single book all things, both corporeal and incorporeal.

Law of Obligations and Actions

The distinction between owning and owing is inherent in the idea of *in rem* and *in personam*: owning involves a direct legal relationship between *persona* and *res*, whereas owing is a legal obligation (*obligatio*) which attaches only to legal subjects. Thus an obligation could relate to a specific *res* inasmuch as such a *res* might be the subject of a contract of sale, hire or loan; but the legal bond did not attach to the thing. A contractor could not vindicate such a *res*.[74] All that such a contractor could do was to ask the court via an *actio in personam* either to order the defendant to convey the thing or to condemn the defendant to pay compensation for failure to perform his obligation. This close interrelation between the categories of obligations and actions *in personam* is confirmed in the *Digest* inasmuch as the two are classified together.[75] This was logical as far as Roman law itself was concerned. But with the disappearance of the law of actions in the later civil law (they were ultimately relegated to codes of procedure) the category of obligations was elevated, as has been mentioned, to one of the three generic institutional categories. The modern codes are thus framed around *persona, res* and *obligatio*, although *res* here, as we have seen, has a more restricted meaning of a category dealing with *owning* and its associated relationships (possession, real rights).

In the *Institutes* of Gaius, obligations are said to arise only from contract and delict.[76] The former were all based on the common denominator of agreement (*conventio*),[77] whilst the latter arose out of a wrong (*ex maleficio*).[78] However, this twofold division was, even for Gaius, unsatisfactory since there were some claims that arose neither out of agreement nor out of a wrong.[79] In the *Digest*, Gaius mentions a third category of 'various causes',[80] but Justinian later extended the sources of obligations to four categories. In addition to contract and delict, obligations could arise out of quasi-contract and quasi-delict.[81] Actions *quasi ex contractu* were used to recover money which had been paid in circumstances where there was no actual contract but where it would be unjust for the payee to retain the money.[82] Claims *quasi ex delicto* are more controversial, since the cases grouped under this heading have no obvious common denominator.[83] Strict and (or) vicarious liability have been suggested and such ideas do at first sight appear to underpin some of the actions;[84] more interesting is the thesis that the quasi-delicts were equivalent to modern administrative liability actions.[85] These four categories are to be found in the *Code civil,* although quasi-delict has little meaning in modern civil law. The BGB has rejected quasi-delict and quasi-contract altogether; the idea of a 'quasi' contract was dismissed as a contradiction in terms and the German jurists adopted, instead, unjust enrichment, a principle also to be found in the Roman sources and associated with quasi-contracts.[86]

In German law, then, obligations are subdivided into the three categories of contract, delict and unjust enrichment. These three categories are also, in many ways, now more representative of French law than the old fourfold division of Justinian. However, where French law does differ in structure from the BGB is in respect of strict liability. The *Code civil* has retained those quasi-delictual actions which represented a liability for damage done by things, with the result that the code chapter entitled *Des délits et des quasi-délits* is based upon two fundamental ideas. There is a general liability for one's own act based upon fault, a liability that is equally to be found in all the other codes (although not necessarily at the same level of generality). But in addition there is a liability for damage caused by persons or things under one's control. This duality is proving a fundamental characteristic of modern French law.[87] Unjust enrichment is, by way of contrast, nowhere to be found in the *Code civil,* although it is a central principle in the BGB and some other codes.[88] The French code, following Roman law, has, instead, a chapter on quasi-contracts. However, the *Cour de cassation* has recognised the principle of unjust enrichment as existing outside of the *Code* and it is this recognition that has brought French law more into line with the other models.[89]

Internal Structure of Private Law

Despite the sharp divide between property and obligations, the two categories remain bound together, if no longer by a 'law of things', then at least by the notion of 'private law'. One can talk therefore of an internal structure to this broad category.[90] The structure is nevertheless complex and it has not been fully thought through, with the result that there is not a complete symmetry between the law of persons, property and obligations. The law of persons, for a start, is a category that by no means fits comfortably within private law. Slavery and status can hardly be said to lack a constitutional dimension, and legal personality was seen by Gaius as raising serious political problems.[91] Nationality sits uneasily in the *Code civil.*[92] Furthermore, the law of property differs in structure from the law of obligations, in that it is concerned, not with legal relations between two persons, but with legal relations between a person and a thing (cf. Chapter 4). However, the law of property is not a subject simply about intangible legal bonds. Property has its foundation in tangible things and thus the first subdivision of property is about the nature and classification of things themselves.[93] The law of obligations, in contrast, is not concerned with the status of people (that belongs to the law of persons). Property, accordingly, deals with both the status of things and the relations in things, while obligations encompasses only the relations between persons. That said, the law of property, having identified and classified different types of property, is concerned primarily with the different types of relationships between people and things. And the paradigm relationship is, evidently, ownership. Yet ownership is not the only relationship between *persona* and *res*. Real rights and possession are equally important in terms of legal rules and technicalities.[94] In Roman law, uninterrupted possession in good faith for a certain period would confer ownership on the possessor and thus an important aspect of possession and the acquisition of ownership was usucapion.[95] Ownership, real rights and possession are, then, the main general sub-categories of legal relations with things and as such are the structural sources of property rights.

The barrier between relations *in personam* and *in rem* is not, in truth, watertight. For a start, as we have already implied, the law of obligations is both an equivalent category to the law of property and a species of property. This may be a far cry from the paradoxes of Borges's scheme discussed earlier, but there is an element of unease. Furthermore, the law of obligations also has an important function in protecting property rights against wrongful invasion. Indeed, in Roman law itself, the delict of wrongfully caused damage was, originally, wholly preoccupied with protecting property interests, since personal injury to a freeman was not recognised as damage. The human body was incapable of valuation,[96] and a person was not deemed owner of his own limbs.[97] The logical structure of the institutional scheme is not therefore as firm as it might at first appear. When viewed from the position of an owner of moveable property, the distinction between the theft, wrongful detention and destruction of the *res* is by no means evident from an economic point of view.[98] Yet the institutional scheme sharply distinguishes between the three situations, not just from a law of actions viewpoint, but equally from a legal relations position. An action for the recovery of a thing is completely different from an action for its wrongful destruction. A more logical distinction from the empirical viewpoint might be one between moveable property and land, since the latter is physically very different from chattels. But this was not the Roman way. In fairness to the Roman jurists themselves, it must be said that their use of a general heading of the law of things does at least make the political point that, for them, private law was largely about property and the protection of property interests. It is the modern civil law that has, perhaps, exaggerated a conceptual scheme which functioned, for the Romans, largely at the level of the law of actions.

Beyond the Institutional Categories

The great strength of the Roman institutional scheme, together with the category of public law, has been its ability to act as a coherent and complete model of law. Any legal rule, legal concept or legal fact can be accommodated within the scheme. This, no doubt, is one reason for the epistemological success of Roman law. However, the price for this success has been the scheme's inability to adapt to the increasing complexity of law. The broad categories of public law, persons, things and obligations and actions have proved too general and abstract for all the detailed rules needed to define and to regulate specialised areas of social welfare, employment, economic and commercial law. In addition, new 'describers', often using an empirical focal point, have given rise to categories which view law from more specialised positions. Alongside persons, property and contract are categories such as employment, consumer and product law.

Specialised Categories and the Institutional Scheme

Some of these specialised categories can be seen simply as species of the institutional categories of Roman law. Indeed, areas such as sale, hire, partnership, loan and deposit are inherited straight from the *Institutes* and are to be found as sub-categories within the law of obligations. Newer forms of contract such as insurance can also be accommodated within the codes by analogy with the Roman specific contracts. Contract is thus subdivided in modern civil law into two main categories: there are the unnamed contracts arising out of the general theory of contract which, in turn, is rooted in the notion of agreement (*conventio*); and there are the named contracts. These named contracts are in form just as dependent upon agreement between the parties, but the special rules come into play as a result of the empirical substance of the transaction. Classification is of course vital, given that the specific nature of the contract can give rise to special rules; yet many of these specialised contracts have a relatively stable unity in that they seemingly reflect long-established empirical transactions. On closer inspection, what distinguishes one transaction from another is often as much an institutional as a factual matter. Thus sale is to be distinguished from hire in that one involves the transfer of ownership and often possession, whereas the other involves the transfer only of possession. One could say that the distinction between sale and hire is to be found in the law of property. The epistemological point to be stressed is that, when new forms of contract begin to emerge within the category of unnamed obligations, they are never just factual situations requiring a new category. They often emerge as a new form, or pattern, of institutional structures within existing legal relations.[99]

Family Law

As for the law of persons, it has already been seen that this institutional category varies in length and content, depending on the code. However, one particular sub-category that has become central is that of family law. In Roman law itself, the family was a fundamental unit which attracted its own rules, even if these rules were not grouped within a category labelled 'family law'. Indeed, the family itself was not a clearly defined independent institution; it was defined indirectly through all the various relations by which it was constituted. Thus Roman family law was a matter of status, filiation and property. In modern civil law, thanks to the Canonists, the foundation of the family is the contract of marriage, but in Roman law the basis was not the actual law of contract; it was consent.[100] Indeed, the word 'contract' was never applied to marriage.[101] Moreover, even in the later civil law the contract of marriage was always special. It operated to change the status of the parties in respect of both their *personae* and their *res*. Matrimonial property is thus communal property, although when viewed in terms of *patria potestas* this in effect meant that, until recent times, the husband had full control. Family law was, then, an institutional structure that was something of a hybrid. It was, and to some extent remains, a 'constitutional' unit within the state, yet the building blocks of this unit are primarily from private law in general, that is to say, status, contract and property. As regards the definition of the family, this remains problematic. Is marriage essential or is cohabitation enough? And if cohabitation is sufficient, must this be between two individuals of different sex? In addition to any questions surrounding the status of adults, there is also the matter of the status of children. They have their own quite independent interests,[102] which, of course, can act as the object of a separate category of child law. Family law can, accordingly, easily fragment into various sub-categories like 'marriage', 'children's rights', 'homosexuality and the law' and 'matrimonial regimes'. And one reason for this fragmentation is that the institutional scheme is 'atomistic' (cf. Chapter 8). The scheme has been erected on the paradigm of the individual human rather than the family.

Commercial Law

Another area where the law of persons and the law of things interrelate to create a hybrid category within the institutional scheme is with regard to commerce. However, relative to family law, the separation between civil and commercial law has even fewer roots in Roman law. As Szladits observes, it is not 'a logical necessity, but originates in historical circumstances'.[103] The division resulted from commercial practice which from the late Middle Ages fashioned its own particular rules, case law and doctrine. This case law and doctrine certainly borrowed from Roman law, but, equally, it took from customary law, from canon law (particularly with respect to isolating the role of the will in contracts) and from its own practices (*consuetudo mercatorum*).[104] In the 17th century, commercial law became the focus of legislative attention in France, where its separation from private (Roman) law was further emphasised by its classification under public law.[105] This public law label has now largely been abandoned – although it could still be argued that commercial and financial regulations have more of a public than a private law character – but the independence of commercial law has survived in the French civilian model. Separate courts and code continue to give expression to the division.

Whether or not commercial law forms part of a delineating boundary of private law is a much more difficult question. According to Szladits, the dichotomy between civil and commercial law is almost universal, but it exists 'as a special branch of private law [which] pre-supposes civil law as its subsidiary law'.[106] Codification, in France, had the effect of incorporating commercial law into private law, but as an exception to the *droit civil*.[107] However, despite this formal position, it is possible to see commercial law as a category which in many ways is turning out to be much more complex than it might once have appeared. It is now acting as a framework for new forms of thought that stretch beyond the old ideas, and this could have an impact upon private law. In the realm of European Union law, for example, it has been argued that traditional ideas about private law are in need of restructuring to take account of the reality that, at the European level, commercial law is as much political as private. Private law is being 'constitutionalised'.[108]

Consumer Law

In addition to these complexities, the arrival of the consumer has added a new level of complexity. There is now in France a consumer code separate from both the *Code civil* and the *Code de commerce*[109] and, while this code can undoubtedly be seen as a subdivision of private law, the category itself of consumer law is one that extends beyond private law. It is a category capable of embracing, in addition to rules of private law, rules from public and from criminal law. Primarily, however, it remains a subdivision within the law of persons. The consumer has, according to Atias, been assimilated to an incapable and thus is to be categorised alongside the minor or mentally ill person.[110] This is perhaps a harsh judgment, but it underlines the continuing importance of status as a category capable of creating new intellectual domains in the law. The law of contract can no longer be viewed as a subject having the same institutional and theoretical unity as it had during the 19th century. It is fragmenting between different status groups and this fragmentation will in its turn influence the way facts are envisaged. Or, put another way, the notion of a 'consumer' transcends its category to become a unit capable of attracting its own interests and rights. A defendant fraudulently sells 98-centilitre bottles of a product as litre bottles, with the consequence that he makes a huge profit. Each individual purchaser of the product will have suffered only a negligible loss, but when viewed from the position of consumers as a class the loss will then match the unjustified profit. If the defendant is a corporation (that is to say, a group with legal personality), why should the defrauded purchasers not equally be envisaged in terms of class interests? Have they not suffered an invasion of a class interest? Consumer law has, then, its own institutional dimension.

Civil Procedure

Categories like commercial and consumer law cut across the old dichotomy between public and private law inasmuch as the *commerçant* or *professionnel* and the consumer act as focal point for rules from private law, administrative law and criminal law. Another category that can in theory give rise to similar difficulties is civil procedure.[111] It is partly public, in that it contains the rules governing the courts system itself – clearly in one sense an area of constitutional law and certainly part of the public service[112] – but it is private, in that procedure has traditionally been seen as ancillary to private rights. From a historical viewpoint, 'civil procedure was no more than an appendix to substantive law and it was classified as a branch of private law, since its purpose was to settle a dispute between private persons'.[113] Civil procedure in the civilian tradition does, however, need to be differentiated from private law in that it does not in theory deal with private law rights. Such rights are the subject matter of the civil codes. Codes of procedure, by way of contrast, concern themselves only with rules that facilitate the revindication of such rights. Nevertheless, this distinction is not always as clear as this dichotomy suggests, in that there are certain areas of civil procedure which directly attach themselves to the substance of private law. The requirement of a 'legitimate interest' in respect of a legal action is one example.[114] It has been observed, accordingly, that civil procedure is situated not just between form and substance but also between law and fact.[115] When dealing with procedural matters, a judge has to become an 'administrator of fact', in that he or she is often working with vague and descriptive concepts such as 'interest' and, in some areas such as family law, the role of the judge is becoming more and more procedural.[116]

This interrelationship between procedure and substantive law is not new. In Roman law, the law of actions was seen as a fundamental part of private law inasmuch as it was the *actio*, rather than any notion of a right, which provided the vehicle for giving expression to a plaintiff's legal claim against another person.[117] 'So great is the ascendancy of the Law of Actions in the infancy of Courts of Justice,' said Maine, 'that substantive law has at first the look of being gradually secreted in the interstices of procedure; and the early lawyer can only see the law through the envelope of its technical forms.'[118] Actions also functioned as much at the level of fact as law, in that they were the means of organising facts so as to reveal whether or not a remedy existed. This is one reason why the *Digest* is so full of concrete examples rather than organised sets of substantive rules. *Ubi remedium ibi ius* (where there is a remedy there is a right) might be said to be the working maxim of a legal system that functions more in terms of procedure and remedies. In the later civil law, when the concept of the subjective right had replaced the objective system of actions, the latter were relegated to separate codes of procedure. *Ubi ius ibi remedium* became the operating maxim which now finds its ultimate expression, as we have said, in codes of substantive rights.

But despite the formal separation between procedure and rights, civil procedure and remedies cannot be entirely excluded from the idea of private law. First, the role of the judge is to apply the law; yet before applying the law it is necessary to categorise the facts. This is both a procedural and a substantive exercise.[119] Secondly, many of the civil codes themselves still exhibit traces of the old Roman forms of action. For example, the named contracts, which take up so much of the civil codes, are hangovers from the old Roman *actiones ex contractu,* where each named contract had its own particular remedy.[120] The distinction between property and obligations remains, equally, one that is given expression as a matter of procedure. Vindication claims are quite separate from compensation actions.

Classification in the Common Law

The procedure and substance division is a useful starting point for an understanding of classification in the common law tradition since this was, until the 19th century, and to an extent remains, a system founded upon a law of actions rather than a law of abstract substantive rights and principles. In the 19th century there was an attempt to marry this very different tradition to the civil law through the notion of legal science. Thus one student 'nutshell' on pleading speaks of the 'Axioms and First Principles of Pleading'.[121] Yet it is unlikely that the book, although introductory, would make that much sense to someone trained in Roman law. Certainly, the distinction between real, personal and mixed actions would cause little trouble. But the statement that 'personal actions, the most usual of which are assumpsit, debt, covenant, detinue, trespass, trespass on the case, trover and replevin', would read like an unintelligible language.[122]

Forms of Action

Unlike Roman law, this system of actions, known as the forms of action, did not, then, respond to an institutional structure in which status was distinguished from patrimony and owing (obligations) was sharply distinguished from owning (property). The forms of action thought in terms of particular types of writ of which the most important general division was the one between trespass and debt. Trespass was an action founded upon a 'wrong', while debt (together with its related writs) was founded upon a 'right'.[123] This latter type of claim was in some respects like the Roman *actio in rem,* in that the plaintiff was revindicating something that was 'his'; but given that the object of the revindication was a sum of money owed, this added an obligation dimension.[124] Equally, where the plaintiff was claiming the return of an item of property this was not necessarily envisaged in terms of a claim against a thing. The plaintiff could be seen as claiming compensation for the interference with his possessory right, which in turn could be envisaged as a wrong.[125] In addition to the *in rem,* and *in personam* characteristics often displayed in a single writ, the whole system was one that was more procedural than substantive.[126] Each writ was in effect a particular procedural process and thus, if the wrong writ was chosen, this could jeopardise the whole claim. Later developments, particularly the expansion of trespass, muddled even more the distinction between compensation and 'revindication' claims. And the result was that, by the time major procedural reforms were introduced in the 19th century, the common law was conceptually and procedurally a rather different framework of remedies than the one to be found in the *Institutes* (cf. Chapter 4).[127]

Legal Reform

However, there were two fundamental reforms during the 19th century that were to bring the common law closer to continental thinking. The first reform was the abolition of the forms of action.[128] The effect is described by a judge of the time:

> What is the foundation of an action? Those facts which it is necessary to state and prove to maintain it, and no others. This really seems a truism: unless those necessary facts exist, the action is unfounded. All other facts are no part of the foundation. There is a further observation. This statute [County Courts Act] passed after the Common Law Procedure Acts. They did not abolish forms of action in words. The Common Law Commissioners recommended that: but it was supposed that, if adopted, the law would be shaken to its foundations; so that all that could be done was to provide as far as possible that, though forms of actions remained, there never should be a question what was the form. This was accomplished save as to this very question of costs in actions within the county court jurisdiction. Until the passing of the statute [County Courts Act] we are discussing, it was necessary to see if an action was assumpsit, case & c. But the Common Law Procedure Act having passed, and the forms of actions being practically abolished, the legislature pass this Act dropping the words 'assumpsit, case,' & c., and using the words 'founded on contract,' 'founded on tort.' This shews to me that the substance of the matter was to be looked at. One may observe there is no middle term; the statute supposes all actions are founded either on contract or on tort. So that it is tort, if not contract, contract if not tort.[129]

The category of 'contract' was of course an import from the civil law,[130] and this mini reception of Roman law was supported by a more general willingness on the part of the judiciary to make specific references to continental doctrine and to the codes.[131] The category of 'torts', it must be said, was in content rather different from the civilian delictual claims, since tort was based on old forms of action. In other words, there was no general theory of tort, only a mass of specific torts such as nuisance, trespass, trover, detinue, slander, libel and so on.[132] However, the idea of a category of 'wrongs' meant that it could be compared in form with the Roman system. As for unjust enrichment, the third sub-category of the law of obligations within the civil law, this was split between the law of equitable remedies and the old quasi-contractual debt claims. With the development of a general theory of contract, these old debt actions were 'relegated ... to the status of an appendix to the law of contract, thereby postponing by a century or so the development of a law of restitution'.[133] Restitution has now been recognised as a third category independent of both contract and tort.[134] But before it is assumed that the English common law now has a law of obligations along civilian lines, it has to be remembered that restitution contains claims that are proprietary rather than obligational.[135] It is, therefore, a category that transgresses the strict frontier between rights *in rem* and *in personam*.

The Roman influence was further intensified by a second reform. In 1846, a Parliamentary Commission on Legal Education had reported that there was no legal education in England worthy of the name and this led to a number of important developments.[136] The Inns of Court established chairs in Roman law, and law faculties, teaching the common law, began to be created within the universities.[137] The model for legal education was the civil law and this gave rise to a range of translated and other imported literature which brought to common lawyers the foundation of *scientia iuris* as understood by continental jurists. As Stein observes, English law may have remained relatively free of Roman law, but 'English jurisprudence has traditionally turned for inspiration to the current continental theories, necessarily based on Roman law'.[138] This kind of Roman science had its effect, and by the end of the century the textbook tradition of expounding the law was established.[139] Cases became the source from which rules could be induced and these rules in turn were assigned to categories which were closer to the institutional model than had been the situation under the old forms of action.[140] Nevertheless, the late development of university law faculties in England meant that their influence on the shape and content of the law was at best rather marginal. Indeed, until recently, there was much hostility from sections of the judiciary and practice towards academic doctrine as a source of law.[141] Things are changing and so, for example, the development of the third category of restitution owes more to doctrine than to practice. Yet this new harmony between judge and academic is now threatened by an evolution in law teaching itself. A law degree today is seen by many university teachers as a social science programme and not as a training designed exclusively for professional lawyers; many in the law faculties are, accordingly, no longer interested in producing a literature for practitioners.[142] One must not exaggerate the situation;

but it is probably true to say that the epistemological assumptions and frameworks are shifting within the law school and this could well produce a new cleavage between judge and academic.[143]

This 'Romanisation' of the common law was, then, only partially effective. Parliament did not intervene with any general codification and this meant that the actual structural substance of private law remained the one inherited from the feudal-influenced past. Viewed from the position of a Romanist, English law was 'irrational'.[144] In particular, the law of property was left unreformed (in a legal science sense) and as a consequence remains a category concerned only with land. Problems of moveable property are shared out amongst the law of contract, tort and equity.[145] At the level of concrete institutions, the most important distinction that exists today is that between the criminal and civil courts (to be discussed below). Indeed, it has been stated in the case law that this is the only division of any real importance in the English system.[146] As a result, it has been asserted in several recent cases that ideas from criminal law ought not to be assumed to be of value in deciding problems of private law.[147] Private law as a category, if it exists at all in English legal thinking, is of value primarily as an area to be contrasted with the criminal law.

Law and Equity

Yet some care must be taken with respect to this 'seamless web' view of the English civil process, for there was once another procedural division which was almost as important as the distinction between the criminal and civil processes. This is the division between 'common law' and 'equity', which represents two systems of judge-made law developed in different courts.[148] The historical independence of the Court of Chancery *vis-à-vis* the common law courts (King's Bench, Common Pleas and Exchequer) has left its mark, in that equity has been fused with the common law only at the level of procedure.[149] Thus, in addition to the criminal and civil distinction, it is of particular importance to recognise that private law is subject to its own internal division between law and equity. This distinction is reflected not just at the level of substantive law but also at the level of remedies.[150] The law of actions can be classified into common law (debt and damages) and equitable (injunction, specific performance, rescission, rectification, account and others) claims and this classification can have real importance within the case law.[151] The internal division between law and equity does not, of course, directly undermine any notion of a 'public law' or an institutionally arranged 'private law', but it does fragment its internal structure. For example, some remedies such as debt or injunction are equally available both in public and in private law, yet the principles which attach to each remedy are very different.[152] In addition, the division between law and equity can transgress the lines between owing and owning. Rights and remedies arising under a trust would not easily be accommodated within a system of categories that rigidly distinguishes between property and obligations.[153]

The difficulty with equity as a category is that it is entirely dependent upon the existence of other fields of law.[154] Accordingly, although one of the foundational subjects of a qualifying law degree is called 'Equity and the Law of Trusts', this subject has little internal coherence. It is simply a box containing the legal sources of trusts and other equitable fiduciary obligations, together with all the various equitable remedies.[155] These substantive rules and remedies are linked by a number of maxims of equity, but many of these remedies make sense only in the context of more fundamental categories such as property, contract and succession. For example, 'equitable ownership' is a notion based upon both the law of contract and the equitable remedy of specific performance; this latter remedy is dependent in its turn on the existence of the law of contract. A person who has contracted to buy land cannot obtain full legal title to the property until it is separately conveyed to the purchaser. However, as a contractor, the purchaser will be entitled, in addition to the common law remedy of damages, to the equitable remedy of specific performance of the contract if the vendor fails to convey.[156] As a result, the purchaser obtains an 'equitable title' to the land.[157] Similarly, a performance artist might not in the eyes of the common law be regarded as the owner of a live performance on stage, but if equity is prepared to grant an injunction preventing others from infringing or interfering with the artist's 'right', this again amounts to a kind of 'equitable ownership', even if it is not formally recognised as such in substance.[158]

One cannot, then, just learn the law of contract or the law of equity. Each subject interrelates at the level of both remedies and substance so as to produce institutional relationships and concepts that are more fluid than in continental systems. Land law, for example, is a mixture of legal and equitable rights and interests.[159] And the rules regarding duress in contract, to give another example, are both legal and equitable because the remedy available is the equitable remedy of rescission.[160] One can learn the rules as contract rules, but the equitable nature of the remedy can bring into play independent notions. Viewed from an institutional perspective, rules attach both to the *persona* (common law of contract) and the *actio* (equitable remedy of rescission).

Administrative Remedies

Many common law and equitable rules and remedies apply equally to private and public bodies. Thus a public body which has abused its power may well find itself faced with a claim in damages based, for instance, on the tort of trespass,[161] or an action for an injunction or similar equitable remedy.[162] Equally, a public body that has caused harm through careless neglect or active breach of promise may be found liable in damages just as if it had been a commercial enterprise in the private sector. In addition, even in cases that can be regarded as falling clearly within the category of public law, the actual reasoning may well be based on concepts originally fashioned within private law.[163] One can state with relative confidence, therefore, that at a general level it is not possible to distinguish private law from public law in England.

However, the position is more complex than it might seem because, even in the days of the forms of action, there were certain writs that applied only to public bodies (mandamus, certiorari and prohibition). Today these administrative remedies have been replaced by a general claim for judicial review[164] and, while it is thus possible to distinguish administrative law from private law, care must be taken.[165] The problem is that this distinction does not cover administrative liability where the ordinary 'private' law of contract and tort applies. Had the English courts shown a consistent disinterest in the status of the parties, the problem would not have been one of categorisation. But this has not been the case. The appeal judgments have in recent years stressed the public law nature of the tort claims against local or central government; yet, equally, the judges have refused to develop a separate set of concepts and relationships to act as the 'describer' of an administrative liability category.[166] This stands in contrast to the situation in France, where such cases, had they arisen in that country, would have found themselves entirely outside of private law and governed by quite different principles with respect to strict liability.[167]

The category of public law is thus of little conceptual value to English law. All that it does is to act as a means by which judges can apply special policy considerations to the solution of concrete contract and tort problems in the public sector. Public law therefore acts as a sub-category within the law of obligations in much the same way as 'product liability' and 'medical negligence' are categories which exert their own particular influence on standard tort and contract concepts. It is a category more concerned with justifying solutions on the grounds of judicial ideology than with constructing an institutional model to separate *imperium* from *dominium*. The constitutional result is that public bodies, or certain public bodies at least, need no specific legislative power to act and can thus do almost anything against an individual once they have been granted immunity from legal claims in tort. Many of these immunities come from statute;[168] others, however, come from the case law and are expressly or implicitly justified by reference to 'public law'.

The incorporation of the Convention for the Protection of Human Rights and Fundamental Freedoms into United Kingdom law will of course modify this position.[169] Moreover, at first sight the legislation does appear to distinguish between public and private law in a number of ways, in particular with respect to the acts of 'public authorities'[170] and the remedies available.[171] However, one leading public lawyer takes the view that, far from consolidating the public–private divide, the Human Rights Act 1998 will have the opposite effect. It seems likely, she says, that the legislation will have horizontal as well as vertical effects; that is to say, it will have an impact not just on the relationship between the individual and the state but also upon the relationships between individuals. This 'cross-fertilisation between public and private law' will, she concludes, 'be in line with the disintegration of other divides in law, for instance the divide between the common law and equity and their remedies'.[172] What cannot be denied is that the Convention rights are now seeping into private law analysis and this in turn is eroding the attempts to erect immunities in the area of public law torts.[173] But of course the whole notion of a 'right' is, as we have seen in Chapter 4, based on a history of *dominium* rather than *imperium* and thus a code of fundamental rights, almost by definition, transgresses the boundary between constitutional and private law. And, given that much constitutional law in the United Kingdom has traditionally been found in the law of tort, it is difficult to see how the Human Rights Act 1998 will do anything more than to add to the complexity of the public and private law question.

Commercial Law and the Common Law

It is no easier to attempt to trace any idea of an English category 'commercial law' that stands in contrast to 'private law'.[174] Historically speaking, the division may once have had some meaning, but in the 18th century it was said that the common law captured and incorporated the *lex mercatoria*.[175] In fact, it is probably closer to the truth to say that the reverse happened, particularly when viewed from the contemporary position.[176] Contract and tort are part and parcel of commercial law itself. It is, as the judges themselves often state, commercial practice that informs civil liability law in England and the judges are therefore reluctant to allow the principles to deviate from commercial expectations.

Private law, if it exists in the common law, is a commercial law and it is these commercial – and to some extent consumer – expectations which tend to inform whole areas of claims for economic and property losses.[177] Only in personal injury and some public law liability cases do the courts apply different sets of criteria.[178]

With respect to these latter situations, however, one cannot easily use the cases as the basis of some rational distinctions between, say, personal injury claims, commercial cases and administrative liability actions since different ideas find expression at the level of reasoning itself. In medical negligence cases, for example, commercial, or at least economic, considerations have their place alongside other ideas, for the defendants are usually public bodies mandated to take account of commercial considerations and their resources are limited. If there are differences, at an empirical level, between public, private and commercial law, they function in a way that will not allow for the isolation of a separate area of private law which will stand in opposition to a public and a commercial law.[179] They are reasoning devices which act as dialectical counterpoints in the judgments themselves.[180] One is continually forced back, therefore, to the idea of the common law as a seamless web which has committed itself to no universal structural pattern of the type that underpinned the *Institutes* of Justinian and the modern codes.[181] However, as we have seen with the criminal–civil divide, the seams can reappear at the level of reasoning and justification. When Lord Goff says that 'in the commercial world contracting parties have to look after their own interests'[182] he is not talking about contract cases in which one party is a consumer or even where one of the parties is a small business. Equally, to state that a person always owes a duty of care with respect to negligently caused physical damage might generally be true as a proposition of private law, yet, where the parties are *commerçants* and the risk is covered by insurance, the general rule may give way to 'commercial reality'.[183]

Civil and Criminal Law

When one turns to the civil–criminal divide, the position at first sight looks much less complex. Civil and criminal is a fundamental division since there are, at the lower levels, two quite separate sets of courts. Thus, in the words of Lord Hobhouse:

> Even though the criminal process is formally adversarial, it is of a fundamentally different character to the civil process. Its purpose and function are different. It is to enforce the criminal law. The criminal law and the criminal justice system exists in the interests of society as a whole. It has a directly social function. It is concerned to see that the

> guilty are convicted and punished and those not proved to be guilty are acquitted. Anyone not proved to be guilty is to be presumed to be not guilty. It is of fundamental importance that the process by which the defendant is proved guilty shall have been fair and it is the public duty of all those concerned in the criminal justice system to see that this is the case. This is the public interest in the system.[184]

By contrast, the civil process is about private interests. Again according to Lord Hobhouse:

> The character of civil litigation is that it involves the assertion by one party that the other has infringed his rights; he seeks a remedy, normally a monetary remedy but sometimes a remedy of declaration of right or specific implement. The court, therefore, has essentially to make a decision between two conflicting parties and determining their respective rights inter se. It is primarily the provision by the state of a service similar to the provision of arbitration services. The public interest does not normally come into it save in so far as the provision of a system of civil dispute resolution and the enforcement of civil rights is a necessary part of a society governed by the rule of law not by superior force.[185]

And thus:

> It is a system of relative justice. It exists in economic terms. The plaintiff complains that he has suffered loss and damage; he claims that the defendant should be required to pay monetary damages to compensate him; the remedy is a redistribution of wealth between the parties. Or he may assert a property right and ask that the court should assist him to enforce it against the defendant.[186]

However, there are problems with this interest approach to the distinction. Lord Hobhouse asserts that the key to criminal law is that it is not concerned with the 'economic interest' of the citizen charged with a criminal offence. The civil courts should thus have no role to play in the criminal process.[187] But from the position of remedies the situation turns out to be more complex. What if a court makes what is called an 'anti-social behaviour order' pursuant to section 1 of the Crime and Disorder Act 1998? Is this a criminal or a civil remedy? The answer is important, since the rules of evidence are less stringent for a civil remedy and, perhaps more importantly, a non-criminal remedy will not attract the protection of article 6 of the Human Rights Convention. If the test is one of economic interest, it is difficult to see how this kind of order falls within Lord Hobhouse's definition of the civil process. Nevertheless, the court of appeal has ruled that the anti-social behaviour order is not a criminal remedy.[188] It is more like an injunction. The 'orders are not about crime and punishment, they are about protection of an identified section of the community'.[189] Moreover, criminal proceedings are begun by an arrest, a charge and the production of the defendant at court, whereas 'anti-social orders are begun by complaint'.[190] Once again, the existence of the remedy (*actio*) as an active institution in the common law legal plan makes any attempt at a conceptualised and closed taxonomy almost impossible. The common law continues to function at the level of a set of forms of action and these forms can define not just the nature of the interests in play but also the categories to be applied.

Taxonomy and Specialisation

Another way of viewing the development of categories outside of the traditional institutional system is through change or movement in legal knowledge. The epistemologist must, as Atias asserts, research these changes and account for the various rhythms and movements.[191] One such change is simply an increase in the amount of law. Every decade there are more texts and more cases and one question that this provokes is as to how such increases are to be handled in terms of taxonomy.

Specialisation and the Institutional Categories

In the civil law tradition the idea of a private law is closely linked linguistically with the Roman law terms of *ius privatum* and *ius civile*. Given the authority with which the Roman sources were treated by the later civilians, these terms must by definition have represented an epistemological (legal knowledge) truth and thus it is not difficult to see why the notion of a private law is so ingrained in the European mentality.[192] Codification only added to the epistemological authority of the Roman terms. For the great codes took as their object an area of law that was, by definition, given the existence of the ancillary codes on commercial law, procedure and criminal law, together with the rigid exclusion of the *ius publicum* in France, existing virtually as an empirical reality.[193] This reality was not just a matter of a juristic space resulting from boundaries created by public, commercial, procedural and criminal law; the Romans themselves had defined private law in terms of *utilitates* attaching to the individual in society (*ad singulorum utilitatem*).[194] Private law was about private interests. In addition to this space and interest dimension, private law had, according to the teaching manuals of Gaius and Justinian (*institutiones*), a structure; and it is this structure which was to act as the foundation for all the codes. Private law, whatever the difficulties of definition and delimitation, could not, seemingly, be accused of lacking either form or substance.

Nevertheless, this rationality has been seriously challenged by the increasing complexity of law caused by the vast expansion of statutory regulations. The institutional categories no longer seem capable of acting as a scheme through which the student can absorb the foundations of legal knowledge, since the structure of these foundations has been undermined by the sheer weight of the detail. Much new legislation is outside the codes.[195] In addition, the cases, in France at any rate, appear more and more to be decided on their facts,[196] something which, according to Atias, is resulting in a decline of legal knowledge.[197] New categories reflecting specialised areas of complexity, or responding to alternative empirical 'describers', are emerging as the foundations of legal knowledge and this process is, according to one modern legal historian, weakening the idea of a comprehensive vision of law and legal science.[198] The emphasis is perhaps shifting away from the institutional scheme towards a specialist view of law in turn based on two apparent empirical realities. The first reality is the sheer increase in the amount of statutory, case law and doctrinal text; it is becoming difficult for a single person to absorb more than a certain amount of legal information. The second reality is seemingly sociological. Categories emphasising different class interests (employees, consumers, women, racial minorities) are tending to become more dominant than the institutional divisions based on *imperium* (sovereignty), *persona* and *res*, in that these latter categories are incapable of distinguishing between different social groups and thus give the impression of being 'ahistorical' and universalist.[199] Much the same is happening with respect to 'things'. The general provisions in the codes are tending to become eclipsed by specialised legislation such as those dealing with traffic accidents, factory injuries and product liability.[200] Some of these specialised provisions have, it must be said, been incorporated into the civil codes.[201] But in emphasising particular classes of person and particular types of thing one is moving towards a new kind of pattern in which monolithic legal relationships are giving way to localised structures. Indeed, in the area of the law of property, some civilians have talked of a return to feudal ideas, with the fracturing of the Roman notion of *dominium*. Others talk of a metamorphosis within private law.[202]

Operational Closure

When this increasing specialisation within law is merged with a methodology that emphasises the rule model and syllogistic logic, the result is what Collins has called 'operational closure of doctrinal subsystems'.[203] Drawing on systems theory,[204] Collins argues that each specialist category of law becomes a closed system that has the effect of isolating itself from the other sub-systems and from any general institutional system of law. Thus:

> Events in the world, presented as claims before courts, must be read by the subsystem within its operational rules. Contract law understands these events by reference to its familiar rules of offer, acceptance, consideration, breach, and so forth, whilst the law of tort simultaneously understands the events by reference to its own categories of duty of care, unreasonable use of land, deliberate interference with business by unlawful means, and many other standards for the attribution of responsibility. The subsystems function like computer software programmes, which can only read the events within their own procedures for comprehending the binary electronic information.[205]

This of course is not so much a problem of systems as such, but of the type of system that is being used. Inference systems are closed systems, since the more open the system the weaker the reliability of the inferences.[206] Collins's analysis is a useful one, of course, and his overall point is most pertinent. However, the epistemological point to be emphasised is that the closure is not just a question of classification and systems. It is equally a question of assuming that the objects to be classified are legal rules. This tendency to emphasise rules seems to increase in the same proportion as the increase in the laws themselves. This, it must be emphasised, is not to suggest that specialisation and method are linked causally, or vice versa; such an explanation would be too simplistic.[207] But it is to suggest that specialisation, detail and the rule thesis are linked within an epistemological model that tends to be predominant in certain professional viewpoints.

Let us return to the position adopted by Professor Birks, discussed in Chapter 2. According to Professor Birks, 'the modern law of tort is still a tangle of criss-crossing categories' where negligence 'is a category based on a degree of fault' and defamation 'is a category based on an interest infringed, as is interference with contractual relations, or interference with chattels'. As for conspiracy, this 'is a category based upon the description of an act'.[208] Professor Birks, as we have seen, illustrates this apparent disorder by reference to the case of *Spring* v. *Guardian Assurance*.[209] The problem with this case, according to Birks, is that two legal categories intersect. Defamation, which is an infringement of the reputation interest, intersects with negligence, which is a wrong based on a species of fault. This leads to a situation where a careless invasion of the reputation interest could give rise to two wrongs, namely defamation and negligence, when a rational system ought to see only one wrong.[210] In order to give intellectual support for claimed rationality, Birks draws an analogy with the zoological sciences:

> My canary is yellow and eats seeds. If all birds are seed-eaters, yellow, or others, my canary counts twice. Are there two birds or one? If there come to be two birds, the double-vision is due to the bent classification. There is only one bird.[211]

Just as there is only one bird, so the 'law cannot tolerate, or should not be able to tolerate, torts named so as to intersect'. Professor Birks goes on to consolidate this canary analogy by making the point that there is no branch of human knowledge which can manage without taxonomy. Whales must not be confused with fish, just as the gender of seahorses must not be confused with that of mammals.[212] Indeed Darwin, it seems, would have despaired at the muddled taxonomy of English law.[213]

Taxonomy in Science and in Law

However, there is a problem with making an analogy between legal classification and taxonomy in the natural sciences. With a subject like zoology, classification relates to specifically identifiable objects which can be said to exist independently of the science. No doubt one has moved on from the older view in the natural sciences of a sharp distinction between the science and object of science; but whales and fish, in the language of Gaius, are *res corporales*. They can be seen and touched. The objects of the empirical sciences, while being abstractions in terms of the scientific scheme itself, never actually lose their link with the senses and this link goes far in regulating the rigour of the science itself.[214] Law as a 'science' is different. It is the discourse of law that creates its own objects such as '*persona*', '*res*', 'contract', 'tort', 'defamation', 'interest', 'fault', 'damage' and so on. Legal science, as Villa has observed, is characterised by 'atypical objects' which escape the observability criteria established for all empirical phenomena and thus the objects of legal science cannot be seen without the aid of concepts and theoretical categories.[215] These concepts and theoretical categories are of course part and parcel of the science of law itself and the objects of science thus merge with the science. Law is the object of its own science.[216] The result is that the taxonomy scheme in law is subject to no rigour emanating from the object of the science; the science can simply construct or deconstruct its own objects to achieve a desired solution. For example, people belonging to minority groups can be declared by a malevolent legislator as non-persons and while this may be politically distasteful, to say the least, no historian can deny the past effectiveness of such treatment. Less extreme, but no less effective, examples can be found in the everyday case law. Claims can be denied simply because the legal science fails to see the existence of some 'damage'[217] or some 'property'.[218]

One might argue that the object of legal science is the facts of cases. Thus 'damage' can be related to a broken arm and 'interest' can be related to some lost profit. Equally, 'defamation' can be seen as a scientific rationalisation of words and reputation. However, the science and object of science dichotomy undermines this kind of rationalisation in two major ways. First, if legal science is the discourse that rationalises 'fact', then what of the discourse that rationalises 'rights' and 'duties'? If the law of tort, contract and property is the science itself, this same science cannot of itself distinguish between the categories it uses. One has need of a meta-science to distinguish contract from tort, real rights from personal rights, property from obligations, public law from private law and so on. This adds a new level of confusion when it comes to the avoidance of intersection of categories, since the meta-science can always be used as a means of avoiding the lower-level science. A good example of this process is to be found in the court of appeal decision of *Beswick* v. *Beswick*. Here the category of 'contract', with its inconvenient rule of privity of contract, was simply avoided through the application of the meta-category of 'real right' whereby the debt was reclassified as a *res* capable of being 'owned'.[219] One can try hard to avoid these ambiguities created by separate layers of legal sciences. Thus some civil law systems refuse to attach real rights to *res incorporales*.[220] Yet the notion of a *res* remains at one and the same time both a concept within the science and an object of the same science. This means in effect that the legal system is never threatened as a scientific discourse if it is decided that a *res incorporales* is capable of supporting a real right.[221] As two jurists have observed, even 'if the notion of a thing is for dogmatic and systematic reasons restricted to corporeals it must be kept in mind that legal development is influenced more by policy considerations than by logic'.[222] In other words it is the science which decides what can be owned and possessed and not the object of the science.[223]

This point can be developed by comparing legal schemes with those of zoology and mathematics. Part of the rigour of a natural science like zoology is the use of exclusive categories that can be arranged hierarchically without contradiction. Concrete objects and materials, whether they are alive or not, natural or artificial, share certain basic properties.[224] The categorisation scheme is able to conceptualise these properties in an exclusive, or near-exclusive way: an animal either has a backbone or it does not. In other words the taxonomical scheme expresses states that are concretely possible and it 'does not create these things or their properties by decree'.[225] A conceptual scheme like law does not and cannot function in this way since it creates its own objects. The things that it recognises are created by decree and as a result the abstract scheme 'has conceptual properties that concrete objects do not possess'.[226] To this extent law is similar to mathematics, as we have seen in Chapter 2.

Where law differs from mathematics is in the kind of concepts that it uses. One can dream, like the German Enlightenment jurist mathematicians, of a hardened legal model where solutions could be deduced from axioms whose rigour left little space for gaps in the logic.[227] But concepts such as *bona fides, ordre public* and *bonnes mœurs* simply belong to another conceptual world because, unlike mathematics, the law does have to take some notice of concrete social reality.[228] This is not to say that it actually schematises this social reality. It cannot do this, since it needs to create a normative rather than a descriptive world. What it does is to create its own abstract model of society which operates quite independently of the real world. As Jacques Ellul observed of Roman law, it 'becomes a kind of reality imposed upon the social situation, putting it into order, and ending up by becoming more "true" than the facts'.[229]

This 'reality' of the legal world is incapable of being consistently rigorous simply because it has need of concepts that themselves are not rigorous. What is more, it uses cumulative categories that are often not exclusive; a piece of property can be both corporeal and moveable or corporeal and immoveable.[230] Now, in order to be rigorous, a category must reflect with respect to its object various particular characteristics and if the category is to be exclusive these characteristics must not be found in objects belonging to another category. The category of 'defamation', if it is to be an exclusive and alternative category to 'negligence', must reflect an object which will not exhibit the characteristics to be found in objects classed under 'negligence'. Peter Birks focuses upon the 'interest' as object. The reputation interest, according to him, is quite different in character from the interests which form the object of the category of negligence.

However, it is with regard to such objects and their categorisation that one comes up against the second major difficulty caused by law in effect being the object of its own science. The abstract scheme has not only the capacity to categorise objects that seemingly exist in social reality but also the ability to alter both the concept and category within the abstract scheme and the nature of these empirical objects themselves. If the jurist chooses to postulate the existence of a new conceptual object such as some new 'interest', this cannot be logically refuted provided it does not undermine the internal coherence of law. If it chooses to invest a live musical performance with the character of 'property', this can be criticised but not *logically* refuted.[231] Equally if the law chooses not to categorise some asset as 'property' then this cannot be attacked on the ground of an absence of scientific logic.[232] Indeed, legal science can even treat a town or a building as a 'person'.[233] This flexibility at the level of the legal concept and legal category is reflected in the 'object' of the legal science by an equivalent flexibility of 'factual' characteristics. The same damage can sometimes be seen as physical and sometimes as purely financial.[234] A pollution incident at sea can be categorised as a negligence case, as a nuisance problem or, perhaps, as damage caused by a thing under the control of another.[235] The placing of an object in a supermarket trolley can be evidence of agreement or of an invitation to treat.[236] Intersection of categories might appear irrational to any observer applying the logic of a natural science like zoology; but it is the observer who is in error in misunderstanding the fundamental differences between the nature of different taxonomy schemes. In fact, were there not to be intersection of categories, the law would become utterly stultified.

Let us return to *Donoghue* v. *Stevenson*,[237] whose facts have been discussed in Chapter 5. If only one legal category were to be applicable, this would have to be 'contract', together with its very restrictive privity rule. The plaintiff would have no action since she had no contract. Happily for the consumer, the facts disclosed other characteristics that permitted categorisation under a different set of relations which, in turn, gave rise to the possibility of someone in the plaintiff's position being able to recover. The same can be said of *Hedley Byrne & Co* v. *Heller & Partners Ltd*,[238] whose facts, under Birks' thesis, would have to be governed strictly by rules from the law of contract. The absence of consideration would mean no action. Once again the law was able to develop because categories intersected as a result of flexible characteristics not only at the level of the abstract legal scheme, but also within the apparent object of the scheme. Special relationships and proximity, seemingly empirical and thus descriptive, are in truth just as much part of the legal science scheme as *persona, res*, implied term, interest, right, contract or duty of care. Such concepts are the objects of the science that creates them and thus cannot be attacked on the ground that they do not 'exist'. In addition, legal development depends upon cumulative categories whereas an empirical science like zoology depends much more upon exclusive categories.

Uncertainty in Systems

All this may be distressing for those who yearn for the 'identification of legal reasoning with formal logic [that] would confer upon it the rigour and the certainty which it often lacks'.[239] But, as Guest pointed out many years ago, when one talks about the meaning of logic it too often centres upon 'the rather barren controversy whether legal reasoning is deductive or inductive in form'.[240] And, as Guest went on to observe, one 'must expect the position to be far more complicated'.[241] In fairness to Professor Birks, however, it is not enough simply to say that things are more complex. Nor perhaps is it sufficient any longer simply to rest with Guest's view that 'logic acts as a kind of geography, explaining the directive force of propositions and their relationship one with the other'.[242] For science is not about creating just abstract models of propositions, but also abstract models of facts. Legal 'logic' is about the construction and schematisation of legal objects and the insertion of this schematisation in a system of concepts and categories. However, what an analysis of the common law cases can show is that this schematisation is very different from the schematisation that takes place in a science like zoology. It is not a matter of moving from empirical object to conceptual scheme, since such a dichotomy does not exist in legal science. The scheme itself, through the institutional model, plays an active role in creating both the major premise and the minor premise in legal logic.

To accuse a legal system of lacking a certain kind of internal symmetry and structure may, then, be a relevant criticism, provided one is clear about the level at which the structure and symmetry should be operating. To accuse it of lacking logic is to risk displaying a misunderstanding not just of the term 'logic' but also of the distinction between closed and open systems. The whole point of a legal system – indeed the whole point of schemes of intelligibility in the social sciences – is that they are not closed.[243] There is virtue in the very uncertainty of the system.[244] Practitioners and judges, perhaps even legislators, cannot say this, of course, since there is an ideological aspect to law whereby rules are supposed to be applied to facts via the *juge automate*. Yet it tends to be forgotten that the systems used in the natural sciences are so strong because not only are their foundations so weak – or perhaps one should more accurately say so precarious (thus obstacles and revolutions) – but also their scope is so limited.[245] Therefore, to equate law with scientific systems, with a *juge automate*, is profoundly to misunderstand both the nature of systems themselves and the way in which they relate to empirical reality.

Scientific facts are, for a start, so different from legal facts that one is talking about two sets of 'virtual facts' that have nothing in common whatsoever.[246] What Darwin classified has no relevance as an object to legal knowledge since the *function* of Darwin's system is quite different to the function of a legal system. As Busino points out, modern research 'shows that truth and falsity, success or probability remain expressions of formal systems and have a legitimacy exclusively within the objectivism of mathematical logic' and it 'is the same for demonstration: it is correct or incorrect'.[247] One can, for example, criticise the decision in the *Pinochet* case on a number of different grounds such as morality or the quality of its argumentation. But to say the decision is either true or false or correct or incorrect would be absurd.[248] Only if a rule is based on a mathematical calculation (for example, the speeding laws) does it become possible to talk in terms of truth and falsity. Again, this is not to say that one cannot classify the decision into either public or private law or, further, into extradition law or even into some other legal category. Moreover, such a classification can of itself bring or exclude certain concepts, institutions and (or) rules. But the classification is not there to determine whether the decision is correct or incorrect in some totally objective fashion. Or, put another way, the classification scheme is not there to model an object like nature, which is stable, permanent and uniform and whose facts cannot be modified by interpretation.[249] Classification is there, amongst other things, to help construct the legal facts which may then *tend* towards one normative solution over another, depending, of course, on the nature of the construction exercise itself.

Notes

1 But cf. Foucault (1966, pp. 137–76).
2 Blanché (1975, p. 152).
3 Bachelard (1938, p. 17).
4 Foucault (1966, pp. 7ff). An excellent translation of the categories can be found in Legrand (1999b, p. 63).
5 Ibid., p. 8.
6 Ibid., pp. 8–9.
7 Bonardel (1996, p. 5).
8 Bergel (1999, paras 199–207).
9 The term is taken from Oléron (1996, p. 88).
10 Oléron (1996, p. 88).
11 Ibid.
12 Bergel (2001, pp. 106–11).
13 Berthelot (1996).
14 See, for example, Birks (1996).
15 Bergel (1999, para. 252).
16 Ibid. See also Bergel (2001, p. 145).
17 Thus, with regard to 'tort', for example, see Winfield (1931), Williams and Hepple (1984), Owen (1995).
18 Birks (1996b).

19 Birks (1997a).
20 Stein (1984, pp. 125–9).
21 G.1.8. See also J.1.2.12; D.1.5.1.
22 J.1.1.4.
23 D.1.1.1.2.
24 D.2.1.3.
25 Lefebvre-Teillard (1996, pp. 99–100).
26 See D.44.7.5.5.
27 Mestre (1985, pp. 140–41).
28 See, for example, Certoma (1985, pp. 22–3).
29 See, generally, Ullmann (1975a), Van Caenegem (1995).
30 Tierney (1982, p. 1).
31 See, generally, Tierney (1982), Van Caenegem (1995).
32 Van Caenegem (1995, p. 293).
33 See, generally, Favoreu (1996).
34 Leca (2000, pp. 60–61).
35 Ibid., p. 61.
36 Jacquemin and Schrans (1982, p. 7).
37 Ibid., p. 90.
38 Jolowicz (1963, pp. 345–7), Leca (2000, pp. 61–5).
39 Carbasse (1990, pp. 29–31, 41–8).
40 D.1.18.13pr.
41 Carbasse (1990, pp. 48–52).
42 D.47.2.93.
43 See, for example, D.1.18.14; D.48.8.1.3.
44 See Bell et al. (1998, pp. 43, 202).
45 *Code de procédure pénale*, arts 2–5.
46 D.1.5.2.
47 D.3.4.2; D.1.8.6.1.
48 D.3.4.7.1.
49 Lefebvre-Teillard (1996, pp. 87–95).
50 D.41.2.2; Samuel (1994, p. 177).
51 'There is however … an abundance of texts which raise the question of the "one" in relation to the "many" in such a way as to show that the two were not simply considered identical' (Jolowicz, 1957, p. 134).
52 D.50.1.25.
53 Lefebvre-Teillard (1996, p. 89), Hilaire (1986, pp. 186–7).
54 D.3.4.1pr; Jolowicz (1957, p. 130).
55 Hilaire (1986, pp. 52–3).
56 Ibid., pp. 208–9.
57 Ibid., p. 215.
58 For example, women were discriminated against as a matter of status (D.1.5.9; D.2.13.12).
59 Jolowicz (1957, p. 113).
60 *The Ampthill Peerage Case* [1977] AC 547, 577.
61 D.1.5.7.
62 In civil law, this question is usually dealt with as a matter of succession, but in English law the estate continues in a remedial legal capacity: Law Reform (Miscellaneous Provisions) Act 1934, s. 1.

63 Terrasson de Fougères (1997).
64 See, for example, CC, arts 9, 16.
65 Edelman (1997).
66 Ourliac and De Malafosse (1971, pp. 47–9).
67 G.2.14.
68 Jolowicz (1957, pp. 75–81).
69 Zenati and Revet (1997, pp. 202–14).
70 G.2.13.
71 D.5.3.25.18; D.50.16.208.
72 D.15.1.32.1; D.50.16.39.1.
73 Cf. Ourliac and De Malafosse (1971, pp. 62–3).
74 Unless, as in some later civil law systems, the contract itself was regarded as capable of transferring title to the thing sold.
75 D.44.7.
76 G.3.88.
77 D.2.14.1.3.
78 D.44.7.4.
79 G.3.91.
80 D.44.7.1pr.
81 J.3.13.2.
82 The principle of unjust enrichment was seen by later civilians as the common denominator (D.12.6.14; D.50.17.206; Zimmermann, 1996a, pp. 873ff).
83 Zimmermann (1996a, p. 16).
84 In particular, the liability of the occupier of a building for things thrown, poured or falling from the building and injuring passers-by (Zimmermann, 1996a, p. 1122).
85 Robinson (1983).
86 D.12.6.14.
87 See, for example, Samuel (2001, pp. 31–3).
88 BGB § 812; Swiss CO, art. 62; Polish CC, art. 405.
89 Zweigert and Kötz (1998, pp. 545–51).
90 Bell (2001, p. 77).
91 D.3.4.1pr.
92 See, in particular, art. 21–7.
93 D.1.8.1 and so on.
94 Zenati and Revet (1997, p. 113).
95 See, generally, *Digest*, book 41.
96 D.9.3.7.
97 D.9.2.13pr.
98 Indeed, the sources themselves continually allude to the overlap and coexistence of real and personal actions.
99 Atias (1994, pp. 84–5).
100 D.35.1.15.
101 Jolowicz (1957, p. 157).
102 See, for example, CC, art. 388–2.
103 Szladits (1969, para. 78).
104 Hilaire (1986, pp. 17–20).
105 Ibid., 80–81.

106 Szladits (1969, para. 78).
107 Hilaire (1986, p. 86).
108 Joerges (1998).
109 Loi no. 93–949 du 26 juillet 1993.
110 Atias (1994, p. 82).
111 Jolowicz (1963, pp. 371–2).
112 Barbiéri (1995, p. 10).
113 David (1981, p. 62).
114 NCPC, art. 31.
115 Barbiéri (1995, p. 10).
116 Ibid., pp. 10–11.
117 Jolowicz (1957, p. 77).
118 Maine (1890, p. 389).
119 NCPC, art. 12.
120 Vescovi (1980, para. 381).
121 Garde (1841, p. vii).
122 Ibid., p. 3.
123 Milsom (1981, p. 243), Ibbetson (1999, p. 87).
124 Milsom (1981, pp. 257–65).
125 Ibid., pp. 366–79.
126 'In the fourteenth century there was no law of England, no body of rules complete in itself with known limits and visible defects ... [The lawyer's] business was procedural, to see that disputes were properly submitted to the appropriate deciding mechanism' (Milsom, 1981, p. 83).
127 Lobban (1991, p. 9).
128 Common Law Procedure Act 1852, s. 3.
129 Bramwell LJ, in *Bryant* v. *Herbert* (1877) 3 CPD 389, 390.
130 Simpson (1975).
131 See, generally, Samuel (2001, pp. 105–10).
132 See also Rudden (1991–2).
133 Lord Goff, in *Henderson* v. *Merrett Syndicates Ltd* [1995] AC 145, 184.
134 *Woolwich Building Society* v. *IRC* [1993] AC 70; *Kleinwort Benson Ltd* v. *Glasgow CC* [1999] 1 AC 153; *Kleinwort Benson Ltd* v. *Lincoln CC* [1999] 2 AC 349.
135 See Samuel (2001, pp. 404–9).
136 Stein (1980, pp. 78–9).
137 Roman law had been taught at Oxford and Cambridge, but not English law.
138 Stein (1980, p. 123).
139 See, generally, Lobban (1991).
140 Cf. Milsom (1981, pp. 392–400).
141 See, generally, Birks (1994).
142 On law teaching today, see Birks (1992), (1993), (1994b), (1996a); Bradney (1998).
143 See, for example, Lord Goff, in *Hunter* v. *Canary Wharf Ltd* [1997] AC 655, 694.
144 Lobban (1991, p. 282).
145 See, for example, *Stevenson* v. *Beverley Bentinck Ltd* [1976] 1 WLR 483; *Waverley BC* v. *Fletcher* [1996] QB 334.

146 *In re Norway's Application* [1990] 1 AC 723, 756. See also *Arthur JS Hall and Co* v. *Simons* [2000] 3 WLR 543.
147 See, for example, *Chamberlain* v. *Lindon* [1998] 1 WLR 1252; *Mansfield* v. *Weetabix Ltd* [1998] 1 WLR 1263; *R* v. *Hinks* [2000] 3 WLR 1590.
148 Weir (1971, para. 87).
149 See Supreme Court of Judicature (Consolidation) Act 1925, ss. 36–44; and now Supreme Court Act, 1981, s. 49.
150 Weir (1971, paras 87–108).
151 See, for example, *Miller* v. *Jackson* [1977] QB 966.
152 See, generally, Samuel (2001, pp. 113–74).
153 See, generally, Cantin Cumyn (1999).
154 Weir (1971, para. 89).
155 ACLEC Report (1996, p. 141).
156 Treitel (1988, para. 62).
157 Gray and Gray (2001, pp. 558–63).
158 See, for example, *Ex parte Island Records* [1978] Ch 122.
159 See Gray and Gray (2001, pp. 77–81).
160 Samuel (2001, pp. 150–52).
161 The classic example is *Cooper* v. *Wandsworth Board of Works* (1863) 143 ER 414.
162 See, for example, *Crabb* v. *Arun DC* [1976] Ch 179.
163 Oliver (2000, pp. 343–5).
164 Supreme Court Act 1981, s. 31.
165 *O'Reilly* v. *Mackman* [1983] AC 237.
166 *X (Minors)* v. *Bedfordshire CC* [1995] 2 AC 633; *Stovin* v. *Wise* [1996] AC 923.
167 See Neville Brown and Bell (1998, pp. 193–202).
168 See, for example, the Security Services Act 1989.
169 Human Rights Act 1998.
170 Section 6.
171 Section 8.
172 Oliver (2000, p. 355).
173 *Barrett* v. *Enfield LBC* [2001] 2 AC 550.
174 See, generally, Samuel (1986).
175 Cf. Baker (1999).
176 Lawson (1953, p. 90).
177 See, for example, *Blackpool & Fylde Aero Club Ltd* v. *Blackpool BC* [1990] 1 WLR 1195.
178 See, for example, *X (Minors)* v. *Bedfordshire CC* [1995] 2 AC 633.
179 But cf. Goode (1988) who argues that 'commercial law does exist and that it embodies a philosophy, not always very coherent but nonetheless present, and fundamental concepts, not always very clearly articulated but nonetheless helping to implement that philosophy and to serve the needs of the business community' (p. 147).
180 See Samuel (1986).
181 Oliver (2000).
182 *The General Capinpin* [1991] 1 Ll Rep 1, 9.
183 See, for example, *The Nicholas K* [1996] 1 AC 211. The expression 'commercial reality' is taken from Lord Wilberforce in *The Eurymedon* [1975] AC 154, 167.

184 *Arthur JS Hall and Co* v. *Simons* [2000] 3 WLR 543, 616.
185 At pp. 614–15.
186 At p. 615.
187 At p. 618.
188 *R (McCann)* v. *Manchester Crown Court* [2001] 1 WLR 1084.
189 At p. 1101.
190 At p. 1091.
191 Atias (1994, p. 91).
192 Bell (2001, pp. 64–101).
193 Carbasse (1998, pp. 324–46).
194 D.1.1.1.2.
195 Halpérin (1996, p. 284).
196 Ivainer (1988, pp. 7–8).
197 Atias (1994, p. 107).
198 Halpérin (1996, p. 290).
199 Ibid., p. 295.
200 Ibid., pp. 342–57.
201 See, for example, CC, art. 1386.
202 Halpérin (1996, p. 324).
203 Collins (1997, p. 58).
204 In particular, Teubner (1993); but cf. Samuel (1997).
205 Collins (1997, p. 60).
206 Bouchon-Meunier and Nguyen (1996, pp. 7–9).
207 Atias (1994, p. 92).
208 Birks (1996c, p. 39).
209 [1995] 2 AC 296.
210 Birks (1996b, pp. 5–6).
211 Ibid., p. 6.
212 Ibid.
213 Birks (1996c, p. 39).
214 Granger (1995, p. 70).
215 Villa (1990, p. 84).
216 Atias (1985, pp. 31–6).
217 See, for example, *Lazenby Garages Ltd* v. *Wright* [1976] 1 WLR 459.
218 See, for example, *In re Campbell (A Bankrupt)* [1997] Ch 14.
219 [1966] Ch 538.
220 Van der Merwe and de Waal (1993, no. 14).
221 See, for example, Libchaber (1997).
222 Van de Merwe and de Waal (1993, no. 14).
223 The various levels of legal science cause endless confusion when it comes to the history and theory of, say, property law. What is the object of a right of ownership or a right of possession: the physical object or the *ius* itself? This becomes completely meaningless once one talks of owning or possessing a *res incorporalis*, for the object of the right is the right itself (see Zenati and Revet, 1997, pp. 58–63, 245–9, 273–5).
224 Bunge (1983, p. 57).
225 Ibid., p. 58.
226 Ibid.
227 Bergel (1999, no. 252).

228 Bergel (2001, pp. 115–20).
229 Ellul (1982a, p. 27).
230 Bergel (1999, no. 200).
231 *Ex parte Island Records* [1978] Ch 122.
232 *Re Campbell (a bankrupt)* [1997] Ch 14.
233 D.50.16.16; *Bumper Development Corporation* v. *Metropolitan Police Commissioner* [1991] 1 WLR 1362.
234 *Anns* v. *Merton LBC* [1978] AC 728; cf. *Murphy* v. *Brentwood DC* [1991] 1 AC 398.
235 *Esso Petroleum Co Ltd* v. *Southport Corporation* [1953] 3 WLR 773; [1954] 2 QB 182; [1956] AC 218. Cf. *Code civil*, art. 1384.
236 Paris, 14.12.1961; JCP.1962.II.12547; Cass.civ.20.10.1964; DS.1965.62. Cf. *Pharmaceutical Society of GB* v. *Boots* [1953] 1 QB 401.
237 [1932] AC 562.
238 [1964] AC 465.
239 Quoting Bergel (1999, no. 252). Professor Bergel goes on to point out, of course, that the reduction of law to equations is a myth.
240 Guest (1961b).
241 Ibid., at p. 182.
242 Ibid., p. 197.
243 Bergel (2001, pp. 115–17).
244 See, generally, Berthelot (1996).
245 Berthelot (1996, p. 259).
246 Busino (1998, p. 87).
247 Ibid.
248 *R* v. *Bow Street Metropolitan Stipendiary Magistrate, Ex p Pinochet Ugarte* [2000] 1 AC 61; *R* v. *Bow Street Metropolitan Stipendiary Magistrate, Ex p Pinochet Ugarte (No 2)* [2000] 1 AC 119; *R* v. *Bow Street Metropolitan Stipendiary Magistrate, Ex p Pinochet Ugarte (No 3)* [2000] 1 AC 147.
249 Busino (1998, p. 59).

7 Theories of Liability

Classification in law is not confined only to a dividing up and categorisation of the areas of law itself. It is a much more subtle process that reaches into the heart of each subject. Different types of behaviour, of transactions, of acts, of things and so on are represented by different terms which in effect mean that they are categorised into groups and sub-groups. These categories, groups and (or) sub-groups then become 'things' in themselves. They become objects of theories. In turn, these theories endow the behaviour, transactions, acts and so on with their social and psychological dimensions that allow them to become the foundations for a normative proposition. Take, for example, the old observation of a Roman emperor: *In maleficiis voluntas spectatur, non exitus* (in crimes it is the intention and not the result that matters).[1] The application of this rule involves the categorisation of an act as 'criminal' and the 'mind' as guilty. Thus, once a behavioural act is classified into *mens rea* (guilty mind) and *actus reus* (criminal act), the foundation of criminal liability is established. What is a 'criminal act' and what is a 'guilty mind' are of course in part determined by the classification scheme itself. The purpose of this chapter is to examine this relationship between taxonomy and theories of liability.

Subjective and Objective Theories

If one returns to the facts of *Donoghue* v. *Stevenson* (Chapter 5), it has already been seen that they can be 'constructed' in a number of different ways. The emphasis on the transactional bond between the consumer and the seller of the ginger-beer is one possible legal relationship; the link between the consumer and the manufacturer is another. The seller might or might not be liable in the law of contract, while the manufacturer could be responsible on the basis of negligence. When viewed from the position of the remedy (damages), however, it makes little difference what relationship acts as the foundation of the duty or obligation. What matters to the injured person is whether they are awarded compensation. Of course, the question of liability is supposedly determined by the pre-existing law; one person will be liable to compensate another only when they have contravened rules primarily set out in the law of obligations. Liability, in other words, is determined by the pre-existing rules. But often these rules can turn out to be much more fluid and open-ended when set in the context of certain factual situations (the 'hard case' perhaps) and judges are then faced with having to decide on the basis of the 'justice' of the case. Are these kinds of liability cases dependent upon theoretical assumptions that stretch beyond those underpinning rule categories such as contract or delict (tort)? Indeed, are the rules themselves dependent upon certain theories of liability?

Fault

The idea that liability may, to some extent at least, be governed by its own theoretical structure is inherent in civil law thinking. The *Code civil* states that the non-performance (*inexécution*) of a contract is resolved by an award of damages.[2] In other words, the aggrieved party is entitled to damages for loss caused by the other party's non-performance.[3] Contractual liability would appear at first sight to be a matter of failure to perform the contract. However, the French code goes on to say that, if the party in default is able to prove that the non-performance is due to an outside cause which cannot be imputed to him, he will have a defence to the damages claim.[4] This suggests that there must be some element of fault before a defendant will be condemned to pay damages. Liability to compensate for harm is a matter of *culpa* (blame).[5] This kind of analysis dates back to Roman law where the jurists dealt with liability problems from the position of the type of behaviour for which a defendant must answer.[6] What the Roman jurists seemed to searching for was a balance between agreement and risk. B asks A for the loan of a slave bricklayer. If the slave falls from B's scaffolding, B will prima facie be liable, unless it was specifically agreed that the slave would work up scaffolding. However, even if it was specifically agreed, B would still be liable to A for the loss of the slave if he fell because the scaffolding was unsafe owing to the fault of B.[7] Again things would be different if A and B had made a specific agreement stipulating that B would be liable for the loss of the slave only if B had committed a wilful wrong.[8]

What endows this kind of analysis with its own theoretical perspective is that *culpa* is a foundation of liability irrespective of the existence or non-existence of a contract.[9] Can one assert, therefore, that the basis of a claim for damages in general is fault? If so, then *culpa* goes some way in suppressing the boundaries between contract and non-contractual liability. French law tackles this problem by erecting what is in essence a procedural barrier; the non-cumul rule prevents a person who has suffered loss from suing in delict if there exists between the plaintiff and defendant a contractual relationship.[10] Nevertheless, the central role of fault in compensation claims allows it to act as a focal point for general theories of liability. Only those persons who are in some way individually responsible for the plaintiff's harm should be required to pay damages.[11] Such a theory reflects both a moral and an individualistic view of liability which in turn connects this kind of theorising to the nominalist revolution.[12] It is the individual who is the actor in society and injuries arising within society are thus to be seen as arising either through the act of another or through some totally independent event often attributed to 'God' ('Act of God').[13] If the injurious event can be imputed to an individual, morality then dictates that liability should attach to the actor only if he committed a 'wrong', that is to say if he is to blame.[14]

Such morality seems to have been the theoretical foundation of the Roman category of actions *ex delicto*, since these were claims based on 'wrongdoing itself' (*id est ipso maleficio*).[15] Moreover, as has been seen, liability *ex contractu* was also closely associated with individual 'human weakness' (*humana infirmitas*).[16] But the moral individualism is also a product of the modern era where jurists have sought to locate the source of all obligations in the autonomy of the individual will. The influence of Kant, the philosophical force behind the will theory, was particularly strong in Germany, but it was to be felt in France as well. The free man is the basis of law and the law of obligations is the means by which this liberty is secured.[17] Translated into the fault principle, it means that each actor is free to act as he or she pleases and will be condemned to pay compensation only when he or she has specifically contracted to pay or when 'human weakness' has been the cause of harm to another. The point to be stressed of course is that theories of liability can act as an arena in which ideological ideas about individualism are acted out in the name of ethics and legal theory. If society does not exist, only individual men and women, the fault theory seems to assume an epistemological and ideological inevitability. Only the individual can act.[18]

Whatever may have been the theory, or theories, underpinning the early common law, there is no doubt that English law was equally influenced in the 19th century by liberal individualism.[19] Can it be said, therefore, that liability in English law is just as dependent on the existence of fault as in Roman law? Certainly, in the field of tort law, negligence has been so dominant with respect to accident liability that it has gone far in suppressing or subverting older torts based on liability without fault.[20] Consequently, it is difficult to imagine an owner of property obtaining damages for its direct accidental destruction unless he can prove carelessness[21] or at least some degree of fault.[22] Perhaps it is best to avoid using sweeping notions such as 'fault' to explain the whole spectrum of tort law in England, since burdens of proof and levels of duty vary according to the cause of action in play.[23] Yet, in what is statistically one of the most important empirical sources of tort liability, road accidents, a victim will have to bear the cost of his or her own injuries (other than the services of the National Health Service) unless fault on the part of another can be established. Cause without blame is not enough.[24] Equally, in medical injury cases, the fault principle is central.

However, when it comes to liability in contract, the position, at first sight, looks quite different: contractual liability is said to be independent of fault since it is based on breach of promise.[25] In truth, the question comes down to what is actually promised and, in respect of a contract of services, the implied obligation is one of skill and care.[26] A contractor is promising, in other words, not to be careless. Moreover, if a contractual party can show that his non-performance of the contractual obligation is to be imputed to an outside event beyond his control, he will be able to claim that the whole contractual obligation has dissipated under the doctrine of frustration.[27] It is possible, then, to formulate a theory of compensation based upon individual responsibility in English law, and such a thesis will find considerable support in the cases.

For the epistemologist, however, what is particularly valuable about fault is the insight it offers into the way the legal structure models society. Liability is a matter that attaches to the individual actors and this indicates that transactions and activities are envisaged only in terms of the individual human (or a corporate body treated as a legal *persona*).[28] The effectiveness of this model in normative terms should not be underestimated. It benefits first of all from a long history whose foundation is very firmly rooted in Roman law. Fault liability is as old as the concept of law and thus appears as indissociable from legal knowledge itself. Secondly, the moral dimension that attaches to the notion of 'wrong' endows the categories of contract and tort with a normative dimension that lies outside the actual categories themselves. It supplies a philosophical justification for the awarding of compensation beyond the positive rules. Thirdly, it provides a political and social justification for limiting compensation claims. Liberty of action is a value enshrined in much Western political thinking and thus the idea that the individual can act relatively free from the economic burden of having to compensate those affected by his activities indirectly endows the idea of a restricted liability scheme with a respectability.

The fact that road accident statistics might be fairly constant from year to year does not seem to affect the model or its metalegal philosophies. Nor, indeed, does the existence of compulsory insurance. Where the group or class does appear to have a role is in respect of the benefit that such activities as driving or manufacturing bring to consumers as a whole.[29] 'Gas, water and also electricity services are well-nigh a necessity of modern life, or at least are generally demanded as a requirement for the common good,' said Sellers LJ in 1964. And he continued: 'It would seem odd that facilities so much sought after by the community and approved by their legislators should be actionable at common law because they have been brought to places where they are required and have escaped without negligence by an unforeseen sequence of mishaps.'[30]

Risk

The moment one abandons the individual as the focal point of liability, a quite different model emerges which turns Sellers LJ's justification on its head. If gas and electricity are a requirement for the common good, why should it be the individual who has to bear the inevitable and associated cost of something that benefits the community as a whole? Ought it not to be the community that bears the burden? This is certainly the view of French administrative law. As one French public lawyer put it: 'the activity of the state is carried on in the interest of the entire community; the burdens that it entails should not weigh more heavily on some than on others'.[31] This principle of equality in the face of public burdens translates into a liability without fault on the part of the public body. Thus, if the facts of some of the English tort cases had arisen in France – cases where the English plaintiff has had to show fault in order to obtain damages – the approach to liability would be quite different. For example, in one case where a citizen lost his shop premises as a result of police action in recapturing a dangerous criminal, the citizen would not have had to prove negligence in order to obtain compensation.[32] The equality principle would have ensured damages on the basis of liability without fault.[33]

It is not just in public law that liability without fault finds expression. In Roman law, the category of quasi-delict gave expression to a number of actions in which the plaintiff did not have to show fault in order to succeed. Perhaps the most famous was the action for things thrown out of buildings. Any person who suffered harm while on a public highway as a result of being hit by something poured or thrown from a building could obtain damages through an action *quasi ex delicto* against the occupier of the building.[34] This liability was not based on fault as such.[35] It rested on the idea that it was in the public interest that anyone should be able to move about the streets without fear or danger.[36] Now, it has to be admitted that the exact basis of liability *quasi ex delicto* is open to debate; the Roman jurists themselves suggest that it is a form of liability whereby one person is liable for the wrongful act of someone under his control or service.[37] Later, civilians came up with a variety of more developed theories.[38] But there is no doubt that it had a community or class orientation, since the action itself was an *actio popularis* which protected public 'rights' (*ius populi*).[39]

Another Roman action which gave expression to a liability without fault was the *actio de pauperie*. The owner of a four-footed animal would be liable for damages without fault on his part for any harm done to another by the animal acting against its nature.[40] The owner could escape liability only by handing over the animal to the victim.[41] A third form of Roman liability, although similar in some ways to liability *quasi ex delicto* and somewhat analogous to the *actio de pauperie*, was in respect of the liability of one person for delicts committed by another. When a slave committed a delict, the owner would be liable to pay damages or to hand over the slave.[42] This form of liability is important inasmuch as it suggests that one person can be directly liable to another on the basis of the relationship between person and slave and thus it is the relationship rather than the fault which acts as the foundation for liability.[43] However, Roman law went further and held that a person might be liable for wrongful damage caused by employees[44] or even guests.[45] This form of liability is based less on the idea of relationship and more on the contractual liability and (or) fault of the employer or invitor; it is a form of *culpa in eligendo*. But it once again gives expression to a structure that can act as an alternative to fault liability; it suggests a form of liability that is corporate in nature.[46]

It was this structure that was to act as the basis for the idea of liability based on risk. Such a liability found little favour in the German civilian tradition which, particularly during the 19th century, was in the grip of the individualist principle of 'no liability without fault'.[47] But in the French tradition the idea of a liability based upon the relationship between person and the instrument of damage (person or thing) found favour and became the basis of an alternative to the fault principle.[48] Article 1384 of the *Code civil* states that 'one is liable not only for the damage that one causes through one's own act, but equally for that which is caused by the act of persons for whom one must have responsibility, or for things that one has under one's control (*sous sa garde*)'. In addition to this general principle, the industrialisation in Europe led to a number of specific statutes, even in Germany, imposing liability for damage done by trains, factory machinery and the like.[49] At first, jurists responded to these new statutes by confining them to regions beyond the code.[50] And with respect to article 1384, adherents to the fault principle simply interpreted the article as a form of *culpa in eligendo*.[51] However, during the 20th century, a new principle emerged based on the idea of profit and risk: *ubi emolumentum ibi onus*.[52]

In French law there is now a very clear alternative to the fault model of liability founded on article 1384 which in turn is justified by reference to the theory of risk itself linked with the widespread existence of insurance. As the advocate general in one recent French case put it:

> The need for security, a characteristic of the present time, has as its consequence that a person who suffers harm wants to be compensated, whatever the circumstances surrounding the cause of the damage. Fatality is no longer accepted and when a person is himself at fault, he looks for others to blame. This is why the courts interpret very widely the notion of liability, and are so much more inclined to do so when in the great majority of cases defendants are covered by insurance.[53]

And he added:

> Strict liability must be accompanied by an insurance obligation already set down in morality. The law of insurance radiates today through the whole of social life. Tomorrow it will come systematically to guarantee the liability of parents.

Professor Viney supported the insurance approach in her comment on the case. She first of all noted that 'the second civil Chamber of the *Cour de cassation* has undertaken a very important change of direction (*un revirement*) in confirming that the mother and father are "strictly liable" for the damage caused by their under-age child living with them and that they can escape this liability only by "proof of *force majeure* or fault of the victim"'. She then later added:

> Is it to be feared that the counterpart will be an excessive increase in the burden of liabilities weighing on the parents and thus a considerable increase in the family debt? It seems not. Indeed, liability insurance for the head of the family, which has always been the only effective guarantee, both for the victims and those liable, is not very onerous at the moment and even if it is to be thought that the premium will rise to take account of the increase in the risk that this new caselaw puts on the parents, this rise will not actually be very much, for the disappearance of the litigation with respect to the proof of the absence of education or supervision fault ought to come close to setting off the extra cost of the move from presumption of fault to strict liability ...

This insurance theory is not without its problems.[54] Nevertheless, it is important inasmuch as it seems able to offer a structural alternative to liability based on the strictly individualistic model. In fact, the legislator in France has gone even further and passed a special law with respect to traffic accidents which has had the effect of reducing considerably the role of individual morality and fault in traffic injury cases.[55] This legislation recognises the reality of the role of the insurance company in road accident compensation and it builds upon this multi-party legal structure to create a new basis for liability founded on the idea of a motor vehicle being 'implicated' in an accident.[56] However, it is to be noted that even this law cannot escape completely from the fault principle. Thus victims will be precluded from obtaining compensation if 'their inexcusable fault ... has been the exclusive cause of the accident'.[57] What the law does is to provide a social morality to act as a counterpoint to the traditional individualistic morality.[58]

Liability for Things

In the middle of the 19th century, it looked as if the English law of tort might adopt a principle similar to article 1384 in respect of dangerous things brought onto land which escaped and did damage. In the famous case of *Rylands* v. *Fletcher*,[59] Blackburn J stated:

> We think that the true rule of law is, that the person who for his own purposes brings on his lands and collects and keeps there anything likely to do mischief if it escapes, must keep it in at his peril, and, if he does not do so, is prima facie answerable for all the damage which is the natural consequence of its escape. He can excuse himself by shewing that the escape was owing to the plaintiff's default; or perhaps that the escape was the consequences of vis major, or the act of God; but as nothing of this sort exists here, it is unnecessary to inquire what excuse would be sufficient. The general rule, as above stated, seems on principle just.[60]

And he continued:

> The person whose grass or corn is eaten down by the escaping cattle of his neighbour, or whose mine is flooded by the water from his neighbour's reservoir, or whose cellar is invaded by the filth of his neighbour's privy, or whose habitation is made unhealthy by the fumes and noisome vapours of his neighbour's alkali works, is damnified without any fault of his own; and it seems but reasonable and just that the neighbour, who has brought something on his own property which was not naturally there, harmless to others so long as it is confined to his own property, but which he knows to be

mischievous if it gets on his neighbour's, should be obliged to make good the damage which ensues if he does not succeed in confining it to his own property ...[61]

However, subsequent case law has severely restricted rather than developed the principles of liability set out by Blackburn J. In 1947 it was made fairly clear that in respect of personal injury there would, save in some limited exceptional situations governed by special rules, be no liability without fault.[62] And more recently the Blackburn J's principle itself has actually been brought within the boundaries of fault. A company was held not liable for damage caused by escaping pollution because such damage was unforeseeable.[63] The general theory of liability is, or soon it seems will be, that a person will be liable only for foreseeable damage.

Of course, fault itself does not necessarily suppress the idea of risk. The latter can be used as a means of importing such a high duty into the area of fault liability that it has the effect of turning fault liability into liability without fault. This has happened to some extent with product liability[64] and with respect to damage caused to passers-by from man-made structures that adjoin the highway.[65] Yet fault can have an impact in a number of ways upon the idea of 'risk'. For example, if one envisages risk in terms of a nominalist approach towards facts, then a farmer who carelessly allows his farm to become overrun with rats will not be liable to a person who suffers a rare and unforeseen illness arising from rats' urine.[66] One is not liable for what cannot be foreseen. Equally, a local authority that leaves a dilapidated and potentially dangerous boat in a place where children play will, at least according to the court of appeal, not be liable to a young person injured when the boat falls off a jack while the young person was trying to restore it.[67] These decisions are not inevitable. They simply depend upon how the judges view the world of fact. If the 'risk' factor is expressed at the level of *res* (thing that does damage) and *injuria* (wrongful harm) then the person suffering from rats' urine or a collapsing boat ought to recover. Accordingly, the House of Lords in the collapsing boat case had little difficulty in overturning the court of appeal's decision.[68] But if a distinction is made between categories of illness, or between the ways accidents actually happen, it becomes much more difficult to link the *injuria* with the *res*. One is facing here, not so much a theory of ethics, but an epistemological (re)construction of the world.

Interestingly, in the area of English contract law the courts have been much more generous in their approach to 'risk' liability. Goods hired or sold to another must be of 'satisfactory quality' and 'reasonably fit for [their] purpose'[69] and the courts have interpreted these terms objectively. That is to say, they have refused to link the state of the *res* with the behaviour of the contracting *persona* and consequently, if the thing is unfit and causes harm, there will be liability.[70] Indeed, even if the unfit *res* causes unforeseeable damage, the case law seems to show that this will not allow a contractor to escape liability.[71] Only if there is sufficient fault on the part of the victim will the courts break the link.[72] At the level of legal structure, liability is based not on behaviour but simply on the relationship between *persona* and *res*. One justification offered for this kind of 'risk' liability was that the structure of the relationship allowed the supplier of goods to protect himself against the risk. Thus, in *Hyman* v. *Nye*, Lindley J held that the supplier of a carriage must furnish a vehicle that is reasonably fit for its purpose. And he continued:

> Nor does it appear to me to be at all unreasonable to exact such vigilance from a person who makes it his business to let out carriages for hire. As between him and the hirer the risk of defects in the carriage, so far as care and skill can avoid them, ought to be thrown on the owner of the carriage. The hirer trusts him to supply a fit and proper carriage; the lender has it in his power not only to see that it is in a proper state, and to keep it so, and thus protect himself from risk, but also to charge his customers enough to cover his expenses.[73]

When one reviews the various classes of defendants across the liability cases it might be said that English law alternates between fault and risk, depending upon the empirical status of the defendant. Suppliers of goods are treated differently from local authorities. However, while there might be some truth in this thesis, it is too simplistic. Local authorities have been held liable in contract in respect of harm that is much less serious than harm from which they have been given protection even though their negligence might have had a role in its cause.[74] Insurance provides some explanation for a court's willingness to find or refuse liability.[75] Yet, in the area of road accidents, the courts have proved, and are still proving, insensitive to the insurance structure.[76] The status of the defendant and the ability to insure against foreseeable risks might seem, accordingly, to be of importance in the formulation of any general theory of liability.[77] But they would not be adequate in themselves.

Protected Interests

Another thesis that is used to ground a theory of liability is the nature of the harm suffered. If the various types of harm are translated into a range of 'interests', it then becomes possible to relate liability to the nature of the interest invaded (cf. Chapter 4). Such a thesis gains particular support from the general liability provision in the BGB. Paragraph 823 states that a 'person who wilfully or negligently injures the life, body, health, freedom, property, or other right of another contrary to law is bound to compensate him for any damage arising therefrom'.[78] In contrast to liability under article 1382 of the *Code civil*, liability in Germany is not grounded just in *culpa*; there must be an invasion of one of the listed interests. This interest thesis lends itself to English law, in that the old forms of action tended to emphasise the nature of the damage. Trespass to the person, nuisance, trover (conversion), defamation (libel and slander) and the like – forms of action which remain the basis of causes of action in modern tort law – all give expression to an invasion of particular kinds of 'interest'.[79] Nuisance, for example, reflects an interest in land, whereas libel deals with reputation; trespass to the person is valuable for remedying, *inter alia*, invasions of personality interests. The tort of negligence admittedly cuts across these old claims.[80] But the requirement of a duty of care has become a means of giving expression to the nature of the interest invaded. Personal injury, nervous shock and pure economic loss each attract different rules within the tort of negligence.[81]

Contractual liability would appear at first sight to be founded in the idea of a *vinculum iuris* rather than in the nature of the interest invaded. Yet interest can play a vital role at the level of damages.[82] Where a plaintiff in a contractual claim is suing for the price of goods sold or for a profit wrongfully obtained by his co-contractor, it is not always viable to express this in terms of harm or loss. The plaintiff may not have actually suffered any 'loss' strictly speaking.[83] In such a situation, it becomes much more plausible to talk in terms of a 'restitution interest' (or, in the case of a claim for a price, 'reliance interest'). Such a 'restitution interest' has the further advantage of transcending the law of contract to act as the basis of a third category of liability reflecting the principle of unjust enrichment. As Denning LJ expressed it in relation to a claim for wrongful interference with goods, if a wrongdoer has made use of goods for his own purpose, then he must pay a reasonable hire for them, even though the owner has in fact suffered no loss. For the 'claim for a hiring charge is ... not based on the loss to the plaintiff, but on the fact that the defendant has used the goods for his own purposes'.[84] It is, he said, an action against him because he has had the benefit of the goods and it 'resembles, therefore, an action for restitution, rather than an action of tort'.[85]

In situations, then, where a person has unjustly profited, but this profit cannot be related to any specific loss on the part of another, the idea of a restitution interest as the foundation of liability becomes particularly attractive. Indeed, it can act as a bridge between 'owing' and 'owning', with the result that the theory of liability can shift from obligation, with its emphasis on 'duty', towards property, with its emphasis on a 'right' (cf. Chapter 4). The interest, so to speak, becomes a form of *res* capable of being claimed by another.[86] This idea has always been latent in the action of debt itself since a debt, being a chose in action, is a form of property.[87] Liability in restitution could thus be said to be based neither on contract nor on a tortious wrong; it is based on the idea of a 'proprietary interest' and the plaintiff is entitled to succeed on the ground of 'ownership'.[88]

Interest does, then, play a key role in formulating liability problems.[89] However, as the basis of a theory of liability, it is much less secure since it is, by its very nature as an essentially descriptive concept, incapable of providing a normative dimension. To say that the plaintiff in a case such as *Spartan Steel*[90] (discussed earlier, in Chapter 5) cannot recover its loss of profit economic interest is not to provide a complete theory of liability because it is very clear that plaintiffs can recover for pure economic loss elsewhere in the delict and tort systems.[91] Of course, one can say that one interest is more valuable, socially and (or) morally,[92] but again this is an indicator of liability that is valuable only when measured against other focal points of liability. Thus the economic interest that was denied in the *Spartan Steel* case makes sense only in the context of unintentional injury. A person who wilfully invades the economic interest of another using behaviour that is *contra bonos mores* will be liable in German law and often English law as well.[93] Indeed, if the plaintiff in *Spartan Steel* had been able to frame his claim as *ex contractu* then the economic loss, or part of it, might well have been recoverable.[94] One cannot state that this or that interest will or will not give rise to liability, since it all depends on other factors besides the nature of the interest.

Take the following examples. A local authority employee is negligent in failing to clear and distribute letters and this results in a local business suffering economic loss; another local authority employee is negligent in failing to discover child abuse and this leads to serious harm to the child. Viewed exclusively from the position of the interest invaded, one would be justified in thinking that the child might recover but the business would not. In fact, according to the English case law, the reverse is true.[95] Now both cases can be explained inasmuch as one involves liability *ex contractu* whereas the other is a problem *ex delicto*; the grounds of liability are thus very different according to the traditional rules of the law of obligations. However, once one attacks these traditional rules as tending to fragment the understanding of liability – something that is particularly tempting with regard to the English law of torts[96] – the theorist's logic is to find a different starting point. Such different starting points, as we have seen, can be normative ideas such as fault or risk (or principles expressing these notions); alternatively, they can be empirical notions such as accident compensation or interest liability. What the case law indicates is that a whole stream of variables come into play in respect of both the construction of facts and the application of liability ideas.

Theory of Variables

A liability theorist can certainly start with structures. Where the emphasis is on, and only on, the *vinculum iuris* between person and person, the pattern of liability is almost by definition individualistic. One looks only at the two parties. Such an approach does not exclude ideas of risk: the resources of the parties could well play a role in any liability theory.[97] But the Western tradition has so emphasised behaviour and will (*voluntas*) that escaping from the idea of *culpa* as the primary normative factor in the determination of liability seems unrealistic. Nominalism and individualism are essential parts of legal knowledge.[98] However, by changing the pattern of the legal model to embrace a third element, either another person or a thing, one can fundamentally alter the whole foundation of liability. The emphasis is no longer on the plaintiff–defendant bond but on the link between defendant and third element. This in turn shifts the emphasis off behaviour and onto control. A defendant can be condemned to pay damages simply on the basis that he had in his control a person or a thing capable of doing damage.[99] This idea can then be reinforced through the idea of activity rather than act; the defendant had in his control persons and (or) things in pursuit of an activity that was, for the defendant, profitable. When one then adds the insurance factor – and road and factory activities have by public law to be covered by insurance – the new pattern is complete. It is capable of acting as an alternative normative basis of liability.

French law sets out these two alternatives very clearly, but English law, in contrast, does quite the opposite. It starts from the idea that the law of torts 'is concerned not with activities but with acts'.[100] Yet it actually retreats from this pattern in a number of ways. Employers are strictly liable for torts committed by their employees while working in the course of employment and some actual negligence and nuisance cases appear to put considerable emphasis on the idea of a liability for persons and a liability for things.[101] However, the principle of liability here is not really a general one in the sense that it expresses a theoretical basis for compensation liability. Thus attempts to use nuisance and *Rylands* v. *Fletcher* as the basis for accident compensation usually fail and one rather interesting use of nuisance as a means of protecting what French law might see as a right of personality has been recently condemned by the House of

Lords.[102] These individualised torts indicate that there is no general theory of liability that attaches to the category of tort.[103]

In order to succeed in a claim, a plaintiff must establish a set of factors that might be described as 'variables'. The behaviour and resources of the defendant, the nature of the interest invaded, the legal concepts and rules applied (foreseeability, causation, contributory negligence and so on), the burden of proof and the construction of the facts (with all its possibilities) are such variables. They inject into the decision making so much complexity that it is impossible to produce a useful theory of liability in the traditional sense. Perhaps Lord Wilberforce was recognising this complexity when he stated:

> It cannot lightly be taken for granted, even as a matter of theory, that the purpose of the law of tort is compensation, still less that it ought to be, an issue of large social import, or that there is something inappropriate or illogical or anomalous (a question-begging word) in including a punitive element in civil damages, or conversely that the criminal law, rather than the civil law, is in these cases the better instrument for conveying social disapproval, or for redressing a wrong to the social fabric ... As a matter of practice English law has not committed itself to any of these theories, it may have been wiser than it knew ...[104]

It is, in other words, a matter of variables. However, in saying this, one is not just stating the obvious, that the question of liability in private law is complex. The point to be made is that decision making in law cannot be explained entirely by reference to theories about interests, morality, individualism, risk, loss spreading, deterrence or whatever. Law is just as much about the construction of facts which itself functions at two levels. At an abstract level, it is a matter of whether one is envisaging the factual situation in terms of two parties (acts) or through the kind of three-element structure given expression by article 1384 of the *Code civil* (the first variable). At a more detailed level, it is then a question of how each judge views the events (the second variable). Is fire to be distinguished from an explosion? Is a disease from rat's urine to be distinguished from a disease by rat bite? Is the sinking of a ship to be seen as a unique event or as a series of events? Is a pair of underpants to be seen as analogous to a bottle of ginger beer? The application of particular legal concepts is another variable (the third). Is the interest invaded of relevance? Is the damage 'too remote'? Was the defendant's behaviour to be classified as 'negligent', 'fraudulent', 'wilful' or 'innocent'? These last questions raise a more general issue of legal schematics. If liability is about individual acts, how is the state of the human mind to be classified in relation to any particular act?

Categorising the Mind

This human mind and human act point is in need of more specific treatment and for this purpose it might be useful to return to the codes. The distinction between paragraphs 823 and 826 of the BGB is simple. One is concerned with damage caused by negligent behaviour while the other is concerned with wilful behaviour. Different types of behaviour can lead to different kinds of liability. This emphasis on behaviour, as we have seen, is one of the fundamental, if not defining, characteristics of Western liability law. In criminal law the state of mind is so fundamental that any act which is unaccompanied by a guilty mind (*mens rea*) is prima facie not a criminal act (*actus non facit reum nisi mens sit rea*). However, intention and negligence are not the only types of behaviour and states of mind of relevance to the law. Negligence itself is subdivided into various degrees in some legal systems and a range of other states of mind and types of behaviour is to be found across the whole spectrum of public and private law in Europe. A fundamental aspect of legal knowledge is thus concerned with the classification and categorisation of behaviour and states of mind.

However, the actual categorisation of states of mind is not of itself the most serious problem for the theorist. What makes this whole area so difficult is that the law is demanding the rational systematisation of an object that is unknowable in any objective sense. The state of a person's mind is no more evident than the state of his or her digestion.[105] The categories used by the law thus represent in a particularly acute form a science which, although by no means detached from social behaviour, is the object of its own science. In other words, a person can be deemed to be, say, 'reckless' for the purposes of the law in situations where a specialist from another profession may take a rather different view.[106]

Intention and Negligence

The categorisation of behaviour in private law goes back to Roman law where, in particular, the distinction between *dolus* (fraud) and *culpa* (malice and negligence) was a fundamental aspect of liability both *ex contractu* and *ex delicto*.[107] Thus a person who gratuitously looked after another person's goods would be liable, if the property was lost or damaged, only for *dolus*; if the depositee received a fee then the standard would change and he would be liable for negligence.[108] Negligence in turn was subdivided into various kinds. *Culpa levis* was a failure to act as a *bonus paterfamilias* would have acted, while *culpa lata* was gross negligence, that is to say, *non intellegere quod omnes intellegunt* (not to realise what everyone realises).[109] This kind of schematisation of behaviour no doubt represented, and represents, discernible behavioural differences and thus could be said to be a rationalisation of social fact. Intentionally killing a pedestrian is clearly different from carelessly causing his death.[110] Yet jurists, in making decisions about behaviour, do not actually indulge in much empirical investigation. What they do is to categorise situations. Thus, as Lawson has observed, Roman 'jurists decided cases on the facts without considering whether the conduct of either or both of the parties was blameworthy; in other words, to do a certain act at a certain time and place was *culpa*, but at another time or place was not'.[111] For example, the jurist Paul, in considering the problem of spreading fire caused by the farmer who was burning off stubble, simply makes a descriptive statement of fact. If he did it on a windy day he was guilty of negligence, if he did not, the fire spreading as a result of a sudden gust of wind, then he was not.[112] Of course one can induce out of such facts the principle of foreseeability.[113] But such a term is being defined entirely in relation to sets of objective facts. Some facts will fall within the category of foreseeable danger, others will not.

Such a question of fact was, in the common law, until relatively recently decided by a jury. They would decide whether the act of the defendant was careless or not. And in criminal law they still perform this role in relation to the state of mind of the defendant. In most civil cases this jury function has now been assumed by the trial judge and this has had the effect of introducing into legal analysis a new dimension. Whereas the jury's decision was simply a yes or no verdict whose formality never embraced the need to give reasons, a judge's decision is something different. A judge's finding of fact forms part of the judgment and if care is not taken it can transcend the facts of the case to become by way of factual analogy a formal precedent.[114] As Weir has noted, 'county court judges ... continue to apply decisions on breach [that is to say on whether the defendant was careless or not] as if they laid down fixed rules ("inching forward into traffic isn't negligence ...")'.[115] What is revealing about this process is the ease with which the boundary between 'fact' and 'law' can become blurred; a factual situation involving reasonableness of behaviour can easily become a rule about foreseeability. This is a point that can so easily become lost in the civil law tradition where the 'law' is seen only as normative propositions (norms, rules and principles). Yet once it is decided, say, that this or that set of facts amounts to a certain category of behaviour, institutional elements in the facts are transformed into the legal discourse. Fire and wind, to go back to the Roman example, are as much legal tools as factual ones; they become the means by which one builds up a picture of behaviour. Motor vehicles, in French law, became one key instrument for translating the abstract proposition of liability for 'things' in article 1384 of the civil code into case law reality.

With regard to negligence, one should not be surprised by such an institutional approach, since it is by no means easy to describe negligence as a 'state of mind'. Indeed, if it were a 'state of mind', it would be much more difficult to hold a corporation liable for negligence. By asking whether or not the defendant acted 'reasonably' it becomes possible to assess liability with reference to an objective figure, the 'reasonable man'[116] or, in French law, *le bon père de famille*.[117] This is not to say that decision making becomes easy or that solutions can in some way be inferred from a reasonable man model. But it does mean that the court can simply assess the facts in a seemingly objective way and categorise them as either negligent or not negligent.[118] In fact, the actual categorisation process (*la qualification juridique*) is viewed in French law as a means by which 'factual' decisions on whether or not a defendant was at fault can be turned into questions of law.[119] 'Intention', on the other hand, is rather different, since this is a state of mind that one associates with a particular actor doing a particular act. Intention implies behaviour in which the actor subjectively wills not just the act which causes (or might cause) injury but also the injury itself.

Where this kind of categorisation becomes particularly difficult is in the subjectivity of the whole exercise. Is the person who sets fire to a house with the intention just of frightening the occupants, but with the result that one of the occupants dies, to be categorised alongside the person who burns down a house with the express intention of killing all the occupants? For the purposes of a civil action for damages such fine distinctions may be of less importance, since the primary aim is to secure compensation rather than to punish the actor. But this is not true of the criminal law. Punishment and states of mind are intricately linked and this forces the courts into categorisation exercises that have then to be reduced to normative (and linguistic) propositions as a result of the maxim *nulla poena sine lege* (no punishment without a pre-existing legal rule).[120]

When viewed institutionally, the problem of intention is that it can be too narrow a concept for categorising all the relevant factual situations. If it is construed only in terms of willing a specific result in the sense of the result being the sole motive for the act, there is a danger that the category will not match the institutional images of 'intended harm'. D blows up an aeroplane in flight with the motive of recovering insurance money. Is D guilty of intentionally killing the aircrew?[121] The deaths may not have been his motive, but they were a side-effect that could not be avoided in achieving the actual result of obtaining the money. Accordingly, the Law Commission have proposed the following definition (with respect to non-fatal crimes at least): 'a person acts ... "intentionally" with respect to a result when – (i) it is his purpose to cause it; or (ii) although it is not his purpose to cause that result, he is aware that it would occur in the ordinary course of events if he were to succeed in his purpose of causing some other result'.[122] Intention is here being applied to a situation that falls short of the specific result desired. D is guilty because he 'intended' to blow up the aeroplane.

Two shifts have taken place here. First, the result is attached to the *res* (aeroplane) rather than to the *persona* (pilot) and this becomes feasible because the destruction of the *res* will inevitably involve the destruction of the *persona*. The aeroplane ends up by embracing the pilot to the extent that they become a single 'universal' unit. Secondly, the notion of 'awareness' brings into play an objective element; one can begin to define 'awareness' with reference to the 'reasonable man'. Would the reasonable man have been aware that the destruction of an aeroplane necessarily entails the death of the aircrew? Difficulties arise, of course, when it becomes problematic to amalgamate the *res* and *persona* (or indeed one event with another event). For example, if D deliberately sets fire to a house, is it an inevitable or necessary consequence that an occupant will die?[123] In order to 'intend' the death of an occupant it is vital that the house and the occupant become a single unit.

Recklessness and Malice

One way of getting around this difficulty is to set up an intermediate category or range of categories such as 'recklessness' and (or) 'malice'. These categories can exist as mental requirements quite independent of 'intention' or they can act as extensions to intention itself. Thus one who recklessly causes death or other kinds of harm could be treated as having intentionally caused it. There may of course be moral objections to such an extension, particularly with regard to a system that distinguishes between the crime of murder and manslaughter. Yet even if recklessness acts as an independent category, it is not free of problems. If recklessness is the doing of an act which creates an 'obvious' or 'serious' risk of causing harm, is the test of awareness of the risk to be subjective or objective?[124] Again, much will depend upon how the facts are envisaged. D does an act (for example, setting fire to some white spirit in a neighbour's shed) which not only causes an immediate event (event 1: for example, a small fire) but results in another event (event 2: for example, the destruction of the whole shed and its contents).[125] If event 2 is absorbed into event 1, then it becomes possible to say that D was 'reckless' or 'malicious' with respect to the destruction of the shed; the act created an obvious or serious risk of the damage. But if the two events are kept strictly separate, a quite different picture can be created. The starting of the small fire might well have been 'negligent' but it would not, particularly from a subjective point of view (if, for example, D was of below average intelligence), necessarily be reckless or even malicious (in the sense of willing destruction).

The category of 'malice' is useful in situations where a person does an act, objectively legitimate, but which is intended to injure another. For example, D deliberately does an act on his land, which of itself is not unreasonable, with the sole intention of disturbing his neighbour whom he detests. Ought the motive to override the legitimacy of the act? In French law, such behaviour can amount to an abuse of a right allowing the party injured by the act to claim damages.[126] In English law, however, the position is more complex. Malice of itself is not a tort and thus one can exercise an established property or contract right 'for a good reason, a bad reason or no reason at all'.[127] That said, malice could function within an established tort to turn a prima facie legitimate act into an unreasonable one. Thus the occupier who plays a musical instrument, or makes some other noise, with the sole intention of disturbing his neighbour will be guilty of the tort of private nuisance simply because of his malicious behaviour.[128] Proof of malice can of course be a matter of great difficulty. Yet one way around this difficulty is to measure behaviour in terms of the concept of an interest. A person who exercises a right in circumstances where it can be said that he has no 'legitimate interest' in the exercise could be deemed to be 'malicious'. The state of mind, in other words, is once again constructed by the institutional pattern of the facts. If the subject (*persona*) who exercises the right has no relational link with an identifiable 'interest' (*res*), then bad faith can be implied.

Indeed, one can take this institutional exercise a step further. Where a person insists on exercising a right in circumstances where the exercise will interfere with another, opposing, interest, the insistence on the exercise can amount to evidence in itself of unreasonable behaviour. In one English case, the buyers of a house, recently constructed adjacent to a cricket field, objected to the playing of cricket because of the risk of injury from cricket balls landing in their garden. The risk was real enough, but when the buyers sought an injunction to prevent the playing of cricket they were faced with this comment from one of the court of appeal judges:

> It is a relevant circumstance which a court of equity should take into account that the plaintiffs decided to buy a house which in June 1972 when completion took place was obviously on the boundary of a quite small cricket ground where cricket was played at weekends and

> sometimes on evenings during the working week. They selected a house with the benefit of the open space beside it ... [T]hey must have realised that it was the village cricket ground, and that balls would sometimes be knocked from the wicket into their garden, or even against the fabric of the house. If they did not realise it, they should have done. As it turns out, the female plaintiff has developed a somewhat obsessive attitude to the proximity of the cricket field and the cricketers who visit her to seek to recover their cricket balls. The evidence discloses a hostility which goes beyond what is reasonable, although as the learned judge found she is reasonable in her fear that if the family use the garden while a match is in progress they will run the risk of serious injury ... It is reasonable to decide that during matches the family must keep out of the garden ...[129]

Admittedly this is a somewhat extreme and not very reliable precedent. Nevertheless, the method remains of interest in that it illustrates how one can build up a behavioural pattern from the pattern of the facts. Had the source of the danger not been cricket ('the manly sport', according to the judge), but, say, industrial quarrying involving blasting, the behaviour of the wife might well have been viewed as perfectly reasonable in the circumstances. Categorisation of behaviour must, accordingly, be considered in the context of the institutional and conceptual model established within any one set of facts. It is a category that interrelates with other categories and notions so as to produce an image of the facts that will conform to the solution in the case.

Psychiatric States of Mind

None of this is to claim that the courts are indifferent to medical evidence about behaviour. The point to be made is that such evidence has to be integrated into a system of thought whose purpose is not to rationalise and explain states of mind, but to create a system of categories which can help infer a result. For example, D negligently kills V in circumstances where the accident is witnessed by P, one of V's parents. P suffers severe shock and depression and subsequently claims compensation from D for this harm. As far as English law is concerned, two distinct states of mind must be identified. If P has suffered 'nervous shock' as a result of D's negligent act, P may in principle have a legitimate claim against D – provided certain conditions are fulfilled – for full compensation.[130] However, if P suffers 'bereavement', then a quite different rule comes into play; P can recover only a fixed sum under statute.[131] In addition to these two psychiatric states of mind, there is the category of 'mental distress'. This is a form of mental damage recognised in English contract law for breaches of a contract whose very object was 'to provide pleasure, relaxation, peace of mind or freedom from molestation'.[132] Thus the victim of a miserable holiday may well be able to claim damages for 'mental distress' if the misery resulted from a failure to provide what the holiday contract promised.[133]

By definition, these three categories imply other categories of mental suffering which, seemingly, do not count as 'damage' for the purposes of law. Damages are not available, for example, in English contract law 'for any distress, frustration, anxiety, displeasure, vexation, tension or aggravation'[134] and it would be tempting to say that this applies in the case of tort as well. Certainly, it has been held that a wife unable to have sexual relations and children as a result of the emasculation of her husband could not claim against the negligent defendant for her mental suffering.[135] However, the position is not quite so simple, since it is often suggested that certain torts which protect rights of a constitutional or quasi-constitutional nature are in truth compensating a mental interest. Thus, if D puts P in fear by threatening to assault him, P can recover damages in trespass even if D does not actually carry out the assault.[136] And the large damages awarded in some defamation cases have been said to have a 'highly subjective element' which suggests that it is mental rather than economic damage that is being repaired.[137] Indeed, one can go further and ask if invasions of personality rights like 'dignity' or 'privacy' are in effect invasions of a mental interest.[138] The general point to be made is that the creation of certain kinds of mental 'states' amounts to damage for the purposes of legal liability. These mental states are not always in themselves in need of empirical proof; in fact they may be unknown as such to medical science. They are states created by the law itself and thus exist, to paraphrase Granger, as a genealogy of 'categories' which make up the object of a science.[139]

Constructing a State of Mind

This ability to 'create' a mental state is particularly evident in a controversial common law criminal case. In *DPP* v. *Ray*,[140] four men who had eaten a meal in a restaurant rushed out of the building, when the waiter had left the dining room, without paying. They had, it seemed, formed the intention not to pay only after they had actually eaten the meal. The House of Lords held by a bare majority that the men were guilty of the statutory offence of obtaining a pecuniary advantage by deception contrary to the (now repealed) section 16 of the Theft Act 1968. No doubt the men had behaved dishonestly, but the question in issue was whether they had actually 'deceived' anyone. There was no actual finding that the waiter was in fact deceived by the men's behaviour and this was crucial to Lord Reid. In his dissenting speech he concluded that dishonest evasion of the debt was not enough: there had to be an actual deception. However, this lack of any actual finding of deception as a fact did not deter the majority of the Law Lords. According to Lord Morris:

> In the present case it is found as a fact that when the respondent ordered his meal he believed that he would be able to pay. One of his companions had agreed to lend him money. He therefore intended to pay. So far as the waiter was concerned the original implied representation made to him by the respondent must have been a continuing representation so long as he (the respondent) remained in the restaurant. There was nothing to alter the representation. Just as the waiter was led at the start to believe that he was dealing with a customer who by all that he did in the restaurant was indicating his intention to pay in the ordinary way, so the waiter was led to believe that that state of affairs continued. But the moment came when the respondent decided and therefore knew that he was not going to pay: but he also knew that the waiter still thought that he was going to pay. By ordering his meal and by his conduct in assuming the role of an ordinary customer the respondent had previously shown that it was his intention to pay. By continuing in the same role and behaving just as before he was representing that his previous intention continued. That was a deception because his intention, unknown to the waiter, had become quite otherwise ... Had the waiter suspected that by a change of intention a secret exodus was being planned, it is obvious that he would have taken action to prevent its being achieved.[141]

Two important epistemological points can be reasserted in relation to this analysis. First, the mental state of 'deception' is not dependent upon any empirical evidence with respect to the waiter's actual state of mind. He may not have cared one way or the other whether the men intended to pay the bill. His being 'deceived' is a matter of legal systematics; that is to say it is assumed that, because of his contractual or status position as a waiter, he cared and it is this assumption which allows Lord Morris logically to arrive at the conclusion that he was deceived. Having arrived at this logical conclusion, Lord Morris was able to work back to the factual premise in order to construct an empirical justification for the existence of the deception. He thus continued:

> It would seem to be clear that if the waiter had thought that if he left the restaurant to go to the kitchen the respondent would at once run out, he (the waiter) would not have left the restaurant and would have taken suitable action. The waiter proceeded on the basis that the implied representation made to him (ie of an honest intention to pay) was effective. The waiter was caused to refrain from taking certain courses of action which but for the representation he would have taken.[142]

The second epistemological point is to be found in the judge's view of the world. Instead of taking a nominalist view of the facts, Lord Morris saw the whole event in univeralist terms. This point is made particularly explicit by one of the other Law Lords, Lord MacDermott, who supported the conviction:

> There is … no sound reason that I can see for restricting the enquiry to this final phase. One cannot, so to speak, draw a line through the transaction at the point where the intention changed and search for evidence of deception only in what happened before that or only in what happened after that. In my opinion the transaction must for this purpose be regarded in its entirety, beginning with the respondent entering the restaurant and ordering his meal and ending with his running out without paying. The different stages of the transaction are all linked and it would be quite unrealistic to treat them in isolation.[143]

Once again it can be seen that legal reasoning was not in essence a matter of interpreting and applying a linguistic proposition dealing with a specific state of mind. It was a question of how one viewed and constructed the world of 'fact'. It was, as Lord MacDermott revealingly put it, a question of being 'realistic'.

Free Will and Consent

Another fundamental 'state' of mind that has a role across the whole spectrum of public and private law is that of free will and consent. Consent (*consensus, consentement*) acts, for example, both as the foundation of modern contract law in the civil law tradition and as a defence to a range of private and public law actions in all Western legal systems. Indeed, there are echoes of this notion in the cricket ball case mentioned earlier. The house buyers had to some extent 'consented' to the danger of cricket balls by buying a house next to a field which they knew, or ought to have known, was used for the playing of cricket. *Volenti non fit injuria*.

In the cricket case it is of course evident that consent is being constructed out of the objective acts of the house buyers rather than out of specific empirical evidence. This is hardly surprising since actual and reliable evidence of internal states of mind is at best difficult to obtain. Accordingly, while legal rules may stipulate that contract is based on consent and the meeting of minds, a contractor is actually judged by his outward behaviour. Consent is a matter of implication flowing, not just from this behaviour, but from certain formal objective requirements attaching to the structure of contract itself. However, the moment that one starts to construct a subjective state of mind out of objective fact, the notion of consent itself is transformed. Merely because a party has 'consented' or 'agreed' to sell a piece of property, it does not follow that there is a contract to sell if certain objective criteria that outwardly define the 'consent' have not been fulfilled.[144] Equally, the apparent absence of consent because of the unconsciousness of one of the parties is not necessarily fatal to the existence of a contractual obligation; for consent can be presumed from a situation where a person acts in the *interest* of the other party.[145] The notion of an interest can thus act as a key concept in the analysis.

This transformation of the notion of consent through recourse to an 'interest' is particularly striking in cases where actual evidence of the existence or non-existence of consent is completely unobtainable owing to the medical condition of the person from whom consent is legally required. Medical treatment such as an operation or sterilisation can be given only when the patient consents, yet what if the patient is unconscious? If the operation is not urgent it is probably the case in many Western systems that consent cannot be implied even if such an operation would be in the interest of the patient. However, if the operation is required as a matter of life-or-death necessity, it immediately becomes possible to argue that the interest in preserving the life of the patient implies of itself consent. The doctor must act in the 'best interests of his patient'.[146] Matters become difficult, of course, if the patient is known to belong to a religious faith that has a strict rule prohibiting, say, a blood transfusion. In this situation the whole consent issue is resolved, in English law at least, by reference to the interests in play. And so, in a case involving the question of whether or not an emergency blood transfusion could be given to a person brought up as a Jehovah's Witness, Lord Donaldson MR reasoned as follows:

> This situation gives rise to a conflict between two interests, that of the patient and that of the society in which he lives. The patient's interest consists of his right to self-determination – his right to live his own life how he wishes, even if it will damage his health or lead to his premature death. Society's interest is in upholding the concept that all human life is sacred and that it should be preserved if at all possible. It is well established that in the ultimate the right of the individual is paramount. But this merely shifts the problem where the conflict occurs and calls for a very careful examination of whether, and if so the way in which, the individual is exercising that right. In the case of doubt, that doubt falls to be resolved in favour of the preservation of life, for if the individual is to override the public interest, he must do so in clear terms.[147]

This introduction of the 'public interest' into the consent problem is, however, more ambiguous than it might at first seem. Lord Donaldson uses it in terms of preserving life. But what if such preservation of life turns out to be economically expensive in a society where resources are limited? Might it not be in the 'public interest' to terminate life? This problem emerges in the controversial Tony Bland case.[148] Bland was left in a condition known as 'persistent vegetative state' (PVS) as a result of the Hillsborough football ground tragedy and according to standard medical opinion there was no chance of his ever regaining consciousness. The parents of Tony Bland held the view that their son would not have wanted to be left in this condition and they thus supported the hospital when it sought a declaration that it would be lawful to terminate the life support procedure.

Although the judges in all three courts were in no doubt about the moral and ethical dimensions in issue, they quickly fixed onto the idea of the unconscious person's 'best interests'. A patient in a state of unconsciousness had two distinct rights: the right of self-determination and the right to be treated in a way that is in his or her best interests.[149] Having set up the 'best interests' structure it was relatively easy to arrive at the conclusion that it would both respect the dignity of the *persona* and be in his (its) best interests that medical treatment be discontinued. Lord Mustill did admit that the 'distressing truth which must not be shirked is that ... he has no best interests of any kind'.[150] Yet this had the effect of allowing attention to shift off the *persona* and consent and onto the 'interests of the community'. 'Threaded through the technical arguments addressed to the House were strands of a much wider position,' said Lord Mustill, 'that it is in the best interests of the community at large that Anthony Bland's life should now end.' For the 'large resources of skill, labour and money now being devoted to Anthony Bland might in the opinion of many be more fruitfully employed in improving the condition of other patients, who if treated may have useful, healthy and enjoyable lives for many years to come'.[151] As far as he was concerned, this was a question that could only be answered by Parliament; yet, despite his personal conviction, Lord Mustill has gone far in articulating the legal route by which compulsory euthanasia could be legally justified were it ever to be in the 'public interest'. Rights belonging to the law of persons are, in the continental codes, strictly to be separated from patrimonial rights defined by the law of things.[152] In the common law tradition, however, patrimonial interests can so easily become the dominant consideration both in private and in public law.

Vitiating Consent

This use of the public interest as a means of overriding the requirement of consent is by no means novel inasmuch as it gives expression to the idea of necessity. Property destroyed without the owner's consent may be justified in the public interest in situations of necessity[153] (although in French law the owner may still be able to obtain compensation). Yet necessity itself has a private interest aspect: if D pulls down P's house, without his consent, to impede a spreading fire, will D be able to resist an action for damages by P? In Roman law there is some authority for this defence on the basis that D was protecting his property rather than acting wrongfully;[154] but this raises an interesting question about the legitimacy of the pursuit of a private interest in relation to free will. Why should D's selfish motive be able to defeat P's claim based on the absence of consent? In the medical examples outlined above, it would be wrong to ascribe private interest motives. But would the position be the same if the hospital or doctor was acting in the private sector and performing operations for profit? To what extent might commercial motives have an impact upon the consent factor? Or what if D uses persuasive techniques to get him or her to 'consent' to something?

The texts and case law in Europe on vitiation of consent form a significant part of private law studies. What is interesting for the epistemologist, however, is the tension between, on the one hand, the subjective and the objective and, on the other, the individual and the class. P, a timid person, is easily coerced into consenting to do something that, in the absence of pressure, P would not have done: ought the law to furnish P with a remedy? Should it make any difference if a reasonably robust person would, in the same circumstances, have easily resisted the coercion? What difference ought it to make if the pressure is economic rather than physical? Should the employer forced to agree to pay higher wages to his employees as a result of their strike action have the opportunity of later repudiating the new wage agreement on the basis of economic duress?[155] If so, should employees who have been pressurised into agreeing to accept much lower wages during a period of high unemployment be able subsequently to repudiate these agreements? What gives these questions an added complexity is that they can be approached in terms either of the individual or of a class. Thus in one English case concerning undue influence exercised by a husband on his wife, a judge in the court of appeal saw the issue as one of status.[156] Ought the law to treat wives who provide security for their husband's debts, and others in an analogous position, as requiring special protection?[157] In the House of Lords, by contrast, the 'legitimate interests' of such wives could be protected, not by treating wives as a status group, but by putting creditors under a duty of inquiry. If a creditor failed in its duty to inquire it might well be held to have had notice of a wife's equity to set aside the transaction. The notion of an individual relationship, both between the husband and the wife (presumed undue influence) and between wife and creditor (duty to enquire), and not the class (wives as a status group), thus becomes the mechanism for constructing and deconstructing the state of mind of the wife.

Such an approach has the advantage of maintaining a clear distinction between the law of persons (families, rights of personality) and the law of things (credit and security). This, in turn, seemingly asserts the private interest over social (law of persons) interests. Yet it would be a mistake to think that it is simply a matter of individual patrimonial interests dependent upon the question of consent. For, behind it all, the public interest was able to reassert itself in a different guise from the one perceived by the court of appeal judge. As Lord Browne-Wilkinson reveals, it 'is easy to allow sympathy for the wife who is threatened with the loss of her home at the suit of a rich bank to obscure an important public interest viz., the need to ensure that the wealth currently tied up in the matrimonial home does not become economically sterile'. And he continued by saying that if 'the rights secured to wives by the law renders vulnerable loans granted on the security of matrimonial homes, institutions will be unwilling to accept such security, thereby reducing the flow of loan capital to business enterprises'.[158] Consent as a state of mind is, then, certainly an important point of focus in determining liability. Yet its construction is often formulated out of the building block of an 'interest'. Such a concept is useful because it appears to be descriptive – and thus the House of Lords appears to be giving effect to Tony Bland's subjective desire to die. The cynic might claim, however, that it is the 'best economic interest' of society that has the most influence when it comes to constructing and reconstructing states of mind.

Notes

1 D.48.8.14.
2 CC, art. 1142.
3 PECL, art. 9:501(1).
4 CC, art. 1147.
5 BGB § 276. See also Swiss Code of Obligations, art. 99(1).
6 See, for example, D.13.6.5.2. And see, generally, Stein and Shand (1974, pp. 128–9).
7 D.13.6.5.7.
8 D.13.6.5.10.
9 See, in particular, CC, art. 1382.
10 Malaurie and Aynès (1999, p. 521): delictual liability exists only in the absence of contractual liability. See also Quebec Civil Code, art. 1458.
11 BGB § 276.
12 Stein and Shand (1974, pp. 117–18).

13 See, for example, *Nichols* v. *Marsland* (1876) 2 Ex D 1.
14 Zimmerman (1996a, pp. 1033–5).
15 D.44.7.4.
16 D.44.7.1.4.
17 Halpérin (1996, pp. 145–6); Zimmerman (1996a, pp. 1033–5).
18 Laurent (1993, p. 103).
19 Stein and Shand (1974, pp. 124–5).
20 See, in particular, *Read* v. *J Lyons & Co* [1947] AC 156; *Cambridge Water Co* v. *Eastern Counties Leather plc* [1994] 2 AC 264.
21 *Rigby* v. *Chief Constable of Northamptonshire* [1985] 1 WLR 1242.
22 *Cambridge Water Co* v. *Eastern Counties Leather plc* [1994] 2 AC 264.
23 Howarth (1995, p. 511).
24 *Mansfield* v. *Weetabix Ltd* [1998] 1 WLR 1263.
25 *Raineri* v. *Miles* [1981] AC 1050, 1086.
26 Supply of Goods and Services Act 1982, s. 13.
27 See, for example, *Joseph Constantine SS Co Ltd* v. *Imperial Smelting Corporation* [1942] AC 154.
28 Cane (1999).
29 Halpérin (1996, p. 167).
30 Sellers LJ in *Dunne* v. *North Western Gas Board* [1964] 2 QB 806, 832.
31 Duguit, extracted and translated in Neville-Brown and Bell (1998, p. 194).
32 *Rigby* v. *Chief Constable of Northamptonshire* [1985] 1 WLR 1242. See also Samuel (1994), pp. 76–8.
33 Jolowicz (1985). For a general survey of the culture of French administrative law, see Bell (2001, pp. 153–98).
34 D.9.3.1.
35 D.9.3.1.4.
36 D.9.3.1.1.
37 See, for example, D.44.7.5.6.
38 Zimmermann (1996a, p. 1129).
39 D.47.23.1.
40 D.9.1.1.7.
41 D.9.1.1.14.
42 D.9.4.1.
43 See, for example, D.9.4.2pr.
44 D.19.2.25.7.
45 D.19.2.11pr.
46 See, in particular, D.19.2.25.7.
47 Zimmermann (1996a, pp. 1034–5).
48 Ibid., p. 1142.
49 Ibid., pp. 1132–3.
50 Ibid., p. 1132.
51 Gazzaniga (1992, p. 261).
52 Ibid., pp. 264–7.
53 Cass.civ.19.2.1997; JCP.1997.II.22848, note Viney.
54 See, in particular, Stapleton (1995).
55 See, generally, Bell et al. (1998, pp. 383–6).
56 Loi no 85–677 du 5 juillet 1985, art. 1.

57 Ibid., art. 3.
58 Tunc (1972).
59 (1866) LR 1 Ex 265 (Ex); (1868) LR 3 HL 330 (HL).
60 (1866) LR 1 Ex 265 at pp. 279–80.
61 Ibid., at p. 280.
62 *Read* v. *J Lyons & Co* [1947] AC 156.
63 *Cambridge Water Co* v. *Eastern Counties Leather plc* [1994] 2 AC 264.
64 *Grant* v. *Australian Knitting Mills Ltd* [1936] AC 85 but see now Consumer Protection Act 1987.
65 See, for example, *Mint* v. *Good* [1951] 1 KB 517.
66 *Tremain* v. *Pike* [1969] 3 All ER 1303.
67 *Jolley* v. *Sutton LBC* [1998] 1 WLR 1546.
68 *Jolley* v. *Sutton LBC* [2000] 1 WLR 1082.
69 Sale of Goods Act 1979, s. 14. See also Supply of Goods and Services Act 1982, ss. 4, 9.
70 *Frost* v. *Aylesbury Dairy Co Ltd* [1905] 1 KB 608.
71 *Vacwell Engineering* v. *BDH Chemicals* [1971] 1 QB 88; *Parsons (Livestock) Ltd* v. *Uttley Ingham & Co* [1978] QB 791.
72 See, for example, *Ingham* v. *Emes* [1955] 2 QB 366.
73 (1881) 6 QBD 685 at p. 688.
74 *Blackpool & Fylde Aero Club Ltd* v. *Blackpool BC* [1990] 1 WLR 1195; cf. *X (Minors)* v. *Bedfordshire County Council* [1995] 2 AC 633.
75 See, for example, *The Nicholas K* [1996] 1 AC 211.
76 See, for example, *Launchbury* v. *Morgans* [1973] AC 127; *Reid* v. *Rush & Tompkins plc* [1990] 1 WLR 212.
77 See, for example, *Smith* v. *Eric Bush* [1990] 1 AC 831.
78 Translation, Lawson (1950, p. 203).
79 See Stanton (1992).
80 See, for example, *Spring* v. *Guardian Assurance plc* [1995] 2 AC 296.
81 See Samuel (2001, pp. 515–21).
82 Ibid., pp. 195–203.
83 See, for example, *Surrey County Council* v. *Bredero Homes Ltd* [1993] 1 WLR 1361.
84 *Strand Electric Co Ltd* v. *Brisford Entertainments Ltd* [1952] 2 QB 246, 254–5.
85 At p. 255.
86 See, for example, the judgments in *Macmillan Inc* v. *Bishopsgate Investment Trust plc (No 3)* [1995] 1 WLR 978, 988–9; [1996] 1 WLR 387, 406–8.
87 See on this point *Beswick* v. *Beswick* [1966] Ch 538 (CA); but cf. [1968] AC 58.
88 *Lipkin Gorman* v. *Karpnale Ltd* [1991] 2 AC 548.
89 Stanton (1992, pp. 59–60).
90 *Spartan Steel & Alloys Ltd* v. *Martin & Co* [1973] 1 QB 27.
91 Weir (2000, p. 567).
92 Ibid.
93 BGB § 826; see Weir (2000, p. 568).
94 *Victoria Laundry (Windsor) Ltd* v. *Newman Industries Ltd* [1949] 2 KB 528.

95 *Blackpool & Fylde Aero Club Ltd* v. *Blackpool BC* [1990] 1 WLR 1195; cf. *X (Minors)* v. *Bedfordshire County Council* [1995] 2 AC 633. But cf. *Phelps* v. *Hillingdon LBC* [2001] 2 AC 619.
96 Stanton (1992, pp. 58–9).
97 Howarth (1995, pp. 514–15).
98 Stein and Shand (1974, pp. 114–41).
99 Note how this idea was comprehensively rejected in *Mangan* v. *Atterton* (1866) LR 1 Ex 239.
100 *Read* v. *J Lyons & Co* [1945] 1 KB 216, 228 per Scott LJ.
101 Samuel (2001, pp. 454–69).
102 *Khorasandjian* v. *Bush* [1993] QB 727; cf. *Hunter* v. *Canary Wharf Ltd* [1997] AC 655.
103 Rudden (1991–2).
104 *Broome* v. *Cassell & Co Ltd* [1972] AC 1027, 1114.
105 Bowen LJ in *Edgington* v. *Fitzmaurice* (1885) 29 Ch D 459, 483.
106 See, for example, *Elliott* v. *C (a minor)* [1983] 2 All ER 1005.
107 Carbasse (1990, pp. 34–41). And see G.3.211.
108 D.16.3.1.8.
109 D.50.16.213.2.
110 Although of course the distinction between gross negligence and recklessness and recklessness and intention is by no means easy to determine. Cf. Cane (2000).
111 Lawson (1950, pp. 37–8).
112 D.9.2.30.3.
113 D.9.2.31.
114 But cf. *Qualcast (Wolverhampton) Ltd* v. *Haynes* [1959] AC 743.
115 Weir (1996, p. 140).
116 *Glasgow Corporation* v. *Muir* [1943] AC 448.
117 Bell et al. (1998, pp. 360–61).
118 See, for example, *Bolton* v. *Stone* [1951] AC 850.
119 Cass.civ.16.7.1953; JCP.1953.II.7792; cass.civ.24.11.1956; Dalloz.1956.163.
120 Expressly set out in the French *Nouveau code pénal*, art. 111–3.
121 Law Commission Consultation Paper No. 122: 'Legislating the Criminal Code' (1992), para. 5.6.
122 Ibid., para. 5.4.
123 See, for example, *R* v. *Nedrick* [1986] 3 All ER 1.
124 Cf. *R* v. *Reid* [1992] 3 All ER 673.
125 See, for example, *Elliott* v. *C (a minor)* [1983] 2 All ER 1005.
126 Cass.req.3.8.1915; S.1920.I.300; Cass.civ.20.1.1964; Dalloz.1964.518.
127 *Chapman* v. *Honig* [1963] 2 QB 502, 520.
128 *Hollywood Silver Fox Farm* v. *Emmett* [1936] 2 KB 468.
129 Cumming-Bruce LJ in *Miller* v. *Jackson* [1977] QB 966, 988–9.
130 See *Alcock* v. *Chief Constable of South Yorkshire* [1992] 1 AC 310; *Page* v. *Smith* [1996] 1 AC 155; *Frost* v. *Chief Constable of South Yorkshire Police* [1999] 2 AC 455.
131 Fatal Accidents Act 1976, s. 1A.
132 *Watts* v. *Morrow* [1991] 1 WLR 1421, 1445; see now *Farley* v. *Skinner* [2001] 3 WLR 899.
133 *Jarvis* v. *Swan's Tours Ltd* [1973] 1 QB 233.

134 *Watts* v. *Morrow* [1991] 1 WLR 1421, 1445.
135 *Best* v. *Samuel Fox & Co Ltd* [1952] AC 716.
136 *Read* v. *Coker* (1853) 138 ER 1437.
137 *Cassell & Co Ltd* v. *Broome* [1972] AC 1027, 1071.
138 CC, arts 9, 16; CE 27.10.1995; JCP.1996.II.22630.
139 Granger (1995, p. 114).
140 [1974] AC 370.
141 At p. 386.
142 At p. 387.
143 At p. 382.
144 See, for example, the French decision, Cass.civ.2.5.1978, Dalloz.1979.317; cf. *Gibson* v. *Manchester CC* [1979] 1 WLR 294.
145 See, for example, Cass.civ.1.12.1969, Dalloz.1970.422.
146 *In re F (Mental Patient: Sterilisation)* [1990] 2 AC 1.
147 *Re T* [1992] 3 WLR 782, 796.
148 *Airedale NHS Trust* v. *Bland* [1993] AC 789.
149 See Butler-Sloss LJ [1993] AC 789 at pp. 816–17.
150 At p. 897.
151 At p. 896.
152 Py (1997, pp. 31–43).
153 *Rigby* v. *Chief Constable of Northamptonshire* [1985] 1 WLR 1242.
154 D.47.9.3.7.
155 *Dimskal Shipping Co* v. *ITWF (The Evia Luck)* [1992] 2 AC 152.
156 *Barclays Bank plc* v. *O'Brien* [1993] QB 109 (CA); [1994] 1 AC 180 (HL).
157 Scott LJ [1993] QB 109 at p. 139.
158 [1994] 1 AC 180 at p. 188; see, generally, Samuel (2001, pp. 398–401).

8 Schemes of Intelligibility in Social Science

In this final chapter an attempt will be made to locate legal knowledge in the wider context, if not of science in the hard sense, then at least of science in the social science sense.[1] This may seem a somewhat daunting project. However, as a result of work published by the French social science epistemologist Jean-Michel Berthelot, there is now a real possibility of locating legal reasoning within a wider epistemological framework.[2] Of course, this attempt at the location of law within a broader framework has not only been directly touched upon in earlier chapters but has been implicit in the analysis of the factual constructions of cases. However, the location of a viewpoint inside or outside law, and its precise positioning within either domain, are by no means the only questions that need to be considered with regard to the theoretical perspective to be brought to bear by the *intellectus* on the *res*. The manner in which the interrogation of the phenomenon (or phenomena) to be studied is to be conducted constitutes 'a linchpin of the research'.[3] Perhaps a change of metaphor is in order, since the term 'theoretical perspective' is too general. In addition to locating a viewpoint, the epistemologist must be aware of the various ways in which one can think about, and study, social reality. The purpose of this chapter, accordingly, will be to consider the various schemes of thought that can be brought to bear on an object of research.

Natural Sciences and Human Sciences

The problem of the various schemes of thought that might be utilised in social science research can be viewed in the context of a larger debate between natural and social science. Is it possible to apply the label of 'science' when it comes to knowledge of human facts? The problem is a complex one, but essentially has its foundation in the difference between objects in the sense of empirical phenomena independent of humans and humans in the sense of objects of research. Clearly, when humans are the objects of their own study the relationship between *intellectus* and *res* becomes much more problematical. Not only is the behaviour of humans complex and cultural contexts so diverse, but the researchers themselves could be said to be actively influencing the behaviour and predictability of their object of research inasmuch as their own scientific investigation is part of the behaviour being investigated. This merging of the *intellectus* and the *res* can deprive social 'science' of its criteria of validity since it risks failing the test of being a true 'critical investigation'.

Critical Approaches

What exactly does 'critical' mean in this context? In the everyday context, it suggests continual fault finding, a negative approach towards the actions or writings of others. However, in the context of philosophy and epistemology, this 'negative' and 'fault-finding' approach is turned into a positive method. It is the means by which the investigator can escape from dogma, bias and pseudo-science. Indeed, the philosopher of science Karl Popper advanced the influential thesis that a theory could *only* be scientific if it was capable of being falsified.[4] In other words, criticism is a fundamental aspect of Popper's scientific methodology; he favoured 'a situation where people disagree' and he saw 'widespread agreement as being unhealthy'. He argued 'that criticism, in so far as it aids us in getting nearer to the truth, is a vital part of our intellectual equipment'.[5] Such an approach has, equally, an important place in social and legal science. Certain social science theories – the causes of suicide for example – can be tested empirically in the Popper sense. That is to say, they can be falsified by reality. However, as Berthelot points out, they cannot normally be falsified in any systematic sense since such theories do not function in a strict true-or-false logic. Thus, to take Popper's most celebrated example, the thesis that 'all swans are white', which will be falsified the moment that a black swan is observed, is different from a social science theory. A thesis linking capitalism to the Protestant ethic will not be falsified the moment that a successful Catholic entrepreneur is discovered in the boardroom.[6]

A critical approach cannot, therefore, be confined to falsification in the Popper sense.[7] Critical theory can equally be based on the idea that, for example, the so-called 'neutral' language, concepts and categories of law are by no means value-free. And it is only by a critical approach to legal texts – for example to judgments in cases – that the value-laden assertions can be discovered, exposed and 'deconstructed'.[8] Yet, if such theories are to be validated, one question that can be asked is the extent to which such critical approaches to law do, themselves, pass the Popper test. Take, for example, the following hypothesis from a critical introductory work to law:

> If there has been a central thesis to this book it has been that the common sense of law both reveals and conceals exercises of power. The argument has been that law, like any other system of power allocation and dispute resolution, plays a central part in reinforcing the particular social reality in which it exists ... There is, we hope, no necessary conclusion to be drawn although we also hope that a suspicion of authority may seem appropriate ... To us an increase in suspicion directed towards hallowed institutions (an increase deplored by the Conservative government) seems entirely healthy. If the result is 'institutional cynicism' ... that seems an excellent starting point from which to move towards a world with very different, and significantly more humane, values than often capitalism presents, and a world in which all individuals may find fulfilment as an integral part of the society in which they live. The 'reality' of the present world hides from us the invalidity of the 'there is no alternative' proposition.[9]

There is no doubt that this work conforms in part to Popper's approach: it adopts a very critical approach towards the Western concept of law. However, it then advances the thesis that such a critical approach will hopefully engender cynicism towards existing institutions and that this cynicism will in turn lead to a better society. Is this thesis a scientific thesis in the Popper sense? No doubt it could be argued that, as a theory, it is capable of being falsified; cynicism regarding institutions might ultimately be shown by history to lead to authoritarian regimes in which it is not possible to say that individuals found fulfilment. But, again, could history 'prove' or 'disprove' this thesis? Might it not be said that a majority of individuals could even find some kind of fulfilment in totalitarian systems? Then again, might it not be said that such a view is simply one interpretation of history?

In fairness to the authors, it has to be admitted that they do not seem to be claiming anywhere in their book that their thesis is a scientific theory. Indeed, they imply that it is all a question of political ideology. Yet this means that 'critical' must be taken in two quite different senses.[10] There is 'critical' in the sense of falsification by observation of a phenomenon; and so a theory explaining the orbit of a comet and predicting its return to the vicinity of the Earth can be, at least in part, validated by observation. In contrast there is 'critical' in an ideological or philosophical sense, where the critic is in truth eschewing any theory that can be validated in the facts. The concepts of 'power', 'authority', 'social reality', 'institutional cynicism', 'fulfilment' and so on are not constructed so as to model facts in the sense of explaining them as facts and predicting their future movements. They are constructed to *'interpret'* (or construe) facts by reference to a philosophical (or ideological) model of an imagined totality (for example, a society where everybody is happy and fulfilled). Social science theorising can thus easily become impossible to falsify as a 'scientific' hypothesis, for, as Berthelot has commented, the 'regularities are of a probabilistic kind and give rise to "weak implications"'. The 'swans are never all white, anymore than capitalist entrepreneurs are all Protestants'.[11]

Models and Schemes

In contrast, science aims accurately to describe, to explain and to predict the behaviour of objects.[12] Now, just as with the social sciences, it does this through the construction of abstract schemes or models which themselves provide the knowledge. The objects of the empirical sciences are not, then, reality itself; they are the schemes and models.[13] However, the effectiveness of the model to explain and to predict becomes in itself a criterion of validity.[14] The trajectory of the orbiting comet is not therefore explained in concepts that directly describe the astrophysical reality. The reality is reduced to a model consisting of concepts, relations and (or) symbols – for example a mathematical model – and it is the manipulation of this model that provides the information about the comet's reappearance. If the model fails to predict correctly, this will make it suspect. Yet, if it does predict correctly, it does not follow that the model is correctly describing the *actual* facts down to the last detail. As Granger explains, it is a matter of *virtual facts*; that is to say, facts schematically created within a scheme of intelligence. Objects of differing weight are said to fall at the same speed. But these objects are *virtual facts* inasmuch as one is talking of ideal conditions which do not take account of cross-winds or whatever that might *actually* result in one object hitting the ground before the other.[15] Many scientists no longer talk, then, in terms of whether a model or a theory is true; the test is whether it is 'adequate' inasmuch as it permits one to explain a phenomenon and to predict its future behaviour.[16]

The problem facing the social or human scientist is that when he or she tries to construct models of social facts a central aspect of these sciences is human behaviour. This is incapable of being translated into objects (*res*) which can form part of an abstract model capable logically and mathematically of being manipulated.[17] Human behaviour cannot be reduced to such models because it is too complex and unforeseeable; it lacks regularity in the sense of being predictable at the level of the individual. It cannot be mathematically predicted if or if not Dr X will assault a patient or if Mr Y will fail to stop at a road junction. Certainly, the number of assaults committed by doctors on patients and the number of road accidents per year can be reduced to statistics and these statistics in turn may well reveal certain regularities allowing prediction. What is the risk of a patient being assaulted or a road user being injured? But the moment one moves to the holistic level other problems emerge. Why do a certain number of doctors assault their patients every year and why are there x number of car accidents every year? Certainly, explanatory theories can be formulated. But these explanations are always contestable because, for example, they are not easily falsified and because they are founded upon premises which are themselves ambiguous. Do doctors assault patients because they belong to the class of doctors, or to the class of professionals, or because they are human beings and a certain number of human beings assault other human beings every year? Do car accidents happen because all humans make mistakes or because there is something about the activity of car driving? The individual and the holistic analysis may well present quite different explanations, each of which seems, in its own way, rationally plausible.

A further problem, of course, is that, as we have seen, such theories are often based on *virtual* rather than *actual* facts. They are facts conceptualised, not in terms of each actual and individual human being, but in terms of 'car driver' – or class of 'car drivers' – and objects simply labelled as 'cars'.[18] One is moving from *ontology* (what exists) to *epistemology* (theory of knowledge) through models that are *ideological* in the wide sense of the term. Does the world consist of billions of individual humans or millions of groups of humans? If one replies by saying groups of humans, is one moving from ontology (individual persons that can be touched) to epistemology (a theory of social relations)?[19] And to what extent is epistemology motivated by ideology (an idealised, holistic view of humans)?

Cause and Effect

All the same, if one had to find a common scheme of analysis between the physical and social sciences, causation would be one focal point. In both the natural and the human sciences a range of theories that explain are based on ideas of causation. What causes comets to circle the sun in a regular pattern? What causes doctors to assault patients and car drivers to have accidents? With respect to the natural sciences, two interrelated points need to be made. First, causation is, for an empiricist, a question of belief rather than fact since cause and effect cannot be directly observed. It is a belief based on past observation, on induction and on faith that the future will repeat the past.[20] This faith may be very rationally based (induction), but it cannot actually be *proved* that, say, cancer cluster spots outside leaking nuclear power stations are caused by the effects of nuclear power. What statistical models show is a probability and this probability factor might be increased by medical research models.[21] Indeed, it might well be argued that the probability is so regular, particularly when supported by the (seemingly) causal effects of radiation on human cells, that it transcends belief to become a 'law'.[22] Yet it is still only a hypothesis; it can be falsified. The second point to be made, therefore, is that a causal theory in science is open – and according to Popper must be open – to falsification.

When one turns to the human sciences, because of the complexities of behaviour and social interaction, causation is much more problematic. A range of causal theories can be advanced in respect, say, of the causes of crime. But these theories, and indeed the notion of crime and criminals, are themselves open to doubt, if only because many cannot in the scientific sense be falsified. Historical theories face the same problems. A thesis that the First World War was prolonged because the soldiers enjoyed the experience cannot really be proved or disproved; it is a matter of interpretation and argumentation. Other equally convincing models can be constructed, each representing a 'singular reality'.[23] In economics, the difficulty has been analysed as being one of the capacity of a social science to constitute theories based on facts since there are problems both with the object and with the method. 'Where the experimental sciences can develop laws from repeated observation,' write two economic theorists, 'the economy (social sciences in general) comes up against the difficulty of separating fictional causes from real causes.'[24]

Models, even scientific models, are not always dependent upon empirical verification. Some systems, such as mathematics, are validated by the internal coherence of the system itself;[25] and it is this coherence that in turn allows mathematics to become a scientific criterion.[26] The point, as we have already seen, is summed up by Bunge: '[if] a mathematician postulates the existence of a new conceptual object and does it without falling into contradiction, nobody will be able to refute it, even if his postulate ends up being ignored or considered wanting in interest'. However, 'if a physicist, a biologist or an historian postulates the existence of a concrete object which has not yet been discovered, they are thus acting in the hope of its discovery'.[27] When this dichotomy is transferred into the social sciences, the problem of the object becomes evident. Is the model one that can be falsified by external reality? If not, then the object's existence is probably one constructed by the theory itself and this forces one back to the 'coherence' of the model or theory and to the plausibility of its explanatory power. What is the internal structure of the model or theory? Is it a model claiming to be based on facts, on abstract concepts or on texts? If it is constructed out of facts, are these *virtual* or *concrete* facts? In short, how can the model and its assertions be *validated*? Can economists predict with accuracy or are their *virtual facts* models simply inadequate? Can historians predict or are their factual models too singular? Granger makes two important points in response to these kinds of question. First, 'a theory dealing with human facts is constantly menaced, if one is not careful, with becoming an ideology, substituting myths for concepts and prescriptions for descriptions'.[28] And secondly, it may be that social facts, like the weather, are too complex. This difficulty may be overcome with simulation and the development of evermore powerful computers.[29]

Typology of Schemes

The complexity of human facts and the impossibility of subjecting these facts to laboratory experimentation have resulted in recourse to a range of other methods of analysis and schemes of intelligibility. These methods and schemes, by no means easy to isolate and enumerate, reflect in turn epistemological perspectives and thus need to be appreciated by jurists as well as social scientists. Law might appear different inasmuch as it is tempting to believe that it has fashioned its own methodology. However, legal technique and method are not in themselves unproblematic. When such methods, as commonly set out in the textbooks, are examined in depth they can prove to be of limited value to the epistemologist (save perhaps as objects of research in themselves), for they often describe legal skills in seductively general terms such as 'problem solving', 'perceptive ability', 'analytical ability', 'creativity', 'logical thinking' and so on.[30] Moreover, recourse to the external point of view is often of no help either. For, as Stuart Toddington points out:

> There is much scope for confusion here: it is not only the idea of the subject matter of law, i.e., law as a phenomenon, which is problematic, but the idea of law as a discipline in the sense of a system of inquiry. From which disciplinary perspective are we supposed to conduct inquiry into legal skills? There seems to be a complacency about method in this regard with some reliance on a broadly 'sociological' approach to supplement the 'traditional' disciplines of law. But the mysteries *of law-as-object* and *law-as-critique* are not solved by recruiting one or even a selection of 'sociologists' to tell [lawyers] what they think law is, or how it should be studied.[31]

Whatever the position, different social science schemes of intelligibility are, perhaps on occasions unconsciously, brought to bear both from within legal technique itself (statutory interpretation as compared to case law analysis) and from an external standpoint (syllogistic method as compared to hermeneutics). Now decoding and enumerating these different schemes of conceptualisation and observation presents serious problems given the diversity and unsystematised (in comparison with those used in the natural sciences) nature of concepts employed.[32] However, a major contribution to the typology of such schemes of intelligibility in the social science has been made by J.-M. Berthelot in his 1990 book entitled *L'intelligence du social*.[33] These schemes, says Berthelot, are to be found *in concreto* in the various procedures used in sociology.[34] The question for the jurist is whether these schemes are also to be found *in concreto* in the various types of legal analysis that are characteristic of judgments, legal opinions and academic writing.

Causal Scheme

Berthelot identifies six basic types of scheme of intelligence. The first scheme identified is the causal scheme, whereby one phenomenon (B) is seen as depending on another phenomenon (A) according to a relation in which it is impossible to have B without A and that in any variation of A there corresponds a variation in B (reciprocal implication). 'It follows,' says Berthelot, 'that A and B are distinct either in reality (different objects or realities) or analytically (different levels of a global reality) and that the element A is conceived as being necessarily prior, chronologically or logically, to the element B.'[35] One example that might be given of this scheme is Durkheim's study of suicide: the number of suicides is seen as being caused by another phenomenon, social cohesion, which is logically prior to the suicides.[36] In the medical sciences the scheme is of importance in diagnosing and treating specific illness and it is of course relevant to the interpretation of statistical data. The phenomena in play (A and B) are not necessarily individualised objects, for the scheme can be applied, as Berthelot observes, to structural systems. Thus the Marxist thesis concerning the relationship between economic infrastructure (A) and social superstructure (B) is one of causality and dependence.[37]

In legal reasoning the causal scheme is particularly prevalent: a victim of harm must prove that the damage (A) was caused by the act or activity of the defendant (B) before the defendant will be liable for the harm. Accordingly, in Roman law, as we have seen in an earlier chapter, the search for liability in the circumstances of the case (*in causa ius esse positum*) was a search for a causal link between victim and the act of another.[38] In other words, one phenomenon (damage) was strictly dependent upon another phenomenon (blameworthy act of another). Modern civil law continues to reflect this causal scheme and thus article 1382 of the *Code civil* states that 'Any human act whatever which *causes* damage to another obliges him by whose fault it occurred to make reparation' (emphasis added). Equally, in the common law tradition it is no different; in order to be able to succeed in a claim for compensation the plaintiff must establish cause and connection between harm and the defendant's act.[39] If the harm would have occurred even in the absence of the defendant's act, the defendant will not be liable.[40] The phenomenon of damage (A) must, as in Roman and modern civil law, be dependent on the act of the defendant (B).

Such causal links are, of course, open to dispute. D's ship carelessly collides with, and damages, P's ship; temporary repairs are carried out in England but more long-term repairs are required which can be effected only in New York. While crossing the Atlantic the ship encounters a bad storm and suffers further damage: is D to be liable for this extra damage?[41] P is hit by a car carelessly driven by D and suffers leg injuries; after this accident P is shot in the damaged leg by gangsters and this second injury necessitates amputation of the leg. Assuming that amputation would not have been necessary if P had suffered just one or other of the injuries, is D the cause of the loss of the leg?[42] How these causal issues are resolved may well depend upon how a particular judge 'sees' or 'constructs' the facts. Thus, if the event is seen as a continuing whole, it may be possible to say that the second damage has been caused by the original act of D. On the other hand, the judge who takes a strictly 'atomistic' view of events may well arrive at a different analysis. The point to be stressed here is that the relationship acting as the focal point of the scheme is one of a particular type of dependence between phenomena each of which is regarded as distinct. The assumption is that but for B there would be no A. However, the intensity of the distinction between A and B might well be a matter of debate.

Functional Scheme

The second scheme is based on the idea that organisms, and indeed machines, are to be understood in terms of their practical functions (rather than, say, their individual parts). This scheme is better known today under the label of 'systems analysis' whereby organisms are seen as being made up of circular relations. 'The logical form symbolised by the *circular relation* (S→B→S) is that of the reciprocal action'; and 'the functional requirements of S require that B fulfils a function useful to S'.[43] A carburettor in a car engine is, for example, to be understood not by a researcher dismantling it into its component parts, but by viewing its function within the car engine, itself seen as a functioning system. In sociology, this scheme has quite old roots inasmuch as it underpins holistic theories of society, in particular those now much-criticised theories which envisaged society as being analogous to biological organisms. However, it has reappeared in a more sophisticated version under the label 'systems theory'. This theory, drawing its inspiration from contemporary scientific thinking, envisages as the object of knowledge, not society itself, but an abstracted model of society viewed as a functioning system.[44] The epistemological strength of this scheme is to be found in its ability 'to go beyond the purely empirical that is to say the study of singular events', and thus to escape the traditional dichotomy between the whole and its parts.[45]

When applied to law, the functional scheme can be seen in two ways. First, it can be seen as little more than a scheme of intelligence whereby legal rules and concepts are understood in terms of their function. Thus in the *Spartan Steel* case,[46] discussed in Chapter 5, Lord Denning MR, after a discussion of various concepts and cases, concluded:

> The more I think about these cases, the more difficult I find it to put each into its proper pigeon-hole. Sometimes I say: 'There was no duty.' In others I say: 'The damage was too remote.' So much so that I think the time has come to discard those tests which have proved so elusive. It seems to me better to consider the particular relationship in hand, and see whether or not, as a matter of policy, economic loss should be recoverable, or not. Thus in *Weller & Co* v. *Foot and Mouth Disease Research Institute* [1966] 1 QB 569 it was plain that the loss suffered by the auctioneers was not recoverable, no matter whether it is put on the ground that there was no duty or that the damage was too remote. Again in *Electrochrome Ltd* v. *Welsh Plastics Ltd* [1968] 2 All ER 205, it is plain that the economic loss suffered by the plaintiffs' factory (due to the damage to the fire hydrant) was not recoverable, whether because there was no duty or that it was too remote.[47]

Lord Denning was adopting a functional approach inasmuch as he was seeing legal concepts as a means of achieving an end rather than as a model that would of itself determine an end. Concepts such as 'duty of care' and 'remoteness of damage' were part of a system that could be understood only in relation to the nature of the damage in turn to be appreciated within particular factual contexts. The notion of 'policy', in other words, was code for a scheme of intelligibility that put the emphasis on a circular relationship: that is to say, 'allowing the understanding of [duty of care or remoteness of damage] from the starting point of the necessity of its effects'.[48]

Secondly, the functional scheme can be seen in terms of systems theory and law. Such an approach can provide important insights into codification, legal classification and indeed the role of law in society and thus is a scheme of analysis that can operate at a variety of levels of legal knowledge.[49] For example, systems theory can be used as a means of understanding law as a discourse in itself; here it has a role in appreciating the nature and definition of law in relation to other knowledge discourses such as economics and political science.[50] Equally, it can be used internally. That is to say, a systems approach can be employed as a form of analysis to explain the functioning of particular areas of law such as 'contract', 'tort' and 'property'.[51] This scheme is not new, of course. Codification is based on the systematic interrelation of legal axioms and concepts and, as we have seen in Chapter 4, the scheme can be used to explain the strength and importance of Roman law, above all the *Institutes* and their *persona, res* and *actiones* structure.[52]

What gives it a special relevance to the epistemologist is that systems analysis can be used to escape, not only the old dichotomy between a whole and its parts, but also the traditional (and two-dimensional) paradigm of logical positivism.[53] Instead of seeing law as an ordered set of propositions and concepts organised into a carefully constructed hierarchy, legal knowledge can be viewed as a circular model of elements between which there are two-way relations.[54] These models do not exist for their own sake. They are both epistemological, that is to say representations through which the *intellectus* can make sense of a phenomenon (*res*), and functional in that the system has a purpose. However, these three aspects – the *intellectus, res* and function – coalesce into what has been described as a 'projective' form of knowledge: that is to say, a form of knowledge that is not exclusively concerned with its 'object' but is equally defined by its 'project' in the sense of function.[55] Moreover, this model permits one to escape from the two-dimensional structure of the hierarchy. Modern systems thinking is, accordingly, less about simplifying complexity than embracing it. A phenomenon can be modelled in terms of a mass of interrelating multidimensional systems whose constructed relations allow for a more sophisticated construction of the object–project. Contradictions and paradoxes can be understood in terms of elements and relations functioning in separate, yet connected, dimensions.[56]

Take, for example, the English law remedy of tracing. The idea upon which this is said to be based is a proprietary relationship between *persona* and *res*. The plaintiff can recover money in the bank account of another on the basis that the plaintiff is 'owner' – that is to say, has a right *in rem* – in the *res* (money claimed) held in the defendant's account.[57] However, the action itself is a claim *in personam*; that is to say, it is based on the *vinculum iuris* between the two legal persons of plaintiff and defendant.[58] In civilian thinking this intermixing of the *in rem* with the *in personam* is unthinkable, since the two kinds of legal relationships, or rights, are kept strictly separate in the logical hierarchy. How, then, does one model the English remedy of tracing within traditional legal science? One might say, of course, that English law is simply 'illogical'. However, systems theory could provide a three-dimensional model by which the substantive *in rem* right or relation is seen to function in a dimension that is conceptually separate from, yet interrelated with, the dimension in which the *in personam* relation functions.[59] The extra dimension, together with the functional project (recovery of money), allows one to model English legal thinking in a way that begins to capture its actual complexity. Moreover, such complex systems models are much more capable of encapsulating the three-dimensional world in which humans actually live. Functional thinking is, then, a scheme of intelligibility that can allow for the construction of a systems model that avoids the simplification of knowledge through loss of information and dimension always incurred through propositional and hierarchical (symbolic) knowledge.[60]

Structural Scheme

Associated with, although independent from, the functional scheme is the structural scheme of intelligibility. 'The main characteristic' of the structural scheme 'is that [the elements] are inserted into a system of oppositions where ... objects, properties, relations ... become signs, elements of a system operating as a code'.[61] This scheme was introduced into social science through linguistics (in particular the work of Lévi-Strauss) since language is perhaps the paradigm example of a closed structure of arbitrary and solid signs, oppositions and correlations.[62] In such a code a term A takes its signification in comparison with terms B, C, D and so on, which are in opposition to it; thus the 'most simple code is one which has only two signs: "red light" ... "green light" ...'.[63] When applied to social science, the structural scheme is used to analyse social behaviour in terms of a code. 'Affection, tenderness, reserve, respect, coldness,' writes Berthelot, 'are attitudes that the kinship system selects (amongst others) in order to signify its component relations through the interplay of their association and their opposition.' However, the significance of the structural scheme goes beyond that of a formal code to embrace the symmetry and pattern of the structure itself, its *isomorphic* qualities.[64] Thus, at its most concrete level, analogy and metaphor would be examples of the use of isomorphic structures as a scheme of reasoning. At more abstract levels the use of structural patterns is fundamental to the understanding and applicability of theoretical structures. Thus Weber's thesis of the relationship between the Protestant ethic and the spirit of capitalism can be seen as an example of the use of an isomorphic model.[65] Another, more general, example is the use of hierarchical structures in social and scientific theory. In this respect one might recall Tierney's observation that the 'human mind has never ceased to be fascinated by natural hierarchy; and the point that hierarchical ordering is a near-universal manifestation among human cultures seems self-evident'.[66]

In the field of law the structural scheme manifests itself in a number of ways. For a start it overlaps with systems theory and accordingly the *Institutes* and the codes can be seen as institutional structures framed around persons, things and actions (obligations). This present enquiry can thus be seen as a work stressing the structural scheme. Just as the 'red light' and 'green light' can be seen as part of a code where one draws its meaning only from its relation to the other, so *persona* (legal subject) and *res* (legal object) are equally part of a code. The legal subject has meaning only in relation to the legal object and vice versa. Indeed, in Gaius, there was a third element, the *actio*. Again, this made sense only when related to *persona* and *res*, just as these two institutions could function in the legal plan only via the *actio*. An important characteristic of a modern code is, then, that it is a 'code' in two senses. There is the original sense of *codex*, which meant book,[67] and there is the structural sense of rules and principles organised into a systematic whole where, in its most perfect manifestation, each concept, article, section, chapter, book and so on interrelates one with another.

In addition, the scheme can be said to underlie the use of analogy and metaphor in legal reasoning. Here structure is being used as a symmetry that can be transferred from one social situation to another social situation even where, in terms of the actual people and things involved, the second situation would appear to have little in common with the first. For example, ships have little in common with cars and the sea has little in common with roads; nevertheless, an analogy has been drawn in law between damage done by ships to an adjacent beach and damage done by cars to property adjacent to a highway (see Chapter 5). Equally, an analogy has been drawn between a lightship and a household chair.[68] What is similar is the symmetry of the structure, that is to say the isomorphic quality of the two situations. Indeed, in one leading common law case it could be said that the whole question turned on the symmetrical, or isomorphic, structure said to be at issue. In *Read* v. *J Lyons & Co*,[69] the plaintiff, an inspector employed by the Ministry of Supply, was injured by an unexplained explosion in a munitions factory where she was carrying out an inspection. She claimed damages from the defendant company which was controlling the factory at the time of the explosion, but did not allege fault in her statement of claim. The question to be decided, accordingly, was whether the defendant could be held strictly liable (that is to say, liable without fault) for her injuries. From a precedent point of view, the case was treated as a claim based on the principle of *Rylands* v. *Fletcher*,[70] where, as has been seen, a landowner had been held strictly liable for the escape of water from a reservoir on his land.

However, counsel for the plaintiff did not rely just upon the language of the rule itself. He tried to go beyond the rule in drawing an analogy with the situation where the keeper of a dangerous animal is strictly liable for any damage resulting from its escape. The relationship, it could be said, between the keeper of a dangerous animal is, in isomorphic terms, the same as a relationship between the controller of a high-explosive shell. This analogy was rejected by the House of Lords. Certainly, said Lord Simonds, it is true 'that if a man brings and keeps a wild beast on his land ... he may be liable for any damage occurring within or without his premises without proof of negligence', but such 'an exception will serve to illustrate the proposition that the law of torts has grown up historically in separate compartments and that beasts have travelled in a compartment of their own'.[71]

The plaintiff's counsel had also developed another isomorphic argument. Counsel had urged that a decision against the plaintiff would show 'a strange lack of symmetry in the law' if compared with a precedent that indicated that, had the plaintiff been standing outside the factory, she would have recovered.[72] Again this was rejected, but not before Lord Simonds was prepared to admit that there was 'some force in the observation'. The difference, then, between the view of the plaintiff's counsel and the final opinions of the judges could be said to be located in the different schemes of intelligibility being applied to the facts. The barrister was advancing an argument based upon a structural analysis; the plaintiff should recover because the plaintiff had been injured by a dangerous *res* under the control of a *persona*. The House of Lords, in contrast, applied a causal and (as we shall see) an actional analysis. This was not a set of facts centring upon the structural relationship between factory and high-explosive shell; it was a matter of one individual injured on the land of another individual. The question thus centred on the actor and not the activity.[73]

Hermeneutical Scheme

The next scheme is the hermeneutical scheme, which has its immediate intellectual foundation in the theological interpretation of old written texts. But it is 'a very ancient scheme of intelligibility, probably one of the first developed by humanity in its attempt to explain reality', and it 'consists of developing systematically a vertical logic of the beyond of appearance or surface of things: B is not only B, for example a tree a little odd in the way it twists its branches into an isolated entanglement'. Thus 'B is simultaneously something else, a force, a spirit, a power which is recognisable by this form.' B and A (this below-the-surface spirit) become one in that 'B and A combine in an animistic ontology where B is both A and B.'[74] However, today the hermeneutical scheme has transcended such pre-scientific thinking: it 'involves B being seen only as a sign, and thus divided into a signifier (what it is) and a signified (what it expresses)'.[75] In the social sciences, it is the human facts which act as the signifier and it is for the particular science to explain the meaning of these signs. Facts, in other words, are only a surface phenomenon; what they need is a science to explain their meaning, their significance.

The idea of interpreting facts is also of relevance to law in that the role of the judge has been said to be 'a hermeneutical process aiming to discover unknown facts from the known facts of every cause'.[76] Théodore Ivainer illustrates this process by analysing a case brought against a satirical magazine which had published a photograph of a well-known right-wing politician in a swimsuit next to a photograph of his ex-wife taken from *Playboy* magazine.[77] The two photographs were placed under a disrespectful headline. The first instance judge had, according to Ivainer, to research out of these known facts – that is to say, the two photographs and headline – the hidden facts. These were the nature and extent of the intention of the journalist and the nature and the extent of the effects produced on the victim. The exposure of these hidden facts involved a double choice for the judge; he had to identify amongst a whole range of values those values deemed relevant and he had to formulate the presuppositions which defined their scope. The first instance judge concluded that for the journalist satire was a manifestation of freedom of expression which allowed the journalist to produce caricatures through exaggeration, irony and distortion. The victim could complain only if such a publication amounted to a serious 'trespass' (*agression*) justifying a legal remedy. On the facts of the present case, the trial judge concluded that the invasion suffered by the victim was equivalent to one arising from a 'simple joke'. The court of appeal took a quite different view of the facts and reversed the decision. The magazine showed an intention to denigrate which constituted an abuse and the fact that it was a satirical publication was no excuse. As for the victim, he had suffered ridicule from the photographs and text. The photographs and headline remain the same known facts for both the trial judge and the court of appeal; but to interpret is 'to choose *one category* of unknown facts F′ F″ in a plurality of virtual categories hidden within the uncontested known facts F^1 F^{2}'.[78]

The hermeneutical scheme is particularly relevant to those human sciences involving the interpretation of texts, since language is literally a sign or set of signs. As Berthelot himself points out, the scheme 'preferentially applies, but not in an exclusive fashion, to data appearing at first sight in a symbolic form'.[79] It is thus a scheme that especially characterises the work of the medieval Roman lawyers – whose object of study (sign) was the *Corpus Iuris* – and the exegetical school of French lawyers whose object of study and interpretation was uniquely the *Code civil*. Van Caenegem makes an interesting comparative and historical point with respect to this tradition.[80] In comparing the historical developments of the civil and common law traditions, he asks the question: which diverged from which? The seemingly obvious answer to this question for many continental jurists, he says, is that it is the common law that diverged from the civil law. For it was the common law which took the un-Roman path. However, he then goes on to make the point that things look different once one escapes the strict viewpoint of European legal history. 'The veneration,' he says, 'enjoyed by the great modern codes – certainly until the end of the nineteenth century – is comparable to that for the *Corpus* in the Middle Ages, and there is little difference between the literal explanation of the one by the glossators and the verbatim scrutiny of the others by the professors of the Exegetical School.'[81] Professor Van Caenegem then observes that this was not the methodology used by the Roman jurists themselves. Their law was developed out of practical reality and problems were dealt with as they turned up. He goes on to say that the 'idea that the law was contained or even half hidden in some old book and had to be ascertained by the exegetical method was quite alien to the Roman world'. It was, he suggests, the European continent that diverged from the rest of the world in seeing 'the law as a timeless revelation contained in a holy book: the *Corpus Juris* and the *Code civil* [which] became the lawyers' bibles'. Legal science was thus 'a bookish science rather than a practitioner's art' which, being based on texts, 'could consist of nothing else than glosses and commentaries'.[82] Viewed from the position of Berthelot's schemes, the comparative observation of Professor Van Caenegem can be seen as a difference of social science methodology. The Roman and common lawyers worked directly on facts (or at least on a direct virtual fact model); they utilised, for example, the causal scheme as the foundation for their analysis and solutions. In contrast, the later civilians worked only on texts. Their scheme was thus quite different and sought to reveal hidden meanings 'through scholastic glosses, disputations and commentaries on this venerable relic of a defunct world'.

If Ivainer is correct, perhaps too much should not be made of this difference of legal sources. Facts as presented in court are, it could be said, as much an object for hermeneutics as case law contained in a text. Berthelot, also, says that one fact (for example a nervous obsession) can be a symbol for some deeper, repressed fact.[83] Moreover, it is clear that the *Corpus Iuris* contains within its practical examples and reasoned solutions evidence of schemes other than hermeneutics. Nevertheless, the civilian jurist's attachment to texts is something that differentiates the civilian tradition from the common law.[84] And it may well be that one cause of this difference is the schematic emphasis on the symbolic (civil law) as opposed to the non-symbolic (common law). The common lawyer is keener to 'construct' facts out of the causal, functional, actional and/or dialectical scheme (these last two to be discussed below), whereas the civilian prefers to think in terms of symbolic linguistic propositions organised into a system and to use these rules and systems as the basis for discovery. Facts are not 'constructed' but 'discovered'. Indeed, one civilian has described case law reasoning in France during the 19th century as the abandonment of the dialectical method in favour of the hemeneutical.[85]

Of course, statutory interpretation in the common law and even the analysis of precedents might equally be labelled *ars hermeneutica* and hermeneutics also characterises the modern school of legal philosophy represented by jurists such as Dworkin (see Chapters 1 and 2). Law, for Dworkin, is interpretation. Yet it has to be asked whether, in, say, a case like *Read* v. *Lyons*, discussed above, the solution was a matter of discovery through a process analogous to the writing of a chain novel. Certainly, Ivainer's idea of hidden categories is more convincing inasmuch as the House of Lords chose to emphasise the categories of 'occupier' and 'visitor' rather than, say, '*persona*' and (dangerous) '*res*'. But it is questionable whether Ivainer's use of the hermeneutical scheme is apt. One could argue that the scheme he is applying to the photographs case is as much a causal (A causes injury to B), actional (A not behaving like the 'reasonable journalist'), functional (journalist's behaviour defined in terms of B's injury) or dialectical (A's interests in contradiction to B's interest, or freedom of the press in contradiction to privacy) scheme. On the other hand, perhaps Ivainer's analysis reveals, if not a weakness in the Berthelot model, then the fact that it is capable of being the object of its own schemes. The causal, functional, structural, actional and dialectical schemes can all be viewed as signs which on deeper analysis reveal hidden meanings; they can, in other words, be read hermeneutically.

Actional Scheme

The emphasis of the actional scheme (*le schème actanciel*) is on the actor. 'The phenomenon B that one wants to study is thought of as the result of the behaviour of the implicated actors' and thus it 'involves the actual recognition of the intentionality of the action, its irreducibility into a causal determination: the *strategic* concepts in politics, and rational calculation in economics, imply a submission of the action to particular desired ends'.[86] A phenomenon, in other words, is studied as resulting from the accumulation of events themselves flowing from the action of a body of actors operating within a particular situation or given system.[87] Economists, for example, build up a specific picture of the actor as *homo rationalis* or *homo œconomicus*. This 'actor' is the fundamental 'atom', that is to say the individual whose behaviour is assumed to conform to a given economic rationality, upon which the collective phenomenon is apprehended.[88] The *homo rationalis* is an individual assumed to be concerned only with his own interests and when placed in the situation of the market will be treated as behaving in such a way as to maximise only his own economic satisfaction.[89] A structural model can be developed on this basis whereby economic behaviour is explained simply in terms of individuals (*persona*), goods (*res*) and price.[90]

Lawyers, of course, have developed a range of actors. The '*bon père de famille*', the 'reasonable man', the 'contracting party' and so on are some of the better-known examples. Indeed, the whole of Western criminal law could be said to be premised on this scheme. Thus one is criminally liable only for one's own act[91] and this act must be founded upon an intention to commit the criminal act.[92] In the English law of tort, negligence is, as we have seen with the case of *Read* v. *Lyons*, based on the idea of the individual act. However, such an act is not judged subjectively. It is a matter of constructing an actor analogous to the *homo œconomicus* and endowing such an individual with a range of qualities. In Roman law these qualities were set out in terms of specific examples: 'to do a certain act at a certain time and place was *culpa*, but at another time or place was not'.[93] In the common law such questions were traditionally dealt with by juries who would not give reasons for their verdict. However, when it came to addressing juries, judges would have recourse to an actional analysis. Thus the 'reasonable man' was described by one judge as 'the ordinary man' whose actions are to be judged 'by the conduct of the man on the top of the Clapham omnibus'.[94] Indeed, the relationship between such a man and the *homo œconomicus* was the subject of a humorous, but revealing, *misleading case* by A.P. Herbert:

> The Common Law of England has been laboriously built about a mythical creature – the figure of 'The Reasonable Man'. In the field of jurisprudence this legendary individual occupies the place which in another science is held by the Economic Man ... This noble creature stands in singular contrast to his kinsman the Economic Man, whose every action is prompted by the single spur of selfish advantage and directed to the single end of monetary gain.[95]

This may have been intended as entertainment rather than analysis, but it has a serious side. Both economics and law could be said to be 'sciences' inasmuch as they are attempts to rationalise social fact;[96] and both use, for this purpose, the individual actor as the methodological starting point. However, the actor in each science is, in relation to the other, endowed with entirely different qualities. The actor in the actional scheme must, accordingly, be understood in the two senses of the word 'actor'. There is the sense first of all of the individual, or body of individuals, whose behaviour is to be understood in terms of intention and effect. A phenomenon is, in short, to be rationalised through the three elements of intention, act and effect. Secondly, however, there is the sense of actor as actor in the artistic meaning of the word; that is to say an individual who adopts the *persona* of another real or fictional person. The actional scheme can thus be identified with the institution of the *persona* in both its legal and its artistic senses. The 'officious bystander' test in English contract law might be one example: the court constructs an imaginary conversation between the parties and thus at one and the same time turns the actors into legal and theatrical subjects.[97] We have seen this method used, in Chapter 5, with respect to statutory interpretation.

The actional scheme is also of importance with regard to legal philosophy. Now Herbert's humorous judgment contrasts the Reasonable Man with the Economic Man. But what if the two were to be combined? That is to say, what if the legal actor was to be endowed with the intentions of the *homo œconomicus*? Instead of seeing the Reasonable Man in terms of an actor whose actions are determined by the consideration of others, he is seen as an actor out to maximise his own self-interests. Such a view has been put forward by Richard Posner:

> I have tried to develop a moral theory that goes beyond classical utilitarianism and holds that the criterion for judging whether acts and institutions are just or good is whether they maximize the wealth of society. This approach allows a reconciliation among utility, liberty, and even equality as competing ethical principles. The approach seems to have played an important role in the growth of the common law, which is not surprising when the limitations of common law as a means of redistributing, as distinct from creating, wealth are taken into account.[98]

What is so effective about this theorising is that it seems at first sight to be linking law as a discourse to social fact. Not only does an area of law like contract become explainable in terms of the society in which it operates, but a rule such as consideration, to be found in the common law, suddenly makes economic sense. 'Why should "economic man" ever make a promise,' writes Posner, 'without receiving in exchange something of value from the promisee ...?'[99] Such a view can evidently be criticised on the grounds of ideology.[100] Yet what is interesting about the actional scheme in this respect is that it indicates how ideology can operate at a range of different levels. At one level, as we shall see, the actional scheme suggests a world populated by individuals rather than groups and this is, in itself, an ideological as well as an epistemological scheme. At another level, however, ideology can function through behaviour and intention. In contrast to Posner, and indeed to the reasonable man thesis, one could propose an actor whose interests and intentions are directed, in any immediate sense, neither towards instant economic gratification nor towards whether digging bear pits in a certain place is *culpa*. John Rawls, for example, has proposed a theory of justice founded on the notion of the rational political man keen to maximise his own interests through social cooperation. This rational political actor is entirely a creature of fiction inasmuch as he or she is inserted into a system – the Original Position – that is by definition imaginary.[101]

Berthelot's actional scheme is not, therefore, a philosophy in the sense that it is a scheme about values. It is epistemological. And even its ideological orientation towards the individual must be treated with a certain amount of care since the action, as linked to intention, is not necessarily confined to the individual. It can, as Berthelot points out, be applied to collective entities and to organisations. The actor can, in other words, be integrated into a system of interrelating groups or classes.[102] Nevertheless, the tendency is to gravitate towards the individual and this is why, in sociology, the scheme appears under the epistemological label of 'methodological individualism'.[103] This methodology is associated, in particular, with

Max Weber (although its epistemological roots are much older). For, as far as Weber was concerned, 'the foundational sociological unit could consist in first analysis only in "single persons", "particular individuals" and even "isolated" or "separated" persons – consequently postulated as social science "atoms"'.[104] This individualist methodology, although associated with the actional scheme, is an area where epistemology and ideology meet. In consequence, it is a methodological perspective of such importance in both the human, and by analogy the natural, sciences that it transcends the actional scheme to warrant its own analysis as an epistemological paradigm. As Berthelot observes, the confrontation between atomism and holism precedes any confrontation between the six schemes of intelligibility themselves.[105]

Dialectical Scheme

The dialectical scheme in many ways stands in opposition to methodological individualism in that it is essentially holistic in its structural form. It is 'a system basically defined by the existence of two terms at one and the same time indissociable and opposed constituting what can be called a contradiction'.[106] It can be expressed in the formula A & non A→B. The method assumes that the object under study contains within it an internal contradiction and that this contradiction will result in an evolution towards a future state of being or situation. Thus a Marxist dialectical analysis sees society as a matter of tension or contradiction between the capitalist (economic property-owning) class and the working class. And the power of the state is simply an ideological means by which the dominant class pursues its own interests at the expense of the other class or classes.[107] This tension will, according to Marx, eventually lead to a withering away of the state and to a classless society where political power will be unnecessary.[108]

This dialectical methodology is associated with the philosopher Hegel (1770–1831) who developed a whole thesis of history based on the idea of a process of internal contradiction. 'Change reflected,' observed Walter Jones, 'the dialectical process through which contradictions were continually being reconciled in a new and wider synthesis.'[109] But as a method *dialectica* was a hermeneutical device used by the medieval scholastic philosophers and lawyers for ironing out apparent contradictions in texts. It is not, then, a methodology that is to be associated only with German metaphysical thinking. The view in the late Middle Ages was that contradictions were only apparent, not real, since 'the unity of the human mind, being a divine creation, could not contradict itself in fundamental matters'.[110] The way to solve these contradictions was through the operation of a *distinctio* which itself could be tested through argumentation (*disputatio*). These arguments would be conducted in a form that emphasised their dialectical nature: a problem would be posed in advance and one group of students would defend while another group would attack.[111] Earlier, Pierre Abelard had developed this scheme as the basic approach towards texts. His *Sic et Non* (yes and no) organised method into a form of rigorous interrogation whereby each question for discussion would be given, first, a positive response (*sic*), then a negative response (*non*) and finally a solution.[112] The results of this scholastic methodology must never be underestimated, as the great work of the canon lawyer Gratian, finished in 1140, bears witness. Entitled *Concordia discordantium canonum*, it harmonised a huge mass of discordant and contradictory texts to become the most influential textbook on canon law during the whole of the early modern period.[113] The dialectical methodology thus became associated with legal studies and with philosophy in general and this was the intellectual foundation for the modern view that reality is riddled with contradictions which must be transcended. Indeed, it has its echo in natural science method as well. The idea that science was to be 'interrogated' through experimentation was an early modernist idea[114] and Popper's theory of falsification could be seen as a descendant of this line of thinking.

The dialectical method still finds central expression in Western legal systems. At the level of general method, dialectical reasoning can be found in conceptual oppositions such as the contradiction between the rights, or interests, of the plaintiff on the one hand and the defendant on the other. Indeed, such a tension can be built into the concepts themselves: the opposition between real and personal rights, between corporal and incorporeal property, between land and chattels, and so on.[115] A notion like the owner's rights thus presupposes the coexistence of a contrary notion such as the tenant's rights. No premise can be admitted, therefore, without admitting the contrary premise and 'no conclusion can be retained without having envisaged the opposite conclusion and without having operated a choice between two possible conclusions: if the right of the tenant is a personal right it must not be transferred with the property being let; if it involves a real right, it is transferred with the property'.[116]

At a procedural level, the dialectical approach can be found in the maxim *audi alteram partem* which translates into the procedural principle of contradiction.[117] This principle of contradiction is a particular characteristic of the common law where every aspect of a case is founded upon the idea of a dialectical opposition. The role of the judge is, traditionally, passive and it is for counsel to advance, and to dispute through cross-examination or through argumentation, not only the facts but also the law.[118] The structure of an English judgment is, accordingly, usually framed around the opposing arguments advanced by each counsel.[119] And such a structure contrasts sharply with that of a French judgment, where the emphasis is put on the (supposed) syllogistic nature of legal reasoning. Yet even the civil law accepts that behind the syllogism there is a fundamental tension between values in conflict which surfaces in the form of judicial disputes.[120] True facts and just solutions are, as a matter of procedural form, assumed to emerge out of a process of internal contradiction. In turn, judicial controversies are, in substance, the result of value conflicts and contradictions inherent within a society that is permanently in a dialectical conflict between the individual and the community.[121]

There are, however, problems with the dialectical method. As a scheme of intelligibility, 'the difficulty consists in actually grasping the internal process at work'. For the 'risk is always to project onto it something which is only an external form: the formula *a*→not *a*→not not *a* often illustrated by biological phenomena (caterpillar→chrysalis→butterfly, bud→flower→fruit) is explicative only if it leads to an effective account of the passage from one state to the other'. And if not, 'it is only descriptive'.[122] The dialectical scheme cannot in itself explain the result of a case. Certainly, it can highlight in a formal way the opposition between principles (freedom of the press versus privacy), between rights (landlord versus tenant), between values (compensation versus freedom of action) or between a whole and its parts (individual versus the community). To this extent it can explain the legal phenomenon in terms of, say, game theory.[123] Furthermore, the dialectical scheme remains of fundamental importance as a methodological device (in the structuring and presentation of a thesis (the two-part French *plan*, for example).[124] However, its epistemological role is architectural only. It can design a formal set of oppositions or states, but it cannot account for the internal movements or processes themselves. Thus the main importance of dialectics as a scheme of intelligibility is to be found in its formal organising quality. It may not explain the internal movement or evolution towards a solution, but it structures oppositions in such a way as to channel a reasoning or argumentation process towards, if not a compromise, then a game-like conclusion[125] whose tactics and strategies are constructed through the employment of other schemes of intelligibility.

Interrelationship of Schemes

The isolation of these schemes of intelligibility implies, then, neither that the typology is exhaustive nor that the various schemes are mutually exclusive. The causal and the actional scheme, for example, might be said to typify much of substantive Western criminal and private law. At the level of procedure, the dialectical scheme is of particular relevance and codification certainly lends itself to a structural analysis, and possibly a functional analysis as well. The hermeneutical scheme, while primarily associated, historically, with theological texts, deserves a special place in the history of legal theory. It was one of the central schemes of intelligibility used by academic lawyers working in the medieval and modern universities.[126] Nevertheless, it has never been a unique scheme. The use of analogy, for example, has an equally respectable pedigree in legal reasoning and this is a form of analysis that is based on the isomorphic qualities to be found in factual situations. Analogy might well then be seen as an aspect of structuralism. The American Realists, while not systems theorists, nevertheless put the emphasis only on the functional role of legal concepts and this functional approach is, so some comparative lawyers have argued, the only methodology that is possible in comparative law.[127] Dialectical methodology would, however, seem to have its relevance for the comparative lawyer as well, since 'he may be able to fashion a new solution, superior to all others, out of parts of different national solutions'.[128] Indeed, dialectical argument and hermeneutics would appear to be the two main schemes which characterised the scholastic methods of the medieval Romanists. In short, legal method involves a *mélange* of social science schemes of intelligibility.

Holistic and Individualistic Methodology

However, if one had to abstract from Berthelot's schemes one fundamental theme or dichotomy, it is perhaps that of the opposition between a 'holistic' and an 'atomistic' analysis of society.[129] The dichotomy is one of ontology, that is to say it is concerned with what exists as a physical reality. Does one view society as a 'thing' in itself or does one view society only as a collection of individual people and physical objects? The debate is an old one and indeed is reflected in a number of Roman legal texts.[130] However, its more immediate foundation is in the nominalist 'revolution' associated, as we have already indicated in earlier chapters, with the late-medieval philosopher William of Ockham (1288–1349). According to Ockham, just to recap, terms such as 'town', 'forest', 'animal' or 'man' were verbal entities only; that is to say, they were nothing more than names (*nomina*).[131] What they referred to had no existence outside the human mind. What existed were individual human beings (*individuum*) and individual trees.[132] A philosopher like Aquinas

(1225–74), in contrast, had seen such universals as realities; thus the categories of genus and species expressed, for a realist philosopher, an ontological – what exists – view of the world.[133] Gradually, however, 'the individualist paradigm began to take shape in the epistemological, then in the "sociological" and ethical, fields, in opposing the realist and holistic philosophy of Saint Thomas Aquinas'.[134] The individual is a unique and separate being who lives only through himself.[135] The Church and the town no longer existed as 'realities' but were simply names to express a collection of individuals.[136] The political birds (so to speak) that took wing in this nominalist revolution finally came home to roost in the celebrated ideological statement of Margaret Thatcher that 'there is no such thing as society'. There 'are individual men and women and there are families'.[137]

The result of this thinking was revolutionary, in that political, social and legal theory no longer started out from the idea of the group as a reality (*ubi societas ibi ius*). It was simply a construction built upon the individual human endowed with natural rights. Philosophical methodology also changed, inasmuch as Ockham took a 'razor' to the multiplication of these entities (*entia non sunt multiplicanda praeter necessitatem*).[138] It was necessary to cut one's way through the mere names and signs in order to arrive at the true ontological foundations of society. What are the basic units in physics, in chemistry, in economics and so on? What is the nature of mathematical entities and the foundational elements used in logic? How does one reconcile the old dichotomy between individual and the state? Is the 'working class' a thing or simply a name?

What holism and individualism have to offer as methodologies are, then, two ways of 'seeing', in turn leading to two different ways of analysis. As Jon Elster has succinctly put it, 'the explanation of the macro by the micro is preferable to that of the macro by the macro', since 'it is always more satisfying to open the black box and to see the cogs of the machine'.[139] Of course, as this back box analogy implies, the individual is not to be taken as an isolated element. The individual is an 'atom' that interrelates with other atoms. It is an individual that reacts with, and relates to, other individuals. The individual is thus never to be envisaged within an empty space; he or she is an 'atom' to be seen within an institutional structure which supports a cultural and social collective.[140] And this institutional and cultural context will certainly act as a restraint upon individual action. What the individualist theorists claim, however, is that this social context is only a restraint; it is never the cause.[141] The social group never determines the conditioning and behaviour of the individual. This, needless to say, is what makes methodological individualism so controversial.

The implications of the nominalist revolution are equally important for epistemology. How are facts to be viewed? Take a simple example. Does the world consist of billions of individual human beings or millions of groups of human beings? Much may depend upon the position from which one is viewing the planet: photographs taken by a satellite tend to emphasise the social nature of human existence, while snapshots at street level suggest the individuality of humans. The question is, however, an important one inasmuch as it can determine the foundations of a whole range of knowledge discourses. What are the basic units in physics, in chemistry, in economics and so on? In mathematics, the old nominalist and universalist debate is revived in the quarrel over the nature of mathematical entities and the foundational elements used in logic.[142] In philosophy, nominalism became the means of asserting empiricism in the battle against metaphysics.[143] In sociology and political science, the debate is fundamental. How one reconciles the old dichotomy between an individual and the state is largely dependent upon the institutional concepts used in giving expression both to society and to theory.[144] Those who think in terms of class are likely to propound quite different theoretical models than those that structure society around the individual. In terms of method, it is the difference between analysing society on the basis of 'words' or on the basis of 'things'. Is the 'working class' a thing or simply a name?

Holistic and Individual Facts

The universalism versus nominalism dichotomy is all-pervasive in that it not only underpins philosophy and methodology but is at the basis of how one 'sees' the world. Not being able to see the wood for the trees, or the trees for the wood, is a question both of understanding and of vision. Woods and forests are easily seen from a suitably distant perspective, whereas trees seem the only objects that surround the hunter crouching deep within the forest. The problem, however, is not just one of distance. What if, over a period of time, all the trees in a wood or forest die, to be replaced by others that spring up in their place? Is it still the same forest after the replacement? This is where the metaphysical element enters the debate so as to turn it from a question of mere perspective into one of relations between objects and of the existence of entities. The question becomes one of ontology. What exists in the world as a factual reality, just the individual entities (for example, individual humans or individual trees) that can be seen and touched, or groups of entities bound together by relations (for example, towns or forests)? And if the relations of place and space are, say, to be included as factual realities, what about other relations not so easily seen? Do families exist as factual realities and, if so, which individual humans will be included in such an entity?

Institutions and Reality

These questions influence lawyers in a number of ways. At a general level, they affect the institutional elements of *persona* and *res*. What do these terms represent in reality? The starting point in Roman law was the physical person and the physical thing, but they soon came to embrace a more metaphysical vision. The institution of the person came to include groups of people such as towns and, once these groups (*universitas*) had been granted the power to sue and be sued, they effectively became a 'person' separate from the human individuals that made up the group. Towns were treated as if they were people.[145] The Post-glossators took this a stage further. The *universitas personarum*, that is to say a group of persons viewed as a single 'person', attracted the name *persona ficta*.[146] And this fictitious person can still be central to the nature and methodology of legal reasoning.[147]

Similar issues arose with the notion of a *res*. Does one own a house or does one own only the bricks, mortar, beams, tiles and so on?[148] A fisherman buys a boat early in his career and over the years gradually replaces, as they wear out, every plank in the boat: at the end of his career does he own the same boat?[149] Roman lawyers started to distinguish between funds of property and the individual items of wealth that made up these funds. Thus Roman jurists began to talk of a person's 'goods' (*bona*) which in turn could be seen as an asset which was capable of being valued in terms of money,[150] and then described as a person's 'patrimony' (*patrimonium*).[151] The Post-glossators and their successors refined this dichotomy between the whole and its parts: the notion of subrogation allows the whole to remain intact as a distinct *res* while its parts, individual things, can come and go.[152]

At the lower level of factual analysis the ontological questions become important in the way they can lead to different constructions of 'factual reality'. Consider the following problem. A man and wife, before leaving to go on a rather exotic tour of the South Seas in a small ship, decide to make a joint will. In the will they provide that, should the death of one of them be 'coinciding with' that of the other, the property is to go to a particular person. Should the deaths not coincide, then the property arrangements would be different. The ship disappears and the couple are never seen or heard of again. The couple are presumed dead, but did the death of one spouse 'coincide with' that of the other? There are two quite different factual images.

The first is of the ship being caught in some catastrophe and sinking with all hands. In this image the sinking and deaths can be envisaged as a single catastrophic event. The alternative picture is a series of events. The ship foundering, some of the crew and passengers take to the rafts or jump into the sea; others are trapped within the sinking boat. Those that make it into the sea survive only for limited periods – some drown, some die of exhaustion and some are eaten by sharks. In the first image it is possible to talk of the deaths coinciding; in the second, however, it is much more difficult. If the catastrophe is envisaged as a series of events it may be that one spouse died when the ship went down, while the other survived perhaps twenty-four hours or longer. How 'coinciding with' is interpreted depends entirely upon the image chosen; and this image in turn will determine who will inherit the property.[153]

Legal Ideology

In the social sciences, the debate between holism and individualism reaches beyond epistemology and into ideology. This raises a general question about the structure of the legal reasoning model as envisaged in Gaius and in the codes. Is it essentially individualist in its view of society or does it function as a holistic model? The traditional response is to say that the Roman model was essentially individualistic, in that it took as its main elements the individual person and the individual thing.[154] Jacques Ellul points out that one should not be surprised by this Roman ideological construction, for obstacles to state authority are to be found in 'the existence of natural groups where man finds his milieu, his protection and the source of his rights'. Thus it is in an individualistic society that authoritarianism flourishes since 'the individual has no protection against the State, and where he receives his rights from the State (the State moreover reorganising the essential groups, which become organs of the State)'.[155] The activity of the individual may be the unit which acts as the source of private law and it may be the interests of the individual which act as the object of the *ius privatum*.[156] 'But,' observed Ellul, 'it is a matter of an abstract individual, whose quality and rights are determined objectively by the State.'[157]

This individualistic ideology is still to be found in private law and is particularly evident when it comes to the treatment of the family. Although the family has featured as a central institution in private law from Roman to modern times, it has never really been seen as a unit in itself. As a French jurist points out, the family is apprehended by the legal model only across the structural relations which underpin it; that is to say, through marriage, filiation and the personal and property relationships which flow from it.[158] In order, then, to protect family interests, the legal reasoner has to construct sets of relations based upon individual members. Take, for example, *Jackson* v. *Horizon Holidays Ltd*.[159] A father, in reliance upon statements made in a tour operator's brochure and over the telephone, booked a holiday for himself and his family. Many of the promised facilities were not available and on the family's return the father sued the tour operator for damages. The tour operator admitted liability but argued that they were liable to compensate only the father, since the other family members were not parties to the contract. The Court of Appeal held that the father could in this case obtain damages for mental distress both for himself and for his family. Lord Denning MR gave some examples of the difficulties arising out of the principle that only those who are parties to a contract have the right to sue for its breach:

> We have had an interesting discussion as to the legal position when one person makes a contract for the benefit of a party. In this case it was a husband making a contract for the benefit of himself, his wife and children. Other cases readily come to mind. A host makes a contract with a restaurant for a dinner for himself and his friends. The vicar makes a contract for a coach trip for the choir. In all these cases there is only one person who makes the contract. It is the husband, the host or the vicar, as the case may be. Sometimes he pays the whole price himself. Occasionally he may get a contribution from the others. But in any case it is he who makes the contract. It would be a fiction to say that the contract was made by all the family, or all the guests, or all the choir and that he was only an agent for them. Take this very case. it would be absurd to say that the twins of three years old were parties to the contract or that the father was making the contract on their behalf as if they were principals. It would equally be a mistake to say that in any of these instances there was a trust. The transaction bears no resemblance to a trust. There was no trust fund and no trust property. No, the real truth is that in each instance, the father, the host or the vicar, was making a contract himself for the benefit of the whole party. In short, a contract by one for the benefit of third persons.[160]

And he continued:

> What is the position when such a contract is broken? At present the law says that the only one who can sue is the one who made the contract. None of the rest of the party can sue, even though the contract was made for their benefit. But when that one does sue, what damages can he recover? Is he limited to his own loss? Or can he recover for the others? Suppose the holiday firm puts the family into a hotel which is only half built and the visitors have to sleep on the floor? Or suppose the restaurant is fully booked and the guests have

> to go away, hungry and angry, having spent so much on fares to get there? Or suppose the coach leaves the choir stranded halfway and they have to hire cars to get home? None of them individually can sue. Only the father, the host or the vicar can sue. He can, of course, recover his own damages. But can he not recover for the others? I think he can.[161]

The law, in other words, seems to take an even more empirical view of society than Mrs Thatcher.[162] The family does not exist as a unit capable of making a contract or of being a plaintiff in a damages case. Only an individual person can sue. This of course is not always very realistic, socially speaking, as Lord Denning has indicated. When a husband or wife is badly injured this has an impact both emotionally and financially on the family as a whole. In fact, when a family member is killed, the dependants might have an individual claim against any wrongdoer thanks to legislation, and what is interesting about this legislation is the way that its starting point is the continued liability of a wrongdoer 'for the benefit of the dependants'.[163] What stays alive, so to speak, is the 'action for damages',[164] but only for the benefit of dependants who, by and large, are the family members of the deceased.[165] Is this a recognition of the family as a group or only a group of individuals linked to the deceased by the bond of dependency?

The Individual and the Group

This individualism does not, of course, apply to Horizon Holidays. These commercial groups are treated as individuals thanks to companies legislation and once properly incorporated a corporation, known as a legal person, can contract in its own name, can own property and can sue to protect its interests. Equally, it can be sued as if it was an individual. Do such groups have a real social existence or are they simply the product of the legal model? The answer to this question has important political implications because, if such entities are only legal constructions, it is more difficult to conceive of groups as social facts. The political initiative remains, in other words, with the ruler rather than the ruled. If, however, they are seen as real, it is more difficult for the political authorities to control their existence. As Jones observed, 'there are few questions bearing upon the nature and function of law, or upon the relation of legal concepts to legal rules and of both to the facts of social life, which have not been raised at some time by the contending theories of corporate personality'.[166] The nominalist will see such corporate groups as fictions – indeed the original basis of legal personality in medieval canon and civil law was to be found in the idea that the corporation was a legal entity only in name (*nomen iuris, corpus intellectuale*) – and this suggests that they are simply a matter of words (*universitas nomen iuris est non facti*).[167]

Nevertheless, there is an image beyond the rules, as both the old civilians and the modern common lawyers have recognised. This is the image of the *persona ficta*. As Denning LJ put it:

> A company may in many ways be likened to a human body. It has a brain and nerve centre which controls what it does. It also has hands which hold the tools and act in accordance with directions from the centre. Some of the people in the company are mere servants and agents who are nothing more than hands to do the work and cannot be said to represent the mind or will. Others are directors and managers who represent the directing mind and will of the company, and control what it does. The state of mind of these managers is the state of mind of the company and is treated by the law as such.[168]

It can certainly be said that corporate bodies obtain their legal personality only as a result of the existence of legislative rules (at least in English law). But it would appear that they are to be envisaged only in the image of the human being. This is the physical 'reality' beyond the rules.

This image of the human being can create problems, since a legal *persona* can exist at one and the same time at the level of the corporation and at the level of each individual that makes up the group. An employee of a company injures a third party: is it the individual or the group that has caused the damage? This problem becomes particularly acute when the individual, during his or her employment time, commits a crime. Consider the following problem. An employee of a supermarket, while resupplying the shelves, inadvertently puts the wrong price on some goods, which results in the supermarket, as a legal person, being prosecuted for an offence under the Trade Descriptions Act 1968. Can the supermarket raise, by way of defence, section 24(1) of the Act? This section states that in 'any proceedings for an offence under this Act it shall ... be a defence for the person charged to prove ... that the commission of the offence was due ... to the act or default of *another person*'.[169] This is a problem that raises directly a conflict between words (rules) and things (facts), since the supermarket assistant is an empirical reality and the supermarket a legal reality, both of whose existence cannot be denied (albeit at the two different levels of things and words). Yet in holding, as the House of Lords did,[170] that the supermarket could escape conviction, the decision illustrates that it is not the rule as such that has engendered the decision, but the factual image in the minds of the judges. The assistant was 'seen' as a separate entity from the supermarket. However, this separation was achieved within the metaphorical image of a company as a human body. 'Mr Clement, being the manager of one of the company's several hundreds of shops, could not,' said Lord Pearson, 'be identified with the company's ego nor was he an alter ego of the company.'[171] Lord Reid was more discursive in his analysis:

> I must start by considering the nature of the personality which by a fiction the law attributes to a corporation. A living person has a mind which can have knowledge or intention or be negligent and he has hands to carry out his intentions. A corporation has none of these: it must act through living persons, though not always one or the same person. Then the person who acts is not speaking or acting for the company. He is acting as the company and his mind which directs his acts is the mind of the company. There is no question of the company being vicariously liable. He is not acting as a servant, representative, agent or delegate. He is an embodiment of the company or, one could say, he hears and speaks through the persona of the company, within his appropriate sphere, and his mind is the mind of the company. If it is a guilty mind then that guilt is the guilt of the company. It must be a question of law whether, once the facts have been ascertained, a person in doing particular things is to be regarded as the company or merely as the company's servant or agent. In that case any liability of the company can only be a statutory or vicarious liability.[172]

Lord Reid then turned to the more junior employees:

> Normally the board of directors, the managing director and perhaps other superior officers of a company carry out the functions of management and speak and act as the company. Their subordinates do not. They carry out orders from above and it can make no difference that they are given some measure of discretion. But the board of directors may delegate some part of their functions of management giving to their delegate full discretion to act independently of instructions from them. I see no difficulty in holding that they have thereby put such a delegate in their place so that within the scope of the delegation he can act as the company.[173]

However, on the facts of the case before him, Lord Reid was not prepared to associate the employee stacking the shelves in a single branch as part of the directing 'mind' of the company. He was to be seen as a separate organ and thus as 'another person':

> The Divisional Court decided this case on a theory of delegation. In that they were following some earlier authorities. But they gave far too wide a meaning to delegation. I have said that a board of directors can delegate part of their functions of management so as to make their delegate an embodiment of the company within the sphere of the

> delegation. But here the board never delegated any part of their functions. They set up a chain of command through regional and district supervisors, but they remained in control. The shop managers had to obey their general directions and also take orders from their superiors. The acts or omissions of shop managers were not acts of the company itself.[174]

What is important about this analysis is that it takes place *within* the image of the human body. The whole of the reasoning is dependent upon the metaphor of the human body and how this body is envisaged. However, if the employee had, instead of committing a trade descriptions offence, done a rather different act which directly caused damage to a third party outside the company then a quite different analysis might have been adopted.

The Group and the Individual

This alternative analysis can be found in a leading Court of Appeal case. An employee working for a firm of dry cleaners, instead of cleaning a customer's valuable mink stole as directed by the manager, stole it. Could the firm of dry cleaners escape liability for the loss of the stole by claiming that it was not their act that caused the loss but the act of 'another person'? When this problem came before the court of appeal, Diplock LJ responded in a way that was rather different from the approach in the supermarket problem. He viewed the image of a corporation from the *outside*:

> If the bailee in the present case had been a natural person and had converted the plaintiff's fur by stealing it himself, no one would have argued that he was not liable to her for its loss. But the defendant bailees are a corporate person. They could not perform their duties to the plaintiffs to take reasonable care of the fur and not to convert it otherwise than vicariously by natural persons acting as their servants or agents. It was one of their servants to whom they had entrusted the care and custody of the fur for the purpose of doing work upon it who converted it by stealing it. Why should they not be vicariously liable for this breach of their duty by the vicar whom they had chosen to perform it? Sir John Holt, I think, would have answered that they were liable 'for seeing that someone must be the loser by this deceit it is more reason that he who employs and puts a trust and confidence in the deceiver should be the loser than a stranger.'[175]

The point to be made about both these examples of crimes committed by employees is that the legal analysis is not just founded in the interpretation of rules. It is not just a question of interpreting words. The decisions in both cases result from how the facts are envisaged and this is a question of imagery and patterns of relationships between persons and, indeed, within persons.[176] It is a matter of how the world is being viewed. In answer to the question about the ontological existence of the corporation, a physical world of brains, limbs and organs needs to be conjured up. There is simply no other way in which the reasoning could possibly begin to function. In the case of the mink stole, however, a different image becomes possible because of the physical existence of the stole and its owner. Diplock LJ did not need to think about the internal structure of the corporation. All that was necessary was the pattern of relationships between owner, stole and cleaning firm. Had he ventured into the internal structure of the dry cleaning corporation, the picture would have become very much more complex. Thus one can compare the reasoning of Diplock LJ with the conclusion of another judge in the same case. According to Salmon LJ:

> A bailee for reward is not answerable for a theft by any of his servants but only for a theft by such of them as are deputed by him to discharge some part of his duty of taking reasonable care. A theft by any servant who is not employed to do anything in relation to the goods bailed is entirely outside the scope of his employment and cannot make the master liable. So in this case, if someone employed by the defendants in another depot had broken in and stolen the fur, the defendants would not have been liable. Similarly in my view if a clerk employed in the same depot had seized the opportunity of entering the room where the fur was kept and had stolen it, the defendants would not have been liable. The mere fact that the master, by employing a rogue, gives him the opportunity to steal or defraud does not make the master liable for his depredations: *Ruben* v. *Great Fingall Consolidated* [1906] AC 439. It might be otherwise if the master knew or ought to have known that his servant was dishonest, because then the master could be liable in negligence for employing him.[177]

In trying to view the corporation at one and the same time from within and without, the result, arguably, was confusion.[178] Why should the liability of the bailee be dependent upon which of the employees stole the stole? Viewed from the outside, it should make no difference who committed the act of appropriation since liability ought to attach to the corporate *persona*. Viewed from the inside, the idea of the directing mind delegating authority to some lesser organ does conform to the image of the human body metaphor and it is possible to appreciate, if not necessarily to approve, the search for a *mens rea* within the corporation. In criminal cases the courts by nature are reluctant to convict in the absence of a guilty mind. However, in civil liability cases, the image of a *mens rea* is surely inappropriate, at least where the law of property is concerned. One might reflect, therefore, on whether

Salmon LJ's rather awkward analysis is the result of an inappropriate image. In other words, working within the facts is by no means an uncreative exercise.

Social Science and Legal Reasoning

The creativity, however, is arguably not special to law. Certainly, the language of the rules employed seems to belong to a specialised knowledge domain and so one does not normally find in works on social science terms such as 'bailee', 'mens rea', 'privity' and so on. But the schemes of analysis are all traceable back to Berthelot's typology, and the same epistemological dichotomies (in particular that between nominalism and holism) surface and resurface in the legal perception, and construction, of factual situations. It is these schemes that take the legal epistemologist beyond the rules. Where law is important, however, is in reminding the social scientist that the individual 'is not just a product of bourgeois society'.[179] The individual is as much a creation of the Roman institutional system as he is of any modernist philosophy. To this extent law is, as others have observed, one of the oldest social sciences.[180] The danger for law, however, is that in forgetting its wider 'scientific' context it can so easily become a discipline whose epistemological assumption is wedded to a single scheme. The thesis that to have knowledge of law is to have knowledge of rules reduces legal method to an *ars hermeneutica*. This is dangerous because law is equally about the causal, functional, structural, actional and dialectical schemes, as the case analysis in this and other chapters has clearly shown. This is not to assume that these schemes are exhaustive or definitive; but they are models that take one beyond texts – written and unwritten (*regulae iuris*) – and thus go far in indicating how legal method cannot be divorced from epistemology in general. In other words, the grand questions about the nature of knowledge – whether it is uniquely symbolic or whether it has a non-symbolic dimension – are as important for law as for any other discipline.

Notes

1 See, generally, Berthelot (2001c).
2 Berthelot (1990).
3 Quivy and Van Campenhoudt (1995).
4 See, for example, Popper (1972).
5 Pheby (1988, p. 26).
6 Berthelot (1996, pp. 203–4).
7 On which see Pheby (1988, pp. 28–9).

8 See Lloyd and Freeman (1994, pp. 935–50).
9 Mansell et al. (1995, p. 144).
10 Granger (1995, p. 98).
11 Berthelot (1996, p. 204).
12 Soler (2000, p. 89).
13 Ibid., pp. 45–7.
14 Granger (1995, pp. 70, 78–84).
15 Ibid., p. 49.
16 Busino (1998, p. 85).
17 Granger (1995, p. 85).
18 Note, however, that Berthelot is not happy with the transfer of Granger's notion of 'virtual facts' to the social sciences. Certainly, the social sciences can manifest the desire for a similar reductive tendency towards facts, but, says Berthelot, such a reduction is always open to challenge on the grounds of the legitimacy of the exercise since social facts are so multidimensional and thus cannot be reduced to one abstract model (Berthelot, 1996, p. 73). It is by no means clear, however, that Berthelot's reservations apply to legal facts.
19 See, generally, Valade (2001).
20 Besnier (1996, pp. 40–43).
21 Blanché (1975, pp. 133–50).
22 Ibid., p. 135.
23 Granger (1995, pp. 86–7).
24 Leroux and Marciano (1998, p. 95). See also Walliser (2001).
25 Empirical truth as coherence: Soler (2000, p. 44).
26 Soler (2000, p. 58).
27 Bunge (1983, p. 60).
28 Granger (1995, p. 99).
29 Ibid., p. 101.
30 See, for example, Jones (1993).
31 Toddington (1996, p. 69 n. 2, emphasis in original).
32 Granger (1995, pp. 87–9).
33 See Berthelot (1990, pp. 62–85). For a summary, see Granger (1995, pp. 90–92).
34 Berthelot (1990, p. 62).
35 Ibid., pp. 62–3.
36 Ibid., p. 63.
37 Ibid., pp. 64–5.
38 D.9.2.52.2.
39 Samuel (2001, pp. 211–46).
40 See, for example, *Barnett* v. *Chelsea and Kensington Hospital Management Committee* [1969] 1 QB 428.
41 *Carslogie SS Co* v. *Royal Norwegian Government* [1952] AC 292.
42 *Baker* v. *Willoughby* [1970] AC 467.
43 Berthelot (1990, p. 65).
44 See Samuel (1994, pp. 157–70; 1997).
45 Lugan (1993, pp. 11, 37).
46 *Spartan Steel & Alloys Ltd* v. *Martin & Co* [1973] 1 QB 27.
47 At p. 37.

48 Berthelot (1996, p. 79).
49 Samuel (1997).
50 See, generally, Teubner (1993).
51 See, for example, Collins (1997).
52 Samuel (1994, 1997).
53 Le Moigne (1995, pp. 24–32).
54 Ibid., p. 91.
55 Ibid., pp. 93–4.
56 Ibid., pp. 97–8.
57 Lawson (1980, pp. 147–60).
58 *Lipkin Gorman* v. *Karpnale Ltd* [1991] 2 AC 548.
59 Samuel (2001, pp. 545–8).
60 Delacour (1995, p. 34).
61 Berthelot (1990, p. 70).
62 Berthelot (1996, p. 79).
63 Berthelot (1990, p. 70).
64 Ibid., pp. 71–2.
65 Ibid., p. 72.
66 Tierney (1982, p. 44).
67 Carbasse (1998, pp. 46–7).
68 *The Mediana* [1900] AC 113, 117.
69 [1947] AC 156.
70 (1866) LR 1 Ex 265 (Ex); (1868) LR 3 HL 330 (HL).
71 [1947] AC 156, 182.
72 Lord Simonds, pp. 182–3.
73 The 'law of torts is concerned not with activities but with acts' (Scott LJ [1945] 1 KB 216, 228).
74 Berthelot (1990, p. 73).
75 Ibid.
76 Ivainer (1988, p. 22).
77 Ibid., pp. 66–7.
78 Ibid., p. 67.
79 Berthelot (1996, p. 79).
80 Van Caenegem (1987, pp. 124–6).
81 Ibid., pp. 124–5.
82 Ibid., p. 125.
83 Berthelot (1996, p. 79).
84 Legrand (1996a, p. 239).
85 Zenati (1991, p. 108).
86 Berthelot (1990, p. 76).
87 Berthelot (1996, p. 80).
88 Leroux and Marciano (1998, p. 83); Jones (1940, pp. 228–9).
89 Granger (1995, p. 90).
90 Berthelot (1996, p. 80).
91 French *Code pénal*, art. 121–1.
92 Ibid., art. 121–3.
93 Lawson (1950, p. 38).
94 McNair J in *Bolam* v. *Friern Hospital Management Committee* [1957] 1 WLR 582, 586.

95 Herbert (1935, pp. 1, 2–3).
96 D.22.6.2.
97 '[I]f he submits a conforming tender before the deadline he is entitled, not as a matter of mere expectation but of contractual right, to be sure that his tender will after the deadline be opened and considered ... Had the club, before tendering, inquired of the council whether it could rely on any timely and conforming tender being considered along with others, I feel quite sure that the answer would have been "of course." The law would, I think, be defective if it did not give effect to that' (Bingham LJ in *Blackpool & Fylde Aero Club Ltd* v. *Blackpool BC* [1990] 1 WLR 1195, 1202).
98 Posner (1983, p. 115).
99 Posner (1977, p. 411).
100 See Lloyd and Freeman (1994, pp. 377–9).
101 Rawls (1972).
102 Berthelot (1990, pp. 78–9).
103 Ibid., pp. 80–81.
104 Laurent (1994, p. 64).
105 Berthelot (1990, p. 152).
106 Ibid., p. 82.
107 Jones (1940, p. 271).
108 Ibid., p. 272.
109 Ibid., p. 203.
110 Ullmann (1975a, p. 121).
111 Laurioux and Moulinier (1998, p. 86).
112 Ibid., p. 17.
113 Ullmann (1975a, p. 121).
114 Barreau (1998, pp. 53–4).
115 Bergel (1999, p. 276), Van de Kerchove and Ost (1992, p. 122).
116 Ibid.
117 NCPC, art. 14.
118 See, for example, *Jones* v. *National Coal Board* [1957] 2 QB 55.
119 For a striking example, see *Blackpool & Fylde Aero Club Ltd* v. *Blackpool BC* [1990] 1 WLR 1195, although almost any weekly copy of the All England or Weekly Law Reports will provide examples.
120 Perelman (1979, p. 84), Zenati (1991, p. 157).
121 Bergel (1999, p. 276).
122 Berthelot (1990, p. 82).
123 Van de Kerchove and Ost (1992, pp. 123–5).
124 Bell et al. (1998, pp. 498–501).
125 Van de Kerchove and Ost (1992, pp. 123–5).
126 Kelley (1990, pp. 132–7, 210–12, 244).
127 Zweigert and Kötz (1998, pp. 34–6).
128 Ibid., p 47.
129 Berthelot (1990, pp. 152–61). And see Valade (2001).
130 See, for example, D.5.1.76; D.41.3.30.
131 Villey (1975, pp. 203–8); but cf. Tierney (1997, pp. 13–42).
132 Ibid., pp. 254–7.
133 Black (1988, pp. 599–600). However, this is not to say that Aquinas did not recognise the individual as an entity: 'Aquinas spoke of individual

and community in terms of "part" and "whole", and insisted upon the duty of the part to shape itself to the "good of the whole"' (Black, p. 600).
134 Laurent (1993, p. 23); but cf. Tierney (1997, pp. 196–8).
135 Note the important role played by both Roman law and criminal and moral responsibility in isolating the individual from the corporation (Black, 1988, p. 599).
136 Black (1988, p. 601).
137 *Women's Own*, 31 October 1987.
138 Knowles (1962, p. 328).
139 Quoted in Laurent (1994, p. 37).
140 Laurent (1994, pp. 37–8).
141 Ibid., pp. 112–13.
142 Blanché (1983, p. 30).
143 Ibid., p. 97.
144 See, generally, Valade (2001).
145 D.50.16.16.
146 Lefebvre-Teillard (1996, pp. 89–90).
147 See, for example, *Tesco Supermarkets* v. *Nattrass* [1972] AC 153.
148 D.41.3.30pr.
149 Cf. D.5.1.76.
150 D.50.16.5.
151 D.27.1.30.1.
152 Zenati and Revet (1997, pp. 107–8).
153 *Re Rowland* [1963] 1 Ch 1.
154 Ellul (1984, pp. 477–8). See also Ourliac and De Malafosse (1969, p. 238), who talk about the individualistic nature of the notion of an obligation.
155 Ellul (1984, pp. 477–8).
156 D.1.1.1.2.
157 Ellul (1984, p. 478).
158 Lefebvre-Teillard (1996, p. 97).
159 [1975] 1 WLR 1468.
160 At pp. 1472–3.
161 At p. 1473.
162 But see now Contracts (Rights of Third Parties) Act 1999.
163 Fatal Accidents Act 1976, s. 1(2).
164 Ibid., s. 1(1).
165 See s. 1(3) of the 1976 Act.
166 Jones (1940, p. 71).
167 Ibid., pp. 166–70.
168 *HL Bolton (Engineering) Co Ltd* v. *TJ Graham & Sons Ltd* [1957] 1 QB 159, 172.
169 Emphasis added.
170 *Tesco Supermarkets Ltd* v *Nattrass* [1972] AC 153.
171 At p. 193.
172 At p. 170.
173 At p. 171.
174 At pp. 174–5.
175 *Morris* v. *CW Martin & Sons Ltd* [1966] 1 QB 716, 732–3.

176 And see now *Lister* v. *Hesley Hall Ltd* [2001] 2 WLR 1311.
177 At pp. 740–41.
178 Cf. *Lister* v. *Hesley Hall Ltd* [2001] 2 WLR 1311.
179 Kelley (1990, p. 280).
180 See Murphy (1997).

Concluding Remarks

This enquiry into what it is to have knowledge of law has arguably confirmed that the rule thesis is inadequate as a knowledge model. There is much more to legal knowledge than knowledge of normative propositions expressed in natural language. Now, such a thesis obviously requires a model through which expression can be given to the legal knowledge said to lie beyond the linguistic proposition. Accordingly, in order to give general expression to the knowledge said to lie beyond the rules, this present work has adopted a dichotomy, used by some cognitive scientists, between symbolic and non-symbolic knowledge.[1] Symbolic knowledge is of a kind that can be expressed in terms of symbols, primarily numbers or words. Non-symbolic knowledge consists of knowledge that cannot be reduced to mathematical figures or natural language; it is knowledge that consists of mental images that reproduce the spatial aspects of an object.[2] Non-symbolic knowledge is pictorial and structural in form and it operates, so this work has tried to show, primarily on, or within, the facts of legal problems.

However, facts, in this respect, must be treated with care since they are not objects external to legal science. They are not things that are 'out there' waiting to be rationalised by a legal science (*intellectus*) that takes them as an independent object (*res*). They are constructions of the science itself (using 'science' in the sense of a rationalising discipline capable in theory of explaining and predicting). This is not to say that facts are completely 'fictional' in the sense of having no connection with the external world. Events in the external world stimulate the construction of a legal-fact model and such a model can thus be said to be a reaction to an external event. But this present enquiry has shown that it is not the external events which act as the object of legal science, but the model constructed by legal science. Law uses, to borrow a notion from a leading epistemologist of science, 'virtual facts'.[3]

These 'virtual facts' are constructed out of three fundamental institutions that were first developed by generations of Roman jurists. These are the institutions of *persona, res* and *actio*. These institutions, it must be stressed at once, are not adequate in themselves to represent a given factual situation. They act as the three main structural elements or anchorage points in a model where it is the relationships between these elements that give expression to the structural and spatial nature of the factual image. Property problems are thus represented through the fundamental structural relationship between person and thing, while contractual situations stress the bond between two *personae*. More detail is provided by a range of seemingly, and equally, descriptive notions such as interest, damage, fault, enrichment, promise or agreement, expectation, causation and so on. In turn, these descriptive notions are integrated within normative propositions which have the effect of turning the whole structure into one capable of producing a normative situation. For example, the juxtaposition of fault, damage and cause within a model involving two persons and perhaps a thing can give rise to a normative model whereby one person is obliged to pay money to another. For any 'human act whatever which causes damage to another obliges the person by whose fault it occurred to make reparation' (article 1382 of the *Code civil*). None of these descriptive notions on its own would trigger a normative response under this article. It is only when two persons, damage, fault and causation are united in the model that the situation becomes normative. In other words, the normative dimension results from the structural interrelationship between these descriptive notions.

This example in itself illustrates that merely learning article 1382 as a linguistic proposition is to have only a partial knowledge of law. Of course, knowledge of such a proposition is of fundamental importance. Yet how it actually relates to a factual situation, and how such a factual situation is constructed so as to conform to the proposition, is equally important. This factual construction is not, however, just a matter of legal institutions. The construction of the institutional model itself – its symmetry or pattern – is of importance. For example, an accident in a munitions factory or even in a supermarket can be constructed in terms of a relationship between two persons, the victim and the owner or controller of the factory or supermarket. In English law this approach would give rise to a pattern of an 'occupier's' normative relationship (duty) with a 'visitor'; and such a pattern would of itself go far in suggesting that the occupier should be liable only if he is at fault.[4] After all, one does not make 'occupiers' everyday accident risk bearers.[5] However, another quite different institutional pattern is possible. The accident might be seen in respect of a relationship between factory or supermarket owner (*persona*) and, say, shell or exploding bottle of lemonade (*res*) which causes the victim's injury. This is quite a different pattern, in that it does suggest a situation where the controller of the thing, particularly a dangerous thing like a piece of military ordnance, ought to carry the risk of its doing damage. For it is a risk activity that is beyond the normal, everyday kind.[6] Indeed, legal systems have long made the owner of dangerous animals liable without fault for the damage they do to others.[7] It is not so much the rules that will determine the solution to the accident case, but the choice of pattern or image.

Other epistemological structures and factors have just as important a role to play. Thus the dichotomy between a nominalist and a realist or holist view of a social reality can be of fundamental importance when it comes to constructing a set of 'virtual facts'. Was the sinking of the *Titantic* a single catastrophic event resulting in a mass of simultaneous deaths? Or was it a whole set of individualistic facts where passengers died at different time intervals? Such a question, as we have seen, was vital when it came to deciding whether property under a will should go to one person or to another.[8] Similarly, in the case involving the resale of a second-hand car, the result was determined by the way the judges viewed the *res*.[9] Was a second-hand car unique as a thing or was it simply indistinguishable from all other cars of the same model and type? If it were unique, any profit or loss on resale would attach to the car itself; if it was not unique, the profit or loss could be calculated in terms of the lost contract (rather than the car).

The structural (isomorphic) pattern produced by an analogy is another important factor in fact construction. Take, for example, mistake in contract. In one English case, a company contracted with two of its directors whereby the two directors agreed to retire in return for a considerable sum of money. Having paid the money, the company discovered grounds upon which they could have forced the directors to resign for misconduct. The jury decided that the two directors had not been dishonest in failing to tell the company of their misconduct and so the question arose as to whether the contract could, alternatively, be set aside for mistake. Now, if one looks at the various rules regarding mistake as set out in a code provision, they are usually so abstract that at first sight they would seem to cover these facts. Thus the UNIDROIT code lays down that mistake 'is an erroneous assumption relating to facts or to law existing when the contract was concluded' (art. 3.4).

In such a situation a party 'may only avoid the contract for mistake if, when the contract was concluded, the mistake was of such importance that a reasonable person in the same situation as the party in error would only have contracted the contract on materially different terms or would not have contracted at all if the true state of affairs had been known' (art. 3.5(1)). The reasonable company would certainly have not contracted with the two directors if it had known the true state of affairs. Yet what if an analogy is drawn with the purchase of a bottle of wine in shop A for £20: can the purchaser demand the setting aside of the contract of sale if he discovers that he could have bought exactly the same bottle of wine for £3 in shop B? It is clear that such a sale cannot be set aside and if this is used as an analogy for the case of the two directors, it would seem, as indeed a majority of the House of Lords decided, that the company got what it bargained for.[10] It is, therefore, not so much abstract rules that decide these kinds of cases. It is the dominant analogy.

Methodological holism, methodological individualism and structural analogies have in their turn been rationalised into schemes of intelligibility by the French social science epistemologist J.-M. Berthelot. What is so important about these schemes for the jurist is that they are applicable, as this enquiry has shown, as much to law as to social science in general. This implies that there is at this level of analysis nothing special about legal reasoning and legal method. It is simply a formalised version of social science methodology.[11] Legal epistemology merges, in other words, into social science epistemology. Now, this does not mean that the whole idea of legal methods and legal epistemology is a fiction; at the level of legal institutions, as we have seen, law can claim a certain 'scientific' autonomy. However, what Berthelot's schemes show is that legal theory itself is founded upon shifting foundations. Dworkin's identification of law with the hermeneutical scheme cannot claim epistemological exclusivity, since a philosophy of law founded on, say, the dialectical or causal schemes would appear, if Berthelot is correct, to be equally valid in knowledge terms. In truth, the position is more complex because a legal philosopher like Dworkin is not employing exclusively the hermeneutical scheme; he also employs other schemes such as the actional when he expresses adjudication through the superhuman judge Hercules.[12] Nevertheless, when legal theory is approached from Berthelot's social science epistemological model, it shows just how theories can be constructed and, of course, deconstructed.

Berthelot's categories represent what could be said to be a synchronic approach to epistemology: that is to say, an approach that is not historically located. However, this present work has also made use of the history of legal thought; it has, in other words, approached legal knowledge from a diachronic perspective. In particular, it has adopted the scheme proposed by Robert Blanché for explaining the development of the sciences. Blanché observed that all the sciences passed through four stages: starting with the descriptive, a science would then pass through an inductive and a deductive stage respectively, to arrive, finally, at an axiomatic stage.[13] In legal science, this final stage is represented by the great European codes. However, this enquiry has also gone beyond Blanché in suggesting that law has moved beyond the axiomatic stage towards a fifth, post-axiomatic stage. This stage sees law as a matter of both symbolic and non-symbolic knowledge. Such a fifth stage is particularly valuable for the comparatist working in the area of European harmonisation (whether positively or negatively) since it offers a model in which contemporary problems can be analysed and dissected.

For example, this post-axiomatic stage could be seen as having a negative effect upon European legal thought, in that it could intensify the cleavages between legal systems, not just in terms of norms applicable but, more importantly, in the fragmentation of methodology and theory. Teubner, for example, has raised doubts about the viability of transplanting some civilian concepts into the common law on the ground that the economic and cultural differences are too great.[14] On the other hand, one could abandon the two-dimensional structure used in the 'axiomatic' stage of legal science and adopt a multidimensional model. In other words, one could abandon the two-dimensional code as a knowledge structure and embrace a more complex pattern capable of giving expression to the kind of knowledge processes that have been investigated in this present work. The idea of a three- or even four-dimensional model might appear novel, yet such a model has been vital for understanding the role of time with regard to real property rights in English law. Estates, trusts and possession function in more complex structures than the ones to be found in the codes.[15]

Is such a model a recipe for instability in the European legal tradition or a new stability? It is, evidently, in relation to this question that the contributions of comparatists such as Legrand,[16] Joerges[17] and Teubner become particularly relevant. These writers argue that legal harmonisation cannot be seen in simplistic terms and they warn that to ignore cultural and economic dimensions could be fatal to European integration. They are in their own ways warning that the traditional epistemological models are inadequate for the future. They are models which have outlived their usefulness. This present work, equally, contributes to this line of thinking, without, for all that, necessarily being hostile to European legal integration.

However, by way of conclusion, and in order to aid the movement from the 'axiomatic' to the 'post-axiomatic', it might be useful to draw an analogy with science, in particular with the science of time. The traditional view of time is that of an arrow in which time flies or flows in a linear and uniform way. Such a model is most valuable in the way it identifies with a commonsense view of the world in which uniformity of movement seems a natural law. However, difficulties soon emerge when it comes to representing space and time in terms of mathematical models. Einstein thus refused to see time in this unidimensional[18] way and, instead, proposed that time should be appreciated through a more complex model where past, present and future did not exist in linear form. They existed in an interrelated model where the past and future might well coexist with the present but in different dimensions. Thus the past might be rediscovered at some point in the future.[19] Of course, drawing an analogy between law and time could be most dangerous, since the history of science is littered with transformations that ultimately proved illegitimate.[20] Nevertheless, the analogy is most useful as a symbol, if not as a conceptual device,[21] to provoke a change in the symmetry of knowledge representation. The new symmetry allows the comparative lawyer to rethink the various European models of law within a single structure that is designed, not to simplify complexity, but to embrace it.

The idea that complex cases involving, say, property and commercial relations – together with the legal 'facts' – can be reduced to a single 'flat' model is far too simplistic for a Europe engaged in reorienting legal systems at a range of different levels. Indeed, it is not just simplistic, it is brittle, and could break under the strain, not just of the give-and-take between the various legal traditions and cultures, but also of a failure to appreciate that legal knowledge stretches beyond symbolic knowledge. What is encouraging, however, is, as this enquiry confirms, that there exists in Europe a rich scientific tradition which is more than adequate to provide the models for any new challenges that political, social and economic events might present. The only obstacle is the lawyer him- or herself. Are lawyers prepared to look at their own rich history in a context that reaches beyond, not just national and geographical boundaries, but intellectual ones as well? Are lawyers – or at least the legal theorists who end up shaping our view of legal knowledge – prepared to accept, for example, that philosophers of science, or social sciences, might have something to say to them? Are they prepared to look beyond rules and hermeneutics and to ask just why AI has not been able to model their minds? This present enquiry, whether or not its conclusions and observations turn out in the end to be useful or valid, has at least tried to do just that.

Notes

1 Delacour (1995, pp. 34–42). And see, generally, Bechtel and Abrahamsen (1991).

2 Delacour (1995, p. 36).

3 Granger (1995, p. 49).

4 *Read* v. *J Lyons & Co* [1947] AC 156; Occupiers' Liability Act 1957, s. 2.

5 *Wells* v. *Cooper* [1958] 2 QB 265.
6 CC, art. 1384.
7 See, for example, Animals Act 1971, s. 2.
8 *Re Rowland* [1963] Ch 1.
9 *Lazenby Garages Ltd* v. *Wright* [1976] 1 WLR 459.
10 *Bell* v. *Lever Brothers* [1932] AC 161.
11 On which see, generally, Berthelot (2001c).
12 See, for example, Dworkin (1986, pp. 238–40).
13 Blanché (1983, p. 65).
14 Teubner (1998).
15 Lawson and Rudden (1982, p. 88).
16 Legrand (1996b, 1997a).
17 Joerges (1998).
18 Piettre (1994, p. 37).
19 Ibid., pp. 70–72.
20 Virieux-Reymond (1972, pp. 71–2).
21 For the difference, see Leroux and Marciano (1998, p. 33).

Bibliography

ACLEC Report (1996), *The Lord Chancellor's Advisory Committee on Legal Education and Conduct: First Report on Legal Education and Training* (April).

Acot, P. (1999), *L'histoire des sciences* (Presses Universitaires de France).

Alder, J. (1993), 'Hunting the Chimera – The End of O'Reilly v Mackman?', 13 *Legal Studies*, 183.

Alexy, R. (1989), *A Theory of Legal Argumentation*, trans. R. Adler and N. MacCormick (Oxford University Press).

Allison, J.W.F. (1996), *A Continental Distinction in the Common Law: A Historical and Comparative Perspective on English Public Law* (Oxford University Press).

Amselek, P. (1995a), 'L'interprétation à tort et à travers', in Amselek (ed.), 11.

Amselek, P. (ed.) (1995b), *Interprétation en droit* (Bruylant).

Araj, H. (1996), 'L'étude du raisonnement analogique par synthèse interdisciplinaire', in Thomasset and Bourcier (eds), 169.

Arnaud, A.-J. (1991), *Pour une pensée juridique européenne* (Presses Universitaires de France).

Astolfi, J.-P. and Develay, M. (1996), *La didactique des sciences*, 4th edn (Presses Universitaires de France).

Atias, C. (1985), *Épistémologie juridique* (Presses Universitaires de France).

Atias, C. (1987), *Théorie contre arbitraire* (Presses Universitaires de France).

Atias, C. (1991), *Science des légistes, savoir des juristes* (Presses Universitaires d'Aix-Marseille).

Atias, C. (1994), *Épistémologie du droit* (Presses Universitaires de France).

Atiyah, P. (1979), *The Rise and Fall of Freedom of Contract* (Oxford University Press).

Atiyah, P. and Summers, R. (1987), *Form and Substance in Anglo-American Law* (Oxford University Press).

Bachelard, G. (1934), *Le nouvel esprit scientifique* (Alcan; 17th edn, Presses Universitaires de France, 1987).

Bachelard, G. (1938), *La formation de l'esprit scientifique* (J. Vrin; reprint J. Vrin, 1989).
Bachelard, G. (1949), *Le rationalisme appliqué* (Presses Universitaires de France).
Baker, J. (1990), *An Introduction to English Legal History*, 3rd edn (Butterworths).
Baker, J. (1999), 'The Law Merchant as a Source of English Law', in Swadling and Jones (eds), 79.
Ball, T., Farr, J. and Hanson, R. (eds) (1989), *Political Innovation and Conceptual Change* (Cambridge University Press).
Barbiéri, J.-J. (1995), *La procédure civile* (Presses Universitaires de France).
Barker, E. (1928), *Political Thought in England 1848–1914*, 2nd edn (Oxford University Press; reprint 1950).
Barreau, H. (1998), *L'épistémologie*, 4th edn (Presses Universitaires de France).
Basedow, J. (1998), 'The Renascence of Uniform Law: European Contract Law and its Components', 18 *Legal Studies*, 121.
Batiffol, H. (1987), *La philosophie du droit*, 7th edn (Presses Universitaires de France).
Beatson, J. (1993), 'Innovations in Contract', The Society of Public Teachers of Law Seminar Paper (16 October).
Bechtel, W. and Abrahamsen, A. (1991), *Connectionism and the Mind* (Basil Blackwell).
Bell, J. (1983), *Policy Arguments in Judicial Decisions* (Oxford University Press).
Bell, J. (1986), 'The Acceptability of Legal Arguments', in MacCormick and Birks (eds), 45.
Bell, J. (1992), *French Constitutional Law* (Oxford University Press).
Bell, J. (1994), 'Comparative Law and Legal Theory', in Krawietz, MacCormick and von Wright (eds), 19.
Bell, J. (1995a), Book review of Samuel (1994), 15 *Legal Studies*, 461.
Bell, J. (1995b), 'English Law and French Law – Not So Different?', 48 *Current Legal Problems*, 63.
Bell, J. (2001), *French Legal Cultures* (Butterworths).
Bell, J., Boyron, S. and Whittaker, S. (1998), *Principles of French Law* (Oxford University Press).
Bengoetxea, J. (1993), *The Legal Reasoning of the European Court of Justice* (Oxford University Press).
Bennun, M. (ed.) (1991a), *Computers, Artificial Intelligence and the Law* (Ellis Horwood).
Bennun, M. (1991b), 'Introduction' to Bennun (ed.).
Bennun, M. (1991c), 'Computerizing Criminal Law: Some Basic Problems', in Bennun (ed.), 60.
Bergel, J.-L. (1999), *Théorie générale du droit*, 3rd edn (Dalloz).

Bergel, J.-L. (2001), *Méthodologie juridique* (Presses Universitaires de France).
Berman, D. and Hafner, C. (1991), 'Artificial Intelligence and Law: Opportunities and Challenges' (Tutorial notes presented at the Third International Conference on Artificial Intelligence and Law, Oxford, June).
Berman, H. (1983), *Law and Revolution: The Formation of the Western Legal Tradition* (Harvard University Press).
Berthelot, J.-M. (1990), *L'intelligence du social* (Presses Universitaires de France).
Berthelot, J.-M. (1996), *Les vertus de l'incertitude* (Presses Universitaires de France).
Berthelot, J.-M. (2001a), 'Les sciences du social', in Berthelot (ed.), 203.
Berthelot, J.-M. (2001b), 'Programmes, paradigmes, disciplines: pluralité et unité des sciences sociales', in Berthelot (ed.), 457.
Berthelot, J.-M. (ed.) (2001c), *Épistémologie des sciences sociales* (Presses Universitaires de France).
Besnier, J.-M. (1996), *Les théories de la connaissance* (Flammarion).
Biondi, B. (1972), *Istituzioni di diritto romano*, 4th edn (Giuffrè).
Birks, P. (1985), 'Unjust Enrichment – A Reply to Mr Hedley', 5 *Legal Studies*, 67.
Birks, P. (1989), *An Introduction to the Law of Restitution*, revised edn (Oxford University Press).
Birks, P. (ed.) (1992), *Examining the Law Syllabus: The Core* (Oxford University Press).
Birks, P. (ed.) (1993), *Examining the Law Syllabus: Beyond the Core* (Oxford University Press).
Birks, P. (1994a), 'Adjudication and Interpretation in the Common Law: A Century of Change', 14 *Legal Studies*, 156.
Birks, P. (ed.) (1994b), *Reviewing Legal Education* (Oxford University Press).
Birks, P. (ed.) (1996a), *Pressing Problems in the Law: Volume 2: What Are Law Schools For?* (Oxford University Press).
Birks, P. (1996b), 'Equity in the Modern Law: An Exercise in Taxonomy', 26 *University of Western Australia Law Review*, 1.
Birks, P. (1996c), 'Harassment and Hubris: The Right to an Equality of Respect' (Faculty of Law, University College Dublin).
Birks, P (ed.) (1997a), *The Classification of Obligations* (Oxford University Press).
Birks, P. (1997b), 'Definition and Division: A Meditation on *Institutes* 3.13', in Birks (ed.), 1.
Birks, P. and McLeod, G. (1987), *Justinian's Institutes* (Duckworth).
Black, A. (1988), 'The Individual and Society', in Burns (ed.), 588.
Blanché, R. (1973a), *Le raisonnement* (Presses Universitaires de France).

Blanché, R. (1973b), *La science actuelle et le rationalisme*, 2nd edn (Presses Universitaires de France).
Blanché, R. (1975), *L'induction scientifique et les lois naturelles* (Presses Universitaires de France).
Blanché, R. (1980), *L'axiomatique*, 6th edn (Presses Universitaires de France).
Blanché, R. (1983), *L'épistémologie*, 3rd edn (Presses Universitaires de France).
Boden, M.A. (ed.) (1990), *The Philosophy of Artificial Intelligence* (Oxford University Press).
Boll, M. and Reinhart, J. (1980), *Histoire de la logique*, 8th edn (Presses Universitaires de France).
Bonardel, F. (1996), *L'irrationnel* (Presses Universitaires de France).
Borkowski, A. (1997), *Textbook on Roman Law*, 2nd edn (Blackstone).
Bouchon-Meunier, B. and Nguyen, H.T. (1996), *Les incertitudes dans les systèmes intelligents* (Presses Universitaires de France).
Bourcier, D. and Mackay, P. (eds) (1992), *Lire le droit: langue, texte, cognition* (Librairie Générale de Droit et de Jurisprudence).
Brachman, R. and Levesque, H. (eds) (1985), *Readings in Knowledge Representation* (Morgan Kaufmann Publishers).
Bradney, A. (1998), 'Law as a Parasitic Discipline', 25 *Journal of Law and Society*, 71.
Buckland, W.W. (1963), *A Text-book of Roman Law*, 3rd edn, revised by P. Stein (Cambridge University Press).
Bunge, M. (1983), *Épistémologie*, trans. H. Donadieu (Maloine).
Burns, J. (ed.) (1988), *The Cambridge History of Medieval Political Thought c.350–c.1450* (Cambridge University Press).
Burns, J. (ed.) (1991), *The Cambridge History of Political Thought 1450–1700* (Cambridge University Press).
Busino, G. (1998), *Sociologie des sciences et des techniques* (Presses Universitaires de France).
Cairns, J. (1984), 'Blackstone, An English Institutist: Legal Literature and the Rise of the Nation State', 4 *Oxford Journal of Legal Studies*, 318.
Calvo García, Manuel (1994), *Los fundamentos del método jurídico: una revisión crítica* (Tecnos).
Cane, P. (1996), *Tort Law and Economic Interests*, 2nd edn (Oxford University Press).
Cane, P. (1997), *The Anatomy of Tort Law* (Hart Publishing).
Cane, P. (1999), 'Fault and Strict Liability for Harm in Tort Law', in Swadling and Jones (eds), 171.
Cane, P. (2000), '*Mens Rea* in Tort Law', 20 *Oxford Journal of Legal Studies*, 533.
Cane, P. and Stapleton, J. (eds) (1998), *The Law of Obligations: Essays in Celebration of John Fleming* (Oxford University Press).

Canning, J. (1987), *The Political Thought of Baldus de Ubaldis* (Cambridge University Press).
Cantin Cumyn, M. (ed.) (1999), *La fiducie face au trust dans les rapports d'affaires* (*Trust vs Fiducie in a business context*) (Bruylant).
Cappelletti, M. (1989), *The Judicial Process in Comparative Perspective* (Oxford University Press).
Cappelletti, M. and Garth, B. (1986), 'Introduction – Policies, Trends and Ideas in Civil Procedure', *International Encyclopedia of Comparative Law*, vol. XVI, ch. 1 (JCB Mohr).
Carbasse, J.-M. (1990), *Introduction historique au droit pénal* (Presses Universitaires de France).
Carbasse, J.-M. (1998), *Introduction historique au droit* (Presses Universitaires de France).
Certoma, G.L. (1985), *The Italian Legal System* (Butterworths).
Chevrier, G. (1952), 'Remarques sur l'introduction et les vicissitudes de la distinction du "jus privatum" et du "jus publicum" dans les œuvres des anciens juristes français', *Archives de philosophie du droit*, 5.
Cocks, R. (1988), *Sir Henry Maine: A Study in Victorian Jurisprudence* (Cambridge University Press).
Cohen, F. (1935), 'Transcendental Nonsense and the Functional Approach', *Columbia Law Review*, 809.
Collins, H. (1997), 'Legal Classifications as the Production of Knowledge Systems', in Birks (ed.), 57.
Cotterrell, R. (1983), 'The Sociological Concept of Law', 10 *Journal of Law and Society*, 241.
Cotterrell, R. (1992), *The Sociology of Law: An Introduction*, 2nd edn (Butterworths).
Cross, R. and Harris, J. (1991), *Precedent in English Law*, 4th edn (Oxford University Press).
Cummings, R. and Pollock, J. (eds) (1991), *Philosophy and AI: Essays at the Interface* (MIT Press).
Dagger, R. (1989), 'Rights', in Ball et al. (eds), 292.
David, R. (1981), 'Sources of Law', *International Encyclopedia of Comparative Law*, vol. II, ch. 3 (JCB Mohr).
Davis, R. and Buchanan, B. (1985), 'Meta-Level Knowledge: Overview and Applications', in Brachman and Levesque (eds), 389.
Degos, J.-G. (1998), *Histoire de la comptabilité* (Presses Universitaires de France).
Delacour, J. (1995), *Le cerveau et l'esprit* (Presses Universitaires de France).
De Libera, A. (1989), *La philosophie médiévale* (Presses Universitaires de France).
Delmas-Marty, M. and Coste, J.-F. (1992), 'L'imprécis et l'incertain:

Esquisse d'une recherche sur logiques et droit', in Bourcier and Mackay (eds), 109.
D'Entrèves, A. (1970), *Natural Law*, 2nd edn (Hutchinson).
Des Graviers, J. (1981), *Le droit canonique* (Presses Universitaires de France).
De Ste-Croix, G. (1981), *The Class Struggle in the Ancient Greek World* (Duckworth).
De Witte, B. (1996), 'The Convergence Debate', 3 *Maastricht Journal of European and Comparative Law*, 105.
De Witte, B. and Forder, C. (eds) (1992), *The Common Law of Europe and the Future of Legal Education* (Kluwer).
De Zulueta, F. (1946), *The Institutes of Gaius: Part I* (Oxford University Press).
De Zulueta, F. and Stein, P. (1990), *The Teaching of Roman Law in England Around 1200* (Selden Society).
Dreyfus, H. (1985), 'From Micro-Worlds to Knowledge Representation: AI at an Impasse', in Brachman and Levesque (eds), 71.
Dreyfus, H. (1992), *What Computers Still Can't Do* (MIT Press).
Dubouchet, P. (1990), *Sémiotique juridique: introduction à une science du droit* (Presses Universitaires de France).
Dubouchet, P. (1991), *La pensée juridique avant et après le code civil*, 2nd edn (L'Hermès).
Duff, P. (1938), *Personality in Roman Private Law* (Cambridge University Press).
Duncanson, I. and Samuel, G. (1980), *Jurisprudence in a Nutshell* (Sweet & Maxwell).
Durand, D. (1992), *La systémique*, 5th edn (Presses Universitaires de France).
Durgnat, R. (1966), *Eros in the Cinema* (Calder & Boyars).
Durgnat, R. (1974), *The Strange Case of Alfred Hitchcock* (Faber & Faber).
Duxbury, N. (1997), *Patterns of American Jurisprudence* (Oxford University Press).
Dworkin, R. (1977), *Taking Rights Seriously* (Duckworth).
Dworkin, R. (1985), *A Matter of Principle* (Oxford University Press).
Dworkin, R. (1986), *Law's Empire* (Fontana).
Ebbesen, S. (1982), 'Ancient Scholastic Logic as the Source of Medieval Scholastic Logic', in Kretzmann et al. (eds), 101.
Edelman, B. (1997), 'La dignité de la personne humaine, un concept nouveau', *Recueil Dalloz*, 23 (12 juin), *Chroniques*, 185.
Ellul, J. (1982a), *Histoire des institutions: 3 – Le Moyen Age*, 9th edn (Presses Universitaires de France).
Ellul, J. (1982b), *Histoire des institutions: 5 – Le XIXe siècle*, 8th edn (Presses Universitaires de France).

Ellul, J. (1984), *Histoire des institutions: 1–2 – L'Antiquité*, 6th edn (Presses Universitaires de France).
Ellul, J. (1987), *Histoire des institutions: 4 – Le XVIe–XVIIIe siècle*, 9th edn (Presses Universitaires de France).
Farber, D.A. (1996), 'The Hermeneutic Tourist: Statutory Interpretation in Comparative Perspective', 81 *Cornell Law Review*, 513.
Fassò, G. (1976), *Histoire de la philosophie du droit: XIXe et XXe siècles*, trans. C. Rouffet (Librairie Générale de Droit et de Jurisprudence).
Favoreu, L. (1996), *Les cours constitutionnelles*, 3rd edn (Presses Universitaires de France).
Finnis, J. (1980), *Natural Law and Natural Rights* (Oxford University Press).
Foucault, M. (1966), *Les mots et les choses* (Gallimard).
Frank, J. (1932), 'Mr Justice Holmes and Non-Euclidean Legal Thinking', 17 *Cornell Law Quarterly*, 568.
Frank, J. (1949), *Law and the Modern Mind* (Stevens & Sons).
Frankenberg, G. (1985), 'Critical Comparisons: Re-thinking Comparative Law', 26 *Harvard International Law Journal*, 411.
Friedmann, W. (1972), *Law in a Changing Society*, 2nd edn (Penguin).
Gaius, *Institutiones*; see De Zulueta (1946), Gordon and Robinson (1988), Muirhead (1895).
Garde, R. (1841), *An Analysis of the First Principles, or Elementary Rules, of Pleading*, 2nd edn (Maxwell).
Garnham, A. (1991), *The Mind in Action: A Personal View of Cognitive Science* (Routledge).
Gaudemet, J. (1986), 'Tentatives de systématisation du droit à Rome', in Terré and Sève (eds), 11.
Gazzaniga, J.-L. (1992), *Introduction historique au droit des obligations* (Presses Universitaires de France).
Geertz, C. (1993), *Local Knowledge* (Fontana).
Gellner, E. (1992), *Postmodernism, Reason and Religion* (Routledge).
Ghestin, J. (1991), 'Note, *sub* Ass. plén., 29 mars 1991', JCP.1991.II.21673.
Ghestin, J. and Goubeaux, G. (1990), *Traité de droit civil: introduction générale*, 3rd edn (Librairie Générale de Droit et de Jurisprudence).
Ginossar, S. (1960), *Droit réel, propriété et créance* (Librairie Générale de Droit et de Jurisprudence).
Glenn, P. (1992), 'Le trust et le jus commune', in Legrand (ed.), 87.
Goffi, J.-Y. (1988), *La philosophie de la technique* (Presses Universitaires de France).
Goode, R. (1988), 'The Codification of Commercial Law', 14 *Monash University Law Review*, 135.
Goodrich, P. (1986), *Reading the Law* (Basil Blackwell).
Goodrich, P. (1990), *Languages of Law: From Logics of Memory to Nomadic Masks* (Weidenfeld & Nicolson).

Gordley, J. (1991), *The Philosophical Origins of Modern Contract Doctrine* (Oxford University Press).
Gordley, J. (1997), 'Contract in Pre-Commercial Societies and in Western History', *International Encyclopedia of Comparative Law*, vol. VII, ch. 2 (JCB Mohr).
Gordon, W. and Robinson, O. (1988), *The Institutes of Gaius* (Duckworth).
Goubeaux, G. (1984), 'Personnalité morale, droit des personnes et droit des biens', *Études Roblot* (Librairie Générale de Droit et de Jurisprudence), 199.
Gough, J. (1957), *The Social Contract*, 2nd edn (Oxford University Press).
Granger, G.-G. (1993), *La raison*, 10th edn (Presses Universitaires de France).
Granger, G.-G. (1995), *La science et les sciences*, 2nd edn (Presses Universitaires de France).
Graubard, S. (ed.) (1988), *The Artificial Intelligence Debate: False Starts, Real Foundations* (MIT Press).
Graveson, R. (1953), *Status in the Common Law* (Athlone).
Gray, K. and Gray, S. (2001), *Elements of Land Law*, 3rd edn (Butterworths).
Griffith, J. (1997), *The Politics of the Judiciary*, 5th edn (Fontana).
Grzegorczyk, C. (1986), 'Évaluation critique du paradigme systémique dans la science du droit', in Terré and Sève (eds), 281.
Guest, A. (ed.) (1961a), *Oxford Essays in Jurisprudence* (Oxford University Press).
Guest, A. (1961b), 'Logic in the Law', in Guest (ed.), 176.
Halpérin, J.-L. (1996), *Histoire du droit privé français depuis 1804* (Presses Universitaires de France).
Hart, H. (1961), *The Concept of Law* (Oxford University Press).
Haton, J.-P. and Haton, M.-C. (1989), *L'intelligence artificielle* (Presses Universitaires de France).
Hayes, P. (1985), 'Some Problems and Non-Problems in Representation Theory', in Brachman and Levesque (eds), 3.
Hedley, S. (1985), 'Unjust Enrichment as the Basis of Restitution – An Overworked Concept', 5 *Legal Studies*, 56.
Hedley, S. (1988), 'Contract, Tort and Restitution; or, On Cutting the Legal System Down to Size', 8 *Legal Studies*, 137.
Hedley, S. (1999), 'How has the Common Law Survived the 20th Century?', 50 *Northern Ireland Legal Quarterly*, 283.
Herbert, A.P. (1935), *Uncommon Law* (Methuen; reprint 1977).
Hilaire, J. (1986), *Introduction historique au droit commercial* (Presses Universitaires de France).
Hofstadter, D. (1980), *Gödel, Escher, Bach: An Eternal Golden Braid* (Penguin).

Hohfeld, W. (1919), *Fundamental Legal Conceptions* (Yale University Press; reprint, 1966).
Holland, T.E. (1924), *The Elements of Jurisprudence*, 13th edn (Oxford University Press).
Holmes, O.W. (1897), 'The Path of the Law', 10 *Harvard Law Review*, 457.
Honoré, A. (1961), 'Ownership', in Guest (ed.), 107.
Honoré, A. (1962), *Gaius* (Oxford University Press).
Howarth, D. (1995), *Textbook on Tort* (Butterworths).
Ibbetson, D. (1999), *A Historical Introduction to the Law of Obligations* (Oxford University Press).
Imbert, J. (1996), *Histoire du droit privé*, 8th edn (Presses Universitaires de France).
Ionescu, O. (1978), *La notion de droit subjectif dans le droit privé* (Bruylant).
Ivainer, T. (1988), *L'interprétation des faits en droit* (Librairie Générale de Droit et de Jurisprudence).
Izorche, M.-L. (2001), *Le raisonnement juridique* (Presses Universitaires de France).
Jackson, B. (1985), *Semiotics and Legal Theory* (Routledge & Kegan Paul).
Jackson, P. and Wilde, D. (eds) (1999), *Property Law: Current Issues and Debates* (Ashgate).
Jacob, J. (1987), *The Fabric of English Civil Justice* (Stevens).
Jacquemin, A. and Schrans, G. (1982), *Le droit économique*, 3rd edn (Presses Universitaires de France).
Jagtenberg, R., Orücü, E. and de Roo, A.J. (eds) (1995), *Transfrontier Mobility of Law* (Kluwer).
Jeauneau, É. (1975), *La philosophie médiévale*, 3rd edn (Presses Universitaires de France).
Joerges, C. (1998), 'European Challenges to Private Law: On False Dichotomies, True Conflicts and the Need for a Constitutional Perspective', 18 *Legal Studies*, 121.
Jolowicz, H. (1957), *Roman Foundations of Modern Law* (Oxford University Press).
Jolowicz, H. (1963), *Lectures on Jurisprudence* (Athlone).
Jolowicz, J. (1968), 'Liability for Accidents', *Cambridge Law Journal*, 50.
Jolowicz, J. (1983), 'Protection of Diffuse, Fragmented and Collective Interests in Civil Litigation: English Law', *Cambridge Law Journal*, 222.
Jolowicz, J. (1985), 'Public Interest and Private Damage', *Cambridge Law Journal*, 370.
Jolowicz, J. (1992), 'Les appels civils en Angleterre et en Pays de Galles', *Revue internationale de droit comparé*, 355.
Jones, J. (1940), *Historical Introduction to the Theory of Law* (Oxford University Press).

Jones, P.A. (1993), 'Skills Teaching in Legal Education – the Legal Practice Course and Beyond', in Birks (ed.), 97.
Justinian, *Corpus Iuris Civilis,* see Mommsen and Krueger (1886), Mommsen et al. (1985), Kolbert (1979).
Justinian, *Digest of Roman Law,* see Kolbert (1979).
Justinian, *Institutiones,* see Mommsen and Kreuger (1886), Birks and McLeod (1987).
Kahn-Freund, O. (1949), 'Introduction', in K. Renner (ed.).
Kahn-Freund, O. (1996), 'Comparative Law as an Academic Subject', 82 *Law Quarterly Review,* 40.
Kelley, D. (1970), *Foundations of Modern Historical Scholarship* (Columbia University Press).
Kelley, D. (1981), *The Beginning of Ideology* (Cambridge University Press).
Kelley, D. (1984), *Historians and the Law in Postrevolutionary France* (Princeton University Press).
Kelley, D. (1990), *The Human Measure: Social Thought in the Western Legal Tradition* (Harvard University Press).
Kelly, J. (1992), *A Short History of Western Legal Theory* (Oxford Univerity Press).
Kelsen, H. (1967), *The Pure Theory of Law,* trans. M. Knight (University of California Press).
Kelsen, H. (1990), 'On the Theory of Interpretation', trans. B. Paulson and S. Paulson, 10 *Legal Studies,* 127.
Kelsen, H. (1997), *Introduction to the Problems of Legal Theory,* trans. B.L. Paulson and S.L. Paulson (Oxford University Press).
Knowles, D. (1962), *The Evolution of Medieval Thought* (Longman).
Kolbert, C. (1979), *Justinian: The Digest of Roman Law* (Penguin).
Koubi, G. (1992), 'La création du droit: image et imaginaire', in Bourcier and Mackay (eds), 85.
Kowalski, A. (1991), 'Case-Based Reasoning and the Deep Structure Approach to Knowledge Representation', *Proceedings,* 21.
Krawietz, W., MacCormick, N. and von Wright, G.H. (eds) (1994), *Prescriptive Formality and Normative Rationality in Modern Legal Systems: Festschrift for Robert Summers* (Dunker & Humblot).
Kretzmann, N., Kenny, A. and Pinborg, J. (eds) (1982), *The Cambridge History of Later Medieval Philosophy* (Cambridge University Press).
Kretzmann, N. and Stump, E. (1988), *The Cambridge Translations of Medieval Philosophical Texts* (Cambridge University Press).
Kuhn, T. (1970), *The Structure of Scientific Revolutions,* 2nd edn (University of Chicago Press).
Lameyre, X. (1993), *L'imagerie mentale* (Presses Universitaires de France).
Lasser, M. (1995), 'Judicial (Self-)Portraits: Judicial Discourse in the French Legal System', 104 *Yale Law Journal,* 1325.

Laurent, A. (1993), *Histoire de l'individualisme* (Presses Universitaires de France).
Laurent, A. (1994), *L'individualisme méthodologique* (Presses Universitaires de France).
Laurioux, B. and Moulinier, L. (1998), *Education et cultures dans l'Occident chrétien: du début du douzième au milieu du quinzième siècle* (Messene).
Lawson, F. (1950), *Negligence in the Civil Law* (Oxford University Press).
Lawson, F. (1953), *A Common Lawyer Looks at the Civil Law* (Ann Arbor, University of Michigan Law School).
Lawson, F. (1977), *Many Laws: Selected Essays, Volume I* (North-Holland).
Lawson, F. (1980), *Remedies of English Law*, 2nd edn (Butterworths).
Lawson, F. and Rudden, B. (1982), *The Law of Property*, 2nd edn (Oxford University Press).
Lawson, F. and Rudden, B. (2002), *The Law of Property*, 3rd edn (Oxford University Press).
Leca, A. (2000), *La genèse du droit (Essai d'Introduction historique au droit)* (Presses Universitaires d'Aix-Marseille).
Lefebvre-Teillard, A. (1996), *Introduction historique au droit des personnes et de la famille* (Presses Universitaires de France).
Legohérel, H. (1994), *Histoire du droit public français*, 3rd edn (Presses Universitaires de France).
Legrand, P. (1989), 'A propos de l'obligatoriété de la Loi sur la vente d'objets: observations et comparaisons', 16 *Canadian Business Law Journal*, 34.
Legrand, P. (ed.) (1992), *Common law d'un siècle à l'autre* (Blais).
Legrand, P. (1995a), 'Comparative Legal Studies and Commitment to Theory', 58 *Modern Law Review*, 262.
Legrand, P. (1995b), 'Questions à Rodolfo Sacco', 4 *Revue internationale de droit comparé*, 943.
Legrand, P. (1995c), 'Legal Traditions in Western Europe: The Limits of Commonality', in Jagtenberg et al. (eds), 63.
Legrand, P. (1996a), 'How to Compare Now', 16 *Legal Studies*, 232.
Legrand, P. (1996b), 'European Legal Systems are not Converging', 45 *International and Comparative Law Quarterly*, 52.
Legrand, P. (1996c), 'Comparer', 2 *Revue internationale de droit comparé*, 279.
Legrand, P. (1996d), 'Sens et non-sens d'un code civil européen', 4 *Revue internationale de droit comparé*, 779.
Legrand, P. (1997a), 'Against a European Civil Code', 60 *Modern Law Review*, 44.
Legrand, P. (1997b), 'The Impossibility of "Legal Transplants"', 4 *Maastricht Journal of European and Comparative Law*, 111.

Legrand, P. (1998), 'Are Civilians Educable?', 18 *Legal Studies*, 216.
Legrand, P. (1999a), *Le droit comparé* (Presses Universitaires de France).
Legrand, P. (1999b), *Fragments on Law-as-Culture* (WEJ Tjeenk Willink).
Leith, P. (1993), 'Review of Mital & Johnson (1992)', *Times Higher Educational Supplement*, 5 February, 35.
Le Moigne, J.-L. (1984), *La théorie du système général*, 2nd edn (Presses Universitaires de France).
Le Moigne, J.-L. (1995), *Les épistémologies constructivistes* (Presses Universitaires de France).
Leroux, A. and Marciano, A. (1998), *La philosophie économique* (Presses Universitaires de France).
Lévy, J.-P. (1972), *Histoire de la propriété* (Presses Universitaires de France).
Libcharber, R. (1997), 'L'usufruit des créances existe-t-il?', *Revue trimestrielle de droit civil*, 615.
Linant de Bellefonds, X. (1992), *L'informatique et le droit*, 3rd edn (Presses Universitaires de France).
Llewellyn, K. (1951), *The Bramble Bush* (Oceana).
Lloyd, D. (Lord) and Freeman, M. (1994), *Lloyd's Introduction to Jurisprudence*, 6th edn (Stevens).
Lobban, M. (1991), *The Common Law and English Jurisprudence 1760–1850* (Oxford University Press).
Lucas, J. (1980), *On Justice* (Oxford University Press).
Lugan, J.-C. (1993), *La systémique sociale* (Presses Universitaires de France).
Luhmann, N. (1985), *A Sociological Theory of Law* (Routledge & Kegan Paul).
MacCormick, N. (1978), *Legal Reasoning and Legal Theory* (Oxford University Press).
MacCormick, N. (1982), *Legal Right and Social Democracy* (Oxford University Press).
MacCormick, N. (1988), 'Institutions, Arrangements and Practical Information', 1 *Ratio Juris*, 73.
MacCormick, N. (1992a), 'Further Thoughts on Institutional Facts', *International Journal for the Semiotics of Law*, 3.
MacCormick, N. (1992b), 'Legal Deduction, Legal Predicates and Expert Systems', *International Journal for the Semiotics of Law*, 181.
MacCormick, N. (1992c), 'A Deductivist Rejoinder to a Semiotic Critique', *International Journal for the Semiotics of Law*, 215.
MacCormick, N. (1992d), 'Le raisonnement juridique en common law: la motivation comme justification', in Legrand (ed.), 309.
MacCormick, N. and Birks, P. (eds) (1986), *The Legal Mind: Essays for Tony Honoré* (Oxford University Press).
Maine, H. (Sir) (1890), *Early Law and Custom* (John Murray).

Maitte, B. (1989), 'Symétrie et matière', in *La symétrie aujourd'hui* (Éditions du Seuil).

Malaurie, P. and Aynès, L. (1999), *Cours de droit civil: Tome VI: Les obligations*, 10th edn (Éditions Cujas).

Mansell, W., Meteyard, B. and Thomson, A. (1995), *A Critical Introduction to Law* (Cavendish).

Markesinis, B. (1990), 'Comparative Law – A Subject in Search of an Audience', 53 *Modern Law Review*, 1.

McCarthy, J. (1985), 'Epistemological Problems of Artificial Intelligence', in Brachman and Levesque (eds), 24.

McCarthy, J. (1988), 'Mathematical Logic in Artificial Intelligence', in Graubard (ed.), 297.

McCarty, T. (1991), 'On the Role of Prototypes in Appellate Legal Argument', *Proceedings*, 185.

McCorduck, P. (1988), 'Artificial Intelligence: An Aperçu', in Graubard (ed.), 65.

McLean, J. (ed.) (1999), *Property and the Constitution* (Hart).

Mendegris, R. (1983), *Le commentaire d'arrêt en droit privé*, 2nd edn (Dalloz).

Mestre, J.-L. (1985), *Introduction historique au droit administratif français* (Presses Universitaires de France).

Millon-Delsol, C. (1993), *Le principe de subsidiarité* (Presses Universitaires de France).

Milsom, S. (1981), *Historical Foundations of the Common Law*, 2nd edn (Butterworths).

Mincke, W. (1992), 'Practical and propositional knowledge as the basis of European legal education', in De Witte and Forder (eds), 285.

Mital, V. and Johnson, L. (1992), *Advanced Information Systems for Lawyers* (Chapman & Hall).

Mommsen, T. and Krueger, P. (1886), *Corpus Iuris Civilis* (Weidmann).

Mommsen, T., Krueger, P. and Watson, A. (1985), *The Digest of Justinian*, 4 vols (University of Pennsylvania Press).

Monro, C. (1904), *The Digest of Justinian* (vol. I) (Cambridge University Press).

Moreau, J. (1986), *La responsabilité administrative* (Presses Universitaires de France).

Motulsky, H. (1948), *Principes d'une réalisation méthodique du droit privé* (Sirey; reprint Dalloz, 1991).

Mucchielli, A. (1985), *Les mentalités* (Presses Universitaires de France).

Muirhead, J. (1895), *The Institutes of Gaius and Rules of Ulpian* (T. & T. Clark).

Müller, F. (1996), *Discours de la méthode juridique* (Presses Universitaires de France).

Murphy, W.T. (1997), *The Oldest Social Science? Configurations of Law and Modernity* (Oxford University Press).
Myrdal, G. (1970), *Objectivity in Social Research* (Pantheon Books).
Neville Brown, L. and Bell, J. (1998), *French Administrative Law*, 5th edn (Oxford University Press).
Nicholas, B. (1962), *An Introduction to Roman Law* (Oxford University Press).
Nicholas, B. (1992), *The French Law of Contract*, 2nd edn (Oxford University Press).
Nozick, R. (1974), *Anarchy, State, and Utopia* (Basic Books).
Oléron, P. (1995), *Le raisonnement*, 4th edn (Presses Universitaires de France).
Oléron, P. (1996), *L'argumentation*, 4th edn (Presses Universitaires de France).
Oliver, D. (2000), 'The Human Rights Act and Public Law/Private Law Divides', *European Human Rights Law Review*, 343.
Ost, F. (1990), *Droit et intérêt: volume 2: Entre droit et non-droit: l'intérêt* (Facultés universitaires Saint-Louis, Bruxelles).
Ourliac, P. and De Malafosse, J. (1969), *Histoire du droit privé 1/Les obligations*, 2nd edn (Presses Universitaires de France).
Ourliac, P. and De Malafosse, J. (1971), *Histoire du droit privé 2/Les biens*, 2nd edn (Presses Universitaires de France).
Owen, D.G. (ed.) (1995), *Philosophical Foundations of Tort Law* (Oxford University Press).
Patault, A.-M. (1989), *Introduction historique au droit des biens* (Presses Universitaires de France).
Pédamon, M. (1985), *Le droit allemand* (Presses Universitaires de France).
Perelman, C. (1979), *Logique juridique: Nouvelle rhétorique*, 2nd edn (Dalloz).
Perelman, C. and Olbrechts-Tyteca, L. (1988), *Traité de l'argumentation*, 5th edn, with a Preface by M. Meyer (Éditions de l'Université de Bruxelles).
Perrot, R. (2000), *Institutions judiciaires*, 9th edn (Montchrestien).
Pheby, J. (1988), *Methodology and Economics: A Critical Introduction* (Macmillan).
Piaget, J. (1987), *Le structuralisme*, 9th edn (Presses Universitaires de France).
Piaget, J. (1988), *L'épistémologie génétique*, 4th edn (Presses Universitaires de France).
Picca, G. and Cobert, L. (1986), *La Cour de cassation* (Presses Universitaires de France).
Piettre, B. (1994), *Philosophie et science du temps* (Presses Universitaires de France).
Popper, K. (1972), *Conjectures and Refutations: The Growth of Scientific Knowledge* (Routledge & Kegan Paul).

Posner, R. (1977), 'Gratuitous Promises in Economics and Law', 6 *Journal of Legal Studies*, 411.

Posner, R. (1983), *The Economics of Justice* (Harvard University Press).

Pound, R. (1923), *Interpretations of Legal History* (Cambridge University Press).

Pound, R. (1959), *Jurisprudence: Volume III* (West Publishing).

Pringsheim, F. (1935), 'The Inner Relationship Between English and Roman Law', *Cambridge Law Journal*, 347.

Proceedings (1991), *The Third International Conference on Artificial Intelligence & Law: Proceedings of the Conference* (ACM Press).

Py, B. (1997), *La mort et le droit* (Presses Universitaires de France).

Quillet, J. (1988), 'Community, Counsel and Representation', in Burns (ed.), 520.

Quivy, R. and Van Campenhoudt, L. (1995), *Manuel de recherche en sciences sociales*, 2nd edn (Dunod).

Rawls, J. (1972), *A Theory of Justice* (Oxford University Press).

Rayar, L. (1993), 'Translating Legal Texts: A Methodology' (Conference Paper, Euroforum, April).

Raz, J. (1985), 'The Problem About the Nature of Law', in Lloyd and Freeman (eds), 419.

Redmond, P. and Shears, P. (1993), *General Principles of English Law*, 7th edn (M & E/Pitman).

Renner, K. (ed.) (1949), *The Institutions of Private Law and Their Social Functions*, trans. A. Schwarzschild (Routledge & Kegan Paul; reprint 1976).

Renoux-Zagamé, M.-F. (1987), *Origines théologiques du concept moderne de propriété* (Droz).

Rissland, E. (1990), 'Artificial Intelligence and Law: Stepping Stones to a Model of Legal Reasoning', 99 *Yale Law Journal*, 1957.

Robaye, R. (1991), *Introduction à la logique et à l'argumentation* (Academia-Erasme).

Robinson, O. (1983), 'Public Law and Justinian's Institutes', in Stein and Lewis (eds), 125.

Robinson, O., Fergus, T. and Gordon, W. (1994), *An Introduction to European Legal History*, 2nd edn (Butterworths).

Roland, H. and Boyer, L. (1986), *Adages du droit français* (2 vols), 2nd edn (L'Hermès).

Roos, N. (1992), 'Review of Samuel & Rinkes (1992)', (unpublished private communication).

Rouland, N. (1998), *Introduction historique au droit* (Presses Universitaires de France).

Rudden, B. (1982), 'Comparative Law as a Remedial Subject', *The Law Teacher*, 141.

Rudden, B. (1991–92), 'Torticles', 6/7 *Tulane Civil Law Forum*, 105.

Rudden, B., Kahn-Freund, O. and Lévy, C. (1991), *A Source-book on French Law*, 3rd edn (Oxford University Press).
Ryle, G. (1949), *The Concept of Mind* (Hutchinson; reprint Penguin, 1963).
Sacco, R. (1991a), *La comparaison juridique au service de la connaissance du droit* (Economica).
Sacco, R. (1991b), 'Legal Formants: A Dynamic Approach to Comparative Law', 39 *American Journal of Comparative Law*, 1.
Salter, M. (1992), 'Towards a Phenomenology of Legal Thinking', 23 *Journal of the British Society for Phenomenology*, 167.
Samuel, G. (1983), 'Public and Private Law: A Private Lawyer's Response', 46 *Modern Law Review*, 558.
Samuel, G. (1984), 'Roman Law and Modern Capitalism', 4 *Legal Studies*, 185.
Samuel, G. (1986), 'Civil and Commercial Law: A Distinction Worth Making?', 102 *Law Quarterly Review*, 569.
Samuel, G. (1987), '"Le Droit Subjectif" and English Law', *Cambridge Law Journal*, 264.
Samuel, G. (1988), 'Governmental Liability in Tort and the Public and Private Law Division', 8 *Legal Studies*, 277.
Samuel, G. (1989), 'Epistemology, Propaganda and Roman Law: Some Reflections on the History of the Subjective Right', 10 *Journal of Legal History*, 161.
Samuel, G. (1990), 'Science, Law and History: Historical Jurisprudence and Modern Legal Theory', 41 *Northern Ireland Legal Quarterly*, 1.
Samuel, G. (1991), 'Epistemology and Legal Institutions', *International Journal for the Semiotics of Law*, 309.
Samuel, G. (1992), 'What is it to Have Knowledge of a European Public Law?', in De Witte and Forder (eds), 171.
Samuel, G. (1994), *The Foundations of Legal Reasoning* (Maklu, Antwerp).
Samuel, G. (1995), 'Entre les mots et les choses: les raisonnements et les méthodes en tant que sources du droit', 2 *Revue internationale de droit comparé*, 509.
Samuel, G. (1997), 'Classification of Obligations and the Impact of Constructivist Epistemologies', 17 *Legal Studies*, 448.
Samuel, G. (1998a), 'The Impact of European Integration on Private Law – A Comment', 18 *Legal Studies*, 167.
Samuel, G. (1998b), 'Comparative Law and Jurisprudence', 47 *International & Comparative Law Quarterly*, 817.
Samuel, G. (1999a), 'The Many Dimensions of Property', in McLean (ed.), 40.
Samuel, G. (1999b), 'Are Property Rights So Simple in Europe?', in Jackson and Wilde (eds), 161.

Samuel, G. (2000a), *Sourcebook on Obligations and Legal Remedies*, 2nd edn (Cavendish).
Samuel, G. (2000b), 'Can Gaius Really be Compared to Darwin?', 49 *International & Comparative Law Quarterly*, 297.
Samuel, G. (2000c), 'English Private Law in the Context of the Codes', in Van Hoecke and Ost (eds).
Samuel, G. (2001), *Law of Obligations and Legal Remedies*, 2nd edn (Cavendish).
Samuel, G. and Rinkes, J. (1992), *Contractual and Non-contractual Obligations in English Law* (Ars Aequi Libri).
Santerres-Sarkany, S. (1993), *Théorie de la littérature*, 2nd edn (Presses Universitaires de France).
Sartorius, R. (1971), 'Social Policy and Judicial Legislation', 8 *American Philosophical Quarterly*, 151.
Sawer, G. (1973), 'The Western Conception of Law', *International Encyclopedia of Comparative Law*, vol. II, ch. 1, pt II (JCB Mohr).
Schauer, F. (1991), *Playing by the Rules* (Oxford University Press).
Schroeder, F.-M. (1978), *Le nouveau style judiciaire* (Dalloz).
Schulz, F. (1936), *Principles of Roman Law*, trans. M. Wolff (Oxford University Press).
Schulz, F. (1946), *History of Roman Legal Science* (Oxford University Press).
Seipp, D. (1993), 'The Reception of Canon Law and Civil Law in the Common Law Courts Before 1600', 13 *Oxford Journal of Legal Studies*, 388.
Sériaux, A. (1992), *Les personnes* (Presses Universitaires de France).
Sériaux, A. (1993), *Le droit naturel* (Presses Universitaires de France).
Simmonds, N. (1984), *The Decline of Juridical Reason* (Manchester University Press).
Simmonds, N. (1986), *Central Issues in Jurisprudence* (Sweet & Maxwell).
Simpson, A. (1975), 'Innovation in Nineteenth Century Contract Law', 91 *Law Quarterly Review*, 247.
Skinner, Q. (1989), 'The State', in Ball et al. (eds), 90.
Sokal, A. and Bricmont, J. (1998), *Intellectual Impostures* (Profile Books).
Sokolowski, R. (1988), 'Natural and Artificial Intelligence', in Graubard (ed.), 45.
Soler, L. (2000), *Introduction à l'épistémologie* (Ellipses).
Stamatis, C.M. (1995), *Argumenter en droit: une théorie critique de l'argumentation juridique* (Publisud).
Stanton, K. (1992), 'Towards an Interest-Based Tort Syllabus', in Birks (ed.), 58.
Stapleton, J. (1995), 'Tort, Insurance and Ideology', 58 *Modern Law Review*, 820.

Stein, P. (1966), *Regulae Iuris: From Juristic Rules to Legal Maxims* (Edinburgh University Press).
Stein, P. (1980), *Legal Evolution: The Story of an Idea* (Cambridge University Press).
Stein, P. (1983), 'The Development of the Institutional System', in Stein and Lewis (eds), 151.
Stein, P. (1984), *Legal Institutions: The Development of Dispute Settlement* (Butterworths).
Stein, P. (1986), 'The Tasks of Historical Jurisprudence', in MacCormick and Birks (eds), 293.
Stein, P. (1988), *The Character and Influence of the Roman Civil Law* (Hambledon).
Stein, P. (1999), *Roman Law in European History* (Cambridge University Press).
Stein, P. and Lewis, A. (eds) (1983), *Studies in Justinian's Institutes in memory of J.A.C. Thomas* (Sweet & Maxwell).
Stein, P. and Shand, J. (1974), *Legal Values in Western Society* (Edinburgh University Press).
Strömholm, S. (1985), *A Short History of Legal Thinking in the West* (Norstedts).
Susskind, R. (1987), *Expert Systems in Law* (Oxford University Press).
Swadling, W. and Jones, G. (eds) (1999), *The Search for Principle: Essays in Honour of Lord Goff of Chieveley* (Oxford University Press).
Szladits, C. (1969), 'The Civil Law System', *International Encyclopedia of Comparative Law*, vol. II, ch. II, pt II (JCB Mohr).
Tellegen-Couperus, O. (1993), *A Short History of Roman Law* (Routledge).
Terrasson de Fougères, A. (1997), 'La résurrection de la mort civile', *Revue trimestrielle de droit civil*, 855.
Terré, F. and Sève, R. (eds) (1986), *Le système juridique* (Sirey).
Teubner, G. (ed.) (1988a), *Autopoietic Law: A New Approach to Law and Society* (de Gruyter).
Teubner, G. (1988b), 'Introduction to Autopoietic Law', in Teubner (ed.), 1.
Teubner, G. (1993), *Law as an Autopoietic System*, trans. A. Bankowska and R. Adler (Blackwell).
Teubner, G. (1998), 'Legal Irritants: Good Faith in British Law or How Unifying Law Ends Up in New Divergences', 61 *Modern Law Review*, 11.
Thiry, P. (1996), 'Du fondement de l'argumentation', in Thomasset and Bourcier (eds), 139.
Thomas, J.A.C. (1975), *The Institutes of Justinian* (North-Holland).
Thomas, J. (1976), *Textbook of Roman Law* (North-Holland).
Thomasset, C. and Bourcier, D. (eds) (1996), *Interpréter le droit: le sens, l'interprète, la machine* (Bruylant).

Tierney, B. (1982), *Religion, Law, and the Growth of Constitutional Thought 1150–1650* (Cambridge University Press).
Tierney, B. (1997), *The Idea of Natural Rights* (Scholars Press for Emory University).
Timsit, G. (1986), *Thèmes et systèmes de droit* (Presses Universitaires de France).
Tissot, P.-A. (1807), *Les douze livres du code de l'empereur Justinien* (Metz; reprint Scientia, 1979).
Toddington, S. (1996), 'The Emperor's New Skills: The Academy, The Profession and the Idea of Legal Education', in Birks (ed.), 69.
Touffait, A. and Tunc, A. (1974), 'Pour une motivation plus explicite des décisions de justice notamment de celles de la Cour de cassation', 3 *Revue trimestrielle de droit civil*, 32.
Treitel, G. (1988), *Remedies for Breach of Contract* (Oxford University Press).
Troper, M. (1986), 'Système juridique et État', in Terré and Sève (eds), 29.
Tuck, R. (1979), *Natural Rights Theories: Their Origin and Development* (Cambridge University Press).
Tunc, A. (1962), 'Jurisprudence en matière de droit civil', 1 *Revue trimestrielle de droit civil*, 305.
Tunc, A. (1972), 'Tort Law and the Moral Law', *Cambridge Law Journal*, 247.
Tunc, A. (1975), 'La méthode du droit civil: analyse des conceptions françaises', *Revue internationale de droit comparé*, 817.
Turing, A. (1950), 'Computing Machinery and Intelligence', 59 *Mind*, 434.
Twining, W. (1973), 'The Bad Man Revisited', 58 *Cornell Law Review*, 275.
Twining, W. (1974), 'Some jobs for Jurisprudence', 1 *British Journal of Law and Society*, 149.
Twining, W. (1985), *Karl Llewellyn and the Realist Movement* (Weidenfeld & Nicolson).
Twining, W. and Miers, D. (1999), *How To Do Things With Rules*, 4th edn (Butterworths).
Ullmann, W. (1962), *The Growth of Papal Government in the Middle Ages*, 2nd edn (Methuen).
Ullmann, W. (1975a), *Medieval Political Thought* (Penguin).
Ullmann, W. (1975b), *Law and Politics in the Middle Ages* (Sources of History).
Valade, B. (2001), 'De l'explication dans les sciences sociales: holisme et individualisme', in Berthelot (ed.), 357.
Van Caenegem, R. (1971), 'History of European Civil Procedure', *International Encyclopedia of Comparative Law*, vol. XVI, ch. 2 (JCB Mohr).

Van Caenegem, R. (1987), *Judges, Legislators and Professors: Chapters in European Legal History* (Cambridge University Press).
Van Caenegem, R. (1988), *The Birth of the English Common Law*, 2nd edn (Cambridge University Press).
Van Caenegem, R. (1992), *An Historical Introduction to Private Law* (Cambridge University Press).
Van Caenegem, R. (1995), *An Historical Introduction to Western Constitutional Law* (Cambridge University Press).
Van de Kerchove, M. and Ost, F. (1988), *Le système juridique entre ordre et désordre* (Presses Universitaires de France).
Van de Kerchove, M. and Ost, F. (1992), *Le droit ou les paradoxes du jeu* (Presses Universitaires de France).
Van den Bergh, G. (1992), 'Ius commune: A history with a future?', in De Witte and Forder (eds), 593.
Van der Merwe, C.G. and De Waal, M.J. (1993), *The Law of Things & Servitudes* (Butterworths, Durban).
Van Gerven, W. (1992), 'Court decisions, general principles and legal concepts: ingredients of a common law of Europe', in De Witte and Forder (eds), 339.
Van Hoecke, M. and Ost, F. (eds) (2000), *The Harmonisation of European Private Law* (Hart).
Van Warmelo, P. (1983), 'The Institutes of Justinian as Students' Manual', in Stein and Lewis (eds), 164.
Védrine, H. (1971), *Les philosophies de la renaissance* (Presses Universitaires de France).
Vescovi, E. (1980), 'Ordinary Proceedings in First Instance: Iberian Peninsula and Latin America', *International Encyclopedia of Comparative Law*, vol. XVI, ch. 6, pt. VI (JCB Mohr).
Villa, V. (1990), *La science du droit*, trans. O. Nerhot and P. Nerhot (Librairie Générale de Droit et de Jurisprudence & Story-Scientia).
Villey, M. (1962), *Leçons d'histoire de la philosophie du droit*, 2nd edn (Dalloz).
Villey, M. (1975), *La formation de la pensée juridique moderne*, 4th edn (Montchrestien).
Villey, M. (1983), *Le droit et les droits de l'homme* (Presses Universitaires de France).
Villey, M. (1986), *Philosophie du droit: I. Définitions et fins du droit*, 4th edn (Dalloz).
Villey, M. (1987), *Le droit romain*, 8th edn (Presses Universitaires de France).
Virieux-Reymond, A. (1972), *Introduction à l'épistémologie*, 2nd edn (Presses Universitaires de France).
Walliser, B. (2001), 'La science économique', in Berthelot (ed.), 117.
Watson, A. (1974), *Law Making in the Later Roman Republic* (Oxford University Press).

Watson, A. (1981), *The Making of the Civil Law* (Harvard University Press).

Watson, A. (1994), 'The Importance of "Nutshells"', 42 *American Journal of Comparative Law*, 1.

Weir, T. (1967), *A Casebook on Tort* (Sweet & Maxwell).

Weir, T. (1971), 'The Common Law System', *International Encyclopedia of Comparative Law*, vol. II, ch. 2, pt. III (JCB Mohr).

Weir, T. (1972), 'Complex Liabilities', *International Encyclopedia of Comparative Law*, vol. XI, ch. 12 (JCB Mohr).

Weir, T. (1974), 'Abstraction in the Law of Torts – Economic Loss', *City of London Law Review* (Michaelmas).

Weir, T. (1992a), 'La notion de dommage en responsabilité civile', in Legrand (ed.), 1.

Weir, T. (1992b), 'Contracts in Rome and England', 66 *Tulane Law Review*, 1615.

Weir, T. (1996), *A Casebook on Tort*, 8th edn (Sweet & Maxwell).

Weir, T. (1998a), 'The Staggering March of Negligence', in Cane and Stapleton' (eds), 97.

Weir, T. (1998b), 'Divergent Legal Systems in a Single Member State', *Zeitschrift für Europäisches Privatrecht*, 564.

Weir, T. (2000), *A Casebook on Tort*, 9th edn (Sweet & Maxwell).

Wieacker, F. (1995), *A History of Private Law in Europe*, trans. T. Weir (Oxford University Press).

Williams, G. and Hepple, B. (1984), *Foundations of the Law of Tort*, 2nd edn (Butterworths).

Wilson, G. (1987), 'English Legal Scholarship', 50 *Modern Law Review*, 818.

Winfield, P.H. (1931), *The Province of the Law of Tort* (Cambridge University Press).

Zander, M. (1999), *The Law-Making Process*, 5th edn (Butterworths).

Zenati, F. (1991), *La jurisprudence* (Dalloz).

Zenati, F. and Revet, T. (1997), *Les biens*, 2nd edn (Presses Universitaires de France).

Zimmermann, R. (1996a), *The Law of Obligations* (Oxford).

Zimmermann, R. (1996b), 'Savigny's Legacy: Legal History, Comparative Law and the Emergence of a European Legal Science', 112 *Law Quarterly Review*, 576.

Zweigert, K. and Kötz, H. (1998), *An Introduction to Comparative Law*, trans. T. Weir, 3rd edn (Oxford University Press).

Index